Grammar, Usage, and Mechanics

Language Skills Practice for Chapters 10–26

- Lesson Worksheets
- Chapter Reviews
- "Choices" Activities
- Proofreading Applications
- Literary Models
- Writing Applications

HOLT, RINEHART AND WINSTON

A Harcourt Classroom Education Company

Austin • New York • Orlando • Atlanta • San Francisco • Boston • Dallas • Toronto • London

STAFF CREDITS

EDITORIAL

Director
Mescal Evler

Manager of Editorial Operations
Bill Wahlgren

Executive Editor
Robert R. Hoyt

Project Editor
Kathryn Rogers

Writing and Editing
Eric Estlund, *Editor;* Randy Dickson, Annie Hartnett, Suzi A. Hunn, Jim Hynes, Kevin Lemoine, Amber M. Rigney, *Associate Editors*

Reviewer
Ed Vavra

Copyediting
Michael Neibergall, *Copyediting Manager;* Mary Malone, *Senior Copyeditor;* Joel Bourgeois, Elizabeth Dickson, Gabrielle Field, Jane Kominek, Millicent Ondras, Theresa Reding, Kathleen Scheiner, Laurie Schlesinger, *Copyeditors*

Project Administration
Marie Price, *Managing Editor;* Lori De La Garza, *Editorial Operations Coordinator;* Thomas Browne, Heather Cheyne, Diane Hardin, Mark Holland, Marcus Johnson, Jill O'Neal, Joyce Rector, Janet Riley, Kelly Tankersley, *Project Administration;* Gail Coupland, Ruth Hooker, Margaret Sanchez, *Word Processing*

Editorial Permissions
Janet Harrington, *Permissions Editor*

ART, DESIGN AND PHOTO

Graphic Services
Kristen Darby, *Manager*

Image Acquisitions
Joe London, *Director;* Tim Taylor, *Photo Research Supervisor;* Rick Benavides, *Assistant Photo Researcher;* Elaine Tate, *Supervisor;* Erin Cone, *Art Buyer*

Cover Design
Sunday Patterson

PRODUCTION

Belinda Barbosa Lopez, *Senior Production Coordinator*
Simira Davis, *Supervisor*
Nancy Hargis, *Media Production Supervisor*
Joan Lindsay, *Production Coordinator*
Beth Prevelige, *Prepress Manager*

MANUFACTURING

Shirley Cantrell, *Supervisor of Inventory and Manufacturing*

Printed in the United States of America

ISBN 0-03-056351-8

22 23 179 09 08 07

Contents

Contents

Contents

Contents

Contents

Contents

Chapter 26
CORRECTING COMMON ERRORS

Using This Workbook

The worksheets in this workbook provide practice, reinforcement, and extension for Chapters 10–26 of *Elements of Language.*

Most of the worksheets you will find in this workbook are **traditional worksheets** providing practice and reinforcement activities on every rule and on all major instructional topics in the grammar, usage, and mechanics chapters in *Elements of Language.*

You will also find in the workbook several kinds of **Language in Context worksheets,** which have been developed to expand the exploration and study of grammar, usage, and mechanics. The Language in Context worksheets include Choices worksheets, Proofreading Applications, Literary Model Worksheets, and Writing Applications.

- **Choices** worksheets offer up to ten activities that provide new ways of approaching grammar, usage, and mechanics. Students can choose and complete one independent or group activity per worksheet. Choices activities stimulate learning through research, creative writing, nonfiction writing, discussion, drama, art, games, interviews, music, cross-curricular activities, technology, and other kinds of projects, including some designed entirely by students.
- **Proofreading Application** worksheets help students apply what they learn in class to contexts in the real world. Students use proofreading symbols like those found in the Writing section of the Quick Reference Handbook in *Elements of Language* to correct errors in grammar, usage, and mechanics in practical documents such as letters, applications, brochures, and reports.
- **Literary Model** worksheets provide literary models that demonstrate how published authors use various grammatical forms to create style or meaning. Students identify and analyze each author's linguistic choices and then use grammatical forms to create style or meaning in their own literary creations. Students are asked to reflect on their own linguistic choices and to draw connections between the choices they make and the style or meaning of their work.
- **Writing Application** worksheets are similar to the Writing Application activities in the grammar, usage, and mechanics chapters in *Elements of Language.* Following the writing process, students use specific grammatical forms as they create a publishable document such as a letter, report, script, or pamphlet.

The Teaching Resources include the **Answer Key** in a separate booklet titled *Grammar, Usage, and Mechanics: Language Skills Practice Answer Key.*

Choices: Exploring Sentences

Here's your chance to step out of the grammar book and into the real world. You may not notice them, but you and the people around you use parts of sentences every day. The following activities challenge you to find a connection between parts of sentences and the world around you. Do the activity below that suits your personality best, and then share your discoveries with your class. Have fun!

CRITICAL ANALYSIS

Everyone's a Critic

Writers love sentence fragments. Find five examples of published sentence fragments, and present them to the class. In each case, lead the class in evaluating whether the fragment or a complete sentence should have been used. Have a debate. You argue for the fragment while a friend argues for a sentence. Let the class be the judge.

DRAMA

Typical Types

Some people speak in sentence fragments quite often. However, some people are more comfortable using complete sentences. How would you describe these two types of people? How would a conversation between them sound? Write a dialogue between two such people. With a friend, tape your dialogue and play it for the class.

CREATIVE WRITING

Four by Four

Write four poems of four sentences each. In each poem, use the different types of sentences (declarative, imperative, interrogative, and exclamatory) once apiece.

DISCUSSION

On Location

While watching the news, have you ever noticed that no matter where a reporter goes in the world, he or she can find at least one person who speaks English? The reporter may even be in some tiny village in Somewhere, Planet Earth, speaking to a person who speaks English just about as well as anyone in Anywhere, U.S.A. What does this observation tell you about the value of English? Where can a knowledge of English take you? Do some research, and report your findings and observations to the class.

MATHEMATICS

X and Y equals Z

Start with ten mathematical equations. Then, translate these equations into sentences and label each subject and predicate. Include some examples showing compound subjects and compound verbs.

ART

Mr. or Ms. D. Clarative

Draw four or five characters. Each character should personify one kind of sentence. In other words, you'll draw one character each for declarative, interrogative, and exclamatory sentences, and one or two for imperative sentences. Name each character. (Yes, a label such as Mr. or Ms. D. Clarative would be acceptable.) Post your drawings in the classroom, and take a bow!

ORIGINAL PROJECTS

Take Charge

Be the one in charge! Create your own project. Begin by asking yourself what puzzles you about sentences. What would your classmates find interesting about sentences? If you're good at something or have a hobby, work it into your project. For instance, if you like dinosaurs, write a dialogue between dinosaurs and use every kind of sentence. How about a dialogue between two people in which one gives the subject and the other gives the predicate? You could make a multimedia presentation. Draw a chart. Discuss your plans with your teacher, sharpen your pencil, and charge ahead!

Sentences and Sentence Fragments A

10a. A ***sentence*** is a word or word group that contains a subject and a verb and that expresses a complete thought.

A *sentence fragment* is a group of words that looks like a sentence but that does not contain both a subject and a verb or does not express a complete thought.

SENTENCE FRAGMENT Giving a speech about whales.

SENTENCE Lori will be giving a speech about whales.

EXERCISE A Decide whether each group of words is a sentence or a sentence fragment. Write *S* if the group of words is a sentence or *F* if the group of words is a sentence fragment.

Examples F **1.** The whales identified by markings on their tails.

S **2.** The whales were identified by the markings on their tails.

S **1.** Water supports the gigantic body of the whale.

F **2.** Unable to survive on land.

S **3.** A beached whale's lungs may be crushed.

F **4.** Prevented by its tremendous weight.

S **5.** Blue whales are the largest mammals.

F **6.** The blue whale, which can weigh over 150 tons.

F **7.** Although some whales have simple teeth.

S **8.** Others have no teeth.

F **9.** The sievelike whalebone in the roof of their mouths.

F **10.** Straining krill from the water for food.

EXERCISE B Each item below shows a sentence fragment. On the line provided, show one way the fragment can be corrected.

Example 1. A walk in the rain. *Let's go for a walk in the rain.*

11. After she spoke. I sat down after she spoke.

12. Her research on whales. Her research on whales was truly amazing.

13. Seen from shore. The large sails could be seen from shore.

14. The girl in the boat. The girl in the boat wobbled uncontrollabl

15. Walking on the beach. Walking on the beach was her favorite passtime.

Sentences and Sentence Fragments B

10a. A ***sentence*** is a word or word group that contains a subject and a verb and that expresses a complete thought.

A *sentence fragment* is a group of words that looks like a sentence but that does not contain both a subject and a verb or does not express a complete thought.

EXERCISE A Write S if the group of words is a sentence or F if it is a sentence fragment.

Example F **1.** Trombones, trumpets, and two bass drums.

F **1.** Marching down the street in perfect rows.

S **2.** Their helmets were topped by tall red plumes.

F **3.** Royal blue uniforms with gold braid.

S **4.** The drum major's baton was keeping the beat.

S **5.** Is that one of John Philip Sousa's marches?

F **6.** The clash of the cymbals and the beat of the drums.

S **7.** The color guard marched in front of the band.

S F **8.** Then ca͏̌me a flo͏ͧat covered with flowers.

F **9.** People sitting on the float, waving to the people in the crowd.

S **10.** What a surprise that was!

EXERCISE B On the line provided, rewrite each of the following sentence fragments as a complete sentence.

Example 1. The freshly washed sheets hanging on the line. *From her room she could see the freshly washed sheets hanging on the line.*

11. Yesterday, a fortunate turn of events. Yesterday, a fortunate turn of events reversed the outcome of the war.

12. The rain dripping from the edge of the roof. The rain dripping from the edge of the roof was filled with wet soot.

13. Waited just inside the front door. Angela quietly waited just inside the front door.

14. His remarkable hat, with a wide brim and a pheasant feather in the hatband. His remarkable hat, with a wide brim and a pheasant feather in the hatband resembled his father!

15. The castle, built with huge, gray stones. The castle, built with huge, gray stones was finally peaceful again.

-1

NAME ____________________ CLASS ____________ DATE ____________

Sentences and Sentence Fragments C

10a. A ***sentence*** is a word or word group that contains a subject and a verb and that expresses a complete thought.

A *sentence fragment* is a group of words that looks like a sentence but that does not contain both a subject and a verb or does not express a complete thought.

EXERCISE A Write *S* if the group of words is a sentence or *F* if the group of words is a sentence fragment.

Example F 1. The leaves floating slowly down the stream.

S **1.** Hoping for good news, she shut her eyes tightly.

F **2.** Finished with the job.

F **3.** Climbing carefully from branch to branch.

F **4.** The young deer at the edge of the clearing.

S **5.** Fireworks lit the sky.

F **6.** Called the electrician after the storm.

F **7.** Want to read the newspaper every morning.

S **8.** Here comes the train!

F **9.** When we thought about his statement for a while.

S **10.** The bird sat on a branch high in the tree, singing merrily.

EXERCISE B On the lines provided, rewrite each of the following sentence fragments as a complete sentence.

Example 1. Disappeared into the woods. *The deer looked around and disappeared into the woods.*

11. At dawn, the mountains in the east. At dawn, the mountains in the east seemed to fade from color to color.

12. Was tossed and turned by the wind. The old flag was tossed and turned by the wind.

13. Because it's snowing. We are sledding happily because it's snowing.

14. Whenever I see a sunset. I say a prayer whenever I see a sunset.

15. The colorful tropical fish. The colorful tropical fish swirled around the coral as if it was a treasure chest.

Subjects and Predicates

Sentences consist of two basic parts: subjects and predicates.

10b. The ***subject*** tells *whom* or *what* the sentence is about.

EXAMPLE In English class **the highlight of the day** was the discussion of Davy Crockett.

10d. The ***predicate*** of a sentence tells something about the subject.

EXAMPLE The class **read several tall tales about this adventurous frontiersman.**

EXERCISE A Decide whether the underlined word or word group is the subject or the predicate. Write *S* if the word or word group is the subject or *P* if it is the predicate.

Examples P 1. Across America, Davy Crockett is a popular legendary hero.

S 2. This native of Tennessee died at the battle of the Alamo.

S P 1. Whether young or old, many people enjoy legends about Davy Crockett.

S 2. In one story, a wild stallion carries Davy on his back for three days.

S 3. Did you ever hear the story about Davy's conversation with a raccoon?

P 4. Most of the remarkable stories about Crockett are obviously not true.

S 5. Still, the legendary Davy Crockett continues to capture our imaginations.

EXERCISE B In each sentence below, draw one line under the complete subject and two lines under the complete predicate.

Example 1. When did the first explorer reach the South Pole?

6. Roald Amundsen led the first successful expedition to the South Pole in 1911.
7. The well-seasoned Amundsen was nearly forty years old at the time.
8. Much earlier in life, Amundsen had planned for a career in medicine.
9. By age twenty-five, the adventurous young man had changed his goal to a life at sea.
10. Who first reached the North Pole?
11. Claiming to be first was the United States explorer Robert E. Peary.
12. Another U.S. explorer, Frederick Cook, made the same claim.
13. Peary's claim was accepted by Congress.
14. The American admiral Richard Byrd made the first flight over the South Pole in 1929.
15. Byrd had made the first flight over the North Pole in 1926 with Floyd Bennett.

NAME ______________________ CLASS ______________ DATE ______________

Simple and Complete Subjects

10c. The ***simple subject*** is the main word or word group that tells *whom* or *what* the sentence is about.

The ***complete subject*** consists of all the words that tell *whom* or *what* a sentence is about.

SIMPLE SUBJECT This **book** on ecology will provide information for my report.

COMPLETE SUBJECT **This book on ecology** will provide information for my report.

Sometimes the simple subject and the complete subject are the same.

EXERCISE A Decide whether the underlined word or word group is the complete subject or the simple subject. Write *CS* for *complete subject* or *SS* for *simple subject.*

Example CS **1.** The study of wildlife is fascinating and fun.

CS **1.** This particular course concentrates on endangered species.

SS **2.** A large variety of plants and animals are endangered.

SS **3.** The U.S. Fish and Wildlife Service provides information on endangered animals.

CS **4.** Some animals are threatened by a change in their surroundings.

SS **5.** Considered the greatest threat to animals are the activities of human beings.

EXERCISE B Underline the complete subject in the following sentences. Then, circle the simple subject.

Example 1. The carnivorous Tasmanian devil grows up to thirty-one inches in length.

6. One fascinating nocturnal animal is the aardvark.

7. That strange name always makes me laugh.

8. Another animal with a strange name is the platypus.

9. One of the biggest moths in the world was named for Hercules, a mythological hero.

10. The ant lion captures ants and other insects in its sand traps.

11. The armadillo lives as far north as Texas and as far south as Argentina.

12. Some armadillos may be up to five feet long.

13. The wingspan of the American crow can reach up to three feet.

14. An intelligent bird, the crow can sometimes learn simple words and phrases.

15. Like the parrot, the crow mimics phrases of human speech.

Simple and Complete Predicates

10e. The ***simple predicate,*** or ***verb,*** is the main word or word group that tells something about the subject.

The *complete predicate* consists of a verb and all the words that modify the verb and complete its meaning.

SIMPLE PREDICATE Aidan **goes** to the movies every weekend.

COMPLETE PREDICATE Aidan **goes to the movies every weekend.**

EXERCISE A Decide whether the underlined word or word group is the complete predicate or the verb (simple predicate). Above each, write *CP* for *complete predicate* or *V* for *verb*.

Examples 1. One hundred years ago, families entertained themselves. CP CP

2. They would have been astonished by television. V

1. Motion-picture cameras and projectors were invented in the mid-1890s. V

2. The first projected movie was shown in Paris in 1895. CP

3. Thomas Edison helped develop the movie projector. CP

4. At first, movies must have amazed people. V

5. For many years, moviegoers watched newsreels at movie theaters. V

EXERCISE B In each of the following sentences, draw one line under the complete predicate, and then circle the verb.

Example 1. Will the temperature reach seventy degrees before breakfast?

6. Our trip took us through misty mountains and shady, green forests.

7. Dairy cows were grazing on the lower slopes of the hills.

8. We arrived at our destination before late afternoon.

9. The whole family was looking forward to a pleasant vacation.

10. Have you ever breathed air as pure as country air?

11. We planned as many outdoor activities as possible.

12. My personal favorite was the daily canoe trip upriver.

13. My older brother had never canoed before.

14. Did he catch fish from the stream for breakfast?

15. My sister caught several trout.

Verb Phrases

Some simple predicates, or verbs, consist of more than one word. Such verbs are called ***verb phrases*** (verbs that include one or more helping verbs).

EXAMPLES I **will be using** the computer for the next hour.
What **does** this error message **mean**?
Have you **contacted** the technical service center?

EXERCISE A Underline the verb phrase in each sentence.

Example 1. Trish didn't have an e-mail account until today.

1. I had used a computer only a few times before this school year.
2. My classmates and I will soon be computer experts.
3. Shouldn't every student have experience with the latest technology?
4. We have been using the computer for research assignments.
5. For example, yesterday I was researching Mark Twain.
6. I had not yet read *The Adventures of Tom Sawyer.*
7. I was surfing the Internet in the computer lab.
8. I had quickly found a complete copy of the book on the Internet.
9. Since then, I have read as much of the story as possible.
10. Can you believe my good fortune?

EXERCISE B In each sentence below, the underlined word group contains a word or part of a word that is not part of the verb phrase. Circle this word or word part.

Example 1. Dylan hasn't checked his e-mail today.

11. Please don't forget my e-mail address.
12. Every day during the holidays, I will check my messages.
13. I have always enjoyed your friendly notes.
14. We will probably exchange e-mails all summer long.
15. Isn't technology becoming part of everyone's social life?

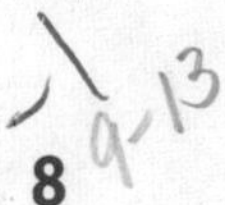

Complete and Simple Subjects and Predicates

10c. The ***simple subject*** is the main word or word group that tells *whom* or *what* the sentence is about.

The *complete subject* consists of all the words that tell *whom* or *what* a sentence is about.

SIMPLE SUBJECT The **study** of small insects is a hobby of mine.

COMPLETE SUBJECT **The study of small insects** is a hobby of mine.

10e. The ***simple predicate,*** or ***verb,*** is the main word or word group that tells something about the subject.

The *complete predicate* consists of a verb and all the words that modify the verb and complete its meaning.

SIMPLE PREDICATE (VERB) Many people **will listen** with interest to facts about bugs.

COMPLETE PREDICATE Many people **will listen with interest to facts about bugs.**

EXERCISE A Underline each complete subject once and each complete predicate twice.

Example 1. Are any of your friends allergic to the dust mite?

1. The microscopic dust mite was discovered less than three decades ago.
2. This eight-legged pest is related to the tick and the spider.
3. Do you ever wash your pillow in very hot water?
4. Someone in your household should probably do so as soon as possible.
5. The daily diet of the dust mite consists of tiny skin flakes on your pillow and sheets.
6. The creatures leave tiny waste droppings in your bed.
7. These microscopic droppings mix with dust in your bedroom and in the house.
8. Unfortunately, this tainted dust may cause an allergic reaction in you or a family member.
9. How can a concerned person remove these pesky flesh-eaters from bedding?
10. Any person with laundry skills can wash bedding in the hottest wash cycle possible.

EXERCISE B Underline each simple subject once and each simple predicate (verb) twice.

Example 1. The tiny bedbug has often found its home in humans' beds.

11. The body of the bedbug is flat and wingless.
12. This bloodthirsty bug belongs to the insect class.
13. The blood of mammals such as humans forms the bedbug's diet.
14. A bedbug may grow to a length of a quarter of an inch.
15. The little insect usually sucks the blood of its host at night.

Compound Subjects

10f. A ***compound subject*** consists of two or more subjects that are joined by a conjunction and that have the same verb.

EXAMPLE Numerous **trees** and **bushes** respond to seasonal weather changes.

EXERCISE A Underline the compound subject in each sentence.

Example 1. The live oak and the Douglas fir remain green year-round.

1. Live oaks and white oaks should not be confused with one another.
2. The redwood and the sequoia are found in California.
3. Douglas firs and other trees of the pine family appeal to Christmas tree shoppers.
4. Most conifers and many broad-leaved plants are evergreen.
5. Does the cypress or the magnolia bear cones?
6. Maples and elms are deciduous trees.
7. In the autumn these and other deciduous trees lose their leaves.
8. Do the reds and golds of autumn trees appeal to your sense of beauty?
9. During the fall my best friend and I always gather colorful leaves.
10. These fragile, beautiful leaves and our original poems make special cards for friends.

EXERCISE B Add a compound subject to each of the following predicates. Use *and* or *or* to join the parts of your compound subjects.

Example 1. *Posters of my favorite singers and photos of my family* decorate the walls of my room at home.

11. Tucked away in my school bag are pens and pencils needed for writing essays.
12. Either Percy or Gertrude will be voted Funniest Student of the Year.
13. Will Nancy Drew and her friend be at your party on Saturday?
14. Frankenstein and the goggle monster came bounding out of the murky darkness straight toward me.
15. In the school cafeteria today, grilled chicken and hamburger patties are the two main dishes.

9-13

NAME ____________________ CLASS ____________ DATE ____________

GRAMMAR

for **CHAPTER 10: THE SENTENCE** *page 327*

Compound Verbs

10g. A ***compound verb*** consists of two or more verbs that are joined by a conjunction and that have the same subject.

EXAMPLE Which mammal **has** wings and **can fly** like a bird?

EXERCISE A Underline each compound verb or verb phrase.

Example **1.** Can a mammal move as fast as a car and rise as high as an airplane?

1. Some bats can fly sixty miles per hour and can also soar to a height of ten thousand feet.

2. Some species of bats fly much slower and cannot reach the same heights as others.

3. In all, more than nine hundred species of bats exist and find habitats worldwide.

4. Bats are the world's only flying mammals and may have wingspans of over five feet.

5. The flying fox hangs in trees and can have a wingspread more than five feet across.

6. The bumblebee bat has a five-inch wingspan and weighs less than a dime.

7. All mammals, including bats and humans, grow fur or hair and nurse their young.

8. Honduran white bats grow long white fur and eat only fruit.

9. The vampire bat drinks cows' blood but seldom consumes human blood.

10. This bat bites its prey and then hungrily laps blood from the wound.

EXERCISE B Add a compound verb to complete each of the following sentences. Use *and, or,* or *but* to join the parts of your compound verb.

Example **1.** *Can* bats *fly and roost* in the darkness of the cave?

11. In the backyard, my puppy chased the cat and scratched the tree.

12. Betty ate pizza but Keisha drank a smoothy during lunch period?

13. Every so often, I allow myself a treat, and eat icecream for dessert.

14. We ran around and giggled loudly at the track after school.

15. Either she broke the window or the seventh graders blamed it on her?

16. Birds and squirrels squack (sp?) and play with each other at the bird feeder.

17. The runners stretched and jumped up and down before they went to the starting line.

18. I can see you and Suzi can talk to me before dinner?

19. Each student wrote and stapled together a paper on a topic of his or her choice.

20. The ball bounced and rolled along the sideline toward the end zone.

9-13 ✓

Compound Subjects and Verbs

10f. A ***compound subject*** consists of two or more subjects that are joined by a conjunction and that have the same verb.

10g. A ***compound verb*** consists of two or more verbs that are joined by a conjunction and that have the same subject.

COMPOUND SUBJECT At sunrise the **farmer** and the **hired hands** arrived at the field.

COMPOUND VERB They **weeded** and **fertilized** the field of peanut plants.

EXERCISE A Underline the compound subject or compound verb in each of the following sentences. On the line provided, write *CS* for *compound subject* or *CV* for *compound verb.*

Examples *CS* 1. Salty peanuts and chewy raisins make a tasty snack.

CV 2. Should I eat a peanut butter sandwich or try a different filling?

_____ 1. Peanuts and soybeans are the two most important sources of vegetable oil.

_____ 2. The U.S. scientist George Washington Carver researched the peanut and found more than three hundred uses for it.

_____ 3. Aren't China and India the two major producers of peanuts in the world today?

_____ 4. Peanut plants are native to South America and belong to the pea family.

_____ 5. Does your family ever make old-fashioned peanut butter or buy it at the supermarket?

EXERCISE B Combine each pair of sentences to create one sentence with a compound subject or a compound verb. Write the new sentence on the line provided. When you create a sentence with a compound subject, you may need to change the verb, too.

Example 1. Than's father is an excellent cook. Lily's mother is an excellent cook, too. _____

Than's father and Lily's mother are excellent cooks.

6. The private eye ducked behind the bookcase. She listened to the suspects' argument. _____

7. The birdbath attracts many birds. So does the small, wooden bird feeder. _____

8. The plumber fixed the pipe beneath the sink. He also checked the water pressure. _____

9. The plane lifted off. It soared quickly out of sight. _____

10. Tweedledum is a character created by Lewis Carroll. So is Tweedledee. _____

NAME ______________________ CLASS ______________ DATE ______________

Subjects and Verbs A

10b. The ***subject*** tells *whom* or *what* the sentence is about.

10e. The ***simple predicate,*** or ***verb,*** is the main word or word group that tells something about the subject.

10f. A ***compound subject*** consists of two or more subjects that are joined by a conjunction and that have the same verb.

10g. A ***compound verb*** consists of two or more verbs that are joined by a conjunction and that have the same subject.

EXERCISE A In each of the following sentences, underline the subject once and the verb twice.

Example 1. A calculator or an abacus will help you and will speed your calculations.

1. Have you or one of your friends ever used an abacus?
2. The abacus is an ancient arithmetic tool and consists of a frame with vertical wires or slots.
3. Beads or balls may be moved up or down in the slots in various combinations.
4. In this way, the user quickly performs calculations such as addition and subtraction.
5. You and your friends can easily find more information about the abacus on the Internet.

EXERCISE B Combine each pair of sentences to create one sentence. Write the new sentence on the line provided. Then, underline the subject once and the verb twice. When you create a sentence with a compound subject, you may need to change the verb, too.

Example 1. Volleyball is a popular sport at my school. Football is also popular.

Volleyball and football are popular sports at my school.

6. Basketball can give you a good cardiovascular workout. Track can do so, too.
   Basketball and track can give you a good cardiovascular workout.
7. Blue is our school color. Gold is our other school color. Blue and gold are our school colors.
8. When will you practice your trumpet? When will you finish your homework? When will you practice your trumpet and finish your homework?
9. Will you go to the game with Sandra's family? Will Bernard go with Sandra's family? Will you and Bernard go to the game with Sandras family.
10. Members of the yearbook staff take photographs at every game. Journalists on the newspaper staff take photographs at every game. Members of the yearbook staff and journalists on the newspaper staff take photographs at every game.

9-13

NAME ______________________ CLASS ______________ DATE ______________

GRAMMAR

Subjects and Verbs B

10b. The ***subject*** tells *whom* or *what* the sentence is about.

10e. The ***simple predicate,*** or ***verb,*** is the main word or word group that tells something about the subject.

10f. A ***compound subject*** consists of two or more subjects that are joined by a conjunction and that have the same verb.

10g. A ***compound verb*** consists of two or more verbs that are joined by a conjunction and that have the same subject.

EXERCISE In each of the following sentences, underline the subject once and the verb twice. Then, on the line provided, write *CV* if the verb is a compound verb, *CS* if the subject is a compound subject, or *CV, CS* if both the subject and the verb are compound. Write *N* if neither is compound.

Example CS 1. My mother and brother want a new puppy.

CS 1. Have you or Kimberly found your tap shoes yet?

B 2. Alec or James will wash and dry the dishes after dinner tonight.

CS 3. In my school, both the Spanish club and the German club have at least twenty members.

N 4. Where are the batteries for this flashlight?

CV 5. At the end of the school year, we will either take a class trip or have a party.

CV 6. She added the numbers and then checked the answer.

CS 7. Neither Steve nor Katya borrowed that book.

B 8. Andrés and Clarence searched the room and looked on all the shelves.

CV 9. You should wear sturdy shoes and pack a raincoat.

N 10. Are you expecting rain during the hike?

CS 11. The newspaper and the radio carried stories about the weather.

CS 12. Fog and rain are expected this afternoon.

CV 13. We could cancel the hike and meet at the museum.

CV 14. The new exhibit about Egypt is open and should be interesting.

B 15. Do you and your sister take the bus or walk to school?

CV 16. We usually take the bus in the morning and walk home in the afternoon.

CV 17. She has band practice and works in the library after school.

CS 18. My friend Nita and I belong to several of the same clubs.

N 19. Nita walks home with my sister and me on Tuesdays and Thursdays.

B 20. Either Max or his brother Sam rented a boat and went fishing last summer.

Classifying Sentences by Purpose A

10h. A ***declarative sentence*** makes a statement and ends with a period.

10i. An ***imperative sentence*** gives a command or makes a request. Most imperative sentences end with a period. A strong command ends with an exclamation point.

10j. An ***interrogative*** sentence asks a question and ends with a question mark.

10k. An ***exclamatory sentence*** shows excitement or expresses strong feeling and ends with an exclamation point.

EXERCISE A On the line provided, write *DEC* if the sentence is declarative, *IMP* if it is imperative, *INT* if it is interrogative, or *EXC* if it is exclamatory.

Example EXC **1.** What a fascinating study ancient cultures are!

IMP **1.** Use Roman numerals whenever you write an outline, Margo.

INT **2.** Did you know Roman numerals consist of seven individual letters used as numbers?

DEC **3.** These letters are *I, V, X, L, C, D,* and *M.*

IMP **4.** Imagine building a boat with no nails or screws.

EXC **5.** What a difficult job that would be!

EXERCISE B On the line provided, write *DEC* if the sentence is declarative, *IMP* if it is imperative, *INT* if it is interrogative, or *EXC* if it is exclamatory. Then, add the correct punctuation to the end of the sentence.

Example IMP **1.** Consider these facts.

DEC **6.** I have recently learned some interesting facts from American history .

IMP **7.** Consider the similarities between President Lincoln and President Kennedy .

DEC **8.** President Abraham Lincoln was elected in 1860 .

INT **9.** Did you know that John F. Kennedy was elected president in 1960 ?

EXC **10.** It is tragic that both Lincoln and Kennedy were assassinated !

DEC **11.** The vice presidents under both Lincoln and Kennedy were named Johnson .

DEC **12.** What a strange coincidence that is .

IMP **13.** Read about the investigations into the deaths of both men .

INT **14.** How many people believe that there was a conspiracy in Kennedy's assassination ?

DEC **15.** There are still unanswered questions about these deaths .

NAME ______ CLASS ______ DATE ______

Classifying Sentences by Purpose B

10h. A ***declarative sentence*** makes a statement and ends with a period.

10i. An ***imperative sentence*** gives a command or makes a request. Most imperative sentences end with a period. A strong command ends with an exclamation point.

10j. An ***interrogative sentence*** asks a question and ends with a question mark.

10k. An ***exclamatory sentence*** shows excitement or expresses strong feeling and ends with an exclamation point.

EXERCISE A On the line provided, write *DEC* if the sentence is declarative, *IMP* if it is imperative, *INT* if it is interrogative, or *EXC* if it is exclamatory. Then, add the correct punctuation to the end of the sentence.

Example INT **1.** Does this pencil belong to you?

DEC **1.** This sculptor recycles metal in her work .

INT **2.** Isn't that the rim of a bicycle wheel ?

IMP **3.** Try to identify as many items as possible .

DEC **4.** She has transformed junk into animals and other recognizable forms .

EXC **5.** What a sense of humor she has !

EXERCISE B On the lines provided, rewrite each of the following sentences according to the instructions in parentheses. Be sure to use correct end punctuation in your new sentences. Hint: You may need to add or delete words.

Example 1. That piece of fabric is from India. *(Rewrite as an interrogative sentence.)*
Is that piece of fabric from India?

6. The colors in the stained-glass windows are brilliant. *(Rewrite as an exclamatory sentence.)*
The colors in the stained-glass windows are brilliant.!

7. Do I have time to get to the store before it closes? *(Rewrite as a declarative sentence.)* I have time to get to the store before it closes.

8. You forgot to bring the library books to school. *(Rewrite as an interrogative sentence.)* Did you forget to bring the library book to school?

9. What an exciting race that was! *(Rewrite as a declarative sentence.)* What an exciting race that was. That was an exciting race.

10. You should turn off the lights when you leave the room. *(Rewrite as an imperative sentence.)*
Turn off the lights when you leave the room.

Review A: Sentences and Sentence Fragments

EXERCISE Decide whether each of the following word groups is a sentence or a sentence fragment. Write *S* if the group of words is a sentence or *F* if the group of words is a sentence fragment.

Examples F 1. Because Dan has a kayak.

S 2. Tatiana is listening to her new CD.

F 1. Thought Roseanne and Steve had missed their flight to Atlanta.

S 2. Pasta salad is especially good on a hot day.

F 3. In the bedroom closet behind the ironing board.

F 4. His latest excuse but definitely not his most original.

S 5. Please take this gift home to your stepsister Lorena.

S 6. I would appreciate some help with this art project.

F 7. The space shuttle on the launching pad.

F 8. Stretching for miles in every direction.

F 9. Whenever he goes out into the bright sunlight.

S 10. That was a dazzling display of fireworks!

F 11. Because of the loud noise.

S 12. After a short while, the beaver began building a dam.

S 13. You must have heard about the mysterious Bermuda Triangle.

F 14. When she wrote her story for the local newspaper.

F 15. Although everyone here had a good reason.

S 16. Scientists keep searching for the answer to the problem.

F 17. On the other side of the basketball court and under the scoreboard.

S 18. Very few people actually saw what happened.

F 19. Without the benefit of modern medicine.

S 20. The car swerved sharply to avoid hitting the pedestrian.

F 21. Mr. Liu, an organic farmer with a large farm in Texas.

S 22. What a sweet rabbit Scooter is!

F 23. Completion unlikely at any point in the near future.

S 24. Watch the satellite traveling across the night sky.

F 25. Saving money in a bank account.

NAME ______________________ CLASS ____________ DATE ____________

for **CHAPTER 10: THE SENTENCE** *pages 317–23*

Review B: Subjects and Predicates

EXERCISE In each of the following sentences, underline the complete subject once and the complete predicate twice. Then, circle the simple subject and the verb.

Example 1. The playful, intelligent dolphin belongs to the toothed whale family.

1. An unusual event occurred at our beach last summer.
2. Two girls were jogging along the beach.
3. They heard a strange sound.
4. Thrashing around in the water was a dark object.
5. A helpless dolphin was being tossed around by the waves.
6. The worried joggers called the Center for Coastal Studies.
7. Two dolphin experts soon arrived at the beach.
8. They moved into the cold surf near the dolphin.
9. Scientists at the local aquarium cared for the dolphin.
10. The healthy dolphin was released into the ocean several months later.
11. Have you ever been to the ocean?
12. Dolphins and whales are mammals, not fish.
13. An aquatic mammal, such as a dolphin or whale, breathes air through a blowhole on top of the head.
14. Fish have gills.
15. Most salmon are born in fresh water but live part of their lives in the ocean.
16. The thousand-mile migration of the salmon fascinates me.
17. Fish "ladders" are built near dams and help the salmon on their voyage.
18. Leaps of more than ten feet have been recorded.
19. The longest spawning trip exceeds two thousand miles.
20. Salmon spawn in fresh water.
21. A Pacific salmon spawns in the stream of its birth and then dies.
22. An Atlantic salmon may spawn as many as three times in its lifetime.
23. The female fish digs several saucer-shaped nests in the bed of a stream.
24. One ten-pound female may deposit up to ten thousand eggs at spawning time.
25. A smolt is a young salmon.

Review C: Compound Subjects and Compound Verbs

EXERCISE Underline the compound verb in each of the following sentences. Then, on the line provided, rewrite the sentence so that it has a compound subject as well. Use *and* or *or* to join the parts of the compound subject. You may need to change the verb, too.

Example 1. Before school each morning, Darnell has been doing push-ups and lifting weights.
Before school each morning, Jalinda and Darnell have been doing push-ups and lifting weights.

1. Today my cousin Luke will hike and take photographs of the land behind his house. Today my cousin Luke and his wife, Jenny, will hike and take photographs of the land behind his house.
2. Before tests, Shanti reviews and summarizes all her notes from class. Before tests, Shanti and Kayla review and summarize all of their notes from class.
3. The pilot smiled and waved at her crew. The pilot and her assistant smiled and waved at her crew.
4. The sleet reduced visibility at the airport and delayed the flight. The sleet and fog reduced visibility at the airport and delayed the flight.
5. The new bus driver joined us at Stonehenge and accompanied us to London. The new bus driver and her bird joined us at Stonehenge and accompanied us to London.
6. The table was cleaned thoroughly and given a fresh coat of paint. The table and woodwork was cleaned thoroughly and given a fresh coat of paint.
7. Rachel is singing a song and dancing for the talent show. Rachel or Samantha is singing a song and dancing for the talent show.
8. Cars filled the roadways and created a massive traffic jam. Cars and buses filled the roadways and created a massive trafic jam.
9. My brother Angelo frowned and sighed but finally did the yardwork. My brothers Angelo and Peter frowned and sighed but finally did the yardwork.
10. Tara takes ice-skating lessons and hopes to skate professionally. Tara and Beverly take ice-skating lessons and hope to skate professionally.

NAME ______________ CLASS ______________ DATE ______________

Review D: **Kinds of Sentences and Sentence Fragments**

EXERCISE Decide whether each group of words is a sentence or a sentence fragment. If it is a sentence fragment, write *F* on the line provided. If it is a sentence, write *DEC* if it is declarative, *IMP* if it is imperative, *INT* if it is interrogative, or *EXC* if it is exclamatory. Then, add the appropriate end punctuation to each sentence.

Examples *F* **1.** Studying Spanish, German, and French next semester

INT **2.** By next semester, will you know the months of the year in three languages?

F **1.** Named for the Roman goddess Juno

IMP **2.** Please bring me that calendar

INT **3.** When will we plan the birthday party for Julio

EXC **4.** How exciting it was to win a gold medal

IMP **5.** Please be careful with the bleach, Suzi

F **6.** After Emily and Rosa climbed slowly up the side of the hill

EXC **7.** How magnificent the view of the valley is

INT **8.** Can you see the village from there

IMP **9.** Hand me the binoculars, please

F **10.** As a hawk soared gracefully over the valley

F **11.** Waiting for fifteen minutes in the rain

IMP **12.** Watch out

INT **13.** How often do you baby-sit for the McCluskys

DEC **14.** I promise that I won't forget about our next appointment

F **15.** Since repairing the broken appliance

IMP **16.** Please don't stand so close to the curb

F **17.** Carrying my little sister all the way across the rickety bridge and to safety

IMP **18.** Put down your pencils and pass your papers forward

F **19.** Will be sitting in front of you tomorrow after lunch

INT **20.** Would you volunteer

Literary Model: Dialogue

When Cloyd was little, he used to talk to his sister about how badly he wanted to find his father, but she didn't seem to need to know him at all, so he had kept his dream inside. . . . Now here he was with his heart pounding, following the nurse down the long hallway to his father's room. . . .

"How did this happen?"

"Car accident," she said. "I don't know any details."

"How long has he been like this?"

"Four years."

"Are you sure he's Leeno Atcitty?"

"Yes, of course."

"Where's he from?"

"I think I heard that once . . . Utah, I think. Monument Valley. I wonder if this could be the man you were looking for."

—from *Bearstone* by Will Hobbs

EXERCISE A Underline each sentence fragment that appears in the above passage.

EXERCISE B

1. Rewrite the dialogue to eliminate all sentence fragments. That is, whenever you come to a sentence fragment, supply words that make it a complete sentence.

When Cloyd was little, he used to talk to his sister about how badly he wanted to find his father. She didn't seem to need to know him at all, so he kept his dreams inside. Now here he was with his heart pounding, following the nurse down the long hallway to his father's room.

"How did this happen?"

"He was in a car accident," she said. "I don't know any of the details."

"How long has he been like this?"

"He has been like this for four years."

"Are you sure he's Leeno Atcitty?"

"Yes, I am sure that this is him."

"Where is he from?"

"I think I heard that he was ~~from~~ Monument Valley, Utah. I wonder if this could be the man that you were looking for."

Literary Model (continued)

2. Read the original passage and your revision. Why do you think the author chose to write the dialogue as a mix of sentences and sentence fragments rather than using only complete sentences?

It was dialogue, so the author could have been trying to portray the way that the person might speak through a mixture of sentences and sentence fragments.

EXERCISE C Write a dialogue in which one person asks questions to try to help a friend who is upset. Have the upset friend speak mostly in sentence fragments to convey his or her feelings or emotions.

"When did your dog, Poodles, die?"

"Two days ago."

"What happened to him?"

"Froze under the deck."

"When did you find him under there?"

"Yesterday."

"Did you notice him missing before you found Poodles?"

"Yeah, two days ago."

"I'm sure you can get a new dog since it wasn't your fault. I know your mom would let you get a new d

EXERCISE D

1. How does the character who uses sentence fragments sound different from the other character in your dialogue?

He sounds sad, upset, and slightly afraid.

2. How would your dialogue sound different if both characters used only complete sentences?

He wouldn't sound as emotional and not as sad.

Writing Application: Letter

Writers use different types of sentences to convey different types of messages. When writers make statements, they use declarative sentences. When they ask questions, they use interrogative sentences.

DECLARATIVE Andrea is playing in the tennis tournament today.

INTERROGATIVE Where is the tournament being played?

Writing Activity

Your teacher has arranged for your class to write to students learning English in Denmark. Each student in your class has been assigned a Danish pen pal. Your assignment is to write a letter to your new pen pal. Using at least five declarative sentences, introduce yourself and tell your pen pal about life in the United States. Using at least five interrogative sentences, ask your pen pal questions about himself or herself and life in Denmark.

PREWRITING Think about what you would like to know about your pen pal, and make a list of your questions. Try to avoid asking only yes-or-no questions. Open-ended questions will give you more information. Your pen pal may have similar questions for you, so you can use your list to help you decide what to write about yourself. Think about what you would like to know about Denmark. What do you think your pen pal would want to know about the United States?

WRITING Decide how to organize your letter. You might tell about yourself in the first half of the letter and ask questions in the second half of the letter. Another way to write your letter is to alternate between telling about yourself and asking related questions about your pen pal. Since your pen pal is still learning English, he or she may not understand slang terms, so be careful with word choice.

REVISING Have a friend read your letter; then, discuss it. Is it interesting? Have you left out any important information about yourself? Can your friend think of any other questions that you should ask your pen pal?

PUBLISHING Check your paragraph for errors in spelling and punctuation. Does each declarative sentence end with a period? Does each interrogative sentence end with a question mark? With your teacher's permission, post your letter with your classmates' letters on the bulletin board. Find or create pictures that illustrate the area where your pen pal lives.

Extending Your Writing

You may wish to extend this activity by finding a real pen pal for yourself or your whole class. Your teacher may be able to help you find Internet sites that help classes from around the United States or around the world set up letter exchange programs. Not only would you get to practice your writing skills, but you would make new friends as well.

NAME CLASS DATE

Choices: Exploring Parts of Speech

Here's your chance to step out of the grammar book and into the real world. You may not notice them, but you and the people around you use the parts of speech every day. The following activities challenge you to find a connection between the parts of speech and the world around you. Do the activity below that suits your personality best, and then share your discoveries with your class. Have fun!

BUILDING BACKGROUND KNOWLEDGE

Every Letter Counts

Have a contest to determine who can find the longest proper compound noun. Entries must be verified in a reliable source such as a dictionary, an atlas, or an encyclopedia.

TIME LINE

First and Last

If you've got a first name and a last name, your name is a compound noun. Not everybody has a compound noun for a name, you know. Plato didn't, Aristotle didn't, and lots of other people don't. However, most people do. Make a time line that your class can use throughout the year. Leave room for additions. Then, pick out some of your favorite historical figures and write their names on the appropriate part of the time line. In small letters under each two-word name, write *compound noun.*

AUDITORY

Begin at the End

Have you noticed that nouns often have certain suffixes, such as *–tion, –ology,* and *–er?* Identify as many of these suffixes as you can. Then, get together with some friends and use your list of suffixes to make up ten new nouns! Here's a question to get you started: What's a good name for those colorful little erasers shaped like dinosaurs, hearts, and other things?

CHARACTERIZATION

Way Back When

Pick three historical periods (such as the Victorian era, medieval times, Ice Age, or Jazz Age). Choose at least ten adjectives that describe each of those time periods. Post your adjectives in the appropriate places on a time line.

COLLABORATIVE LEARNING

Betty the Boa Constrictor

There's a big difference between saying, "I took an animal with me," and "I took my pet boa constrictor Betty with me." *Animal* is a general noun that could refer to anything from an elephant to a tarantula. Choose a partner. Then, in a page or less, write a description of a day on safari, and use only general nouns. Then, trade papers with your partner, and revise the description so that every noun is a specific noun. Trade again, and compare results.

FOREIGN LANGUAGES

Las, Les, Der, and *The*

Why do we need articles, anyway? Do other languages use articles? How does Spanish use articles? German? Japanese? Find out about at least one other language. Interview someone who speaks another language, or conduct a library search. Then, write a one-page essay explaining how another language uses articles and comparing it with English. Read your essay to the class.

VISUAL PRESENTATION

Documentation

Get together with a group of friends or lead the class in a brainstorming session. Your goal is to make a poster listing nouns that name every kind of document that exists. Concentrate especially on documents that you and your friends are most likely to create in the future. Your list should include job application forms, personal letters, business cards, reports, recipes, and directions. Don't limit yourself to print media; try to include documents that can be produced in other media like videos, cassettes, and electronic media. When you've finished your list, organize it into categories and create a poster to display in class.

The Noun

11a. A ***noun*** is a word or word group that is used to name a person, a place, a thing, or an idea.

A ***compound noun*** is a single noun made up of two or more words used together. The compound noun may be written as one word, as a hyphenated word, or as two or more words.

PERSONS Diana Chang, poet, police officer, Cherokees
PLACES living room, town, New South Wales, island
THINGS sandwich, television, Father's Day, Statue of Liberty
IDEAS fear, self-control, truth, sympathy

EXERCISE A Underline each noun in the following sentences.

Example 1. A volcano is a hole in the crust of the earth through which lava and gases may erupt.

1. When a volcano erupted in the Sunda Strait of Indonesia, the whole world felt the effects.
2. The noise from the eruption of Krakatoa could be heard at great distances.
3. The force from the blast could be felt as far away as Hawaii.
4. A cloud of ash circled the globe and created spectacular sunsets.
5. Volcanic eruptions are powerful forces that can affect the entire planet and its living creatures.

EXERCISE B Underline each noun in the following sentences. Then, identify each compound noun by writing *CN* above it.

CN
Example 1. A letter from Uncle Rufino arrived yesterday.

6. Please put these new books in the bookcase over there.
7. Takako Mioshi, an exchange student, is here from Japan for the year.
8. Mr. Morales was fascinated by the koalas at the San Diego Zoo.
9. Manuel is the new goalie on the team.
10. Stephanie is having a party after the football game.
11. Did your grandparents go to Hawaii for a convention or a vacation?
12. The storm interrupted the final game of the World Series.
13. The journalists learned to have faith in their editor in chief.
14. Lucy, a young chimpanzee, learned several words in sign language.
15. Ryan always puts a little humor into his term papers.

NAME ______________________ CLASS ______________ DATE ______________

Common and Proper Nouns

A *common noun* names any one of a group of persons, places, things, or ideas and is generally not capitalized. A *proper noun* names a particular person, place, thing, or idea and begins with a capital letter.

COMMON pilot, book **PROPER** Willa Brown, *The Once and Future King*

EXERCISE A Underline each common noun once and each proper noun twice in the sentences below.

Example 1. My favorite book, *Twenty Thousand Leagues Under the Sea,* was written by Jules Verne.

1. Jules Verne must have loved adventure.
2. Born in France, he worked on a ship when he was a boy.
3. Later he studied law in Paris, but he preferred a career in literature.
4. He wrote a popular play, which provided only a little income.
5. Verne found a job as a stockbroker, but he also pursued his literary dreams.
6. He wrote books about imaginary adventures, such as *A Journey to the Center of the Earth.*
7. The public loved these stories and eagerly awaited each new novel.
8. Many of his books, including *Around the World in Eighty Days,* have been made into movies.
9. These novels by Verne influenced another famous writer, H. G. Wells.
10. Wells wrote over one hundred books, including *The War of the Worlds.*

EXERCISE B Revise the following sentences by substituting a proper noun for each common noun. You might have to change some other words in each sentence. You may make up proper names.

Example 1. That parrot belongs to my sister. *Oscar belongs to Lucinda.*

11. Don't forget to take this book to your next class. Don't forget to take A World of Science to your next class.
12. I would love to travel to two other countries. I would love to travel to Germany and Switzerland.
13. To get to that city, you need to get on a highway. To get to Louisville, you need to get on a highway.
14. Before we go to the theater, I should tell my uncle where we'll be. Before we go to the theater, I should tell Uncle Bert where we'll be.
15. I am learning to speak two more languages. I am learning to speak Spanish and German also.

9-20

GRAMMAR

Concrete Nouns, Abstract Nouns, and Collective Nouns

A ***concrete noun*** names a person, place, or thing that can be perceived by one or more of the senses (sight, hearing, taste, touch, smell). An ***abstract noun*** names an idea, a feeling, a quality, or a characteristic.

CONCRETE song, hubcap, dog **ABSTRACT** loyalty, dishonor, trust

A ***collective noun*** is a word that, even when it is singular, names a group.

COLLECTIVE audience, family, batch, herd, class

EXERCISE A Decide whether each of the following nouns is concrete or abstract. Identify each one by writing *CON* for *concrete* or *ABS* for *abstract.*

Examples CON 1. locker

ABS 2. enthusiasm

ABS 1. humor

CON 2. Brazil

CON 3. computer

ABS 4. sympathy

CON 5. Great Barrier Reef

CON 6. bridge

ABS 7. dishonesty

CON 8. Jupiter

ABS 9. procrastination

CON 10. Queen Elizabeth II

EXERCISE B Underline each collective noun in the following sentences.

Example 1. The choir practiced in the new auditorium.

11. I sing tenor in a quartet.
12. Everyone in the group received a door prize.
13. The team arrived early and went to the locker room.
14. As I watched, a flock of geese flew overhead.
15. The jury filed into their seats and listened to the judge's instructions.
16. During lunch today the committee will meet to plan fund-raising events.
17. Can you find your way through this thick grove of trees?
18. The cat and her litter found a home in my dog's abandoned doghouse.
19. When Jared hit the beehive with a stick, a swarm of angry bees flew out.
20. For this short flight, the plane needs a crew of only three.

NAME ____________ CLASS ____________ DATE ____________

Identifying Kinds of Nouns

A ***common noun*** names any one of a group of persons, places, things, or ideas and is generally not capitalized. A ***proper noun*** names a particular person, place, thing, or idea and begins with a capital letter.

COMMON city, monarch **PROPER** Boston, Queen Victoria

A ***concrete noun*** names a person, place, or thing that can be perceived by one or more of the senses (sight, hearing, taste, touch, smell). An ***abstract noun*** names an idea, a feeling, a quality, or a characteristic.

CONCRETE hat, water, finger **ABSTRACT** shyness, fear, need

EXERCISE Identify each underlined noun in the following sentences by writing above it *COM* for *common* or *PRO* for *proper* and *CON* for *concrete* or *ABS* for *abstract*.

COM, CON

Example 1. Have you ever seen a blindfish?

1. Mrs. Perry was planning a field trip to Carlsbad Caverns in New Mexico.

2. Parts of Carlsbad Caverns are still unexplored.

3. The giant formations produce feelings of awe in many visitors.

4. She captured our interest by describing cave-dwelling animals and fish.

5. Blindfish live in dark areas such as caves and underground streams.

6. A distinguishing characteristic of these fish is blindness.

7. They have nerves on their bodies that have a special sensitivity.

8. When tiny animals such as amphipods move, the blindfish senses the movement.

9. In this way, the fish can find and eat smaller animals without using sight.

10. A blindfish may eat its own offspring if it senses their movement.

11. These young fish stop moving when they feel something swimming nearby.

12. Blindfish may be found in Mammoth Cave in Kentucky and in other caves across the U.S.

13. Mammoth Cave is part of the longest known cave system in the world.

14. As a result of our field trip to the caves, I developed a desire to learn more.

15. I learned that geologists study caves and the stalactites and stalagmites within.

16. The Geology Department at Idaho State University has an interesting Web site.

17. It contains photos, information, and links to other Web sites about geology.

18. All of this fascinating information has increased my enthusiasm and curiosity.

19. My cousin belongs to a group of cave explorers.

20. Before I join, I will have to conquer my fear of the dark.

Pronouns and Antecedents

11b. A ***pronoun*** is a word used in place of one or more nouns or pronouns.

The word or word group that a pronoun stands for (or refers to) is called its *antecedent*. Sometimes the antecedent is not stated.

EXAMPLE **John** said **he** would wash **his** car this afternoon.

I told **myself** not to worry.

EXERCISE A In the following sentences, underline each pronoun once. If a pronoun has a stated antecedent, draw an arrow from the pronoun to the antecedent.

Examples **1.** Natasha forgot to bring her notebook.

2. I will tell you about interesting and funny moral tales.

1. You have probably read or heard Aesop's fables.

2. Aesop was once a Greek slave; he may have lived on the island of Samos.

3. Aesop told stories about animals with human traits; they spoke and thought like people.

4. One well-known story is about a boy who cried "Wolf!" even though he saw no wolf.

5. Later, when the boy was in real danger from a wolf, he again cried "Wolf!"

6. The villagers had grown tired of the boy's false alarms, and they ignored his cries.

7. Have you heard the story about the ant and the grasshopper?

8. The grasshopper chirps and plays during summer, and it does not prepare for winter.

9. The ant works hard at storing food, and this food saves it from starving in the winter.

10. Reading these tales is enjoyable, and it doesn't take long.

EXERCISE B Cross out the repeated word or word group in each of the following sentences, and write an appropriate pronoun above it.

Example **1.** Riding a bike is good exercise, but ~~riding a bike~~ *it* can be difficult in cold weather.

11. Larry, will ~~Larry~~ you please work this math problem?

12. These plants do not bear flowers, nor are ~~these plants~~ they poisonous.

13. My ten-year-old cat is jealous, and ~~my ten-year-old cat~~ it has not accepted the new kitten.

14. When Amanda and Kirsten got to class, ~~Amanda and Kirsten~~ they realized they were late.

15. Learning to type is slow, but ~~learning to type~~ it is worthwhile.

NAME CLASS DATE

Personal, Reflexive, and Intensive Pronouns

A ***personal pronoun*** refers to the one speaking *(first person),* the one spoken to *(second person),* or the one spoken about *(third person).* A ***reflexive pronoun*** refers to the subject and is necessary to the meaning of the sentence. An ***intensive pronoun*** emphasizes a noun or another pronoun and is unnecessary to the meaning of the sentence.

PERSONAL **I** would like to invite **you** to a party.

REFLEXIVE I allowed **myself** a budget of fifty dollars.

INTENSIVE She **herself** delivered the invitations.

EXERCISE Underline the pronoun or pronouns in each of the following sentences. Then, identify the kind of pronoun each is. Above each pronoun write *P* for *personal, R* for *reflexive,* or *I* for *intensive.*

Examples **1.** I will call Farid after school myself.

2. Lucia smiled at herself in the mirror.

1. Sara picked up a handout for herself.

2. Are you aware of the dangers of smoking?

3. We should not let ourselves overlook the plight of the homeless.

4. "I will not tolerate lateness," the band leader told us.

5. The principal himself called me with the good news.

6. "Jogging is not for me," said Dr. Wong.

7. The cat found a hiding place for itself.

8. After the twins frosted the cake, they looked for candles to put on it.

9. Before you mop the floor, please move the chairs.

10. Don't wear the new boots until you waterproof them.

11. I can't believe they won the contest!

12. Sometimes I make myself laugh.

13. Max asked, "Are you ready to come with me and do our homework now?"

14. Ms. Lin found herself looking forward to the afternoon classes.

15. Where will you find yourself a sweater like Kerry's?

16. The choir director said that he himself would sing a solo.

17. If you want to join us, call him now.

18. The dog itself opened the gate!

19. Have you met them?

20. The climbers pulled themselves onto the narrow ledge.

Demonstrative Pronouns and Relative Pronouns

A ***demonstrative pronoun*** points out a person, a place, a thing, or an idea. A ***relative pronoun*** introduces a subordinate clause.

DEMONSTRATIVE **These** are the best strawberries of the summer!
That was the worst movie I have ever seen.

RELATIVE Apricots, **which** are smaller than peaches, make tasty pies.
The fence **that** borders our property needs repair.

EXERCISE In each of the following sentences, underline the demonstrative or relative pronoun. Above each pronoun write *D* if it is *demonstrative* or *R* if it is *relative.*

Examples **1.** This (D) is an updated map of Africa.
2. Africa, which (R) is the second largest continent, has several deserts.

1. The equator, which crosses Africa, is at 0° latitude.

2. These are the Atlantic and the Indian Oceans.

3. Chinua Achebe, whose native country is Nigeria, won the Nobel Prize in literature in 1989.

4. The water that lies to the west of Africa is the Atlantic Ocean.

5. "That is the small African republic, Togo," Mr. Lawson told us.

6. The Mediterranean Sea, which borders Africa to the north, is the largest inland sea in the world.

7. Commercial fishers who work in the Mediterranean Sea catch tuna, sardines, and anchovies.

8. These are among the four hundred species of fish in this sea.

9. Is that the Kalahari Desert or the Sahara?

10. The country in Africa that fascinates me most is Egypt.

11. Joseph Conrad, whom I studied in English class, wrote a novel about the Congo.

12. Captain Marlow, who is the main character of *Heart of Darkness,* is a sailor.

13. Libya, which lies south of the Mediterranean Sea, borders the western side of Egypt.

14. "Is this Madagascar?" I asked, pointing to an island east of Africa.

15. The map doesn't show the Tropic of Capricorn, which runs through Madagascar.

16. That is not possible!

17. The Tropic of Capricorn is an imaginary line that marks the southern edge of the tropics.

18. That is the Tropic of Cancer, the northern boundary of the tropics.

19. They are the southernmost and northernmost points at which the sun is directly overhead.

20. These are really hard to see on this map.

Indefinite Pronouns and Interrogative Pronouns

An ***indefinite pronoun*** refers to a person, a place, a thing, or an idea that may or may not be specifically named. An ***interrogative pronoun*** introduces a question.

INDEFINITE	He said that **anyone** can do this simple trick.
	Most of my friends drink milk.
INTERROGATIVE	**Who** knows the words to the song?
	Which of these books have you read?

EXERCISE A Identify each underlined pronoun in the following sentences by writing above it *IND* if it is *indefinite* or *INT* if it is *interrogative*.

Examples **1.** Do both (*IND*) of these costumes belong to you?

2. What (*INT*) did you and Tom do on Friday night?

1. Will many attend the school play?

2. Several of my friends are attending with me.

3. Who did you say is the lead actor?

4. Nobody is more excited about the play than I!

5. Which of the costumes do you prefer?

EXERCISE B In each sentence, underline the indefinite or interrogative pronoun. Identify each pronoun by writing above it *IND* if it is *indefinite* or *INT* if it is *interrogative*.

Examples **1.** Did she say that either (*IND*) of these answers is correct?

2. "Whose (*INT*) is this sweater?" asked Ms. Martin.

6. Whom are you tutoring in Spanish?

7. Everything is starting to make sense now.

8. Few could restrain their laughter at the unexpected joke.

9. Will somebody erase the chalkboards, please?

10. Others are low-fat, such as the baked chicken and rice.

11. Who will volunteer as a tutor this semester?

12. Whose is this backpack blocking the aisle?

13. Many of the dishes in the cafeteria are vegetarian.

14. Which of these science experiments is yours?

15. The principal announced that all will participate in the fund-raising event.

Identifying Kinds of Pronouns

A ***personal pronoun*** refers to the one speaking (first person), the one spoken to (second person), or the one spoken about (third person). A ***reflexive pronoun*** refers to the subject and is necessary to the meaning of the sentence. An ***intensive pronoun*** emphasizes a noun or another pronoun and is unnecessary to the meaning of the sentence.

PERSONAL Will **you** call **me**?

REFLEXIVE Give **yourself** a pat on the back.

INTENSIVE He **himself** won after all.

A ***demonstrative pronoun*** points out a person, a place, a thing, or an idea. A ***relative pronoun*** introduces a subordinate clause.

DEMONSTRATIVE **This** is my favorite poem.

RELATIVE The novel **that** Ms. Ingram assigned is interesting.

An ***indefinite pronoun*** refers to a person, a place, a thing, or an idea that may or may not be specifically named. An ***interrogative pronoun*** introduces a question.

INDEFINITE **All** is lost!

INTERROGATIVE **Who** will read this passage aloud?

EXERCISE Underline the pronoun or pronouns in each of the following sentences. Identify each by writing above it *PER* for *personal, REF* for *reflexive, INTEN* for *intensive, DEM* for *demonstrative, REL* for *relative, IND* for *indefinite,* or *INTER* for *interrogative.*

Example 1. (INTER) What has (PER) she learned about peaches?

1. These are Elberta peaches, which are very popular in the United States.
2. Nobody really knows where the fruit came from originally.
3. We read a story that may or may not be true.
4. Who started the story?
5. A man in Georgia, whose name was Samuel Rumph, grew peaches.
6. One of them was particularly beautiful.
7. The man named the peach after his wife, Elberta.
8. He soon found himself at the forefront of commercial peach production in Georgia.
9. He developed ways to ship peaches so they would arrive in good condition.
10. The Elberta peach itself is very firm and ships well.

NAME CLASS DATE

Adjectives and Articles

11c. An ***adjective*** is a word that is used to modify a noun or a pronoun.

An adjective tells *what kind, which one, how much,* or *how many.*

WHAT KIND Anzu bought **red** shoes. **HOW MUCH** There is **no** water there.

WHICH ONE Viktor is my **oldest** brother. **HOW MANY** I discovered **several** photos.

The adjectives *a, an,* and *the* are called ***articles***. *A* and *an* are called ***indefinite articles*** because they refer to any member of a general group. *The* is called the ***definite article*** because it refers to someone or something in particular.

INDEFINITE Julio went to see **a** movie. **DEFINITE** **The** U.S. flag is red, white, and blue.

EXERCISE A In the following sentences underline each adjective once, and underline each article a second time. Then, above each article write *D* for *definite* or *I* for *indefinite.*

Example 1. The ripe berries attracted two birds and many squirrels.

1. Yes, Sylvia has an older brother.
2. The sudden wind chilled us.
3. Someday you may own a small electric car.
4. Edna ordered a large sandwich with extra onions.
5. The mysterious noises terrified everyone.

EXERCISE B Underline all the adjectives except the articles. Then, draw an arrow from each underlined adjective to the word that it modifies.

Example 1. I love scary stories!

6. Mary Shelley wrote a horror story.
7. The plot of the story was imaginative.
8. One rainy summer, she had listened to several stories about ghosts.
9. Friends had made up scary stories about monsters.
10. Someone challenged the group to write a ghost story.
11. Mary thought about the stories all night and had a strange nightmare.
12. She dreamed of a young scientist who created a monster.
13. Mary wrote a story of the ghastly nightmare and called it *Frankenstein.*
14. The eerie novel was very successful.
15. Several movies have been made from it.

Noun or Adjective?

Many words that can stand alone as nouns can also be used as adjectives modifying nouns or pronouns.

NOUN school, summer **ADJECTIVE** **school** bus, **summer** vacation

EXERCISE A Decide whether the underlined word in each of the following sentences is used as a noun or an adjective. Above each write *N* for *noun* or *A* for *adjective*.

Example 1. Please place your lunch boxes on the shelf. A

1. This town needs a good dress shop. A
2. Allison bought a white dress for the dance.
3. The glass top on that table is difficult to clean. A
4. This glass is still dirty. N
5. Tomorrow is my birthday.
6. Ramona mailed a birthday card to her grandmother.
7. Put some of this good Texas barbecue sauce on your sandwich. A
8. Sam Houston was the president of Texas before it became a state.
9. Many attended the holiday festival. A
10. I received many cards during the holiday.

EXERCISE B Use each of the following words in two sentences. In the first sentence, use the word as a noun. In the second sentence, use the word as an adjective.

Example 1. apple Would you like an apple in your lunch?
I would prefer apple juice.

11. silver ______

12. telephone ______

13. paper ______

14. mouse ______

15. hat ______

NAME ______________________ CLASS ______________ DATE ______________

Demonstrative Adjectives

This, that, these, and *those* can be used both as adjectives and as pronouns. When they modify a noun or pronoun, they are called ***demonstrative adjectives***. When they are used alone, they are called ***demonstrative pronouns***.

ADJECTIVES **These** bags are heavy.
That sound is annoying.

PRONOUNS Please hold **these** for me.
Why won't she stop **that**?

EXERCISE A Identify each underlined word in the following sentences by writing above it *DA* for *demonstrative adjective* or *DP* for *demonstrative pronoun*.

Examples **1.** This (DA) wind cuts like a knife.

2. This (DP) must be the coldest day of winter.

1. Is that cloth as soft as silk?

2. Those peppers burn like fire!

3. These are as valuable as gold.

4. Listen to this girl sing.

5. That is as black as coal.

EXERCISE B Underline the demonstrative adjective or demonstrative pronoun in each of the following sentences. Then, identify each one by writing above it *DA* for *demonstrative adjective* or *DP* for *demonstrative pronoun*.

Examples **1.** I asked whether that (DP) would be on the test.

2. Will you help me with this (DA) homework?

6. These marigolds are a rich shade of gold.

7. On the other hand, those are pale yellow.

8. My windowsill garden contains these herbs: chives, parsley, and basil.

9. Those pepper plants will provide us with plenty of jalapeños.

10. This is the perfect place for the bed of pansies.

11. That plant is poisonous, so don't let the dog chew it.

12. How deeply should I plant these?

13. Should I plant those sunflowers near the fence?

14. That is where I'll place the birdbath.

15. Will those survive the first frost?

for **CHAPTER 11: PARTS OF SPEECH OVERVIEW** ***page 349***

Common and Proper Adjectives

Common adjectives are generally not capitalized. A ***proper adjective*** is formed from a proper noun. Like a proper noun, it is capitalized.

COMMON ADJECTIVE Did you see **beautiful** butterflies?

PROPER NOUN This butterfly is found in **Africa.**

PROPER ADJECTIVE The **African** giant swallowtail is a large butterfly.

EXERCISE A In the following sentences, underline all common adjectives once and all proper adjectives twice. Do not underline the articles *a, an,* and *the.*

Example 1. I have learned to prepare delicious Japanese sushi.

1. I like melodious and eerie Celtic music.
2. Do you prefer Spanish architecture?
3. I'm fascinated by the stories from Greek mythology.
4. Would you come to my New Year's Eve party?
5. Was T. S. Eliot American or English?
6. I love your Australian accent!
7. I am studying Roman architecture as well as modern styles of building.
8. I asked for a gray pony for my thirteenth birthday, but I didn't get one.
9. Ashley Bryan is a master storyteller.
10. Bryan has also illustrated books such as *It's Kwanzaa Time!*

EXERCISE B Change each of the following proper nouns into a proper adjective, and use the adjective to modify a noun.

Example 1. Asia Asian friend

11. Italy ______
12. Buddhism ______
13. Midwest ______
14. Labor Day ______
15. California ______

9/26

Noun, Pronoun, or Adjective?

11a. A ***noun*** is a word or word group that is used to name a person, a place, a thing, or an idea.

11b. A ***pronoun*** is a word used in place of one or more nouns or pronouns.

11c. An ***adjective*** is a word that is used to modify a noun or a pronoun.

NOUNS When will **Tracy** ride her **bicycle** in **Central Park** and relieve some **stress**?

PRONOUNS **She** will go when **he** can go with **her,** and **I** will watch the baby.

ADJECTIVES I usually prefer **mild** cuisine, but I'll try **this spicy Southwestern** dish.

EXERCISE Identify each underlined word in the following sentences by writing above it *N* for *noun*, *P* for *pronoun*, or *A* for *adjective*.

Example 1. The museum is featuring an exhibit on Egyptian mummies.

1. Many have heard about how the pony express carried the mail in 1860 and 1861.
2. However, the pony express lasted only eighteen months.
3. Among its young riders was William Cody, later known as Buffalo Bill.
4. The arrival of transcontinental telegraph lines put an end to the pony express.
5. Even the fastest riders could not compete with the telegraph.
6. Silkworms thrive on a diet of mulberry leaves and form cocoons of silk fiber.
7. A scarf made of wool may be warmer than a silk scarf.
8. These plants have poisonous leaves.
9. I can't believe you said that!
10. This is just a summer shower, so it won't last long.
11. Louis Braille invented a special alphabet that allows people with visual impairments to read.
12. The alphabet uses raised dots that the visually impaired can feel.
13. The dots are arranged in patterns, with different patterns standing for individual letters or sounds.
14. A person reads Braille by rubbing one or two fingertips over the elevated dots.
15. Using a pointed stylus and a metal slate, a person can write Braille by hand.
16. People also use Braille typewriters and computers.
17. These are the short stories that my friends and I wrote.
18. This story is especially funny, and I wrote it.
19. All of us are going to enter the annual short story contest.
20. One of us is sure to win the prize, which is a scholarship to a summer writing workshop.

GRAMMAR

Review A: Nouns

EXERCISE A Underline the nouns in the following sentences.

Example 1. O. Henry wrote "The Gift of the Magi," a short story.

1. William Sydney Porter had talent.
2. The man was a writer.
3. His pen name was O. Henry.
4. Porter spent three years in jail.
5. His first story was published by St. Paul Pioneer Press while he was a prisoner.
6. Owney was a stray dog found behind a post office in New York.
7. The clerks in the post office gave food to the friendly animal.
8. Owney traveled all over the United States, hitching rides on trains.
9. Soon, his collar jingled with metal tags from cities all over the country.
10. Owney traveled to Europe by boat and then was given a jacket to hold all the tags.

EXERCISE B Decide whether each underlined noun in the following sentences is common or proper, concrete or abstract. Then, on the line provided, write *COM* for *common* or *PROP* for *proper* and *CON* for *concrete* or *ABS* for *abstract.*

Example COM, CON **1.** You can find maps in encyclopedias and on the Internet.

_______ **11.** Maps change over time.

_______ **12.** Some changes are caused by human beings.

_______ **13.** Old maps do not show the Suez Canal.

_______ **14.** Nature changes the outlines of continents and oceans.

_______ **15.** The Caspian Sea is a good example.

_______ **16.** This small inland sea is filling up with sediment.

_______ **17.** Centuries ago, the Caspian Sea was larger.

_______ **18.** The Red Sea seems to be growing.

_______ **19.** Many different forces affect the surface of the earth.

_______ **20.** Wind, water, and movement of the earth's crust are powerful forces.

Review B: **Pronouns and Antecedents**

EXERCISE A In the following sentences, underline each pronoun once. If a pronoun has a stated antecedent, underline the antecedent twice. Then, identify the type of pronoun by writing above it *P* for *personal*, *R* for *reflexive*, or *I* for *intensive*.

Example 1. Did Maria buy herself a silver bracelet yesterday? (R)

1. The instructor herself first demonstrated the dive.

2. Aaron cooked the entire meal himself.

3. The proud athlete will display her trophy in the school's trophy case.

4. A frightened hedgehog curls itself into a ball.

5. The artist wanted you to come to the gallery opening.

6. Tyra baked two loaves and then sliced them.

7. The swim team outdid itself in the freestyle relay.

8. Consuela smiled and said, "I know the words to the song."

9. The senator herself signed the letter.

10. Is the sponge you bought natural or artificial?

EXERCISE B Underline each pronoun in the following sentences. Then, identify each by writing above it *DEM* for *demonstrative*, *INT* for *interrogative*, *IND* for *indefinite*, or *REL* for *relative*.

Examples 1. This (DEM) is the dog that (REL) Marcus found last weekend.

2. Who (INT) is the person most admired by all (IND)?

11. Who is the boy who wore the red wig in the first act?

12. Hairstyle is one of the personal details that Janet always notices.

13. Everyone who enters the lab must wear a coverall.

14. Whom will the class choose as a representative?

15. Lily was the only person who voted against the measure.

16. These are the best photographs that Pat has ever seen!

17. Jamal called the house, but no one answered.

18. Please put away the boxes that are on the floor, and then help Marvin move this.

19. What should Susan bring to the party?

20. Of all the fruits, these have the most vitamin C.

Review C: Adjectives and Articles

EXERCISE A Underline each article in the following sentences. Identify each article by writing above it *D* for *definite* or *I* for *indefinite*. Then, circle each adjective that is not an article.

Example 1. Most people consider the rose a beautiful flower.

1. Have you ever seen the huge rosebush in Tombstone, Arizona?
2. Every spring, the bush is covered with white flowers.
3. The bush was brought over from Great Britain.
4. It is a specimen of the Lady Banksia rose.
5. It has a thick trunk and many branches.
6. The plant is very old now.
7. Many people travel to Tombstone to see this bush.
8. It grows beside the old Rose Tree Inn.
9. The rosebush covers a large area.
10. One source calls it the largest rosebush in the world.

EXERCISE B In the following sentences, underline each adjective and draw an arrow from the adjective to the noun or pronoun it modifies. Do not include the articles *a, an,* and *the.*

Example 1. Aunt Laurie has a beautiful cameo that is quite old.

11. A cameo is a carving on a striated gemstone, semiprecious gem, or shell.
12. A striated gem or shell has veins of different colors.
13. The artist cuts the carving on the lighter color.
14. The darker color forms a complementary background.
15. Nowadays most cameos feature the profile of a head.
16. The history of cameos traces back to ancient Egypt, Greece, and Etruria.
17. The ancient Egyptians placed carved stone seals in their tombs.
18. The carved pattern on these seals was the scarab beetle.
19. The scarab was a mystic symbol.
20. Ancient Egyptians sometimes wore a carving of a scarab as a charm.

Literary Model: Poem

Mama Is a Sunrise

When she comes slip-footing through the door,
she kindles us
like lump coal lighted,
and we wake up glowing.
She puts a spark even in Papa's eyes
and turns out all our darkness.

When she comes sweet-talking in the room,
she warms us
like grits and gravy,
and we rise up shining.
Even at nighttime Mama is a sunrise
that promises tomorrow and tomorrow.

—by *Evelyn Tooley Hunt*

EXERCISE A Underline the nouns in the above poem. Then, fill in the blanks below so that each noun is listed in its appropriate category. Note: Do not write the same noun twice in one category.

Common Nouns

Proper Nouns

EXERCISE B

1. A *metaphor* is a comparison between two unlike things in which one thing is said to be another thing. In the poem above, to what does the poet compare the character Mama? (Hint: Your response to Exercise A should contain the answer.)

2. What do you think the poet is trying to communicate about Mama and the impression that she has on her family? How do words such as "lump coal" and "grits and gravy" support the poet's characterization of Mama?

Literary Model (continued)

EXERCISE C

1. Choose a family member to be the subject of a poem. At the top of the following space, write the name of the family member. Reflect on him or her for a few minutes. Then, thinking in terms of one or more metaphors, brainstorm a list of nouns that relate to this person and write them under the name. You will use some or all of these nouns in the poem. As Evelyn Tooley Hunt did, try to include nouns that have an unusual connection to a human being.

2. Write the poem on the lines below.

EXERCISE D How did you use nouns to describe the family member? Why did you use these particular nouns and not any others?

Writing Application: Journal Entry

When writers use common nouns, they could be referring to any member of a general group. Sometimes, though, writers want to name a specific person, place, thing, or idea. To do this, writers use proper nouns. Substituting proper nouns for common nouns can make nearly any piece of writing more memorable.

GENERAL The girl lives in the city.

SPECIFIC Judy Martin lives in San Francisco.

In the first sentence, the common noun *girl* does not name a young female in particular. It could refer to any girl, just as the common noun *city* could refer to any city. In the second sentence, the proper noun *Judy Martin* tells exactly whom the author means, and the proper noun *San Francisco* tells exactly where she lives. Notice that proper nouns are capitalized.

Writing Activity

Your class is gathering material for a time capsule to be opened in a hundred years. Your teacher has asked you and your classmates each to write a journal entry describing the everyday life of a student. Your journal entry will be a historical document when it is unearthed in a hundred years. Historians look for the specific names of people, places, things, and ideas when studying the past. To give the historians a clear picture of your life, include at least ten proper nouns in your journal entry. For example, provide interesting details about your friends, your school, your neighborhood, or your favorite books and music.

PREWRITING You cannot include every moment of the day in your journal entry, so make a list of the highlights of your day. Think of details that you can add to flesh out events and personalize your description.

WRITING Decide how to organize your journal entry. For example, you could write about events in chronological order. Another option is to arrange topics by subject. However you decided to organize your entry, do not just list events, but create a narrative with smooth transitions between topics.

REVISING Read through your journal entry, pretending that it was written by a stranger. Do you gain a sense of what a day in this "other person's" life was like? If not, what is missing?

PUBLISHING Check your journal entry for errors in spelling and punctuation. Remember to capitalize all proper nouns. Compare your journal entry with those of your classmates. Are your experiences similar? What specific things do you have in common? What specific things are different? After you and your classmates have compared journal entries, consider including your journal entries in a real time capsule.

Extending Your Writing

You may wish to develop this writing exercise further. You might write about your personal opinions or reactions to current events, making sure to choose events that you think people might be interested in a hundred years from now. Or you might write down your guesses as to what everyday life will be like a hundred years from now.

Choices: Investigating Parts of Speech

Here's your chance to step out of the grammar book and into the real world. You may not realize it, but people around you use parts of speech every day. The following activities challenge you to find a connection between parts of speech and the world around you. Do the activity below that suits your personality best, and then share your discoveries with your class. Have fun!

RESEARCH/ETYMOLOGY

Deep Roots

Look up the etymologies of the words that name these parts of speech—*verb, adverb, preposition, conjunction,* and *interjection.* Where and when did these words originate? What are their roots? If it is available in your school library, check the *Oxford English Dictionary.* Present your research to your classmates, and pass out copies of your findings. Post appropriate notes on a time line.

LINGUISTICS

Staples, Hinges, and Glue

Conjunction is a pretty cool word, but maybe you can think of a better one. With a friend, brainstorm some new names for the coordinating conjunctions. First, think about what conjunctions do. Then, ask yourself what other things join things together. Are these joints permanent or temporary? How strong are they? Then, tell your classmates about your new terminology.

CREATIVE WRITING

Who Am I?

If you could bring the parts of speech to life, how would you make them act? If you were an interjection, what would you be like? Would you prefer philosophy or sports? Would you be organized and calm or impulsive and emotional? Write a personality profile for three parts of speech. Then, share (or perform) your profiles.

VISUAL LEARNING

Apples to Oranges

Who says you can't compare apples to oranges? Use colors to code the parts of speech in a paragraph. Then, choose a famous poem and color-code it. When you show your code to the class, also tell them which task (color-coding the paragraph or color-coding the poem) was harder.

PERFORMANCE

Walk On

Have you ever heard the words *traipse* and *sashay*? They are both synonyms for *walk.* Use a thesaurus to look up the word *walk.* Make a list of all the synonyms. Then, show your classmates that adverbs aren't the only words that show *how.* The right verb can do the job, too. Demonstrate how to walk in at least five different ways.

MATHEMATICS

The X Factor

Consider the following questions as you write a one-page essay that compares math to grammar: In mathematics, what elements of equations or formulas could function as parts of speech? For instance, what part of speech would a number be? How about a plus sign? Choose several math symbols, and tell whether each of your choices acts like a certain part of speech. Explain your comparisons to the class.

SPORTS REPORTING

It's *How* That Counts

What would sports reporting be without adverbs? Write a newspaper account of a sporting event at your school. First, write the account without using any adverbs. Then, revise the account to include as many adverbs as you can without sounding silly. Which version is easier to write? Don't forget the headline (and the byline)!

ORIGINAL PROJECT

One of a Kind

Make up your own project. Illustrate transitive verbs, draw a cartoon of a preposition and a verb having a conversation, develop an electronic slide show, use a Venn diagram to compare transitive and intransitive verbs, or invent some other project. Be sure to get your teacher's permission.

NAME CLASS DATE

The Verb

12a. A ***verb*** is a word that expresses action or a state of being.

EXAMPLES The giraffes **munched** on fresh leaves.
They **are** herbivores.

EXERCISE Underline each verb in the following sentences.

Examples **1.** The giraffe is the tallest mammal in the world.

2. It eats from high tree branches in the African savanna.

1. The giraffe's neck forms about half of its height.

2. The giraffe has a short tufted mane on its long neck.

3. A mature giraffe is approximately eighteen feet tall.

4. All giraffes develop two to four horns.

5. Reddish brown splotches highlight their pale brown coats.

6. The glass snake is actually a legless lizard.

7. Some people call them glass lizards.

8. These lizards live in North America, Eurasia, and Africa.

9. Their smooth skins are usually brown or green.

10. A groove runs along each side of the glass snake's body.

11. The glowworm is a wingless female beetle.

12. Organs inside these beetles and their larvae emit a glow.

13. *Firefly* is the term for the male.

14. The male, not the female, flies.

15. Hares are large members of the rabbit family.

16. Many adult hares weigh up to ten pounds.

17. The ears of a hare are longer than its head.

18. The fur of the arctic hare turns white in winter for camouflage.

19. Its ears are shorter than the ears of the Mediterranean brown hare.

20. The jack rabbit is a familiar North American hare.

Action Verbs

12b. An ***action verb*** is a verb that expresses either physical or mental activity.

EXAMPLES John Muir **wrote** about Yosemite National Park.
Eileen **imagined** the scene.

EXERCISE A Underline the action verb in each of the following sentences.

Examples **1.** Jon and I hiked for several miles.

2. Both of us admired the brilliant fall foliage.

1. Jon collected gold, red, and yellow leaves.

2. He carefully placed them in his backpack.

3. I wondered why.

4. Later, he told me about his plan.

5. He knew of a market for these beautiful leaves.

6. A local craft shop buys the leaves for craft classes.

7. For example, the class on greeting cards uses colorful leaves regularly.

8. The art classes always want leaves, too.

9. Artists incorporate the foliage into collages.

10. People enjoy the "back to nature" tone of this artwork.

EXERCISE B Underline each action verb in the following sentences. Then, identify the type of action of the verb by writing above it *P* for *physical action* or *M* for *mental action.*

Examples **1.** My mother makes (P) delicious red beans and rice.

2. Today, however, I crave (M) Cajun gumbo.

11. I remember my great-grandmother's recipe for gumbo.

12. The shrimp, vegetables, and spices simmer together.

13. I always drop a little hot pepper sauce into the pot.

14. Meanwhile, white rice steams until tender.

15. I prefer this mild rice along with the spicy gumbo.

Linking Verbs

12c. A ***linking verb*** is a verb that expresses a state of being. A linking verb connects, or links, the subject to a word or word group that identifies or describes the subject.

LINKING VERB Your painting **is** beautiful!

Some verbs may be either action verbs or linking verbs, depending on how they are used.

ACTION VERB Paco **tasted** the soup.

LINKING VERB Those vegetables **tasted** fresh.

EXERCISE A Underline the linking verb in each of the following sentences. Then, draw an arrow showing which words are joined by the linking verb.

Example 1. The old house looked deserted.

1. The huge diamond mine is now a museum.
2. The computerized voice sounds human to me.
3. After the storm, the islanders grew nervous at the sight of all the dark clouds.
4. Some of the bristlecone pine trees are very old.
5. The farm animals looked quite content.

EXERCISE B Underline the verbs in the following sentences. Then, identify each as an action verb or a linking verb by writing above it *A* for *action verb* or *L* for *linking verb.*

Example 1. Aaron Burr was the third Vice President of the United States.

6. Burr became one of the most colorful characters in U.S. history.
7. Burr came from a well-known Puritan family.
8. At age twenty-one, he was a commanding officer of an entire regiment.
9. He resigned in 1779 because of ill health.
10. Later, Burr practiced law.
11. He almost always looked wealthy and successful.
12. Burr and Alexander Hamilton were longtime enemies.
13. Burr fought a duel with Hamilton.
14. Hamilton died from his wound.
15. Burr's political career was soon over.

GRAMMAR

Helping Verbs and Main Verbs

12d. A ***helping verb*** *(auxiliary verb)* helps the main verb express action or a state of being.

EXAMPLE Christopher **can** sing beautifully.

A ***verb phrase*** contains one main verb and one or more helping verbs. Sometimes a verb phrase is interrupted by another part of speech.

EXAMPLES The code **was hidden** inside an old book. [The helping verb is *was*.]
Sparky **will** not **bite** you. [The helping verb is *will*.]

EXERCISE A Underline the verb phrase in each sentence. Then, draw another line under each helping verb.

Examples 1. People have celebrated birthdays in many different ways.

2. I didn't forget your birthday.

1. Perhaps we should learn more about birthday celebrations in various countries.
2. Mexicans will sometimes buy a piñata for a birthday party.
3. The piñata is filled with small treats and gifts.
4. In Mexico, families will usually celebrate a girl's fifteenth birthday with a special party.
5. This traditional celebration is called a *quinceañera.*
6. In the United States, a girl's sixteenth birthday is often treated as a special birthday.
7. Some people do not like birthday celebrations.
8. They might not tell you their age.
9. Other people have celebrated in spectacular ways.
10. Maybe I will celebrate my birthday in a new way this year.

EXERCISE B Underline the verb phrases in the following paragraph. Then, draw a second line under the helping verb in each phrase. Hint: The paragraph contains ten verb phrases. 10

Example A storm will sometimes produce thunder and lightning.

Scientists can explain the causes of thunder. The sound of thunder is caused by the heat of lightning. A bolt of lightning can heat nearby air molecules. The air molecules will then expand, and they will also move. Their movement can create sounds and echoes. Because light can travel faster than sound, you will first see the lightning. The flash will occur almost immediately; only afterward will you hear the thunder.

Transitive and Intransitive Verbs

12e. A ***transitive verb*** is a verb that expresses an action directed toward a person, a place, a thing, or an idea.

12f. An ***intransitive verb*** expresses action (or tells something about the subject) without the action passing to a receiver, or object.

TRANSITIVE Ingrid **left** her sneakers in the gym.
INTRANSITIVE The runner **stretched** before the race.

A verb may be transitive in one sentence and intransitive in another.

TRANSITIVE The settlers **endured** many hardships.
INTRANSITIVE Many died, but a few **endured** for years.

EXERCISE A Identify the underlined verb by writing above it *T* for *transitive* or *I* for *intransitive*.

Example 1. Ira finished (T) his homework.

1. At this airport, no planes land after dark.
2. My sister and I planted tomatoes and onions.
3. Rick's parrot screams all day long.
4. Everyone ran quickly toward the exit.
5. Of all the contestants, Ming Chin caught the largest fish.

EXERCISE B Add a word or word group to each of the following sentences to change each intransitive verb into a transitive one. Write your expanded sentences on the lines provided.

Example 1. Amos is driving to Seattle. *Amos is driving a truck to Seattle.*

6. Erin will not forget. ______________________
7. Ernesto will recite next. ______________________
8. Today we will draw with charcoal. ______________________
9. While one partner works, the other watches. ______________________
10. Michael, can you cook? ______________________

Identifying Kinds of Verbs

12b. An ***action verb*** is a verb that expresses either physical or mental activity.

ACTION I **memorized** the definitions and then **wrote** them perfectly on the test.

12c. A ***linking verb*** is a verb that expresses a state of being. A linking verb connects, or links, the subject to a word or word group that identifies or describes the subject.

LINKING The test **was** pretty hard.

12d. A ***helping verb*** (***auxiliary verb***) helps the main verb express action or a state of being.

HELPING Ms. Mandell **will** grade the tests tonight.

12e. A ***transitive verb*** is a verb that expresses an action directed toward a person, a place, a thing, or an idea.

TRANSITIVE Ms. Mandell **wrote** the answers on the chalkboard.

12f. An ***intransitive verb*** expresses action (or tells something about the subject) without the action passing to a receiver, or object.

INTRANSITIVE Ms. Mandell **wrote** on the chalkboard.

EXERCISE A Identify each underlined verb by writing above it *A* for *action verb* or *L* for *linking verb*. Then, circle any helping verbs.

Example 1. Please (do) paint the doghouse on Saturday. [A]

1. We are late, Tony.
2. That would be wonderful!
3. Terrence sings in the school choir.
4. I have traveled to Scotland twice.
5. I dreamed vividly last night.
6. Throw the football!
7. How far is the park?
8. Guess again, Lori.
9. She has become quite famous.
10. Will you come to my party?

EXERCISE B Identify each underlined verb by writing above it *T* for *transitive* or *I* for *intransitive*.

Example 1. My parakeet has been quiet today. [I]

11. Several songbirds chirped sweetly outside my window.
12. This weekend we will build a bird feeder.
13. I will fill it with birdseed daily.
14. Dozens of birds will visit our backyard soon.
15. I can relax while listening to bird songs.

NAME ______________________ CLASS ______________ DATE ______________

The Adverb

12g. An ***adverb*** is a word that modifies a verb, an adjective, or another adverb.

An adverb tells *where, when, how, how often, how long, to what extent,* or *how much.*

EXAMPLE **Yesterday** my next-door neighbor was **extremely** kind. [*Yesterday* modifies the verb *was,* and *extremely* modifies the adjective *kind.*]

EXERCISE A Underline the adverb in each of the following sentences. Then, circle the word or words that each adverb modifies.

Example 1. You can rarely get tickets for this horse show.

1. Vivi Malloy rides her horse daily.
2. She has always wanted to make the U.S. Equestrian Team.
3. Vivi rides a very attractive chestnut horse named Penny Red.
4. Vivi usually cleans the horse's stall after school.
5. Then she grooms her horse.
6. Vivi mounts Penny Red cheerfully.
7. Penny Red trots briskly around the ring.
8. Penny Red and Vivi especially enjoy jumping.
9. They have competed successfully in several shows.
10. Vivi's parents always attend her shows.

EXERCISE B Provide appropriate adverbs to fill the blanks in the following sentences.

Example 1. Medieval castles have ___always___ fascinated me.

11. Castle walls were ______________ thick.
12. Many medieval castles were protected ______________ by moats.
13. The moats were ______________ filled with water.
14. People ______________ crossed the moats on drawbridges.
15. These bridges could ______________ be raised.

Adverbs and the Words They Modify

12g. An ***adverb*** is a word that modifies a verb, an adjective, or another adverb.

Adverbs may come before, after, or between the words they modify.

EXAMPLES Armand **quickly** mowed the yard.

He rested **briefly.**

He has **faithfully** worked in the Fosters' yard all summer.

EXERCISE On the line provided, rewrite each of the following sentences, adding one or more adverbs. Then, identify the word or words being modified and tell whether each is a verb, adjective, or adverb.

Example 1. Armand and I have been earning pocket money. *Armand and I have been earning pocket money daily. [Daily modifies have been earning, a verb.]*

1. Most of the kids we know are spending money.
2. They are also complaining about not having enough money.
3. They get their allowance.
4. They spend it all.
5. Armand and I do not want to spend every cent we have.
6. Armand mows lawns in his neighborhood.
7. Mowing lawns isn't practical for me because I live in an apartment building.
8. Instead, I walk dogs and run errands for people in my building.
9. I can earn extra money and meet new neighbors.
10. I am saving my earnings in a bank account.

NAME CLASS DATE

GRAMMAR

Adverb or Adjective?

Many adverbs end in *–ly*. These adverbs are generally formed by adding *–ly* to adjectives.

ADJECTIVES loud shocking great
ADVERBS loudly shockingly greatly

However, some words ending in *–ly* are used as adjectives.

ADJECTIVES **early** arrival **friendly** smile

EXERCISE Draw an arrow from each underlined word to the word it modifies. Then, identify each underlined word by writing above it *ADV* for *adverb* or *ADJ* for *adjective.*

Example 1. The ADJ ghastly rodent frightened us all.

1. The ADJ kindly stranger helped the lost child.
2. At noon, the whistle blew ADV shrilly.
3. I ADV carefully tested the heat of the water.
4. My young niece's ADJ frilly dress was handmade by her mother.
5. I rose ADV early and jogged three miles.
6. The ADJ early bird catches the worm.
7. Candace had ADV rarely been late.
8. For some reason, I laughed ADV uncontrollably.
9. I pack my own lunch ADV daily.
10. My ADJ daily lunch is fruit, pretzels, and a sandwich.
11. This ADV brightly lit room will be perfect for my art studio.
12. The air over the city is ADV refreshingly clear of smog.
13. The ADJ timely bell saved me from a dozen more sit-ups in gym class.
14. I was ADV extremely tired by the end of the day.
15. The ADJ monthly meeting was held in the cafeteria.
16. The club meets ADV monthly, doesn't it?
17. With a ADJ queenly smile, she dismissed the knight.
18. John smiled ADV shyly and then started to laugh.
19. Our ADJ yearly trip to Vermont was postponed.
20. He ADV easily lifted the cabinet.

Ask Emily

The Preposition

12h. A ***preposition*** is a word that shows the relationship of a noun or pronoun to another word.

EXAMPLE The dog jumped **through** the hoop.

EXERCISE A Underline the preposition in each of the following sentences.

Example 1. This article about oceans is surprisingly interesting.

1. The bottom of the ocean is very dark.
2. In most places, it is also cold.
3. However, in some places the ocean floor is warm.
4. One such place is near the Galapagos Islands.
5. Scientists discovered a crack in the ocean floor.
6. They found that heat poured from this crack.
7. The heat was rising from the earth.
8. Many plants and animals lived around this spot.
9. Tiny bacteria lived near giant worms.
10. These life forms lived eight thousand feet below the water's surface.

EXERCISE B Write a preposition that correctly completes each blank in the following sentences.

Example 1. My pet lizard ran ___behind___ the door.

11. Should the dog be allowed ______________ the sofa?
12. You will find a patch of flowers ______________ the bridge.
13. Please store the fruit ______________ the vegetables, Gary.
14. ______________ the water, I saw a faint light glowing.
15. I finished the race several seconds ______________ Jay.
16. Both cats came racing ______________ the corner.
17. Did your parents park the car ______________ the building?
18. The squirrel quickly climbed the trunk ______________ the tree.
19. ______________ the beginning of the school year, we have been assigned to the same seats.
20. The runner ______________ me almost tripped just before the finish line.

NAME ______________________ CLASS ______________ DATE ______________

Prepositional Phrases

A ***prepositional phrase*** includes a preposition, a noun or pronoun called the ***object of the preposition,*** and any modifiers of that object.

EXAMPLE Dr. Okana peered **through the huge telescope.** [*Through* is the preposition, and *telescope* is the object of the preposition. The adjectives *the* and *huge* modify *telescope.*]

EXERCISE A Underline the prepositional phrase in each sentence. Then, circle the preposition.

Example 1. I looked for a key under the muddy doormat.

1. A copper-colored snake slithered along the rotting log.
2. During a crisis David sometimes loses his temper.
3. The pigs found their food under the shallow water.
4. That ancient bridge was built 155 feet above the Gard River.
5. The newscaster slipped on the ice as he hurried along.

EXERCISE B Prepositional phrases can be used to add interesting information to sentences. Add prepositional phrases to the following sentences. Rewrite the sentences on the lines provided.

Example 1. We sailed slowly.

At dawn, we sailed slowly through the rocky channel.

6. The frightened soldier hid. ______________________

7. Canditha wore a beautiful scarf. ______________________

8. Suddenly, the prisoners heard a faint scratching noise. ______________________

9. The creature had hideous green tentacles. ______________________

10. The noisy helicopter landed. ______________________

Preposition or Adverb?

Some words may be used either as prepositions or as adverbs. Remember that a preposition always has an object. An adverb never does.

PREPOSITION Please step **aboard** my boat.

ADVERB Please step **aboard.**

EXERCISE Identify the underlined word or word group in each sentence by writing above it *ADV* for *adverb* or *PREP* for *preposition*.

Example 1. Why did you tell me to get out? ADV

1. The poison ivy climbed around the trunk of the tree. Prep
2. I looked up but didn't see the source of the noise. ADV
3. The ship slowly sailed away. ADV
4. Do not put the bread bag near the hot burner on the stove. Prep
5. When did you say you are coming over? Adv
6. I could go to your house instead. Prep
7. If I inherited a million dollars, I would spread my wealth around a little. Prep bit
8. For example, I would give all my friends a shopping spree in their favorite stores. Prep
9. My brother got a ticket for parking in front of a fire hydrant. Prep
10. He was able to pay the fine through the mail. Prep
11. Should I flip the pancake over yet? ADV
12. I could barely squeeze through. ADV
13. Once upon a time, there was a very hungry dragon. Prep
14. Without you and Jessie, I couldn't have done it. Prep
15. I can sprint to that tree or beyond it. Prep
16. I have never seen anything like this before! ADV
17. Our star party will last from dusk till dawn. Adv
18. Is there really a ghost in *Wuthering Heights*? Prep
19. Yes, the ghost of Catherine tries to get inside Heathcliff's house during a storm. Prep
20. With the dog close behind, the cat scrambled up the fence and out of its reach. Prep

The Conjunction A

12i. A ***conjunction*** is a word that joins words or word groups.

COORDINATING CONJUNCTION You can eat **or** sleep first.

CORRELATIVE CONJUNCTION Your tropical fish **not only** will survive **but also** will thrive.

EXERCISE A Underline the conjunctions in the following sentences.

Example 1. Neither the cantaloupe nor the pineapple appealed to me.

1. I pressed the button, but the elevator did not stop.
2. Either Eddie or Pang will deliver the furniture.
3. We wanted to go sledding, but the snow was starting to melt.
4. Jennifer repeated the caller's number and wrote it on the pad.
5. Neither strawberries nor raspberries are in season right now.
6. Pandora was curious but frightened.
7. Don't sail now, for the winds are too strong.
8. The children are not only tired but also cranky.
9. Leotie wondered whether she should go or stay home.
10. Do you want me to make the fruit punch or blow up the balloons?

EXERCISE B Provide an appropriate conjunction for each blank in the following sentences.

Example 1. ___Both___ Lewis ___and___ his sister like the taste of seafood.

11. I don't know whether it's too cool __________ not cool enough in here.
12. Lightning bolts struck the tree, __________ it remained standing.
13. I do not want a cat, __________ do I want a dog.
14. __________ a parrot __________ a snake is the pet for me!
15. Parrots can speak, __________ they can be very noisy.
16. __________ the actor __________ the director were exhausted by the end of the play.
17. I like to sew, __________ getting the details right takes patience.
18. We will drive to Santa Fe, __________ she decides to come with us __________ not.
19. __________ did she win the election, __________ she __________ won it by a huge margin!
20. Carrie knows this area better than anyone else, __________ she will lead the expedition.

The Conjunction B

12i. A ***conjunction*** is a word that joins words or word groups.

(1) ***Coordinating conjunctions*** join words or word groups that are used in the same way.
(2) ***Correlative conjunctions*** are pairs of conjunctions that join words or word groups that are used in the same way.

COORDINATING My dog Neptune is afraid of thunder, **so** he is hiding under the bed.
CORRELATIVE **Whether** we rent a movie **or** see one at the theater does not matter to me.

EXERCISE Combine each pair of sentences by using one or more conjunctions.

Example 1. You can bus the tables. You can wash the dishes. *You can either bus the tables or wash the dishes.*

1. Rudy plays the trumpet. Rudy plays the trombone. __________

2. The horse bucked. The horse reared. __________

3. Scott served the first course. Paco served the first course. __________

4. My sister does not speak Russian. My sister does not read Russian. __________

5. The building trembled. The building did not collapse. __________

6. Daniel played basketball. Daniel played baseball. __________

7. The birds ate from the bird feeder. The squirrels ate from the bird feeder. __________

8. A large bear waded into the water. A large bear caught a salmon. __________

9. The candle flickered. The candle went out. __________

10. Shannon studied the trees in the forest. Shannon studied the plants in the forest. __________

The Interjection

12j. An ***interjection*** is a word that expresses emotion.

Usually an interjection is followed by an exclamation point. Sometimes an interjection is set off by a comma or by two commas.

EXAMPLES **Hey!** Come back here!

Well, you could try a lighter bat.

I'd guess**, oh,** twenty pounds.

EXERCISE Underline the interjections in the following sentences.

Example 1. Yikes! A spider almost crawled on my foot.

1. Ouch! I stubbed my toe.
2. Oh, maybe we should wait.
3. Help! My experiment blew up!
4. Well, it isn't raining as hard now.
5. You won that much? Wow!
6. Eureka! I have found it!
7. Well, it sounds like fun, but I have to work.
8. Hooray! We won first place!
9. Oops! I spilled juice on the floor.
10. Shucks, that's not so fast.
11. She swung the bat and, bam, the ball flew out of the park.
12. Pow! Every time he hits the bag it pops back.
13. Oh, that isn't so impressive.
14. After it started raining, well, we went home.
15. Aha! So you're the mysterious good Samaritan!
16. Okay, I'll go to the park with you.
17. Uh-oh, here comes trouble.
18. Goodness! I hope everyone is unhurt.
19. You ran a marathon? Whew!
20. Wow, I didn't even know that bird could whistle.

for CHAPTER 12: PARTS OF SPEECH OVERVIEW page 379

Determining Parts of Speech

12k. The way a word is used in a sentence determines what part of speech it is.

VERB Please **place** the bowl of flowers on the table. [*Place* can also be a noun.]

ADVERB May we go **within**? [*Within* can also be a preposition.]

PREPOSITION All **but** one finished. [*But* can also be a conjunction.]

CONJUNCTION I wanted to **but** couldn't. [*But* can also be a preposition.]

INTERJECTION **Goodness!** It's completely dark in here. [*Goodness* can also be a noun.]

EXERCISE Each of the following sentences contains one or more underlined words. Identify the part of speech of each underlined word or word group by writing above it *V* for *verb*, *ADV* for *adverb*, *PREP* for *preposition*, *C* for *conjunction*, or *I* for *interjection*.

Example 1. <u>Expertly</u> following the map, she led us to the cave.

1. Maps are <u>very</u> popular with collectors.
2. Some <u>have sold</u> for very high prices.
3. High prices have encouraged the publication of special books <u>and</u> magazines.
4. Valuable maps must be <u>carefully</u> protected from light and dust.
5. Many of the most valuable maps are kept <u>inside</u> closed drawers.
6. <u>Oh</u>, that really is a treasure map.
7. The Library of Congress houses the world's largest collection <u>of</u> maps.
8. <u>Within</u> its vault are more than 4.5 million maps.
9. In the Geography and Map Division, you may use <u>either</u> an atlas <u>or</u> a globe.
10. In this collection <u>are</u> many unusual maps.
11. Some of the maps <u>there</u> are on public display.
12. <u>Carefully</u>, the librarian opened the first volume of Ptolemy's *Guide to Geography*.
13. <u>Later</u>, he showed us a globe from the eighteenth century.
14. The archaeologist looked <u>inside</u> the cave and thought she saw a map on the wall.
15. In ancient times, the Babylonians drew maps <u>on</u> clay tablets.
16. <u>Wow</u>! Look at this Inuit map painted on an animal skin!
17. This old map shows <u>both</u> the northern hemisphere <u>and</u> the southern hemisphere.
18. <u>Say</u>, do you know how to read this road atlas?
19. The bold print in the atlas can be read <u>easily</u>.
20. <u>Yesterday</u> we used the road atlas to find a route to St. Louis.

Review A: Verbs

EXERCISE A Identify each underlined verb by writing above it *A* for *action verb* or *L* for *linking verb.*

Example 1. We were fearful of the unusually violent winds.

1. The apartment has been too warm all week.
2. Before diving, always look below you for possible hazards.
3. In his old age, my dog has become quite gray around the muzzle.
4. As he climbed the tower, Willis felt totally confident.
5. Most of the test subjects dreamed about flying or sailing.
6. My father is glad about it.
7. Quartz crystals vibrate at a constant rate.
8. Alicia wore kneepads and a helmet while she was in-line skating.
9. The baby rabbit remained still until the dog passed by.
10. We may be lost, because this area doesn't look familiar to me.

EXERCISE B Identify each underlined verb by writing above it *T* for *transitive verb* or *I* for *intransitive verb.* Then, circle any helping verbs.

Example 1. The lion was shaking his mane in the wind.

11. The end of the rope fell into the water.
12. All the antelopes raised their heads.
13. Sean has received an award for bravery.
14. During the scavenger hunt, we raced into every store on Main Street.
15. Mu Lan finished her picture just in time for the show.
16. A chameleon's body may grow to be twenty-five inches long.
17. The reptile's tongue can be as long as its body.
18. This long tongue stays rolled up inside the mouth.
19. The chameleon can unroll its tongue very quickly.
20. Chameleons have caught insects many inches away.

Review B: Adverbs, Prepositions, Conjunctions, Interjections

EXERCISE A In each of the following sentences, underline the prepositional phrase. Then, draw a second line under each object of the preposition.

Example 1. The stadium was filled with shouting, enthusiastic fans.

1. Mildred Didrikson Zaharias came from Texas.
2. She was better known as Babe.
3. During her teens, she played basketball.
4. She also excelled in swimming and figure skating.
5. At eighteen, she was a major track star.
6. Before the year's end, she won two Olympic medals.
7. Babe won one medal for the javelin throw.
8. She played baseball with equal skill.
9. Until her early death, she played golf.
10. She won seventeen straight golf tournaments in 1947.

EXERCISE B Identify the underlined word or word group in each of the following sentences by writing above it *ADV* for *adverb*, *C* for *conjunction*, or *I* for *interjection*.

Example 1. Walking energetically (ADV) on the beach is fantastic exercise.

11. Sometimes beachcombers find interesting things on beaches.
12. They are likely to find both bottles and driftwood.
13. A woman found a narwhal tusk there.
14. People once thought the tusks were unicorn horns.
15. But aren't narwhals really imaginary creatures?
16. No, a narwhal is a small arctic whale.
17. The males often grow a single, long tusk.
18. Wow! Some tusks are almost nine feet long.
19. The narwhal may use the tusk for play-fighting or digging.
20. That tusk is not only uncommon but also quite interesting.

NAME ______________________ CLASS ______________ DATE ______________

Review C: Verbs, Adverbs, Prepositions, Conjunctions, Interjections

EXERCISE In each sentence, identify the underlined word or word group by writing above it *V* for *verb, ADV* for *adverb, PREP* for *preposition, C* for *conjunction*, or *I* for *interjection*.

Example 1. I ate too much but, oh, it was good! (*I*)

1. Zap! The dragon's breath burned the fence.
2. My sister trains police dogs.
3. A technician is fixing the computer now.
4. A fire burned in the fireplace, but no one was in the room.
5. Three different Pharaohs built those pyramids.
6. During the operation, the nurse looked neither nervous nor pale.
7. Margarita grabbed the horse by its mane.
8. Breathlessly everyone watched the stunt parachutist.
9. Dr. Levine handed the new eyeglasses to the woman.
10. The mechanic checked the wires, yet he found nothing wrong.
11. Everyone wore a different kind of costume.
12. Yum, your entire house smells spicy.
13. Latrice is helping me catalog the books.
14. With one swift stroke, the chef chopped the onion into two pieces.
15. The students at my new school seem friendly.
16. In science, we are studying vampire bats.
17. These bats are found in Central America and South America.
18. Vampire bats rarely bite humans.
19. Instead, a vampire bat will make a tiny cut on an animal's skin.
20. Usually, a bat will lap only a small amount of blood.

Literary Model: Using Adverbs in a Description

The opinions of this club were completely controlled by Nicholas Vedder, a patriarch of the village, and landlord of the inn, at the door of which he took his seat from morning till night, just moving sufficiently to avoid the sun and keep in the shade of a large tree; so that the neighbors could tell the hour by his movements as accurately as by a sundial. It is true he was rarely heard to speak, but smoked his pipe incessantly. His adherents, however, perfectly understood him, and knew how to gather his opinions. When anything that was read or related displeased him, he was observed to smoke his pipe vehemently, and to send forth short, frequent, and angry puffs; but when pleased, he would inhale the smoke slowly and tranquilly, and emit it in light and placid clouds; and sometimes, taking the pipe from his mouth, and letting the fragrant vapor curl about his nose, would gravely nod his head in token of perfect approbation.

—from "Rip Van Winkle" by Washington Irving

EXERCISE A List ten adverbs that appear in this passage.

EXERCISE B

1. Underline the adverbs in the passage. Then, read the passage aloud, leaving the adverbs out.
2. Explain how leaving adverbs out changes the description. Is it better with the adverbs or without them?

Literary Model (continued)

EXERCISE C Imagine that you are at a park with a younger sibling, cousin, or other relative. Write a paragraph in which you describe his or her actions. Use several adverbs in your description.

EXERCISE D

1. Rewrite your paragraph, leaving out the adverbs.

2. How is your paragraph affected by deleting the adverbs?

Writing Application: Personal Description

Adverbs come quickly to the writer's aid when verbs, adjectives, and even other adverbs need further clarification. In fact, speakers often use them without even thinking about it. In writing, however, replace overused adverbs like *really, very,* and *so* when you can.

OVERUSED ADVERB The athletes performed really well.

FRESHER ADVERB The athletes performed brilliantly.

Writing Activity

This year, the school's yearbook staff has come up with a fun idea. During English class, each student will write a paragraph for a "Where Are They Now?" chapter in the yearbook. Imagine yourself ten years in the future. Where will you be? What will you have accomplished? Imagine yourself ten years from now, and write an optimistic paragraph for your peers to read. Describe your future self with at least five carefully chosen adverbs.

PREWRITING Find some quiet, uninterrupted time to imagine yourself ten years from now. High school will be behind you—what were you known for during those years? After high school, will you go to college, start a career, begin a family? Since you're imagining, imagine the best life you can. Jot down the possible futures as you allow yourself to think ahead.

WRITING You only have one paragraph in which to share your dreams with your friends, so choose your favorite future from your prewriting. Describe the future in third person, writing about yourself as someone else might. Although you are writing only one paragraph, organize it well, as if it were an essay in miniature. Decide on the best order for the facts about yourself.

REVISING Now that you have the basic paragraph structure, add clarifying detail to your description. Use at least five strong, specific adverbs—no weak *really, very,* or *so* for this stellar report on your life!

PUBLISHING Check your paragraph for errors in punctuation and spelling. The yearbook staff will let you know how to submit your paragraph—on disk, perhaps, or online. Follow these instructions. But why wait until the yearbook comes out to share your paragraph and read others' dreams? With your teacher's permission, make a bulletin board display with paragraphs and pictures.

Extending Your Writing

This exercise could lead to a more developed writing project. In two or three years, you will leave your current school and head to high school. Write a personal essay in which you outline the goals you would like to accomplish by that time. In your concluding paragraph, set a few distant goals for your high school years, too.

Choices: Exploring Complements

Here's your chance to step out of the grammar book and into the real world. You may not notice complements, but you and the people around you use them every day. The following activities challenge you to find a connection between complements and the world around you. Do the activity below that suits your personality best, and then share your discoveries with your class. Have fun!

BUILDING BACKGROUND KNOWLEDGE

To Give or Not to Give?

If you've tried to write sentences with indirect objects, you know that not every verb takes an indirect object. Which ones do? Make a list of these verbs, and give the list to your classmates. Leave room for additions to the list.

FOREIGN LANGUAGES

The Order of the Day

How do other languages present subjects, verbs, and objects? In what order do they appear? What differences and similarities can you find between the sentence structures of English and those of, for instance, Spanish? Write a short essay detailing several of these points, or give a presentation to the class.

MUSIC

Beyond Firefighters and Cowboys

Do you remember when grown-ups used to ask you, "What do you want to be when you grow up?" Well, you're growing up now. Do you have an answer? Perhaps what you have is a lot of questions and a few dreams. Write a song about the problems of choosing a career. Include plenty of predicate nominatives and predicate adjectives. Then—you guessed it—sing your song to the class!

REPRESENTING

Four Branches, One Tree

Make a flowchart or decision tree that illustrates the process of identifying complements. Begin by noting the questions that you ask yourself at each step of the process. Transfer your chart to poster board. Use colors and other graphic techniques to help viewers understand your chart. With your teacher's permission, post your chart in the classroom where everyone can use it.

ART

Catch a Wave

Your classmates will remember direct objects better if you provide illustrations of specific situations. If you have access to a computer, page through the clip art and look for situations that may be described with direct objects. Print them out and make a collage, writing appropriate sentences under each one. If you prefer, cut out appropriate pictures from magazines and newspapers and assemble them into a poster. With your teacher's permission, hang your poster in the classroom.

WRITING

The Sincerest Form of Flattery

Do you have a saying or a sentence that you live by, one that you admire? Analyze the structure of that sentence. Identify its subject, verb, and other important elements. Then, taking that sentence as a model, write five more sentences that use that exact structure. You just might be surprised at what a fine writer you can be.

LINGUISTIC ANALYSIS

The Force Is with Him

Hey, *Star Wars* fans, have you ever noticed that Yoda talks rather strangely? Why is that? Check out a *Star Wars* book or listen to one of the videos, and write down some of Yoda's speeches. How did George Lucas make Yoda sound so special? What elements of the standard subject-verb-object order did Lucas invert or reverse? Begin by identifying the subject, verb, and object of each of Yoda's sentences. Then, identify the adverbs. Look out for the way Yoda uses *not!*

Complements

13a. A ***complement*** is a word or word group that completes the meaning of a verb.

A complement may be a noun, a pronoun, or an adjective.

NOUN I enjoy **books** of all types.

PRONOUN I read **them** at every opportunity.

ADJECTIVE This book is **suspenseful.**

EXERCISE A Complete the meaning of each verb by adding a complement.

Example 1. Yesterday I read *Watership Down*.

1. This poem is ______________________.
2. I greatly admire ______________________.
3. I recently composed a ______________________.
4. I'll give ______________________ the books they wanted.
5. My skills as an author are ______________________.
6. In the ghost story, the weather was always ______________________.
7. The ancient ghost haunted the ______________________.
8. When I told you, did you believe ______________________?
9. A mystery story should be ______________________.
10. Tell ______________________ the rest of the story.

EXERCISE B Underline the complements in each of the following sentences.

Example 1. Do you smell smoke?

11. John built these shelves.
12. Russell grows basil in his garden.
13. Spooky is our new cat.
14. Is Spike your pet iguana?
15. These pecans are very crunchy.
16. My sister enjoys grapes enormously.
17. Marcia has a new kitten.
18. Last summer we built a birdhouse.
19. Was Rafael happy about his new bicycle?
20. Suzi and Eric gave us a ride to the park.

Direct Objects

13b. A ***direct object*** is a noun, pronoun, or word group that tells *who* or *what* receives the action of the verb.

EXAMPLES Alexander Graham Bell invented the **telephone.** [What did Bell invent?]
Mia took **Brent** and **Lenice** to the play. [Whom did Mia take?]

Because a linking verb does not express action, it cannot have a direct object.

EXERCISE A Underline the direct objects in the following sentences. Some sentences contain a compound direct object. If a sentence does not contain a direct object, write *none* on the line provided.

Example __________ **1.** Have you ever seen a cotton gin?

__________ **1.** In 1793, Eli Whitney invented a machine for cotton farmers.

__________ **2.** His machine was the cotton gin.

__________ **3.** The machine separates seeds and small sticks from the cotton fibers.

__________ **4.** It combs the fibers with tiny, fine-toothed rakes.

__________ **5.** Whitney's invention was important to the economy of the South.

EXERCISE B Underline the direct objects in the following sentences. Some sentences contain compound direct objects.

Example [1] Ms. Costa explained faults and earthquakes to my class.

[6] Thick plates of solid material form the earth's crust, and sometimes these plates move. **[7]** The movement causes cracks in the earth's surface, such as the famous crack known as the San Andreas fault in California. **[8]** Sudden movements along this crack caused a terrible earthquake in 1906. **[9]** It ruined many homes and other buildings in San Francisco. **[10]** Thousands of people lost their lives. **[11]** Natural gas pipelines exploded, and fires devoured homes and other structures. **[12]** Courageous firefighters fought blazes throughout the city. **[13]** Unfortunately, they didn't have enough water and equipment. **[14]** The earthquake destroyed lives and property. **[15]** Eventually, however, the city repaired the damage.

Indirect Objects

13c. An ***indirect object*** is a noun, pronoun, or word group that sometimes appears in sentences containing direct objects.

Indirect objects tell *to whom* or *to what*, or *for whom* or *for what*, the action of the verb is done.

EXAMPLES He fed the **dog** a biscuit. [To what did he feed the biscuit?]
I gave **Jaime** and **Alameda** their tickets. [To whom did I give the tickets?]

EXERCISE A Each of the following sentences contains both a direct object and an indirect object. For each sentence, underline the direct object once. Then, underline the indirect object twice. Hint: Some sentences may contain a compound indirect object.

Example 1. I promised Hortensia and Mary two slices of cake.

1. The president gave the astronaut a medal.
2. The weather report promised us sunshine for the weekend.
3. After a long delay, the store sent Mr. Wong a refund.
4. Virgil and Mike sent Chim a birthday card.
5. María gave the carpenters and bricklayers clear directions.

EXERCISE B In each sentence, circle the verb. Then, underline the direct object once and the indirect object twice. Hint: Some sentences do not have indirect objects. Some sentences have no objects.

Example 1. I gave Fido and Cheeky a bath.

6. The governor gave her staff a party.
7. Carlos showed Delia pictures from his vacation.
8. The witness gave the jury additional information about the crime scene.
9. Shizuo has been my friend for years.
10. Felice threw the ball to me.
11. The scary movie gave us the shivers.
12. Melissa gave the waitress her order.
13. Please tell me a story, Arthur.
14. My friend Heather is the secretary of the Hiking Club.
15. Give the speaker your complete attention.

NAME ____________ CLASS ____________ DATE ____________

Direct Objects and Indirect Objects A

13b. A ***direct object*** is a noun, pronoun, or word group that tells *who* or *what* receives the action of the verb.

13c. An ***indirect object*** is a noun, pronoun, or word group that sometimes appears in sentences containing direct objects.

DIRECT OBJECTS After sitting down, I studied my **program.**
I adore the **costumes** and **songs** in opera productions.

INDIRECT OBJECTS Later, I lent **Melissa** my opera glasses.
She gave **Eddie** and **Carlos** a turn with the glasses, too.

EXERCISE A Identify each underlined word by writing above it *DO* for *direct object* or *IO* for *indirect object.* Add *C* if the word is part of a compound object.

Example 1. Will you send Grandma (IO, C) and Grandpa these tickets, please?

1. Pierre gave me a ticket to the opera *Madama Butterfly.*
2. We took a bus to the opera house.
3. An usher showed Pierre and me our seats.
4. The orchestra began the overture.
5. The opera tells a sad and touching story.
6. A woman marries a man who is in the navy.
7. Soon after their marriage, the man sails his ship to faraway places.
8. He leaves the woman and her little child.
9. Sadly she watches the sea, hoping for his return.
10. The performers tell us the entire story through their beautiful songs.

EXERCISE B In each of the sentences, circle the verb. Then, underline the direct object once and the indirect object twice. Some sentences do not contain indirect objects.

Example 1. Each afternoon after school, I (give) Willy food and water.

11. My neighbor across the hall has an interesting pet.
12. The Stoneham Zoo gave her a chinchilla whose name was Willy.
13. For years, the zoo featured the chinchilla in its Children's Zoo.
14. When Willy grew old, the zoo needed a new home for him.
15. Ms. Jefferson, my neighbor, volunteered her home for Willy.

NAME ______________________ CLASS ______________ DATE ______________

Direct Objects and Indirect Objects B

13b. A ***direct object*** is a noun, pronoun, or word group that tells *who* or *what* receives the action of the verb.

13c. An ***indirect object*** is a noun, pronoun, or word group that sometimes appears in sentences containing direct objects.

EXERCISE A In each of the following sentences, underline each direct object once and each indirect object twice. Some sentences contain compound objects.

Example 1. Before entering the room, Maya gave the guard her camera.

1. The museum does not allow cameras.
2. According to our guide, that diamond caused its owner some trouble.
3. She finally gave the museum the diamond and some other gems.
4. Did you see the rubies and the emeralds?
5. Color, brilliance, and weight determine a gem's value.
6. A lapidary, or gem cutter, gives a gem its final shape.
7. This museum also has an exhibit and books about famous gems.
8. Indian and Persian rulers possessed the famous *Koh-i-noor* diamond for centuries.
9. The British East India Company gave Queen Victoria the *Koh-i-noor* in 1850.
10. Show the teacher and the class your postcards from the exhibit.

EXERCISE B In each of the following sentences, underline the direct object. Then, on the lines provided, rewrite each sentence so that it has both a direct object and an indirect object.

Example 1. Will you write a letter today? *Will you write your grandmother a letter today?*

11. Throw the football. ______________________________

____

12. Lani will show her project tomorrow morning. ______________________________

____

13. Mr. Garcia told a story about his childhood. ______________________________

____

14. Please bring a glass of water. ______________________________

____

15. Did she send a birthday card? ______________________________

____

NAME CLASS DATE

Subject Complements

13d. A ***subject complement*** is a word or word group in the predicate that identifies or describes the subject.

A subject complement is connected to the subject by a linking verb.

EXAMPLES The world's oldest surviving religion is **Judaism.** [*Judaism* is a noun that identifies the subject *religion*.]

This prayer book looks **new.** [*New* is an adjective that describes the subject *book*.]

EXERCISE Circle each verb, and underline each subject complement in the following sentences. Some sentences do not contain a subject complement.

Examples **1.** Is Taoism a religion of the East?

2. I attend a Catholic church.

1. Jerusalem is the capital of Israel.
2. That beautiful Islamic mosque appears ancient.
3. I visited Vatican City in Rome once.
4. The church bells sounded pleasantly harmonious in the night air.
5. Many magnificent structures become tourist attractions.
6. The Eiffel Tower was an attraction at the World Exposition in 1889.
7. In ancient Greece the Parthenon honored the goddess Athena.
8. The Forbidden City in China became open to the public.
9. The Statue of Liberty stands majestically in New York harbor.
10. The Great Wall of China seems almost endless!
11. It stretches nearly 1,500 miles.
12. The North Pole is not a land mass.
13. In fact, the Arctic Ocean covers the North Pole.
14. The South Pole remains frozen year round.
15. Unlike the North Pole, the South Pole lies on an icy land mass.
16. The winds of Antarctica feel bitter.
17. The biggest lake in the world is the Caspian Sea.
18. The Caspian Sea is not an arm of the ocean.
19. However, the water tastes salty.
20. Lake Baikal is much deeper.

NAME ______________________ CLASS ______________ DATE ______________

Predicate Nominatives

13e. A ***predicate nominative*** is a word or word group in the predicate that identifies the subject.

A predicate nominative may be a noun, a pronoun, or a word group that functions as a noun. A predicate nominative is connected to the subject by a linking verb.

EXAMPLES A tiger is a wild **animal.**

The guilty people in the room were **he** and **she.**

That is **what I wrote.**

EXERCISE A Circle the linking verb in each of the following sentences. Then, underline the predicate nominative. Some predicate nominatives may be compound.

Example 1. Jacques Cousteau (has) always (been) one of my role models.

1. Jacques-Yves Cousteau was a French underwater explorer.
2. His main interests were ocean life and conservation.
3. The fish and plants of the sea were his topics of study.
4. Underwater exploration is sometimes a dangerous occupation.
5. Cousteau's explorations have become the subjects of films and books.

EXERCISE B In the sentences below, circle each verb. Then, identify each underlined word or word group by writing above it *PN* for *predicate nominative* or *DO* for *direct object.*

Example 1. My brother (may become) a doctor. [PN]

6. Lyndon Johnson became president in 1963.
7. That story describes him exactly.
8. Tomás Ortega is the best student in our class.
9. A leopard has spots on its coat for camouflage.
10. A rake is a useful tool in a garden.
11. Billie Holiday is Kevin's favorite jazz singer.
12. The class elected Jennifer.
13. She was probably the best candidate.
14. Her friend Martin managed the campaign.
15. That is what she promised before the election.

Predicate Adjectives

13f. A ***predicate adjective*** is an adjective that is in the predicate and that describes the subject.

A predicate adjective is connected to the subject by a linking verb.

EXAMPLES Yesterday I felt **sick.**

The cider was **cold** and **refreshing.**

EXERCISE A Circle the linking verbs in the following sentences, and underline the predicate adjectives. Some predicate adjectives are compound.

Example 1. Your dog appears tired or ill.

1. The ocean looks calm tonight.
2. The governor seemed happy with the meeting.
3. After roller-skating, the children were hungry and tired.
4. Traffic on my street becomes quite heavy during rush hour.
5. The committee's plan is very complicated.

EXERCISE B Underline each predicate adjective or compound predicate adjective in the following sentences. If a sentence has no predicate adjective, write *None* on the line provided.

Examples ____________ 1. Reading is fun and relaxing.

None 2. These books are about adventures.

____________ 6. Scott O'Dell is a fantastic writer.

____________ 7. His books have become famous.

____________ 8. *Island of the Blue Dolphins* is excellent in my opinion.

____________ 9. The main character is an American Indian girl.

____________ 10. Alone on a deserted island, she feels lonely and scared.

____________ 11. Fierce, wild dogs are inhabitants of the island, too.

____________ 12. They seem very frightening to her.

____________ 13. She then becomes intent on leaving the island in a canoe.

____________ 14. Her journey becomes dangerous when the canoe springs a leak.

____________ 15. She is a brave person but wisely turns back.

Predicate Nominatives and Predicate Adjectives A

13e. A ***predicate nominative*** is a word or word group that is in the predicate and that identifies the subject.

13f. A ***predicate adjective*** is an adjective that is in the predicate and that describes the subject.

PREDICATE NOMINATIVE Yesterday was my **birthday.**
PREDICATE ADJECTIVE Yesterday was **sunny.**

EXERCISE A Identify each underlined word by writing above it *PN* for *predicate nominative* or *PA* for *predicate adjective.* Add *C* if it is part of a compound complement.

Example 1. My favorite movies are old and musical. (PA, C)

1. Fred Astaire was an actor and a dancer.
2. When he danced, he seemed very light on his feet.
3. Astaire's first dancing partner was his sister Adele.
4. His solo dances were sophisticated and improvisational.
5. In many movies, Ginger Rogers was his dancing partner.
6. The movies they made together became very famous and popular.
7. My two favorites are *Top Hat* and *Swing Time.*
8. Astaire's career was long and brilliant.
9. He became an actor in 1933 and continued to make films until 1981.
10. He was the winner of a special Academy Award, several Emmys, and two lifetime achievement awards.

EXERCISE B In each of the following sentences, underline each predicate nominative once and underline each predicate adjective twice.

Example 1. Adrienne seems especially happy and excited today.

11. The clouds on the horizon looked dark.
12. She is both a swimmer and a dancer.
13. Those pears are inexpensive and delicious.
14. My favorite sports are hockey and lacrosse.
15. Is the girl in the green parka your sister?

Predicate Nominatives and Predicate Adjectives B

13e. A ***predicate nominative*** is a word or word group that is in the predicate and that identifies the subject.

13f. A ***predicate adjective*** is an adjective that is in the predicate and that describes the subject.

PREDICATE NOMINATIVE Mammals are **vertebrates.**
PREDICATE ADJECTIVE Mammals are **warm blooded.**

EXERCISE A Identify each underlined word by writing above it *PN* for *predicate nominative* or *PA* for *predicate adjective.* Add *C* if it is part of a compound.

Example 1. Is this script comic or tragic? *PA, C*

1. Lawrence Kasdan's writing is skillful and clever.
2. His works are not books, poems, or articles.
3. Many of Kasdan's works become exciting films.
4. One of the first movies that he wrote was *Raiders of the Lost Ark.*
5. To many people, that movie seemed exciting and funny.
6. Harrison Ford was wonderful as the leading man, Indiana Jones.
7. Kasdan's script for *Return of the Jedi* led to a film that is full of adventure and colorful characters.
8. The western *Silverado* is another film by Kasdan.
9. The actor Kevin Kline is one of the stars of *Silverado.*
10. Kasdan was once a student at the University of Michigan.

EXERCISE B Complete each sentence by writing a predicate nominative or a predicate adjective on the line provided. You may have to write more than one word for a sentence to be meaningful. Above each complement, write *PN* for *predicate nominative* or *PA* for *predicate adjective.*

Example 1. Tuesday was *my birthday* (PN).

11. These lemons and grapefruit taste ______.
12. My cousin Isaiah is ______.
13. My uncle Nathan is ______.
14. Mario and Marco are ______.
15. The little girl felt ______.

Review A: **Identifying Complements**

EXERCISE Identify the underlined word in the following sentences by writing above it *DO* for *direct object, IO* for *indirect object, PN* for *predicate nominative,* or *PA* for *predicate adjective.* Add *C* if it is part of a compound object or subject complement.

Example 1. This tall tale is silly yet entertaining! PA, C

1. I'll tell you and your friends an American tale or two.
2. According to legend, Pecos Bill was the inventor of the lasso.
3. Coyotes raised the young Pecos Bill.
4. His horse was Widow-Maker, and his wife was Slue-Foot Sue.
5. According to another tale, Sally Ann Thunder Ann Whirlwind rescued Davy Crockett.
6. Then she married him.
7. While growing up, she had given her brothers strong competition in wrestling, running, and fishing.
8. The physically powerful Paul Bunyan issued lumbermen their orders.
9. In one meal he devoured half of a wagon load of vegetables and several sides of beef.
10. Paul Bunyan's pet ox Babe was huge and blue.
11. John Henry was incredibly strong as well.
12. In tall tales, he is a railroad worker in West Virginia and other areas.
13. In one tale, he challenges a machine to a contest of strength and speed.
14. Tall tales may seem impossibly far-fetched.
15. Some legends and tales, however, feature characters from real life.
16. Two real-life heroes were Johnny Appleseed and Davy Crockett.
17. Johnny Appleseed offered animals his friendship.
18. He also planted apple trees throughout Pennsylvania.
19. The dates of Appleseed's birth and death are 1774 and 1845.
20. Davy Crockett's life spanned the years from 1786 to 1836.

Review B: Identifying Complements

EXERCISE A Identify the underlined word in the following sentences by writing above it *DO* for *direct object, IO* for *indirect object, PN* for *predicate nominative,* or *PA* for *predicate adjective.* Add *C* if the word is part of a compound object or subject complement.

Example 1. Old Yeller is the name of a dog in one of my favorite books. (PN above "name")

1. Fred Gipson wrote a wonderful book called *Old Yeller.*
2. I know the book will give you hours of pleasant reading.
3. The main character and narrator is Travis, a teenage boy.
4. The setting is Texas, just after the Civil War.
5. Travis is responsible for the farm during his father's absence.
6. One day, a stray dog steals some meat.
7. To Travis, the dog seems ugly and useless.
8. However, the dog soon becomes a companion and a hero.
9. The dog gains the family's affection and gratitude.
10. I will lend you my copy of *Old Yeller* if you want to read a terrific book.

EXERCISE B Underline the complement in each of the following sentences. Then, identify the complement by writing above it *DO* for *direct object, IO* for *indirect object, PN* for *predicate nominative,* or *PA* for *predicate adjective.* Some sentences have more than one complement.

Example 1. Are onions the pizza topping? (PN above "topping")

11. Rumpelstiltskin spun straw into gold for the miller's daughter.
12. Earth is not the only planet in the solar system with a moon.
13. That house has a lovely porch.
14. My older brother is now a sophomore at Princeton University.
15. Please send Sarah a postcard while you are traveling.
16. This apple tastes slightly sour.
17. Mark Twain's home in Hartford, Connecticut, has become a museum.
18. We read the class a ballad about John Henry.
19. Many of the magician's tricks were unbelievable.
20. Was the pep rally before the game fun?

Review C: Identifying Complements

EXERCISE A Identify the underlined word in the following sentences by writing above it *DO* for *direct object, IO* for *indirect object, PN* for *predicate nominative,* or *PA* for *predicate adjective.* Add *C* if it is part of a compound object or subject complement.

IO, C
Example 1. Tell Marianne and me a pirate story!

1. One of New England's early pirates was Dixie Bull.
2. He attacked ships and trading posts in Maine until 1633.
3. Before he turned to piracy, Bull had been a trader and a fisherman.
4. But French pirates stole all of his supplies and boats.
5. Angered at this, he became a pirate as well.
6. Key West, Florida, is famous for the pirates who once sailed in and out.
7. The ocean off Key West is often violent and dangerous.
8. The harsh waves and huge rocks gave ships a terrible beating.
9. Pirates would watch the ships as they passed through the rough waters.
10. They would give the officers and crew aid, but they would also take the cargoes.

EXERCISE B Underline the complement in each of the following sentences. Then, identify the complement by writing above it *DO* for *direct object, IO* for *indirect object, PN* for *predicate nominative,* or *PA* for *predicate adjective.*

DO
Example 1. I have just discovered the thought-provoking writings of Thoreau.

11. Henry David Thoreau wrote *Walden.*
12. It is a book about his experiences near Walden Pond in Massachusetts.
13. Thoreau was a teacher in Concord, Massachusetts.
14. In 1845, he left his home and went to the woods near Walden Pond.
15. His cabin in the woods was small.
16. He was seeking a life of simplicity.
17. His life at Walden Pond was an experiment in quiet solitude.
18. For Thoreau, nature seemed peaceful and instructive.
19. His daily journal about his life and thoughts became *Walden.*
20. I will read you one of the inspiring quotations about his search for personal freedom.

Literary Model: Poetry

Living Tenderly

by May Swenson

My body a rounded stone
with a pattern of smooth seams.
My head a short snake,
retractive, projective.
My legs come out of their sleeves
or shrink within,
and so does my chin.
My eyelids are quick clamps.

My back is my roof.
I am always at home.
I travel where my house walks.
It is a smooth stone.
It floats within the lake,
Or rests in the dust.
My flesh lives tenderly
inside its bone.

EXERCISE A Make a list of the predicate nominatives that appear in the poem. After each one, write the subject that the predicate nominative identifies. (Hint: In the first and third lines of the poem, the linking verb *is* is understood to follow the subject.)

EXERCISE B This poem is a riddle poem. Why is the use of predicate nominatives particularly effective in this type of poem?

Literary Model (continued)

EXERCISE C Using May Swenson's poem as a model, write a riddle poem. Use several predicate nominatives as you create clues for the riddle.

EXERCISE D

1. Make a list of the predicate nominatives that appear in your poem. After each one, write the subject that the predicate nominative identifies.

2. Swenson uses predicate nominatives to create metaphors. Are there any metaphors in your poem? If so, list and explain them below.

NAME ______ CLASS ______ DATE ______

for **CHAPTER 13: COMPLEMENTS** *pages 386–89*

Writing Application: Report

Direct and indirect objects complete a sentence's meaning when transitive verbs are involved. Without them, meaning can be incomplete and even beyond understanding.

BEYOND UNDERSTANDING The emcee handed.
INCOMPLETE MEANING The emcee handed the award.
COMPLETE MEANING The emcee handed the glamorous actress the award.

Sometimes, of course, a sentence can do without an indirect object, as in this example: "The actress accepted the award with many thanks." Read each sentence aloud, listening for complete meaning.

Writing Activity

Every month or so, some awards show makes its way to television. Hollywood chooses the best of recent movies, music video stations count down the top ten songs of the year, or people go online to vote for a favorite episode of a popular show. In "real life," too, awards ceremonies occur, from an elementary school awards assembly to the honors of graduation. Choose an awards ceremony, on television or in your area. Watch or attend it; then write a report for your school or local paper. Use direct and indirect objects as you list who won what.

PREWRITING First, choose the awards ceremony on which you will report. Then watch or attend it, but not as a passive observer. Take active and thorough notes of every announcement. Get a program from the ceremony, if possible; or you might be able to get information online. Gather all the data you can to use as you write your report.

WRITING Journalistic writing is brief, so write a sentence or two of introduction in which you tell readers the when, where, and why of the awards ceremony. Then list the awards, organizing them by category to avoid simply writing a list. Write a few sentences of concluding material, too, commenting on the interest or value of the ceremony.

REVISING You could write "The award for new artist went to Starla Lane," using a prepositional phrase to tell who got the award. However, since newspapers have strict space limitations, using object complements can make your writing more concise: "Starla Lane received the new artist award" or "The host gave Starla Lane the statuette."

PUBLISHING Check your report for errors in punctuation and spelling, especially capitalization of proper nouns and adjectives. Follow all instructions for submitting your report to the paper.

Extending Your Writing

This exercise could lead to a more developed writing project. For a speech class, investigate the appeal (or lack of it) of television awards shows. Interview people who like the shows, and talk also to some who dislike them. Consider why those little gold-plated statuettes grab the attention of so many people.

Choices: Looking at Phrases

Here's your chance to step out of the grammar book and into the real world. You may not notice phrases, but you and the people around you use them every day. The following activities challenge you to find a connection between phrases and the world around you. Do the activity below that suits your personality best, and then share your discoveries with your class. Have fun.

FINDING EXAMPLES

Appreciating Appositives

Journalists like to use appositives because these phrases are informative and save space. Instead of writing an additional sentence, journalists often insert an appositive. Look through some newspapers or magazines, and cut out or copy examples of sentences that include an appositive. Paste your examples on poster board. With your teacher's permission, display them in the classroom.

VIEWING AND REPRESENTING

Mother Goose

Many nursery rhymes use prepositional phrases. Take a trip down memory lane, and read some Mother Goose nursery rhymes again. Find several examples of adjective prepositional phrases and adverb prepositional phrases, and copy them onto notecards. On the copies, underline each prepositional phrase and draw an arrow to the word or words it modifies. With your teacher's permission, display your notecards on your classroom wall.

HISTORY

To Be or Not to Be

Many famous quotations begin with or include an infinitive. How many can you remember? List as many as you can. Then, look through a dictionary of quotations. Pick several famous or interesting quotations that include infinitives. Write each quotation on a card. Include the author, date, and the work in which the quotation appears. Then, have your class vote on their favorite quotation.

MUSIC

Praising Phrases

Did you know music can contain phrases? If you are familiar with music, tell the class what a musical phrase is. If possible, provide the class with some examples. How can you tell where a musical phrase ends? Make a chart that compares musical phrases to grammatical phrases. With your teacher's permission, post your chart in the classroom.

DEMONSTRATION

Human Flashcards

Here is a demonstration that will help everybody in the class understand how adverb phrases can move around in a sentence. First, get together with a team. You will need several large cards. On each card, write an adverb phrase. Create other cards that contain the word or words each phrase modifies along with cards for the subjects, verbs, and complements of sentences. Each person on the team holds up a card and stands in correct sentence order in front of the class. Then, move the adverb phrase (the person holding the card) to different positions and read the resulting sentences. In addition, make a couple of adjective phrase cards, and demonstrate that these phrases usually cannot be moved.

ART

A Babbling Brook

Have you ever heard a brook talk too much? If you like a joke and like to draw, try this project. Illustrate participles that don't necessarily mean what they seem to say. For example, you could draw the expression *balanced meal* as a scale with food on either side. Display your images, but without the participles. Then, let your classmates write their guesses next to your pictures.

NAME ______________ CLASS ______________ DATE ______________

Phrases

14a. A ***phrase*** is a group of related words that is used as a single part of speech and that does not contain both a verb and its subject.

PREPOSITIONAL PHRASE	in a boat
PARTICIPIAL PHRASE	rowing swiftly
INFINITIVE PHRASE	to swim daily
VERB PHRASE	will have gone

EXERCISE A On the line provided, identify each word group by writing *P* for *phrase* or *NP* for *not a phrase.*

Examples _P_ **1.** with chocolate frosting

_NP_ **2.** while the cake baked

_____ **1.** over the rainbow

_____ **2.** since the alarm rang

_____ **3.** as a baby sitter

_____ **4.** to warn us

_____ **5.** was repaired

_____ **6.** the cat sat

_____ **7.** on the mat

_____ **8.** has been singing

_____ **9.** under pressure

_____ **10.** where my friends are

_____ **11.** stricken with the measles

_____ **12.** to check randomly

_____ **13.** had been whistling

_____ **14.** since you didn't call

_____ **15.** ending happily after all

_____ **16.** to study the stars through a telescope

_____ **17.** because you don't ever miss track practice

_____ **18.** listening to really good music

_____ **19.** has smashed

_____ **20.** to understand my innermost feelings

EXERCISE B In each of the following sentences, identify each underlined word group by writing above it *P* for *phrase* or *NP* for *not a phrase.*

Example 1. The train arrived (NP) at the platform (P).

21. The troll under the bridge opened his eyes.

22. Thinking carefully, Sinead arrived at the right answer.

23. Has anyone looked outside since the rain stopped?

24. The antibiotics should have stopped the infection.

25. Carla knows how to order dinner in Korean.

for **CHAPTER 14: THE PHRASE** *pages 402–403*

The Prepositional Phrase

14b. A ***prepositional phrase*** includes a preposition, the object of the preposition, and any modifiers of that object.

EXAMPLES during the days with us of noble deeds about them

A prepositional phrase can have more than one object.

EXAMPLE for the **parents** and their **children**

EXERCISE A Underline each prepositional phrase in the following paragraph.

Example [1] In this book you can read about Camelot and its king.

[1] Many legends are told and retold about King Arthur and his knights. **[2]** Through his strength, King Arthur proved his right to the British throne. **[3]** He removed a great sword, Excalibur, from a solid rock. **[4]** The knights who gathered around King Arthur were known throughout the land for their courage and goodness. **[5]** They dedicated themselves to honorable and noble ideals.

EXERCISE B Complete each sentence by adding a prepositional phrase where the blank is. Write your new sentence on the line provided.

Example 1. _____ we will get refreshments.
After the game we will get refreshments.

6. We are listening _____ on the radio.

____

7. We're going home _____.

____

8. _____ was a pile of newspapers.

____

9. Last week's game _____ ended in a tie.

____

10. The oil painting _____ is priceless.

____

The Adjective Phrase

A prepositional phrase used as an adjective is called an ***adjective phrase.***

14c. An ***adjective phrase*** modifies a noun or a pronoun.

EXAMPLES Someone **in my class** lent me a wonderful story. [The prepositional phrase *in my class* modifies the pronoun *Someone*.]

The story **about Scrooge and Tiny Tim** has become famous. [The prepositional phrase *about Scrooge and Tiny Tim* modifies the noun *story*.]

EXERCISE A Underline the adjective phrases in the following sentences. Then, draw an arrow from each phrase to the noun or pronoun it modifies.

Example 1. Charles Dickens wrote many tales about poverty.

1. *A Christmas Carol* is the story of a rich man's repentance.
2. Ebenezer Scrooge was a man of wealth and property.
3. His clerk, Bob Cratchit, led a difficult life in poverty.
4. Spirits from the past, present, and future warned Scrooge.
5. One of the spirits showed Scrooge the poor, yet happy, Cratchit family.
6. Dickens also began writing a story about a mysterious disappearance.
7. A character in the story, Edwin Drood, disappears.
8. Unfortunately, the death of Charles Dickens cut short the story.
9. The mystery of Edwin Drood's disappearance remains unsolved.
10. The possible fate of the young man has fascinated countless readers.

EXERCISE B Underline each adjective phrase in the following sentences, and draw an arrow from the phrase to the word it modifies.

Example 1. Microorganisms in the bodies of people and animals cause disease.

11. Louis Pasteur was dean of a university's science faculty.
12. The process of sterilization of milk is called pasteurization.
13. Bacteria as the cause of disease was a new idea then.
14. Pasteur's studies of infectious diseases in animals helped him formulate his germ theory.
15. Pasteur developed a vaccine against rabies in humans.

The Adverb Phrase

A prepositional phrase used as an adverb is called an *adverb phrase*.

14d. An ***adverb phrase*** modifies a verb, an adjective, or an adverb.

EXAMPLES **In the morning**, my sister and I jog five miles. [The adverb phrase *In the morning* modifies the verb *jog*.]

Jessica is active **in several sports**. [The adverb phrase *in several sports* modifies the adjective *active*.]

EXERCISE Underline the adverb phrases in the following sentences. Draw an arrow from each adverb phrase to the verb, verb phrase, adjective, or adverb it modifies.

Example 1. The Ford Motor Company was founded by Henry Ford in 1903.

1. Cars have not always been made in factories.
2. At one time, cars were manufactured by hand.
3. People were ready for a change.
4. Through mass production, Henry Ford changed the world.
5. By 1908, the company was producing one hundred cars in a day.
6. In 1913, the Ford Motor Company was manufacturing cars on an assembly line.
7. A moving-belt conveyor was used in the assembly process.
8. This new method added speed to the manufacturing process.
9. Henry Ford put workers on assembly lines.
10. The employees worked repeatedly at the same tasks.
11. Early in the 1900s, low-priced cars were selling rapidly.
12. The Model T was popular for its affordability.
13. For almost twenty years, the Model T outsold all other cars.
14. Under Ford's leadership, the Ford Motor Company grew into a highly successful business.
15. In 1945, Henry Ford II became the head of the company.
16. He directed the company for the next thirty-four years.
17. During the 1950s, the automobile became increasingly important.
18. Performance and styling became more important to consumers.
19. Ford cars and trucks are still driven in America today.
20. Throughout the world, Henry Ford is known as a great innovator.

NAME ______________________ CLASS ______________ DATE ______________

Adjective and Adverb Phrases A

14c. An ***adjective phrase*** modifies a noun or a pronoun.

14d. An ***adverb phrase*** modifies a verb, an adjective, or an adverb.

ADJECTIVE PHRASES The house **with the driveway of red brick** is ours.

ADVERB PHRASES **After school** I rode my bicycle **to a friend's house.**

EXERCISE A On the line provided, identify the underlined prepositional phrase by writing *ADJ* for *adjective phrase* or *ADV* for *adverb phrase.* Then, draw an arrow from each underlined prepositional phrase to the word or words it modifies.

Example ADV **1.** At her first Olympic competition, Sonja Henie was eleven years old.

______ **1.** Sonja was the daughter of a Norwegian fur dealer.

______ **2.** Trained as an ice skater, she competed in the 1924 Olympics at age eleven.

______ **3.** Her costume, a knee-length, flared skirt, made an impression on observers.

______ **4.** This skirt might have been considered improper on an adult.

______ **5.** However, opinions at the Olympics four years later had changed.

______ **6.** Sonja left the 1928 Olympics with her first gold medal.

______ **7.** Sonja introduced the elements of dance and showmanship to skating.

______ **8.** Furthermore, Sonja did jumps that had been performed only by men.

______ **9.** Sonja preferred to be treated like someone of great celebrity.

______ **10.** She was considered temperamental by many.

EXERCISE B For each sentence below, underline each adjective phrase once and underline each adverb phrase twice.

Example 1. On weekends, many members of my family enjoy ice-skating.

11. Last winter we went to the ice-skating rink many times.

12. Once, my cousins Sarah and Cameron came with us.

13. The ice-skating rink in their hometown closed a few years ago.

14. My mother did figure eights in the center of the rink.

15. Sarah and Cameron especially enjoyed the music from the 1950s.

Adjective and Adverb Phrases B

14c. An ***adjective phrase*** modifies a noun or a pronoun.

14d. An ***adverb phrase*** modifies a verb, an adjective, or an adverb.

ADJECTIVE PHRASES We climbed a mountain **with a steep slope on the west side.**

ADVERB PHRASES **On Saturday night**, we went **to a jazz concert.**

EXERCISE A Underline each prepositional phrase in the following sentences, and draw an arrow from the phrase to the word it modifies.

Example 1. The first perfect score in Olympic Games history was earned by Nadia Comaneci.

1. Nadia Comaneci competed in the 1976 Olympic Games in Montreal.
2. Her performance on the uneven bars occurred during the first game day.
3. This fourteen-year-old girl from Romania received a judges' mark of 10.00.
4. In the gymnastic events, Nadia earned a total of three gold medals and seven perfect scores.
5. Nadia was very happy about the first perfect score in Olympic history.
6. Nadia's achievements led many young girls to gymnastics classes.
7. In 1980, she won two gold medals and two silver medals.
8. She was also enjoying her fame in Romania.
9. She came to the United States in 1989.
10. There, she met a fellow gymnast, Bart Conner, whom she later married in Bucharest, Romania.

EXERCISE B For each sentence below, underline each adjective phrase once and underline each adverb phrase twice.

Example 1. How often do you go to the movies?

11. I recently saw an excellent movie about space travel.
12. In the movie, the travelers explored distant planets.
13. They visited one planet with rings that resembled Saturn.
14. Across its surface, the planet also had huge mountain ranges.
15. I really enjoyed the scenery in that movie.

NAME CLASS DATE

The Participle

14e. A ***participle*** is a verb form that can be used as an adjective.

(1) *Present participles* end in *–ing.*

(2) *Past participles* usually end in *–d* or *–ed.* Some past participles are formed irregularly.

PRESENT PARTICIPLES **Concentrating** carefully, Steve hit the **speeding** ball.

PAST PARTICIPLES An **experienced** player, Josh was the **chosen** pitcher.

EXERCISE A In each of the following sentences, circle the participle that modifies the underlined noun or pronoun.

Example 1. The stretched net suddenly broke.

1. The elected captain thanked her teammates.
2. The shouting fans encouraged the runners.
3. The painted goal posts were hard to miss.
4. The cheering crowd stomped their feet in the bleachers.
5. The lines on the track, newly painted, guided the runners.
6. Spiking the volleyball, she scored another point for her team.
7. The sports equipment, mistreated all year, looked old.
8. Smiling cheerleaders stepped in front of the crowd.
9. The popcorn vendor, calling loudly, climbed the bleachers.
10. Feeling hungry, I bought popcorn and a bottle of water.

EXERCISE B Underline the participle that is used as an adjective in each of the following sentences, and draw an arrow to the noun or pronoun it modifies.

Example 1. I covered the shivering child with a blanket.

11. Playing in the sand, the children laughed happily.
12. Cheryl's chosen career is engineering.
13. Is all this used furniture for sale?
14. Tad's older sister, talking excitedly, explained the joke to us.
15. The fallen leaves still covered the ground in early spring.

The Participial Phrase

14f. A ***participial phrase*** consists of a participle together with its modifiers and complements. The entire phrase is used as an adjective.

EXAMPLE **Standing in a long line**, the group of teenagers waited to see the new movie.

EXERCISE A Underline each participial phrase in the following sentences, and draw an arrow from it to the noun or pronoun it modifies.

Example 1. Born in 1899, Alfred Hitchcock lived eighty-one years.

1. Alfred Hitchcock, respected by his colleagues, earned an important place among film directors.
2. Known as the "master of suspense," he created dark, suspenseful moods in his films.
3. Remaining faithful to this trademark tone, he directed movies throughout five decades.
4. Hitchcock's films, criticized by some, maintained a dramatic flair.
5. Some of the movies directed by Hitchcock are *Dial M for Murder, Rear Window,* and *The Birds.*
6. Turning to the television format, Hitchcock also hosted a series for television.
7. The television show hosted by Hitchcock was *Alfred Hitchcock Presents.*
8. It was a mystery series featuring a different story and different actors each week.
9. Still airing as reruns, episodes feature actors such as Robert Redford.
10. Never honored with an Academy Award for best director, Hitchcock remains best director to many fans.

EXERCISE B On the lines provided, write sentences using the following word groups as participial phrases. Then, circle the noun or pronoun that each participial phrase modifies.

Example 1. talking to her friends *Talking to her friends, Jen walked by me without stopping.*

11. painted a bright yellow ______
12. blowing wildly in the wind ______
13. frozen solid as a rock ______
14. singing in the shower ______
15. stuffed into my tiny locker ______

Participles and Participial Phrases A

14e. A ***participle*** is a verb form that can be used as an adjective.

PARTICIPLE The **crying** child asked for his mother.

14f. A ***participial phrase*** consists of a participle together with its modifiers and complements. The entire phrase is used as an adjective.

PARTICIPIAL PHRASE The record **broken by José Canseco** was impressive.

EXERCISE Circle each participle used as an adjective in the following sentences. If the participle has modifiers or complements, underline the complete participial phrase.

Examples **1.** Scattered evidence was found in the house.

2. Hammering the nails, Midori envisioned the treehouse she would have.

1. The baking bread smelled delicious.

2. Shaped like a flag, the sand sculpture won first prize.

3. Under a pile of magazines lay the forgotten letter.

4. Frozen blueberries are his favorite dessert.

5. Devoted soccer fans are looking forward to the season.

6. Waking slowly, the dog stretched its legs.

7. From behind the tree came a screeching sound.

8. The lion basking in the sun looked sleepy.

9. Surrounded by the smell of apples, I walked through the orchard.

10. I heard something pounding against the windowpane.

11. Leaping into the air, the dancer thrilled the audience.

12. The athlete, sweating heavily, grabbed a towel and a bottle of water.

13. I did not want to eat the burned potatoes that my sister had cooked.

14. Stapled in the corner, the test booklet contained ten pages.

15. Closely written, the words filled every space on the diary pages.

16. Jake, slipping on a banana peel, let out a shriek.

17. Smiling, I opened my birthday present.

18. Examined by a doctor, his wrist will heal soon.

19. I shook the brightly wrapped gift before opening it.

20. The pet chosen by Trisha is a baby rabbit.

for CHAPTER 14: THE PHRASE pages 410–12

Participles and Participial Phrases B

14e. A ***participle*** is a verb form that can be used as an adjective.

EXAMPLES Did you see the **flying** bird?
Perhaps we will find a **hidden** treasure.

14f. A ***participial phrase*** consists of a participle together with its modifiers and complements. The entire phrase is used as an adjective.

EXAMPLE The tree **struck by lightning** has fallen.

EXERCISE Underline once the participles and participial phrases used as adjectives in the following sentences. Then, underline twice the word or words each participle or participial phrase modifies.

Example 1. Excited by the good news, Sherry called all her friends.

1. The clown entertaining the children at the party was funny.
2. He had a surprised look on his face.
3. We were awakened last night by a barking dog.
4. Students participating in the event will meet after school.
5. The woman wandering down the street was wearing a red hat.
6. Surrounded by her closest friends, Jane enjoyed her birthday party.
7. As we entered the room, we noticed the broken vase on the floor.
8. Her dad comforted her with a reassuring smile.
9. The wooded site was a perfect place to camp for the night.
10. Startled by the noise, the cat scrambled under the chair.
11. Finally, they could see the train approaching in the distance.
12. Everyone involved in the discussion expressed his or her opinion.
13. We were happy with the services provided by that company.
14. The married couple set out on their honeymoon.
15. When we were young, my friends and I always hoped to find buried treasure.
16. Damaged by the storm, the car no longer ran.
17. The school threw a huge party for the teacher retiring this year.
18. We have to turn in our written work by the end of the week.
19. The man jogging up the hill is my grandfather.
20. Beatriz has always been a committed person.

The Infinitive

14g. An ***infinitive*** is a verb form that can be used as a noun, an adjective, or an adverb. Most infinitives begin with *to.*

INFINITIVE USED AS NOUN	**To heal** was the athlete's first priority.
INFINITIVE USED AS ADJECTIVE	The player **to watch** this season is Rodney.
INFINITIVE USED AS ADVERB	This speech will be easy **to memorize.**

EXERCISE Underline the infinitives in the following sentences. If a sentence does not contain an infinitive, write *none* after the sentence.

Examples **1.** Which is the healthier meal to eat?

2. Will you give your dessert to me? *none*

1. When you need help with math, Maddie is the one to ask.

2. When I play racquetball, I play to win.

3. Robin Hood stole from the rich and gave to the poor.

4. To interrupt was not my intention.

5. If you start the project, you must be sure to finsh.

6. In my opinion, the fashion accessory to have this season is a silver charm bracelet.

7. I go to the local thrift store to shop.

8. The clothing to donate is in a box.

9. Our plan for the day is to hike.

10. The place to shop is the new mall downtown.

11. We plan to go first thing in the morning.

12. To whom should I address this letter?

13. Some people think it is refreshing to swim.

14. I don't know which film to recommend.

15. Have you decided what you want to eat?

16. Going to the YMCA is fine with me.

17. To exercise is one of my goals this semester.

18. Has Juanita begun to study?

19. Shelly recommended a great poem to read.

20. Roberto went home early to rest.

The Infinitive Phrase

14h. An ***infinitive phrase*** consists of an infinitive together with its modifiers and complements. The entire phrase may be used as a noun, an adjective, or an adverb.

NOUN **To stay in shape** requires dedication and discipline.
ADJECTIVE The thing **to do first** is an activity you enjoy.
ADVERB I came to Austin **to see the art exhibit.**

EXERCISE A For each of the following sentences, underline the infinitive phrase. If a sentence does not contain an infinitive phrase, write *none* after the sentence.

Example 1. The place to go for information is the library.

1. At the library I found a book about yoga to read over the weekend.
2. The goal of yoga is to relieve stress and tension.
3. Around test time, I definitely need to reduce stress!
4. Yoga also helps to increase flexibility and muscle tone.
5. To most people, beginning a yoga routine is easy.
6. The yoga positions to practice first can be learned from a book or video.
7. To do the more difficult movements and stretches requires more experience.
8. At that point, it is probably better to work with a yoga instructor.
9. For now, I've chosen to learn a routine that increases flexibility.
10. After I master the basics, I'll train to become a yoga instructor.

EXERCISE B On the lines provided, write sentences using each of the following infinitive phrases.

Example 1. to make the honor roll *To make the honor roll, I must improve my grades.*

11. to wake me up in the morning ______
12. to arrive at La Guardia Airport in New York ______
13. to surprise my best friend ______
14. to plan the party for Saturday night ______
15. to succeed in my goals ______

Infinitives and Infinitive Phrases A

14g. An ***infinitive*** is a verb form that can be used as a noun, an adjective, or an adverb. Most infinitives begin with *to*.

14h. An ***infinitive phrase*** consists of an infinitive together with its modifiers and complements. The entire phrase may be used as a noun, an adjective, or an adverb.

NOUN **To swim before school** is refreshing.
ADJECTIVE The request **to make to Mom** is for a new coat.
ADVERB Janet was too shy **to answer**.

EXERCISE Underline the infinitives and infinitive phrases in the following sentences.

Example **1.** Elston went to the library to write his paper.

1. Pepita decided to join the track team.

2. Lamont wants to learn Spanish before fall.

3. Courtney is planning to sell more tickets to our school play.

4. Robert Fulton, who built the first successful steamboat, tried to invent a practical submarine.

5. To learn about agriculture was George Washington Carver's goal.

6. Krista was happy to finish the art project.

7. Elena offered to wash the car.

8. Justin was reluctant to try raw fish.

9. To fly was Wilbur Wright's dream.

10. Some astronauts have had the opportunity to journey into space.

11. The time to begin a paper is long before the paper is due.

12. The option to choose is the one that causes the least trouble.

13. To do research in the library can be very productive.

14. That car was the first one to be sold this year.

15. The effort to rescue the kitten ended in success.

16. Elian was laughing too hard to speak.

17. Press the button to ring the doorbell.

18. To see the ocean for the first time is a thrilling experience.

19. We are ready to start the race.

20. He was the first person to run a four-minute mile.

Infinitives and Infinitive Phrases B

14g. An ***infinitive*** is a verb form that can be used as a noun, an adjective, or an adverb. Most infinitives begin with *to.*

14h. An ***infinitive phrase*** consists of an infinitive together with its modifiers and complements. The entire phrase may be used as a noun, an adjective, or an adverb.

EXERCISE A Underline the infinitives and infinitive phrases in the following sentences.

Example 1. Theo wanted to build a treehouse.

1. Roberta sliced the bread to serve it to her dinner guests.

2. My mother's favorite dish to cook is lasagna.

3. To remove stains from clothes, I recommend washing them in hot, soapy water.

4. Justin likes to conduct research on the Internet on the weekends.

5. To travel to Argentina was Elena's wish for the new year.

6. We called Peter and Laura to ask them about our homework assignment.

7. The number to call for that information has been changed.

8. Rafael and Alex were happy to meet their new neighbors.

9. We peeked at the baby in the crib to see her.

10. David told his little sister a vivid story to entertain her after dinner.

EXERCISE B Write sentences using each of the following infinitives and infinitive phrases.

Example 1. to learn more about South American history *I went to the library to learn more about South American history.*

11. to try new things ______

12. to create ______

13. to plan a trip ______

14. to enjoy ______

15. to work hard ______

Verbal Phrases A

Two types of *verbal phrases* are participial phrases and infinitive phrases.

14f. A ***participial phrase*** consists of a participle together with its modifiers and complements. The entire phrase is used as an adjective.

14h. An ***infinitive phrase*** consists of an infinitive together with its modifiers and complements. The entire phrase may be used as a noun, an adjective, or an adverb.

PARTICIPIAL PHRASE **Becoming thirsty from the heat,** I looked for a water fountain.

INFINITIVE PHRASE My only concern was **to quench my thirst**.

EXERCISE A On the line provided, identify each underlined phrase by writing *inf* for *infinitive phrase* or *part* for *participial phrase*.

Example *part* **1.** Tired from the walk, Aurelio lay down for a short nap.

______ **1.** Eric hopes to see the Great Wall of China someday.

______ **2.** Singing a happy tune, Marcia strolled down the street.

______ **3.** Built last year, one new home sits proudly on top of a hill.

______ **4.** To travel to India is Devorah's goal.

______ **5.** A classical music concert is a joy to attend on a relaxing weekend.

EXERCISE B Underline the verbal phrase in each of the following sentences. Then, on the line provided, identify the phrase by writing *part* for *participial phrase* or *inf* for *infinitive phrase*.

Examples *part* **1.** The languages commonly spoken in Canada are French and English.

inf **2.** To speak fluent French is my goal.

______ **6.** One requirement of airline pilots is to speak and understand English.

______ **7.** People speaking Chinese outnumber those who speak English.

______ **8.** To learn a second language is certainly worthwhile.

______ **9.** Signs posted in international airports are often in several languages.

______ **10.** To visit a foreign country is the desire of many young people.

______ **11.** They want to experience different customs, foods, and environments.

______ **12.** Knowing Spanish, a person can travel in Mexico and South America without a language barrier.

______ **13.** I would also like to go to São Paulo, Brazil.

______ **14.** If you like to travel by boat, perhaps you should visit Venice.

______ **15.** Tourists looking for beautiful views might visit Denmark.

Verbal Phrases B

Two types of ***verbal phrases*** are participial phrases and infinitive phrases.

14f. A ***participial phrase*** consists of a participle together with its modifiers and complements. The entire phrase is used as an adjective.

14h. An ***infinitive phrase*** consists of an infinitive together with its modifiers and complements. The entire phrase may be used as a noun, an adjective, or an adverb.

PARTICIPIAL PHRASE **Pressed for time**, Susan quickly bought her ticket and boarded the plane.

INFINITIVE PHRASE She felt lucky **to have a seat next to the window**.

EXERCISE A On the line provided, identify each underlined phrase by writing *inf* for *infinitive phrase* or *part* for *participial phrase*.

Example part 1. Struggling intensely, the toddler finally took his first step.

______ **1.** I would like to know the name of that singer.

______ **2.** Sarah and Katie stood in line to see the band.

______ **3.** Susan and Michelle, returning from their trip, told stories about their adventures.

______ **4.** To buy a car is Laura's main objective this summer.

______ **5.** Recently released on video, the highly praised movie quickly became a big seller.

EXERCISE B Underline the verbal phrase in each of the following sentences. Then, on the line provided, identify the phrase by writing *part* for *participial phrase* or *inf* for *infinitive phrase*.

Examples part 1. The raw vegetables, chopped into bite-sized pieces, made a crunchy snack.

inf 2. After the concert, we decided to go for a walk around the lake.

______ **6.** I caught my younger sister eavesdropping behind my bedroom door.

______ **7.** The anvil, dropped from a great height, hit the sidewalk hard.

______ **8.** Splashing in the shallow water, the children enjoyed their day at the beach.

______ **9.** The city passed a law to protect endangered animals.

______ **10.** Juanita was happy to find the letter.

______ **11.** We raked all the leaves fallen from the trees during autumn.

______ **12.** Ending the speech, the candidate received loud applause.

______ **13.** "If you want to know the end of the story," Gloria said, "read the book."

______ **14.** The dog, covered in mud from the backyard, left tracks as he ran through the house.

______ **15.** To end the game well was Kevin's only wish.

Review A: Identifying Phrases

EXERCISE A Underline each prepositional phrase in each of the following sentences. Then, draw an arrow from the phrase to the word or words it modifies.

Example 1. A bath in warm water before bed relaxes your muscles.

1. Scientists have studied patterns of human sleep.

2. Our nightly rest consists of light sleep and deep sleep.

3. Some people sleep on their backs.

4. Other people rest on their sides quite comfortably.

5. The origin of dreams has interested some people.

6. One theory is that we write our own script for each dream.

7. Some dreams appear in color.

8. The amount of sleep a person gets affects how often he or she dreams.

9. Some nightmares may be caused by tension, worries, and nervousness.

10. Most adults dream at regular intervals.

EXERCISE B Underline the verbal phrase in each of the following sentences. Then, identify the phrase on the line provided by writing *part* for *participial phrase* or *inf* for *infinitive phrase.*

Example _part_ **1.** The rain, falling gently, had a steady rhythm.

_____ **11.** To forecast the weather is not a simple process.

_____ **12.** Gathered from weather stations and satellites, data change continually.

_____ **13.** Barometers, designed for measuring air pressure, detect weather changes.

_____ **14.** The clouds forming in the sky also indicate weather conditions.

_____ **15.** To measure precipitation, gauges are used.

_____ **16.** Instruments indicating wind speed and direction are important tools.

_____ **17.** Monitoring temperature changes, local news stations report current information throughout the day.

_____ **18.** To study weather changes is the job of a meteorologist.

_____ **19.** Using maps and technical equipment, meteorologists forecast weather conditions and changes.

_____ **20.** Hurricanes and floods, feared for their destructiveness, attract national attention.

Review B: Identifying Phrases

EXERCISE A Underline each prepositional phrase in the following sentences, and draw an arrow from the phrase to the word or words it modifies.

Example **1.** The submarine beneath the sea lies in wait.

1. Submarines can travel on the surface of the water.

2. They also move quite well beneath the surface.

3. Submarines deploy in times of war.

4. Many modern submarines run on nuclear power.

5. During operations, nuclear-powered submarines remain deep under the water's surface.

6. Satellites bounce back information from distances high above the earth.

7. In the future, more and more information will be sent by satellite.

8. The news on television comes to us by satellite.

9. Cables under the ocean carry messages to our homes.

10. During the 1920s, few people would have dreamed of such marvels in our own homes.

EXERCISE B Underline the verbal phrase in each of the following sentences. Then, identify the phrase by writing *part* for *participial phrase* or *inf* for *infinitive phrase*.

Example *part* **1.** Tennessee, admitted to the Union in 1796, is in the South.

______ **11.** Planning a family trip to Tennessee, my grandfather gathered information.

______ **12.** He wrote the tourist information center a letter asking for information.

______ **13.** My sisters wanted to visit Nashville.

______ **14.** They wished to see the Grand Ole Opry House.

______ **15.** My cousins wanted to visit different places in Tennessee.

______ **16.** Gatlinburg, located at the entrance of the Great Smoky Mountains National Park, was a popular choice.

______ **17.** Topping the list of second choices, Memphis received many votes.

______ **18.** To hike in the mountains was my choice.

______ **19.** The destination finally agreed upon by my entire family was Nashville.

______ **20.** It was difficult to choose the location of our trip in such an interesting state.

NAME ______________________ CLASS ______________ DATE ______________

Review C: Identifying Phrases

EXERCISE A In each of the following sentences, identify the underlined phrase by writing above it *prep* for *prepositional phrase* or *part* for *participial phrase*.

Example 1. *part* Traveling in Thailand, Faith learned a great deal about this Eastern nation.

1. The Kingdom of Thailand is one of ten nations in Southeast Asia.
2. Bangkok, located near the Gulf of Thailand, is Thailand's capital.
3. Producing vehicles and agricultural crops, Thailand is a rapidly developing nation.
4. Thailand is the world's largest producer of natural rubber.
5. Named Siam until 1938, Thailand is a constitutional monarchy.
6. Thailand is bordered by Myanmar, Laos, Cambodia, and Malaysia.
7. Colored red, white, and blue, the Thai flag has five horizontal stripes.
8. The monsoon season in Thailand lasts from May to October.
9. Founded in the sixth century B.C., Buddhism is Thailand's principal religion.
10. Covering approximately 198,000 square miles, Thailand is smaller than the state of Texas.

EXERCISE B Underline the verbal phrase in each of the following sentences. Then, identify the phrase by writing above it *part* for *participial phrase* or *inf* for *infinitive phrase*.

Example 1. *inf* To take better notes in class is one of my goals this year.

11. Hopping slowly across the dirt road, the frog finally reached the pond.
12. The concerto composed by the cellist was performed at the recital.
13. The best room to use for the spring dance is the large ballroom.
14. Yesterday, we saw a squirrel collecting food for the winter.
15. Scattered on the ground, the fall leaves added color to the landscape.
16. Will all of these names and dates be too difficult to remember for the test?
17. I wanted to watch television, but I wrote my science report instead.
18. My raincoat, soaked in the downpour, dripped onto the floor.
19. I finally found Kris jogging through the park.
20. Arching its back, the cat hissed angrily at the snake.

Literary Model: Participles in Poetry

The 1st

By Lucille Clifton

what I remember about that day
is boxes stacked across the walk
and couch springs curling through the air
and drawers and tables balanced on the curb
and us, hollering,
leaping up and around
happy to have a playground;

nothing about the emptied rooms
nothing about the emptied family

EXERCISE A Write the two participles that are not part of a phrase. One is used twice. Then, write the four participial phrases and underline the participle found in each one.

Participles:

Participial phrases:

EXERCISE B

1. Which nouns in this poem are modified by participial phrases?

2. Which pronoun is modified by a participle and participial phrase?

EXERCISE C Using Lucille Clifton's poem as a model, write a short poem about an event from your childhood. Use several participles and participial phrases.

Literary Model (continued)

EXERCISE D

1. Rewrite your poem so that all participles and participial phrases are replaced with verbs or verb phrases.

2. Compare the use of verbs in your rewritten poem and the use of verbals in your original poem. Explain how the actions and events you describe seem different in the two poems.

Writing Application: Narrative

Participles and participial phrases allow writers to create a sense of action with modifiers. Present or past, participle or participial phrase, these modifiers pack a sentence with more interesting action.

EXAMPLES **Standing in the wings of the theater,** I fought my nervousness and waited for my cue.
The leading man, **slightly distracted by the bright lights and murmuring audience,** stood next to me.

Writing Activity

As part of your training in a student leadership workshop, you are writing a narrative about a time when you faced an unnerving situation but eventually overcame your fear with action. You will present your narrative to the other students in a dramatic reading as the group investigates leadership qualities. Use at least five participial phrases as you describe the situation.

PREWRITING First, think about challenging circumstances in which you have recently found yourself. Choose one such circumstance, and brainstorm to recall all the details that you can. Use the *5W-How?* questions to think of information you need, and focus also on how you felt in that situation and how you overcame your hesitation and did what needed to be done.

WRITING As you organize your narrative, you can choose from several structures. For example, you could use a problem-solution structure, relating events as they unfolded in time, or you could try a flashback structure, starting in the present and casting back to an earlier time. Outline several structures, and then choose the most suspenseful and exciting one.

REVISING Stories tell well when they are descriptive and packed with verbals and action verbs. "Brown and furry, the bear's head was in the tent door" is not as interesting as "Slobbering and grunting, the bear shoved its head through the tent door." Use participial phrases as you would use vivid verbs—to create a sense of action and a sense of excitement.

PUBLISHING Check your narrative for errors in grammar, usage, punctuation, and spelling. You don't want errors to trip you up as you read aloud! Practice delivering your narrative dramatically to yourself and to a friend or family member. It may be that standing up and speaking before a group is a challenge for you—practice will make it less nerve-racking.

Extending Your Writing

This exercise could lead to a more developed writing project. Using your narrative as a springboard, create a fifteen-minute presentation discussing how people overcome their fears. Then, offer to give your presentation at a meeting of a youth organization or a teen support group.

for **CHAPTER 15: THE CLAUSE** *pages 423–31*

Choices: Exploring Clauses

Here's your chance to step out of the grammar book and into the real world. You may not notice clauses, but you and the people around you use them every day. The following activities challenge you to find a connection between clauses and the world around you. Do the activity below that suits your personality best, and then share your discoveries with your class. Have fun!

CREATIVE WRITING

Mix and Match

Have you seen those sets of magnets that have a word or two written on each piece? By mixing and matching the words, anyone can create a catchy saying or a short poem. Think about the words that would be most useful, interesting, flexible, or funny in such a set. Then, make a set for the classroom. You can cut out strips from flat magnet sheets, which can be found at a craft supply store, and glue paper onto them. Be sure to include relative pronouns, subordinating conjunctions, and transitional expressions.

PERFORMANCE

Mad Scientists

Have you got a sense of humor? Well, here's your opportunity to use it. Write a skit about mad scientists dissecting a sentence. Naturally, you'll need to get white lab coats and create a special effect or two. Videotape or perform your skit in front of the class. During your video or performance, you'll be cutting up a sentence and identifying each of its parts. Since you'll be going to some trouble for this project, make the sentence you dissect one with several subordinate and independent clauses.

VISUAL

Subject to Approval

Finding the verb in a subordinate clause is fairly easy, but those subjects can sometimes blend into the scenery. Create a poster-sized illustration in which you highlight the subjects of at least five adjective clauses and at least five adverb clauses. Use color and other design elements to highlight the subject of each clause. Finally, with your teacher's permission, post your illustration to share with your classmates.

WRITING

In the Beginning

Some people have a hard time thinking of a story idea. Help your classmates get started. Think up twenty subordinate clauses with which to begin a story. Make some of them fantastic, such as "When strange flashing lights first appeared on that fateful day some twenty-odd years ago. . . ." Make some of the clauses more ordinary, such as "Before Mr. Wiley and his five dogs moved in next door. . . ." Type or neatly write your beginning clauses, and hand out copies to your classmates.

LITERATURE

If at First You Don't Succeed

Many an old proverb begins with a subordinating conjunction. How many of these proverbs can you remember? Working with a friend or two, write down as many as you can. Open your textbook to a list of subordinating conjunctions. It'll help jog your memory.

WRITING

If Wishes Were Horses

When you read tales of a person who made three foolish wishes, weren't you angry with the rotten choices that the character made? You could do better, couldn't you? Well, do so. With your teacher's permission, prepare strips of paper large enough for three sentences. Give everyone in the class a strip of paper. Write *I wish* . . . on the board, and tell everyone to write down three wishes, each expressed in a noun clause. Collect all the strips. Tape them together, write *Noun Clauses* at the top, and display the list in the classroom.

GRAMMAR

Clauses

15a. A ***clause*** is a word group that contains a verb and its subject and that is used as a sentence or as part of a sentence.

A clause that expresses a complete thought is called an *independent clause*. A clause that does not make sense by itself is called a *subordinate clause*.

NOT A CLAUSE I enjoy **writing in purple ink.** [This word group is not a clause because it does not contain both a verb and its subject.]

INDEPENDENT CLAUSE **I write** when I am angry or confused.

SUBORDINATE CLAUSE I write **when I am angry or confused.**

EXERCISE A For each of the following sentences, identify the subject and the verb in the underlined part of the sentence. Above the subject write *S*, and above the verb write *V*.

Example 1. At the local bookstore I bought a blank book. (S above "I", V above "bought")

1. An antique map of the world is on the cover of my journal.

2. To me, this map represents the undiscovered areas of my mind.

3. When I read entries from months ago, I usually learn something about myself.

4. I often write about experiences because I need an outlet for my emotions.

5. I vent my frustrations in writing, and I feel better afterwards.

EXERCISE B For each of the following sentences, identify the underlined word group by writing above it *C* for *clause* or *NC* for *not a clause*.

Example 1. Writing down the angry comments that I think of is better than saying them aloud to a friend. (NC)

6. If I let a few days go by, I usually do not feel the same anger.

7. I then wonder what would have happened if I had actually said those things aloud!

8. During the past two years, I have filled four blank books with journal entries.

9. I know that many fascinating novelists and poets kept journals.

10. Sometimes the writer will use his or her own experiences to inspire a story.

11. Although I do not enjoy feeling sadness or fear, I am able to write about them convincingly.

12. I can write convincingly because I have experienced these emotions myself.

13. Several of my friends have told me that my stories should be published.

14. Not even my best friend, whom I have known for three years, has ever read my journal.

15. I believe that everyone deserves a certain amount of privacy.

The Independent Clause

15b. An ***independent*** (or ***main***) ***clause*** expresses a complete thought and can stand by itself as a sentence.

EXAMPLES **Sheldon can make homemade pizzas.**
Sheldon can make homemade pizzas, and **he made one for me.**

EXERCISE A Underline the independent clause or clauses in each of the following sentences.

Examples **1.** Sheldon opened a can of pizza dough, and then he spread the dough in a pan.

2. He used a nonstick pan because he wanted cleanup to be easy.

1. After he prepared the dough, Sheldon washed mushrooms, green peppers, and an onion.

2. He peeled the onion, and he chopped the vegetables into bite-size chunks.

3. The next step was sautéing the vegetables until they were tender.

4. I wanted to make myself useful, so I grated the mozzarella and Parmesan cheese.

5. Now we had two bowls of ingredients, which were the vegetables and the cheese.

6. I also opened a jar of pizza sauce, and I spread the sauce on the dough.

7. Then came the fun part!

8. Sheldon spread the vegetables evenly across the sauce, and I added the cheese on top.

9. After baking at 450° for twenty-five minutes, the pizza was ready.

10. What a delicious pizza it was!

EXERCISE B For each of the following sentences, identify the underlined word group by writing above it *I* for *independent clause* or *NI* for *not an independent clause.*

Example **1.** NI Since I met you, I've become more interested in baseball.

11. I never watched baseball games on television before meeting you.

12. We then watched games for several weekends in a row.

13. Now I understand the game much better.

14. When the game makes sense, it is suspenseful and enjoyable.

15. Since I have never played baseball, you can teach me!

The Subordinate Clause

15c. A ***subordinate*** (or ***dependent***) ***clause*** does not express a complete thought and cannot stand by itself as a complete sentence.

A subordinate clause must be joined with at least one independent clause to make a sentence and express a complete thought.

EXAMPLES **Since I was curious about acupuncture,** I looked it up in an encyclopedia.
The information **that I found** was fascinating.

EXERCISE A Identify the underlined clause in each of the following sentences by writing above it *SUB* for *subordinate clause* or *IND* for *independent clause.*

Example 1. Acupuncture, which is my research topic, is a Chinese medical technique. SUB

1. Although acupuncture is an ancient medical technique, it is still in use today.
2. The treatment is based on the idea that it helps bring into balance the yin and the yang.
3. Many areas of the world, including China, use this technique.
4. If you have a fear of needles, do not try acupuncture.
5. Acupuncture involves the insertion of tiny needles, which are made of metal, into the skin.
6. Since this technique uses no medication, some people may prefer it to prescription medicines.
7. For example, someone suffering mental depression might choose acupuncture over medication.
8. Other disorders that acupuncture treats are swollen joints, nosebleeds, and heart pains.
9. In China, patients who have surgery may choose acupuncture as anesthesia.
10. Until I'm braver, I won't try acupuncture.

EXERCISE B Underline the subordinate clause in each sentence.

Example 1. I studied the philosophy of yin-yang because it emphasizes balance.

11. According to ancient belief, the yin and the yang are two forces that make up all aspects of life.
12. The symbol of the yin and yang, which is a circle with intertwining black and white teardrop shapes, is familiar to many people.
13. Since yin, the female half, represents earth and darkness, it is the black half.
14. Because the yang, the male half, represents brightness and the heavens, it is the white half.
15. In yin-yang philosophy, which values harmony and balance, the black and the white are equally important.

Independent and Subordinate Clauses A

15b. An ***independent*** (or ***main***) ***clause*** expresses a complete thought and can stand by itself as a sentence.

15c. A ***subordinate*** (or ***dependent***) ***clause*** does not express a complete thought and cannot stand by itself as a complete sentence.

INDEPENDENT CLAUSE If you need me, **I will help you.**
SUBORDINATE CLAUSE **If you need me,** I will help you.

EXERCISE For each of the following sentences, identify the underlined word group by writing above it *IND* for *independent clause* or *SUB* for *subordinate clause*.

Example 1. The friend who is visiting this weekend is Melody. (SUB)

1. When Jeremy called last night, I was not at home.
2. I know the woman who owns that store.
3. John is the boy who is on the swim team.
4. It is hot today; please water the garden.
5. If he finishes his report on time, he can go to the beach Saturday.
6. This is the poem that I memorized last year.
7. The student whom I recommend for class president is Lindsey.
8. I can't concentrate when you practice the trumpet with your door open.
9. Although these colors are beautiful, I don't like the painting.
10. The man whom you met is the president of the group.
11. The girls who painted that mural live in my neighborhood.
12. When you reach the end of the hallway, turn right.
13. Please fold these clothes before they become wrinkled.
14. After we wrapped the presents, we hurried to the post office.
15. We didn't go to her party because we went camping that weekend.
16. The trees that my great-grandfather planted still shade the farmhouse.
17. Whenever you dust the shelves, I sneeze.
18. My aunt stays at our house when she comes to the city for business meetings.
19. The CD that you borrowed last week is due at the library today.
20. Preheat the oven to 350°, and take the chicken out of the refrigerator.

Independent and Subordinate Clauses B

15b. An ***independent*** (or ***main***) ***clause*** expresses a complete thought and can stand by itself as a sentence.

15c. A ***subordinate*** (or ***dependent***) ***clause*** does not express a complete thought and cannot stand by itself as a complete sentence.

INDEPENDENT CLAUSE When you call Jane, **ask her for that book.**
SUBORDINATE CLAUSE **When you call Jane,** ask her for that book.

EXERCISE On the lines provided, add independent clauses to the following subordinate clauses to express complete thoughts. Make sure each sentence begins with a capital letter and has end punctuation.

Example 1. after we left the pizza parlor *We went to a movie after we left the pizza parlor.*

1. when I graduate from high school ______

2. whose sweater was lost ______

3. which is a good book ______

4. until Mark moved to Chicago ______

5. after the game was over ______

6. that caused the accident ______

7. since I met you in art class ______

8. until I call you on Friday ______

9. whom I assist as a student aide during my free period ______

10. because I didn't think before I spoke ______

NAME CLASS DATE

The Adjective Clause A

15d. An ***adjective clause*** is a subordinate clause that modifies a noun or a pronoun.

Unlike an adjective phrase, an adjective clause contains both a verb and its subject.

ADJECTIVE PHRASE a shirt **with stripes** [has no subject or verb]

ADJECTIVE CLAUSE a shirt **that has stripes** [has a subject and verb]

EXERCISE A For each of the following sentences, identify the underlined word or word group by writing above it *ADJ* for *adjective*, *AP* for *adjective phrase*, or *AC* for *adjective clause*.

Example 1. The house with peeling paint is at the end of the street. [AP]

1. This thick sweater should keep me warm in the snow.
2. The CD that Thomas scratched will no longer play.
3. The puppy with white paws was chewing on your shoe.
4. The people whom I invited to my study session are bringing snacks.
5. Go find your waterproof boots.
6. The subway station that is near my apartment is closed for repairs.
7. The patient in the wheelchair has a broken leg.
8. That team member who raises the most funds will receive an award.
9. The injured bird was taken to the veterinarian.
10. This shade of paint, which is not very pretty, was on sale at the hardware store.

EXERCISE B Underline the adjective clause, and circle the word or words that it modifies.

Example 1. The sport that I tried out for is softball.

11. Softball is a popular game that is played throughout the United States.
12. The game, which comes from an 1880s indoor baseball game, resembles baseball.
13. People who play softball are aware of slight differences in the two games.
14. The field that is used for softball is smaller than a baseball field.
15. The game, which lasts only seven innings, is shorter than a baseball game.
16. A softball is larger and softer than the ball that is used for baseball.
17. Those who play softball are familiar with a variation called slow pitch.
18. Softball pitching, which is done underhand, is different from baseball pitching.
19. Players whom I especially envy can hit the ball out of the park!
20. The pitcher, whose pitches determine the course of the game, is my favorite player.

NAME ______ CLASS ______ DATE ______

The Adjective Clause B

15d. An ***adjective clause*** is a subordinate clause that modifies a noun or a pronoun.

Unlike an adjective phrase, an adjective clause contains both a verb and its subject.

ADJECTIVE PHRASE a picnic spot **with shade** [has no subject or verb]

ADJECTIVE CLAUSE a picnic spot **that has shade** [has a subject and verb]

EXERCISE For each of the following sentences, identify the underlined word or word group by writing above it *ADJ* for *adjective, AP* for *adjective phrase,* or *AC* for *adjective clause.* Then, circle the word or words the adjective, adjective phrase, or adjective clause modifies.

Example 1. The test, which lasted only one hour, was not difficult. [AC; *test* circled]

1. Nico wanted to find a chess set with magnetic pieces.
2. This cat has long, silky fur.
3. The soccer field in the park needs to be mowed.
4. I should have warned you about the chair with the broken leg.
5. The story that she told us was certainly fascinating.
6. The boys found the old map in a box underneath the bed.
7. The ship sank in a violent storm.
8. My mother introduced us to her uncle, whom we had never met.
9. The telephones in that office ring constantly.
10. How much is the jacket with the red stripes on the sleeves?
11. The bread, which was still warm from the oven, tasted wonderful.
12. The weather announcer warned everyone about the hurricane that was near the coast.
13. We will need to paint this old table, which my father bought at a garage sale.
14. Don't forget about the clothes in the dryer!
15. The new shoes, which he had left out in the rain, were ruined.
16. Tricia and her sister made the decorations that you see on the walls.
17. Did you remember to turn off the lights in the classroom?
18. The student who sits next to me was born in China.
19. The cathedral had magnificent stained-glass windows.
20. The novel, which will be made into a movie, was hard to put down.

Relative Pronouns

An adjective clause is usually introduced by a ***relative pronoun.***

RELATIVE PRONOUNS that, which, who, whom, whose

ADJECTIVE CLAUSES the book **that I read;** the man **who called**

EXERCISE A Each of the following items is a noun modified by an adjective or an adjective phrase. On the lines provided, rewrite each item so that it contains an adjective clause instead of an adjective or adjective phrase.

Example 1. the boy with the torn jacket *the boy whose jacket is torn*

1. the player with the bat ______

2. the softball field at our school ______

3. the best team ______

4. the fastest runner ______

5. the player with the best batting average ______

EXERCISE B Complete each of the following sentences with an adjective clause. Then, circle each relative pronoun.

Example 1. The concession stand, *(which) sells hot dogs and pretzels*, is open.

6. In the crowd I looked for the player ______.

7. I envied the ticket holders ______.

8. The banners ______ distracted me from the game.

9. Arriving late, the father and son sat in the seats ______.

10. They ordered the hot dogs ______.

11. The home team's pitcher, ______, was playing well.

12. The first batter, ______, struck out.

13. Did you see the home run ______?

14. Will the outfielder catch the balls ______?

15. The shortstop is the one ______.

The Adverb Clause A

15e. An ***adverb clause*** is a subordinate clause that modifies a verb, an adjective, or an adverb.

Unlike an adverb phrase, an adverb clause contains both a verb and its subject.

ADVERB PHRASE **With great speed,** Tomás ran the race.

ADVERB CLAUSE **Because Tomás ran the race with great speed,** he won.

EXERCISE A For each of the following sentences, identify the underlined word or word group by writing above it *A* for *adverb, AP* for *adverb phrase,* or *AC* for *adverb clause.*

Example 1. I started painting early so that I would finish by 3:00 P.M. *AC*

1. The employee at the hardware store mixed the paint carefully.
2. He matched the paint sample I brought with me.
3. As much as I enjoy painting, I have other things to do.
4. Do not paint the fence until you scrape off the old paint chips.
5. You should also sand the wood so that the new paint adheres evenly.
6. Before you start, spread an old towel or sheet under the work area.
7. The dropcloth will catch paint if it drips from your brush.
8. Because I did such a great job on our fence, the neighbor asked me to paint his fence.
9. I can paint his fence sometime during summer vacation.
10. As soon as I finish cleaning these brushes, I'm taking the rest of the day off.

EXERCISE B Underline the adverb clause in each of the following sentences. Then, identify the question the adverb clause answers by writing above it *how, when, where, why, how much,* or *under what condition.*

Example 1. Please come over whenever you finish your homework. *when*

11. I ate a bowl of popcorn while I did my homework.
12. We will have to hurry if we want to catch the 5:30 bus.
13. From the top of the hill, you can see trees wherever you look.
14. I need to borrow a pencil because I left mine at home.
15. The puppies act as if they are hungry.
16. A giraffe is taller than an elephant is.
17. Before we left for our vacation, we unplugged the computer.
18. Since I love mystery stories, I enjoy books by Agatha Christie.
19. They watch more television programs than I do.
20. Set the potted plants where they will get plenty of light.

The Adverb Clause B

15e. An ***adverb clause*** is a subordinate clause that modifies a verb, an adjective, or an adverb.

Unlike an adverb phrase, an adverb clause contains both a verb and its subject.

ADVERB She shoots the basketball **accurately.**
ADVERB PHRASE She shoots the basketball **with accuracy.**
ADVERB CLAUSE She made the basket **because she shot the ball accurately.**

EXERCISE For each of the following sentences, identify the underlined word or word group by writing above it *ADV* for *adverb, AP* for *adverb phrase,* or *AC* for *adverb clause.* Then, circle the word or words the adverb, adverb phrase, or adverb clause modifies.

Example 1. AC Although he ran as fast as he could, he (missed) the bus.

1. The stonecutters worked slowly and carefully.
2. Sweep the floor after you finish the project.
3. We sleep with the windows open whenever the weather is pleasant.
4. Before Sam went skating with his friends, he finished his homework.
5. In August, it is really hot at four o'clock.
6. The guide's canoe glided silently across the lake.
7. I usually write in my journal after everyone else has gone to bed.
8. The lioness crouched warily in the tall grass.
9. After a hard day's work, I always sleep soundly.
10. Yesterday I left my jacket in my locker.
11. I raised my hand because I knew the answer.
12. My father always waters his flower garden before he goes to work.
13. On Tuesdays and Thursdays, we practice after school.
14. The audience cheered and clapped enthusiastically.
15. The fly buzzed around the room.
16. As soon as you finish that book, please lend it to me.
17. Tom and Julie met us at the restaurant.
18. Never ride your bicycle without wearing a helmet.
19. Call me after you have finished your chores.
20. The lights went out during the thunderstorm.

Subordinating Conjunctions

Adverb clauses begin with ***subordinating conjunctions***. Common subordinating conjunctions include *after, although, as if, as soon as, because, before, if, since, than, unless, until, when, wherever,* and *while.*

Some subordinating conjunctions, such as *after, as, before, since,* and *until*, can also be used as prepositions.

SUBORDINATING CONJUNCTION **After** I weed the garden, I put mulch around my new plants.

PREPOSITION It becomes too hot to garden **after** two o'clock.

EXERCISE A For each of the following sentences, indicate how the underlined word is used by writing above it *SC* for *subordinating conjunction* or *PREP* for *preposition.*

Example 1. After the rain soaked the earth, many seedlings appeared. (SC)

1. I have been trying to finish shelling these beans since yesterday.

2. Until you have read the instructions, do not prune that tree.

3. As the moon rose, coyotes slipped out of the trees.

4. I expected more flowers in the garden after I had planted so many seeds.

5. After this long, hot afternoon of garden work, I need a nap.

EXERCISE B Underline the adverb clause in each sentence, and circle each subordinating conjunction.

Example 1. I patched the garden fence (after) I noticed the rabbits' entry point.

6. As soon as the ground softens in the spring, plant your garden.

7. Some seeds take more time to sprout than others do.

8. If you want to grow morning glories, start the seeds under lights.

9. When the seeds sprout, you can transplant them into the garden.

10. Plant them near a fence or wall so that the plants can climb.

11. After the young plants grow strong, they will produce flowers.

12. The flowers will look as if they are big blue trumpets.

13. They're called morning glories because they open each morning.

14. When they are warmed by the morning sun, they open.

15. If the day is dark or stormy, they stay tightly shut, like umbrellas.

Adjective and Adverb Clauses A

15d. An ***adjective clause*** is a subordinate clause that modifies a noun or a pronoun.

15e. An ***adverb clause*** is a subordinate clause that modifies a verb, an adjective, or an adverb.

ADJECTIVE CLAUSE Did you hear about the cow **that jumped over the moon**?

ADVERB CLAUSE I feel **as if I've heard that nursery rhyme a hundred times.**

EXERCISE A For each of the following sentences, identify the underlined clause by writing above it *ADJ* for *adjective clause* or *ADV* for *adverb clause*. Circle the word or words that the clause modifies.

Example 1. Because I enjoy reading to my baby nephew, I bought a book of nursery rhymes. (ADV)

1. The rhyme that I like the most is about Jack and the candlestick.
2. Although I can't remember all the words, I like the poem about Mary and her garden.
3. The woman whom I baby-sit for decorated her nursery with a Mother Goose theme.
4. You'll probably overlook the tiny, thoughtful details unless you look closely.
5. The night light, for example, turns on automatically whenever the overhead light goes out.
6. The night light, which is made of plastic, bears the image of a cow jumping over the moon.
7. Stars are painted on the ceiling with special paint that glows in the dark.
8. Where the wall meets the ceiling, the letters of the alphabet are painted as a border.
9. A chalkboard has been attached to the wall so that the child can write on the "wall."
10. The child whose room this is must enjoy spending time in his room.

EXERCISE B Underline the subordinate clause in each sentence. Then, identify the clause by writing above it *ADJ* for *adjective clause* or *ADV* for *adverb clause*.

Example 1. Linguistics, as I learned recently, is the study of language. (ADV)

11. Some words that are in the English language come from people's names.
12. Because Adolphe Sax invented the saxophone, it was named for him.
13. Most American trains had steam engines until Rudolf Diesel invented the diesel engine.
14. From *Caesar,* which was the title of Roman leaders, comes *czar.*
15. Theodore Roosevelt, who was President of the United States, inspired the term *teddy bear.*
16. We have the word *sideburns* because Ambrose Burnside had bushy whiskers.
17. Many words that we use every day are borrowed from other languages.
18. American Indians who lived in the Northeast gave us the word *chipmunk.*
19. Although the French word *bureau* means "desk," we use it to mean "chest of drawers."
20. From Spanish comes the word *patio,* which means "an open courtyard."

Adjective and Adverb Clauses B

15d. An ***adjective clause*** is a subordinate clause that modifies a noun or a pronoun.

15e. An ***adverb clause*** is a subordinate clause that modifies a verb, an adjective, or an adverb.

ADJECTIVE CLAUSE Do you recognize the people **who are in that photograph**?

ADVERB CLAUSE **Before you answer,** study their faces for a few minutes.

EXERCISE For each of the following sentences, identify the underlined clause by writing above it *ADJ* for *adjective clause* or *ADV* for *adverb clause.* Circle the word or words that the underlined clause modifies.

Example 1. ADV Although I shut the door tightly, the wind (blew) it open again.

1. Are these the videotapes that you wanted to borrow?
2. Please give that coat, which is too small for you, to your cousin.
3. Whenever I hear that song, I remember my last birthday party.
4. If we knew the telephone number, we could call the store for directions.
5. Laura, whom we saw at the movies last night, lives next door to our teacher.
6. My little brother, who is only three years old, knows the words to a lot of songs.
7. Before we got out of bed, my father had already cleared the snow off the sidewalk.
8. When I am older, I would like to travel in South America.
9. Although she didn't mean to be unkind, her words hurt Camilla's feelings.
10. Those documents, which had been missing for more than twenty years, were discovered in a kitchen drawer.
11. Until we learned how to use the compass, we wandered around the woods for hours.
12. That story is about a giant whose favorite food is Limburger cheese.
13. My young cousins laugh whenever I read the story to them.
14. People who like to fish must have a lot of patience.
15. Please address the envelopes before you leave this afternoon.
16. We brought this puppy to you because we know how much you like animals.
17. The mail carrier who delivers the mail to our house is always in a good mood.
18. The boys crouched behind the fence until they heard the car drive away.
19. My garden includes some flowers that bloom all year long.
20. The rug, which was woven by hand, once belonged to my grandmother.

NAME ______ CLASS ______ DATE ______

Review A: **Clauses**

EXERCISE A For each of the following sentences, identify the underlined clause by writing above it *IND* for *independent clause* or *SUB* for *subordinate clause.*

Example 1. Although I don't like Brussels sprouts, I politely ate them. (IND)

1. The student who owns the wallet may claim it at the school office.
2. This weekend we will wash the car, which badly needs a good scrub.
3. The plant has small orange flowers that open every morning.
4. As soon as I finish my report, let's go to the movies.
5. Although she had never taken piano lessons, she could play very well.
6. Do you know the name of the boy whom we saw on the train?
7. We stopped for a picnic, which was very pleasant.
8. Please accept this gift that I made for you.
9. We practiced our roles in the play until we were sure of our lines.
10. I wonder where we should put the new plant we just bought.

EXERCISE B For each of the following sentences, underline the adjective clause and circle the relative pronoun. Then, draw an arrow from the clause to the noun or pronoun it modifies.

Example 1. Several friends who enjoy music are attending a concert with me.

11. The concert that we'll hear tonight includes music by George Gershwin.
12. George Gershwin, who was a great American composer, wrote *Porgy and Bess.*
13. This opera, which is set in South Carolina, features jazz rhythms.
14. "Summertime," which is a beautiful song, is a highlight of the show.
15. Gershwin did not write the lyrics that went with his songs.
16. The lyricist whom Gershwin most preferred was his brother, Ira.
17. George wrote the music, but it was Ira who wrote the words.
18. The Gershwin concert piece that I like the best is *An American in Paris.*
19. Gene Kelly stars in the movie that is based on this composition.
20. Kelly, who sings and dances to Gershwin's music in the film, is superb.

Review B: Clauses

EXERCISE A Underline the adverb clause and circle the subordinating conjunction in each of the following sentences. Above the clause, write whether the clause tells *how, when, where, why, how much, how long,* or *under what condition.*

Example 1. Before the parade, I polished my trumpet until it shone. *(how long)*

1. Because I am in the high school band, I will march in the parade.
2. The parade will begin after all the bands and floats are in position.
3. Our band is larger than the band from Zavala Junior High School is.
4. Since we are larger, we will play "The Star-Spangled Banner."
5. The parade will officially begin as soon as we finish the anthem.
6. After the parade, meet me where the band's buses are parked.
7. If it is raining, meet me in the lobby of city hall.
8. The sky filled up with storm clouds as if it might rain.
9. Wherever I go, the weather seems to work against me!
10. As soon as I start to play my horn, the weather becomes a music critic.

EXERCISE B Underline the subordinate clause in each sentence. Then, identify the clause by writing above it *ADJ* for *adjective clause* or *ADV* for *adverb clause.*

Example 1. The performer whom I researched is Will Smith. *(ADJ)*

11. Will Smith, who has acted in films and television, has also made musical albums.
12. One of Smith's songs, a rap solo performance that he made in 1998, won a Grammy.
13. Before he won this Grammy, he had costarred in a movie.
14. An actor with whom Smith has costarred is Tommy Lee Jones.
15. Before he started performing solo, Smith had been part of the duo called DJ Jazzy Jeff and the Fresh Prince.
16. After he and his partner won the first Grammy award for a rap performance, Smith starred in a popular television show.
17. If you have never seen a Will Smith performance, you have missed some fun.
18. Some of the movies that Smith has made are action-adventure films.
19. One film starring Smith was number one the year that it opened.
20. Smith's nickname was Prince Charming until he changed it to Fresh Prince.

Review C: Clauses

EXERCISE A For each of the following sentences, identify the underlined clause by writing above it *IND* for *independent clause* or *SUB* for *subordinate clause.*

Example 1. SUB After I found the lost dog, I put up posters to find her owner.

1. The research report that was assigned last month is due tomorrow.
2. Since the bicycle was on sale, I bought it.
3. I voted for the candidate who lost the election.
4. I'll let you know as soon as your package arrives.
5. Did you read the book before you saw the movie?
6. The flag should be brought indoors when the weather is bad.
7. After the final performance of the play, the cast had a party.
8. William Shakespeare is the best-known playwright in the world today.
9. You may borrow my book overnight if you'd like.
10. Please help me when it is time to decorate the gym for the dance.

EXERCISE B For each of the following sentences, underline the adjective clause or adverb clause. Then, circle the relative pronoun or subordinating conjunction.

Example 1. Juanita, (who) is my cousin, organized a fantastic party.

11. What costume did you wear to the party that Juanita had?
12. My costume, a chicken suit, won a prize because it was very well-made.
13. My cousin, whom I took to the party, went as a huge mosquito.
14. Since the guests were in costume, I couldn't recognize many of the people there.
15. Did you recognize Hilary when you saw her in the gorilla costume?
16. The person whom I didn't recognize was Mingan.
17. His costume, which was quite original, was a large cardboard box.
18. The box, which was painted white and covered with clear plastic, was very shiny.
19. Mingan, who was hidden inside the box, kept saying, "I'm melting!"
20. As soon as I saw him, I got it—he was supposed to be an ice cube!

Literary Model: Description

I can still remember the smell of the first girl I ever fell in love with when I was twelve. . . . Because I wanted to make a wondrous impression on this girl, grooming was suddenly important to me. Before puberty, happiness in appearance for me was pants that didn't fall down and a football that stayed pumped; but now I started taking three long baths a day and washing my own belt until it was white and shining my shoes until I could see in them a face that was ready for romance.

—from *"The Only Girl in the World for Me"* by Bill Cosby

EXERCISE A Underline the four adjective clauses and four adverb clauses that appear in this passage. [Hint: One of the adjective clauses is part of an adverb clause.]

EXERCISE B

1. Rewrite the passage so that it no longer includes any adjective or adverb clauses.

2. Without the subordinate clauses, does the paragraph sound different? How?

Literary Model (continued)

EXERCISE C Write a paragraph in which you describe an acquaintance. Use three adjective and three adverb clauses to help make your paragraph descriptive and to keep your style from being choppy. Underline each adverb clause once and each adjective clause twice.

EXERCISE D If you deleted all of the adjective clauses and adverb clauses in your paragraph, how would your paragraph be different?

Writing Application: Contract

Just as adjectives and adverbs can be used to make your writing more detailed and specific, adjective clauses and adverb clauses can, too. Your writing will be more interesting if you use subordinate clauses to vary your sentence patterns and to add descriptive details.

ADJECTIVE CLAUSE I bought the paint, **which was bright blue,** on sale.

ADVERB CLAUSE **When I dipped the brush into the paint,** several bristles fell out.

Writing Activity

Gone are the days when teddy bears, ducklings, or firetrucks decorated your room. Now it's even more *your* room, and you would like to personalize it. Your family, however, isn't sure about your plan to paint and decorate. To earn their support, draw up a contract in which you list what you would do to decorate and take care of your room. Use at least three adjective clauses and at least three adverb clauses as you detail your plans for your room.

PREWRITING First, imagine the perfect room—the room in which you'd like to study, sleep, and chat with friends. Describe it on paper; in fact, you could even draw it. List the changes you would need to make to bring your room closer to the ideal room you have imagined. Then, list the supplies that would be needed. You want to renovate as cheaply as possible!

WRITING A contract, even between family members, is a formal and serious document that clarifies expectations. Use formal language and a committed tone so that your family will sense your readiness to make your room your own distinct space. Like all writing, the contract requires organization. Write about what you will change in your room, then about what you will do to maintain your room. If you share your room with a sibling or two, work together on a plan that meets everyone's needs as fully as possible.

REVISING Sometimes writers are advised to avoid using first-person pronouns. In this case, however, first person is very appropriate. You are the one who will undertake the responsibilities listed in the contract, so make sure you have used *I, me, my, mine,* and *myself* where needed. Ask a friend or family member to read your draft and make suggestions to improve clarity or to make it more convincing.

PUBLISHING Check your contract for errors in grammar, usage, spelling, and punctuation. Mature, error-free writing is itself convincing! Give the final draft of the contract to your family, remaining open to suggestions they may make.

Extending Your Writing

This exercise could lead to a more developed writing project. For a class in art, you could check out research on rooms. What sorts of room shapes are comfortable? What effects do different paint colors have on a room's inhabitants? Investigate how interior environments influence our daily lives.

for **CHAPTER 16: KINDS OF SENTENCE STRUCTURE** pages 440–447

Choices: Investigating Sentence Structure

Here's your chance to step out of the grammar book and into the real world. You may not always notice sentence structures, but you and the people around you use them every day. The following activities challenge you to find a connection between kinds of sentences and the world around you. Do the activity below that suits your personality best, and then share your discoveries with your class. Have fun!

CONTEST

The Long and Short of It

A simple sentence can be longer than a compound-complex sentence. Prove the point. Hold a contest to see who can write the longest simple sentence. With your teacher's permission, post the best entries in the hall where everyone can see them.

VISUAL

Lay It Out

For many people, nothing beats a diagram for understanding sentences. Prepare four sentence diagrams—one for each type of sentence structure. You may want to print the subjects and verbs in contrasting colors so that they stand out.

LOGIC

Common Denominators

All of the different sentence structures have some things in common, but each of the structures has its own unique features. What are these similarities and differences? Draw a Venn diagram or some other type of chart, and present it to the class.

LITERATURE

First Things First

Have you ever read a book or article that grabbed you with its very first sentence? How did that sentence do it? Find out. Identify the sentence structure of twenty different introductory sentences. Choose sentences from works that are special to you, to your friends, or to literary history. When you do your analysis, also note the purpose of each introductory sentence—is it declarative, imperative, interrogative, or exclamatory? Gather your findings together in a chart to post in the classroom.

PERSUASIVE WRITING

Madison Avenue Ace

Are you the sort of person who thinks that people don't understand the complex issues of our times? Or are you the sort who thinks the world would be a lot better if everybody just kept things simple? Use advertising to get what you want! Create an ad campaign for the type of sentence structure that best suits our times. Check with your teacher, and then post your ads throughout the classroom.

COMPARISON

Like a Pro

How do real writers use sentence structure in different situations? Get together with a group. Brainstorm several common speaking or writing situations, such as newscasts, editorials, and advertisements. Assign one of these situations to each group member, and have each member select and write down five sentences from his or her situation. (Reading articles and watching recordings of television are great ways to find material.) As a group, identify each sentence as *simple, compound, complex,* or *compound-complex*. Make a bar chart of your results, and discuss with the class reasons why your chart turned out the way it did.

ANALYSIS

How About You?

You've studied some of the world's great writers, but how do *you* use sentence structure? Look through your portfolio or journal. Pick out a few pieces of writing that are at least four paragraphs long. Then, count the types of sentence structures that you find. When you're finished, ask yourself, "Do I need to change my ways?"

Simple Sentences

16a. A ***simple sentence*** contains one independent clause and no subordinate clauses.

A simple sentence may have a compound subject, a compound verb, or both.

EXAMPLES **Thelma sells** automobiles.

Thelma and **Leo buy** and **sell** automobiles.

EXERCISE Circle each subject and underline each verb in the following sentences.

Example 1. Claudia smiled sweetly and motioned the guests inside.

1. Carmen skated at the pond after school.
2. Iris and Phil took a train to Chicago.
3. The pattern of every snowflake is unique.
4. During the Renaissance, Italian women shaved the front part of their heads and kept the rest of their hair long.
5. Federico and Garth rowed over to the island last summer.
6. Emily Dickinson published very few poems in her lifetime.
7. After the harvest, the workers and their families have a dance and play music in the barn.
8. *Cats* takes place in a junkyard.
9. The well-known musical is based on T. S. Eliot's poems.
10. Jupiter, Saturn, Uranus, and Neptune have rings.
11. Christina played the guitar and sang songs from Chile.
12. Leaves and branches lay beneath the trees in our front yard and blocked the driveway.
13. Jill and Erica campaigned energetically and raised the needed funds.
14. My favorite snack is graham crackers and milk.
15. Jordan should wash the dishes and put them away.
16. Lupe raked the leaves in the backyard.
17. We congratulated Rosa on her achievement.
18. I read the draft of the paper and did a thorough revision.
19. This month's school newspaper includes a list of new books in the library.
20. Where will Tim and Eric ride their bicycles this weekend?

NAME ________________ CLASS ________________ DATE ________________

Compound Sentences

16b. A ***compound sentence*** contains two or more independent clauses and no subordinate clauses.

The independent clauses of a compound sentence are usually joined by a comma and a coordinating conjunction (*and, but, for, nor, or, so,* or *yet*). Independent clauses also may be joined by a semicolon.

EXAMPLES Mark Twain wrote fiction**, and** T. S. Eliot wrote poetry.

My brother does the dishes and takes out the trash**;** my chores include vacuuming and dusting.

EXERCISE A Each of the following compound sentences contains two independent clauses joined by a comma and a conjunction. Underline each subject once and each verb twice. Then, circle the conjunction.

Example 1. Kiyo likes the beach, and she often goes there with her brothers.

1. The ice-covered sidewalk was slippery, and several people fell down.
2. Some students ate in the cafeteria, but others went outside in the sunshine.
3. The talk show host was silly, but his show had a large audience.
4. The waves were enormous, yet the surfer rescued his new surfboard.
5. Mr. Kumamoto has uncovered some great fossils, for he is an experienced fossil hunter.

EXERCISE B Rewrite each of the following pairs of simple sentences as one compound sentence. Use the coordinating conjunction in parentheses, and write your sentences above the original sentences. Be sure to add the correct punctuation where necessary.

Ants are small, but they are powerful.
Example 1. Ants are small. They are powerful. *(but)*

6. We can go to a movie. We can watch a videotape at home. *(or)*
7. Angel wrote a poem about his girlfriend. He did not show it to her. *(but)*
8. Dark clouds gathered above the baseball field. Rain fell steadily. *(and)*
9. The bears stole all our food. We left the campground early. *(so)*
10. Outside, a storm howled. We were warm inside the igloo. *(yet)*
11. Aretha has never taken a drawing class. She can sketch almost anything. *(but)*
12. They wanted to surprise her. They gave her a gift the day before her birthday. *(so)*
13. Joe can wait for us at the entrance. He can go in and find us a seat. *(or)*
14. Suddenly, Sparky ran to the window. We wondered what he saw. *(and)*
15. Last night the house felt chilly. I drank hot tea and curled up with a book. *(so)*

GRAMMAR

Simple or Compound?

16a. A ***simple sentence*** contains one independent clause and no subordinate clauses.

16b. A ***compound sentence*** contains two or more independent clauses and no subordinate clauses.

The independent clauses of a compound sentence are often joined by a comma and a coordinating conjunction, but they also may be joined by a semicolon.

SIMPLE SENTENCE I went outside and looked at the sky.

COMPOUND SENTENCES The sky looked threatening**,** **so** I expected a storm.

The sky looked threatening**;** I expected a storm.

EXERCISE A For each of the following sentences, underline each subject once and each verb twice. Then, identify the sentence by writing *S* for *simple sentence* or *CD* for *compound sentence* on the line provided.

Example CD **1.** Geronimo was an Apache; he struggled to preserve the Apache way of life.

______ **1.** Geronimo was born in No-doyohn Canyon, Mexico.

______ **2.** Geronimo defended his homeland against colonization by Mexicans and North Americans.

______ **3.** Mexican bounty hunters killed his mother, his wife, and his children in 1858.

______ **4.** Geronimo wanted revenge, so he gathered a band of men.

______ **5.** He led the band of Apaches in raids against Mexican settlements.

______ **6.** The Mexicans called him Geronimo; that name in English is Jerome.

______ **7.** The Apaches used his name as their battle cry.

______ **8.** In 1874, U.S. authorities forcibly moved about four thousand Apaches to a reservation.

______ **9.** Geronimo led these Apaches in attacks on U.S. settlements and soldiers.

______ **10.** The United States sent five thousand soldiers after Geronimo, but the small group of Apaches did not surrender for more than four months.

EXERCISE B For each of the following sentences, underline each subject once and each verb twice. Then, identify the sentence by writing *S* for *simple sentence* or *CD* for *compound sentence* above the item number.

Example S **[1]** The army finally tracked Geronimo to his camp in the mountains.

[11] He was imprisoned in Florida and later in Oklahoma; he never returned to Arizona and to his Apache life. **[12]** He told his story to S. M. Barrett in 1905–1906, and Barrett wrote a book about it. **[13]** Geronimo would not permit a stenographer at the interviews, so Barrett took notes. **[14]** The name of this book is *Geronimo: His Own Story*. **[15]** Geronimo died in 1909; he was a courageous man to the end.

Complex Sentences

16c. A ***complex sentence*** contains one independent clause and at least one subordinate clause.

A subordinate clause cannot stand alone as a sentence. The following words are often used to introduce subordinate clauses: *who, whose, whom, which, that, after, as, because, if, since, before, when.*

INDEPENDENT CLAUSE I often go to the library
SUBORDINATE CLAUSE because I like to read
COMPLEX SENTENCE **Because I like to read,** I often go to the library.

EXERCISE A The sentences in the following paragraph are complex sentences. For each sentence, underline the independent clause once and the subordinate clause twice.

Example **[1]** Mr. Morales, who is my English teacher, encouraged me to be a writer.

[1] Since I was five years old, I have read in bed at night. **[2]** For my twelfth birthday I received *A Light in the Attic*, which is a book of poems. **[3]** Before I go to sleep, I sometimes read my favorite poems to my little brother. **[4]** As he listens to me, he closes his eyes and falls asleep. **[5]** When he wakes up in the morning, he usually asks about the ending of a poem. **[6]** I may be a writer or an editor when I grow up. **[7]** My Aunt Sabrina, who lives in Dallas, is a copyeditor for a newspaper. **[8]** If I study hard, I can become an editor, too. **[9]** A job as an editor makes sense for me because I love words. **[10]** The books that I love most sit on a special shelf in my room.

EXERCISE B The sentences in the following paragraph are complex sentences. For each sentence, underline the independent clause once and the subordinate clause twice.

Example **[1]** When I read some Greek myths last summer, I learned a lot of interesting things.

[11] As I read, I learned about Arachne, a character in a famous Greek myth. **[12]** In the stories, she weaves tapestries that are very beautiful. **[13]** When people see her work, they are really impressed. **[14]** Because Arachne is such a good weaver, she begins to boast about her skill. **[15]** Athena, who is the goddess of arts and crafts, hears about Arachne's boastfulness and decides to pay Arachne a visit. **[16]** After Athena arrives, she warns Arachne not to be so boastful. **[17]** Because Arachne refuses to listen, the goddess Athena challenges her to a weaving contest. **[18]** The contest that Athena proposes ends in a draw. **[19]** Because Athena feels sorry for Arachne, she turns Arachne into a spider. **[20]** According to the myth, spiders, who are also excellent weavers, are descended from Arachne.

Compound or Complex?

16b. A ***compound sentence*** contains two or more independent clauses and no subordinate clauses.

16c. A ***complex sentence*** contains one independent clause and at least one subordinate clause.

INDEPENDENT CLAUSE My mom drinks coffee
SUBORDINATE CLAUSE because she likes hot beverages
COMPOUND SENTENCE My mom will drink tea, but she prefers coffee.
COMPLEX SENTENCE Because she likes hot beverages, my mom drinks coffee.

EXERCISE For each of the following sentences, underline each independent clause once and each subordinate clause twice. Then, identify the sentence by writing *CD* for *compound* or *CX* for *complex* on the line provided.

Example CX **1.** Because the cardinal was bright red, I could see it clearly.

______ **1.** When Abe Lincoln gave a stump speech, he stood on a real stump.

______ **2.** Many trees lose their leaves in the fall, and they look cold and forlorn.

______ **3.** When we lived in southern Maryland, we visited Annapolis often.

______ **4.** Brian is mild tempered, and he makes friends easily.

______ **5.** If you move your knight to that square, I will capture him.

______ **6.** My new wool sweater shrank when I washed it in hot water.

______ **7.** Don't give me any excuses; I don't want to hear them!

______ **8.** If I wash the dishes, will you cook the meal?

______ **9.** Cameron, who is my cousin, is the new captain of the soccer team.

______ **10.** I dropped my sandwich on the floor, so I threw it in the garbage.

______ **11.** The movie was really scary, yet I could not stop watching.

______ **12.** Janet Jackson, whose music I enjoy, will be in town next week.

______ **13.** I washed the rug with detergent, but the red stain would not come out.

______ **14.** Since you asked me nicely, I will lend you some paper for the test.

______ **15.** Give your dog a bath, or do not let him inside the house.

______ **16.** Call me tonight, and we'll make plans for the weekend.

______ **17.** I'll ask my mother after she gets home from work.

______ **18.** The book that he is reading is about ancient Egypt.

______ **19.** My grandfather, whom I respect very much, will be ninety this summer.

______ **20.** Jane is eager to begin her new music class, but she'll have to wait another week.

Compound-Complex Sentences

16d. A ***compound-complex sentence*** contains two or more independent clauses and at least one subordinate clause.

INDEPENDENT CLAUSES	I will decorate for the party you can prepare the food
SUBORDINATE CLAUSE	when we get to my house
COMPOUND-COMPLEX SENTENCE	When we get to my house, I will decorate for the party, and you can prepare the food.

EXERCISE In each of the following compound-complex sentences, underline the independent clauses once and the subordinate clause or clauses twice.

Example 1. Jane was late to the party, as I predicted, and Ron came too early.

1. When we planned our holiday party, we planned a small one, and we invited only a few friends.
2. We were expecting about eight people, but we were very surprised when ten extra guests showed up.
3. Luckily, we found out about the extra people in time; we raced to the grocery store just before it closed.
4. We got carried away and bought plenty of extra food; we were certain that most of our guests would be hungry.
5. Although I don't like raw vegetables, we included them in the menu; healthy snacks please some people.
6. My friend Dennis is outgoing and creative, so I asked him to plan some group games that we would all enjoy.
7. The Wilson twins, who are not identical, arrived together, but they left with different friends after the party.
8. Before the party began, I borrowed a collection of CDs from friends, and I set up a CD player.
9. The music that I chose was a hit, and everyone enjoyed dancing to it.
10. Since they enjoyed the evening so much, Wayan and J.C. stayed afterward; they stacked dishes and bagged trash with me.

for **CHAPTER 16: KINDS OF SENTENCE STRUCTURE** *pages 445–47*

Complex or Compound-Complex?

16c. A ***complex sentence*** contains one independent clause and at least one subordinate clause.

16d. A ***compound-complex sentence*** contains two or more independent clauses and at least one subordinate clause.

COMPLEX After she leaves school, Kiesha takes ice-skating lessons.

COMPOUND-COMPLEX After she leaves school, Kiesha takes ice-skating lessons, and she stays at the rink for two hours.

EXERCISE Identify each sentence by writing *CX* for *complex* or *CD-CX* for *compound-complex* on the line provided.

Example CD-CX **1.** Kiesha never misses a practice, but she is occasionally late because the rink is so far from her home.

______ **1.** When she was young, Kiesha roller-skated on sidewalks, and she begged for ice skates.

______ **2.** Although she had never skated on ice before, she had watched ice-skating competitions on television.

______ **3.** She dreamed about skating in competitions, yet she still needed ice skates before she could start lessons.

______ **4.** Her parents could not afford skates, which were very expensive, but they encouraged her to earn money herself.

______ **5.** Before the week was out, Kiesha had begun finding odd jobs that would pay a few dollars each.

______ **6.** She saved almost every dollar, although it required perseverance.

______ **7.** When she entered junior high school, Kiesha was skating in competitions, for she had bought her own skates.

______ **8.** The skates were paid for, yet she continued working odd jobs because she now paid for her own lessons.

______ **9.** After I heard Kiesha's story, I admired her.

______ **10.** Although I can't and don't want to skate, I have learned a lot from Kiesha's story, and I will pursue my own dream.

Review A: **Kinds of Sentence Structure**

EXERCISE A Identify each sentence by writing *S* for *simple* or *CD* for *compound* on the line provided.

Example __CD__ **1.** Beavers and squirrels are rodents, yet many people don't know this fact.

______ **1.** A rodent's teeth never stop growing.

______ **2.** Rodents gnaw hard things, so their teeth don't get very long.

______ **3.** The capybara is the largest rodent of all.

______ **4.** Capybaras can grow to four feet and weigh one hundred pounds.

______ **5.** In prehistoric times, capybaras lived in North America, but now they are found only in Panama and South America.

EXERCISE B Underline each independent clause once and each subordinate clause twice. Then, identify each sentence by writing *S* for *simple*, *CD* for *compound*, *CX* for *complex*, or *CD-CX* for *compound-complex* on the line provided.

Example __CX__ **1.** After I studied past presidents, history became my favorite subject.

______ **6.** David Atchison may have been the president of the United States for one day.

______ **7.** President Polk's term had ended on March 4, 1849, which was a Sunday.

______ **8.** Because it was a Sunday, the new president, Zachary Taylor, did not take the oath of office until March 5.

______ **9.** Under an old law, the president pro tempore of the Senate became the president of the United States if no one else held the office.

______ **10.** Today if the president and vice-president cannot do their jobs, the Speaker of the House takes over.

______ **11.** Here's another interesting fact.

______ **12.** Technically, George Washington was not the first president of the U.S. government.

______ **13.** That honor belonged to a man who had been Maryland's representative to the Continental Congress.

______ **14.** The first and only president of the Congress of the Confederation, which managed the first U.S. government, was John Hanson, and he was elected by the Congress in 1781.

______ **15.** Hanson's title was "President of the United States in Congress Assembled," and he served for one year.

Review B: Kinds of Sentence Structure

EXERCISE A Identify each sentence by writing *CD* for *compound* or *CX* for *complex* on the line provided.

Example __CD__ **1.** I can't fix a leaky faucet, nor can I fix a faulty electrical outlet.

______ **1.** When we have plumbing problems, we call Señor Rodriguez.

______ **2.** Sometimes Señor Rodriguez comes himself, and sometimes he sends one of his employees.

______ **3.** Elaine Blum, who lives across the street, is an electrician.

______ **4.** She has a pickup truck, which she uses to carry her tools and supplies.

______ **5.** We enjoy Elaine's company, and she is a helpful neighbor, too.

EXERCISE B In the following sentences, underline each independent clause once and each subordinate clause twice. Then, identify each sentence by writing *S* for *simple, CD* for *compound, CX* for *complex,* or *CD-CX* for *compound-complex* on the line provided.

Example __CX__ **1.** When I studied the globe, I located Peru in South America.

______ **6.** During the summer I will visit Australia, which people call the Land Down Under.

______ **7.** While I am there, I'll also visit New Zealand.

______ **8.** New Zealand is a small country that lies southeast of Australia.

______ **9.** I am not afraid of flying, and I am not afraid of long ocean voyages.

______ **10.** In fact, I may become a flight attendant.

______ **11.** Flight attendants get discounts on airfare; their families are also eligible for lower fares.

______ **12.** Have you ever been to England?

______ **13.** Since globes make me wonder about life in different countries, I like to study them; I enjoy maps as well.

______ **14.** Ireland is located off the western coast of England, but Scotland is north of England on the same landmass.

______ **15.** If you see the waters of the Caribbean Sea, you will fall in love with their gemlike color and clarity.

NAME ____________ CLASS ____________ DATE ____________

Review C: **Kinds of Sentence Structure**

EXERCISE Rewrite each of the following sentences on the lines provided. Follow the directions in parentheses.

Example **1.** Television news is fascinating. Newspapers often provide more in-depth coverage. (Rewrite as a compound sentence. Use the conjunction *but.*) *Television news is fascinating, but newspapers often provide more in-depth coverage.*

1. We found out about the shelter. Mona and I began helping the people there. (Rewrite as a complex sentence. Begin the first clause with *After.*) ____________

2. We gathered our outgrown clothes and toys. We put them neatly in boxes. (Rewrite as a compound sentence. Use the conjunction *and.*) ____________

3. My mother drove us to the shelter. She helped us carry the boxes inside. (Rewrite as a simple sentence.) ____________

4. The shelter director saw our gifts. She seemed very happy. She thanked us. (Rewrite as a compound-complex sentence. Use the conjunction *and.* Begin the first clause with *When.*) ____________

5. In the evenings we usually watch the news. We are interested in world events. (Rewrite as a complex sentence. Begin the second clause with *because.*) ____________

Literary Model: Narration

The tall man stood at the edge of the porch. The roof sagged from the two rough posts which held it, almost closing the gap between his head and the rafters. The dim light from the cabin window cast long equal shadows from man and posts. A boy stood nearby shivering in the cold October wind. He ran his fingers back and forth over the broad crown of the head of a coon dog named Sounder.

—from *Sounder* by William H. Armstrong

The night passed, and the next day, after dinner, Redruth and I were afoot again and on the road. I said good-bye to Mother and the cove where I had lived since I was born, and the dear old "Admiral Benbow"—since he was repainted, no longer quite so dear. One of my last thoughts was of the captain, who had so often strode along the beach with his cocked hat, his sabre-cut cheek, and his old brass telescope. Next moment we had turned the corner and my home was out of sight.

—from *Treasure Island* by Robert Louis Stevenson

EXERCISE A In these two passages, underline each simple sentence once, underline each compound sentence twice, and circle each complex sentence. Then, complete the chart below by writing the number of times each kind of sentence appears in each passage.

	Simple	Compound	Complex
Sounder			
Treasure Island			

EXERCISE B Compare the styles of the two passages. What is the effect of including many compound and complex sentences? of including many simple sentences?

NAME ____________ CLASS ____________ DATE ____________

Literary Model (continued)

EXERCISE C

1. Write a brief paragraph that might be the beginning of a short story about an event that took place at your house or apartment. Include both description and action. Try to use mostly simple sentences.

____

____

____

____

____

____

2. Rewrite your paragraph so that you use only compound and complex sentences.

____

____

____

____

____

____

____

EXERCISE D Which version of your paragraph do you think would appeal more to readers? Explain your answer.

____

____

____

____

____

____

____

Writing Application: Children's Story

Many fairy tales and stories written for children use choppy, short sentences—all in similar structures. Such writing may be appropriate for children, but it is not interesting enough for more mature readers. Avoid choppy writing by using the techniques you have learned to combine and vary sentence length and pattern.

CHOPPY The fiddler played his fiddle. His tabby cat suddenly began to dance. It danced on its front paws. The people shouted and clapped in astonishment.

REVISED When the fiddler played, his tabby cat suddenly began to dance. As it danced on its front paws, the people shouted and clapped in astonishment.

Writing Activity

Retell your favorite fairy tale or childhood story—first in short, simple sentences for an audience of little children and then in more varied, complex sentences for your own peers. Keep the events of the story the same; the only change should be in sentence variety and complexity.

PREWRITING Of all the stories you heard when you were a young child, which is your favorite? Outline the story—what are the events of the plot? Who are the characters? What is the conflict, and how is it resolved? If your memory lacks detail, head to the library to rediscover the story. Organize the events of the story chronologically, making sure to include the important particulars.

WRITING Retell the story you have chosen, first for an audience of young children. You may discover that it's harder to keep the story's energy going when you write in short, simple sentences! Using energetic verbs will help. When you finish the children's version of your story, use it as the basis for the more advanced version you will write next. Keeping your audience in mind, rewrite your story using sentence structure that appeals to students your own age. Write several versions of the sentences, trying out different sentence-combining techniques.

REVISING Read your two narratives aloud to a willing audience, making note of their responses and comments. Consider these comments for a day or two, and then prepare your final draft. When revising the children's draft, watch out for fragments. When revising the advanced version, make certain that you have not written any run-on sentences.

PUBLISHING Check both stories for errors in punctuation and spelling. Prepare both neatly, in handwriting or on a computer printout, and turn them in to your teacher. Then, work with a partner to create a children's book. Choose the story that you would most like to illustrate, and work together to design a book that combines words and pictures in an appealing, easy-to-read way.

Extending Your Writing

This exercise could lead to a more developed writing project. In a group of three or fewer, choose a fairy tale and find a creative new way to tell it. Perform the story as a modern-day drama, turn the tale into a comic book, describe the events in a news broadcast, illustrate the plot on a storyboard, or come up with your own format. Share your new fairy tale with the class.

NAME CLASS DATE

for CHAPTER 17: AGREEMENT pages 457–78

Choices: Investigating Agreement

The following activities challenge you to find a connection between agreement and the world around you. Do the activity below that suits your personality best, and then share your discoveries with your class.

DISCUSSION

What If . . . ?

What happens when a pronoun-antecedent error slips by a writer or speaker? What if you were reading a cookbook that said, "Take one egg and beat them for one minute"? What would you do? Would you beat one egg or two? Prepare at least ten examples such as this. Then, discuss with your classmates the confusion (and ruined recipes) agreement errors can cause.

VISUAL

Peace and Harmony

What does the word *agreement* mean? What are its roots? What are synonyms for *agreement*? Make a list of these synonyms. Look them up in a dictionary. Think about the ways they differ. Then, design a chart like a wheel, with the word *agreement* at the hub. At the end of each spoke, place a synonym and its definition. Pass out copies to the class.

CONTEST

STOP!

Prepare a dialogue or monologue on audiotape or videotape. Sprinkle subject-verb agreement errors and pronoun-antecedent agreement errors throughout the script. Then, divide the class into two teams. Play your tape. When someone hears an error, he or she yells "STOP!" Stop the tape, and ask the person to correct the error. Proper corrections earn a point. Incorrect "stops" lose a point. The team with the most points wins, of course.

BUILDING BACKGROUND KNOWLEDGE

Rock-and-Roll

There are quite a number of pairs of nouns that go together, but actually name only one thing. These pairs even have a name—*binomial nouns.* Get together with a friend, and brainstorm a list of at least ten of these pairs. You could start with *macaroni and cheese* or *horse and carriage.* When you're done, pass out copies of your list for the class to insert in their English notebooks.

MATHEMATICS

Vital Statistics

Using measurements as subjects of sentences takes some getting used to. Give your classmates a chance to hear how measurements used as subjects sound with verbs. Choose a topic—the space shuttle, the *Enterprise,* or some other vehicle or structure. Write ten sentences that use measurements as subjects or antecedents. Remember to spell out numbers that begin sentences.

MUSIC

In Tune

Give a short oral explanation comparing the agreement of subjects and verbs to the tuning of a stringed instrument such as a guitar, violin, cello, or harp. If possible, bring your instrument to class and demonstrate how strings sound when they are in tune and agree. Then, demonstrate how they sound when they don't agree and are not in tune.

SURVEY

Guilty Parties

Polish your listening skills. Listen for subject-verb agreement errors around school, at home, with friends, and out shopping. Which subjects seem to cause the most problems? Let your classmates in on your findings, and give everybody a list of the guilty parties. No, not the people—pass out a list of the subjects!

USAGE

Number

Number is the form a word takes to indicate whether the word is singular or plural.

17a. When a word refers to one person, place, thing, or idea, it is ***singular*** in number. When a word refers to more than one, it is ***plural*** in number.

SINGULAR	circle	he	one	woman	loss
PLURAL	circles	they	some	women	losses

EXERCISE A Above each of the following words, write *S* for *singular* or *P* for *plural.*

Examples **1.** oxen (P) **2.** fox (S)

1. she	**11.** shelves
2. beach	**12.** people
3. we	**13.** many
4. men	**14.** guesses
5. mouse	**15.** geese
6. cities	**16.** chickens
7. I	**17.** loaf
8. mouth	**18.** us
9. plateau	**19.** prophecies
10. parentheses	**20.** citizen

EXERCISE B Change each singular word to the plural form, and change each plural word to the singular form. Write the new word on the line provided.

Examples ___leaves___ **1.** leaf ___virus___ **2.** viruses

____________ **21.** roof	____________ **26.** him
____________ **22.** box	____________ **27.** man
____________ **23.** e-mails	____________ **28.** sheep
____________ **24.** French fry	____________ **29.** puppies
____________ **25.** calves	____________ **30.** stereo

USAGE

Subject-Verb Agreement A

17b. A verb should agree in number with its subject.

(1) Singular subjects take singular verbs.
(2) Plural subjects take plural verbs.

EXAMPLES Mexican **art is** interesting. [The singular verb *is* agrees with the singular subject *art*.]

Mexican **holidays are celebrated** in the Southwest. [The plural helping verb *are* agrees with the plural subject *holidays*.]

EXERCISE In each of the following sentences, underline the verb or helping verb in parentheses that agrees with its subject.

Example 1. Mr. Frank *(has, have)* been studying Mexican culture.

1. Cinco de Mayo *(is, are)* an important Mexican holiday.

2. We *(celebrates, celebrate)* the Mexican victory at the Battle of Puebla on May 5, 1862.

3. Some people *(watches, watch)* these celebrations in Los Angeles, California.

4. Others *(sees, see)* them in San Antonio, Texas.

5. The celebrations *(includes, include)* parades and dancing.

6. The women dancers *(wears, wear)* swirling skirts or brilliant colors.

7. Strolling bands *(plays, play)* traditional mariachi music.

8. Spectators *(lines, line)* the streets of the parade route.

9. The floats *(seems, seem)* lively and colorful.

10. Mexican Americans *(views, view)* the festivities with pride.

11. We *(has, have)* learned about Mexican traditions.

12. Many immigrants *(has, have)* brought new traditions from their homelands.

13. Mexican ballads *(is, are)* heard in the Southwest.

14. In Spanish, ballads *(is, are)* called *corridos*.

15. What subjects *(does, do)* these ballads describe?

16. In them, heroes' lives *(has, have)* been recorded.

17. Everyday people *(does, do)* appear in ballads, too.

18. Historians *(has, have)* begun to record these ballads.

19. They *(is, are)* trying to save these ballads.

20. *(Does, Do)* Horacio know any *corridos*?

Subject-Verb Agreement B

17b. A verb should agree in number with its subject.

(1) Singular subjects take singular verbs.
(2) Plural subjects take plural verbs.

EXAMPLE **Is she taking** biology class this year? [The singular helping verb *Is* agrees with the singular subject *she*.]

USAGE

EXERCISE Underline the verb in each of the following sentences. If the subject and verb do not agree, write the correct verb form above the error. If the sentence is already correct, write *C*.

Example 1. My cousins *are* is bringing that delicious cinnamon bread.

1. Two of the sparrows is eating at the bird feeder.
2. Each morning I look out my window at the sunrise.
3. No, he do not sing and dance.
4. After three months, the experiment have been judged a success.
5. The children smile for the camera.
6. The singers is applauding for the winners.
7. They wave to the audience.
8. That tree have still not lost all its leaves.
9. After every performance, she bow.
10. Outside on the playground, children laugh.
11. This evening, Frank are not needed at rehearsal.
12. The geese leaves our town during the winter.
13. Mario wants the last orange.
14. We has been waiting for more than two hours.
15. Her sister have that CD.
16. They run together every morning.
17. Sophia need a new winter coat.
18. He always eat breakfast.
19. Jeremy does not expect any problems with the new equipment.
20. That bread smell delicious.

USAGE

Subject-Verb Agreement C

17c. The number of a subject is not changed by a phrase following the subject.

EXAMPLE The phases **of the moon** are caused by changes in the amount of sunlight reflected by the moon. [The plural helping verb *are* agrees with the plural subject *phases.*]

EXERCISE A In each of the following sentences, circle the phrase following the subject. Then, underline the verb in parentheses that agrees with the subject.

Example 1. The moon (in the night sky) (*are, is*) a beautiful sight.

1. People throughout history (*has, have*) been fascinated by the moon.

2. The distance to the moon (*is, are*) 384,403 kilometers (238,857 miles).

3. The features of the moon (*is, are*) seen through powerful telescopes.

4. The sun, like the earth, (*influences, influence*) the moon's motion.

5. The moon's orbit around the earth (*takes, take*) about 27 days, 8 hours.

6. The earth, at the same time, (*moves, move*) around the sun.

7. A full moon, on the average, (*occurs, occur*) every 29 1/2 days.

8. Tides on the earth (*rises, rise*) according to the moon's gravitational pull.

9. Photography from lunar-orbiting vehicles (*shows, show*) features on the moon's surface.

10. Exploration of the moon (*continues, continue*).

EXERCISE B In each of the following sentences, circle the prepositional phrase following the subject. Then, underline the verb in parentheses that agrees with the subject.

Example 1. The contributions (of immigrants) (*has, have*) enriched many countries.

11. The names of some American Jewish authors (*is, are*) well known.

12. A famous author of short stories and novels (*is, are*) Bernard Malamud.

13. Jewish writers of fiction (*includes, include*) Saul Bellow.

14. A Nobel Prize in literature (*was, were*) awarded to Saul Bellow.

15. Another writer of Jewish descent (*is, are*) Philip Roth.

Subject-Verb Agreement D

17d. The following indefinite pronouns are singular: *anybody, anyone, anything, each, either, everybody, everyone, everything, neither, nobody, no one, nothing, one, somebody, someone,* and *something.*

17e. The following indefinite pronouns are plural: *both, few, many, several.*

17f. The indefinite pronouns *all, any, more, most, none,* and *some* may be either singular or plural, depending on their meaning in a sentence.

EXAMPLES **Nobody** on our street **throws** a better fastball than Otis.
Many of his pitches **blaze** past the batter.
None of Jana's effort **is** wasted.
Some of Mr. Green's tomatoes **are** prize winners!

EXERCISE A Circle the indefinite pronoun in each of the following sentences. Then, underline the correct form of the verb in parentheses.

Example 1. Either of the vegetables *(are, is)* a good choice for the salad.

1. One of my brothers *(plants, plant)* tomatoes every year.
2. No one on my block *(believes, believe)* his plants will grow.
3. Everyone in the neighborhood *(says, say)* the soil is not good enough.
4. Most of the plants *(does, do)* not do very well.
5. A few of them *(reaches, reach)* full size.
6. Usually everyone in the family *(eats, eat)* these tomatoes in a salad.
7. Most of the salad *(is, are)* greens.
8. Several of us *(prefers, prefer)* blue cheese dressing on the salad.
9. None of us *(likes, like)* that kind of salad dressing.
10. All of the tomatoes *(is, are)* eaten before they spoil.

EXERCISE B Circle the indefinite pronoun in each of the following sentences. Above the pronoun write *S* if it is singular or *P* if it is plural. Then, underline the correct form of the verb in parentheses.

Example 1. Everyone in a successful band *(practices, practice)* frequently.

11. Some of my cousins *(is, are)* in musical bands.
12. All of my classmates *(listens, listen)* to them.
13. Any of the bands *(plays, play)* for private parties.
14. None of our neighbors ever *(complains, complain)* when they practice.
15. Most of their music *(is, are)* enjoyable.

Subject-Verb Agreement E

A pronoun that does not refer to a definite person, place, thing, or idea is called an ***indefinite pronoun***.

USAGE

17d. The following indefinite pronouns are singular: *anybody, anyone, anything, each, either, everybody, everyone, everything, neither, nobody, no one, nothing, one, somebody, someone,* and *something.*

17e. The following indefinite pronouns are plural: *both, few, many, several.*

17f. The indefinite pronouns *all, any, more, most, none,* and *some* may be either singular or plural, depending on their meaning in a sentence.

EXERCISE A In each of the following sentences, underline the correct indefinite pronoun in parentheses.

Example 1. *(All, Many)* of the fruit has been put in the refrigerator.

1. *(One, Several)* of my sisters runs in the marathon every year.
2. *(Many, Nobody)* is predicting rain for tomorrow.
3. *(Everyone, Several)* wears a coat in this weather.
4. *(One, Many)* of us sometimes forget to bring lunch.
5. *(Both, Each)* of my brothers like algebra.
6. *(None, No one)* of the performances take place outside.
7. *(Someone, Few)* are strong enough to swim across the English Channel.
8. *(All, Neither)* have seen that movie.
9. *(Each, Most)* has an opinion about the review in the newspaper.
10. *(Somebody, Both)* have been given that responsibility.

EXERCISE B Circle the indefinite pronoun in each of the following sentences. Then, underline the correct form of the verb in parentheses.

Example 1. Most of the potatoes *(has, have)* been harvested.

11. Everybody *(is, are)* welcome at the skating party.
12. I hope nobody *(forgets, forget)* to bring skates.
13. Many of my friends *(is, are)* good skaters.
14. All of us *(enjoys, enjoy)* the music at the skating rink.
15. Most of the music *(is, are)* popular dance music.

Subject-Verb Agreement F

17g. Subjects joined by *and* usually take a plural verb.

A compound subject that names only one person or thing takes a singular verb.

17h. Singular subjects joined by *or* or *nor* take a singular verb.

Plural subjects joined by *or* or *nor* take a plural verb.

17i. When a singular subject and a plural subject are joined by *or* or *nor*, the verb agrees with the subject nearer the verb.

EXERCISE A Above the compound subject, write *S* if it is singular or *P* if it is plural. Then, underline the correct form of the verb in parentheses.

Example 1. Acids and bases *(is, are)* interesting. [P above "and"; "are" underlined]

1. Acids and bases *(is, are)* one of our topics in science class.
2. Red litmus paper and blue litmus paper *(is, are)* used to show the presence of acids or bases.
3. Some food and common household items *(contains, contain)* acids.
4. *(Does, Do)* macaroni and cheese contain acids?
5. Citrus fruit and vinegar *(make, makes)* good test items.
6. Either a lemon or a lime *(is, are)* easy to test.
7. Lemon juice and other acids *(turns, turn)* blue litmus paper red.
8. Vinegar and lemon juice *(contains, contain)* acids.
9. Neither lemons nor limes *(is, are)* bases.
10. Acids and bases *(combines, combine)* to make salts.

EXERCISE B If the underlined verb in each of the following sentences does not agree with the subject, write the correct form of the verb above it. If the verb form is already correct, write *C* above it.

Example 1. Experiments and observations <u>plays</u> an important role in science. [play written above]

11. Either baking soda or soap <u>are</u> a salt.
12. Fats or oils <u>is</u> added to bases to make soap.
13. <u>Are</u> plaster and cement made with bases?
14. The acidity or alkalinity of a solution <u>are</u> expressed as a pH value.
15. A pH value as low as 0 or one as high as 7 <u>indicates</u> acidity.

Subject-Verb Agreement G

17j. A collective noun may be either singular or plural, depending on its meaning in a sentence.

A *collective noun* is singular in form but names a group of persons, animals, or things. It takes a singular verb when it refers to the group as a unit. It takes a plural verb when it refers to the individual parts or members of the group.

EXAMPLES The **family is** closely knit. [The family as a unit is closely knit.]

The **family are** meeting in Rochester. [The individual members are meeting.]

USAGE

EXERCISE A Above each noun, write *Coll* if it is collective or *Not* if it is not collective.

Examples 1. jury (*Coll*) **2.** leaves (*Not*)

1. flock

2. team

3. boards

4. faculty

5. book

6. group

7. house

8. batch

9. squadron

10. clothes

EXERCISE B Identify the collective noun in each of the following sentences, and write above it *S* for *singular* (if it refers to the group as a unit) or *P* for *plural* (if it refers to the parts of the group). Then, underline the correct form of the verb in parentheses.

Example 1. The crew (*P*) (*arrive, arrives*) at work at different times.

11. The pack of wild dogs (*has, have*) scattered in all directions upon hearing the noise.

12. Each morning the herd (*go, goes*) all together to the watering hole.

13. The audience (*was, were*) taking notes, sitting quietly, or sleeping.

14. The fleet (*sail, sails*) home tomorrow.

15. The group of students (*sit, sits*) one by one on the bench outside the school.

16. (*Are, Is*) the visiting chorus staying at several guest houses?

17. During the semester the faculty (*is, are*) helping the students with fund-raisers.

18. The faculty (*is, are*) meeting with their team captains in their classrooms.

19. The flock (*fly, flies*) over this area each autumn.

20. The set (*is, are*) all in perfect condition except for the one you cracked.

Subject-Verb Agreement H

17k. When the subject follows the verb, find the subject and make sure that the verb agrees with it.

The subject usually follows the verb in questions and in sentences beginning with *here* or *there*.

EXAMPLES When **are Oscar** and **Ana** leaving for the party?
There **are** the **gifts.**
Here**'s** the **invitation** to the party.

USAGE

EXERCISE A Underline the subject and the correct word or word group in parentheses in each of the following sentences.

Example 1. Where *(is, are)* the substitute teacher?

1. Here *(is, are)* the worksheets for today's class.

2. *(There's, There are)* an answer key in the locked desk drawer.

3. On the chalkboard *(is, are)* written the instructions.

4. Where *(is, are)* the other assignments for the class?

5. Oh, there *(is, are)* the dictionary.

6. *(Who's, Who are)* the student assistant today?

7. *(Is, Are)* both of you assistants?

8. Over here *(is, are)* the papers for the students.

9. *(Was, Were)* there enough copies for everyone?

10. *(Here's, Here are)* one more copy.

EXERCISE B In each of the following sentences, underline the subject once and the verb twice. Above the verb, write *C* for *correct* if the subject and verb agree. If they do not agree, write the correct form of the verb.

Example 1. Here's the donations for the relief fund. (*are*)

11. There are several places in need of volunteers in our community.

12. What is the types of volunteer activities available?

13. Here's a list of community centers and hospitals.

14. On one of these pages are a parental consent form.

15. There's several locations in immediate need of your help.

NAME ______________________ CLASS ______________ DATE ______________

for **CHAPTER 17: AGREEMENT** page 471

USAGE

Subject-Verb Agreement I

17l. Some nouns that are plural in form take singular verbs.

EXAMPLE **Physics is** my sister's major in college.

17m. An expression of an amount (a measurement, a percentage, or a fraction, for example) may be singular or plural, depending on how it is used.

EXAMPLES **Five dollars is** a good price for that football.

Two of these dollars **are** torn at the edges.

EXERCISE Underline the correct form of the verb in parentheses in each sentence.

Example 1. Chickenpox *(is, are)* common among young children.

1. *(Is, Are)* eighteen weeks the length of the typical semester?
2. Seven dollars *(is, are)* the price of a movie ticket.
3. Two thirds of the students *(has, have)* finished the work already.
4. Three fourths of the watermelon *(was, were)* eaten immediately.
5. Two thousand pounds *(equals, equal)* one ton.
6. Three tons *(is, are)* the weight of Ed's truck.
7. *(Does, Do)* thirty-six inches equal a yard?
8. Two quarters *(is, are)* lying on the floor next to the vending machine.
9. Two quarters *(is, are)* the price of a granola bar from the machine.
10. The news about the hurricane *(was, were)* alarming.
11. *(Was, Were)* 3,500 pounds stated as the amount of the elevator's load limit?
12. Two days *(is, are)* not enough time for my test preparation!
13. Unfortunately, both of the days *(was, were)* spent in panic.
14. Mathematics *(is, are)* my strongest subject.
15. Loose curls *(is, are)* Mindy's everyday hairstyle.
16. *(Is, Are)* her curls natural?
17. Pets *(was, were)* the topic of my research report.
18. Two hundred square feet *(is, are)* the size of this room.
19. Forty hours *(makes, make)* a workweek.
20. Genetics *(is, are)* a science that has always fascinated Tina.

Subject-Verb Agreement J

17n. Even when plural in form, the title of a creative work (such as a book, song, film, or painting), the name of an organization, or the name of a country or city generally takes a singular verb.

EXAMPLES ***The Birds* is** a scary but entertaining movie.
The **Los Angeles Lakers is** my favorite basketball team.

USAGE

EXERCISE Underline the correct form of the verb in parentheses in each sentence.

Example 1. *(Was, Were) The Three Musketeers* made into a movie?

1. "Trees and Snow Fields" *(is, are)* the title of my poem.
2. Calico Creations *(is, are)* a crafts store owned by my aunt.
3. Hanging in the museum, *Water Lilies (was, were)* more beautiful than I expected.
4. *(Does, Do) Elements of Literature* contain excerpts from "The Raven" by Poe?
5. The Association of Veterans *(has, have)* an office on Crescent Street.
6. Written by Nancy Farmer, *The Ear, the Eye, and the Arm (takes, take)* place in Zimbabwe.
7. Founded in 1860, Alice Springs *(is, are)* a town in Australia.
8. *Anna and David (was, were)* painted on steel and aluminum by the artist Miriam Schapiro.
9. *(Is, Are)* the Parks and Recreation Department located in this building?
10. The Ganges *(is, are)* a river in northern India.
11. The Blenville Junior High Fighting Falcons *(was, were)* named best football team.
12. At the video store, *101 Dalmatians (was, were)* not on the shelf.
13. Pets Helping Humans *(sponsors, sponsor)* a pet adoption day each month.
14. Rising Hills *(is, are)* my hometown.
15. The Panthers *(is, are)* the name of my little sister's soccer team.
16. Daughters of Mercy Hospital *(accepts, accept)* teenage volunteers.
17. The United States *(shares, share)* a border with Canada.
18. The Harlem Globetrotters *(was, were)* formed in 1927.
19. Painted on silk by Toko, *Cat and Spider (shows, show)* a fluffy gray cat stalking a spider.
20. *The Fat-Cats at Sea (is, are)* a book of funny poems about cats sailing to the Island of Goo.

Subject-Verb Agreement K

17o. *Don't* and *doesn't* should agree in number with their subjects.

Use *don't* with all plural subjects and with the pronouns *I* and *you*. Use *doesn't* with all singular subjects except the pronouns *I* and *you*.

EXAMPLES **Plaids don't** match with stripes.
Brown doesn't go well with purple.

USAGE

EXERCISE A In each sentence, underline the subject and the correct form of *don't* or *doesn't* in parentheses.

Example 1. Temperatures in the equatorial zone *(don't, doesn't)* get cold.

1. Snow *(don't, doesn't)* fall in the tropics, except at high elevations.
2. Hurricanes *(don't, doesn't)* travel very far inland.
3. *(Don't, Doesn't)* tornadoes look like funnel-shaped clouds?
4. You *(don't, doesn't)* want to get near a tornado.
5. A rainbow usually *(don't, doesn't)* appear on a bright, sunny day.
6. *(Don't, Doesn't)* rainbows form from the reflection of light in rain or fog?
7. It *(don't, doesn't)* rain much in the Atacama Desert in Chile.
8. Without lightning, thunder *(don't, doesn't)* occur.
9. *(Don't, Doesn't)* sleet form from frozen rain?
10. I *(don't, doesn't)* enjoy shoveling the walks after a snowstorm.

EXERCISE B In each sentence, underline the subject in parentheses that agrees with the form of *don't* or *doesn't* in the sentence.

Example 1. Why don't the *(teacher, teachers)* eat the food in the cafeteria?

11. Don't the *(locker, lockers)* have to be cleaned out by three o'clock?
12. My *(dog, dogs)* doesn't obey my commands.
13. Why don't *(she, you)* tell me what happened?
14. Doesn't *(he, they)* remember who I am?
15. The *(plants, plant)* in the window don't need more water yet.

Pronoun-Antecedent Agreement A

A pronoun usually refers to a noun or another pronoun called its *antecedent.*

17p. A pronoun should agree in number and gender with its antecedent.

EXAMPLES **Dolores** lost **her** scarf.
The **snake** shed **its** skin.
Shoppers filled **their** baskets with food.
Each **one** of the teenagers paid for **his or her** ticket.

EXERCISE A In each sentence, underline the pronoun or pronouns in parentheses that agree in number and gender with the antecedent.

Example 1. High in the tree's branches, the bird built *(their, its)* nest.

1. Billy loaned *(their, his)* bike to Phillip.
2. The captain of the girls' softball team accepted *(her, his or her)* award.
3. In the evening the chickens return to *(its, their)* roost.
4. The cats sunned *(itself, themselves)* contentedly in the grassy yard.
5. The microscopes in the science lab still have *(its, their)* price tags attached.
6. The workers at the pizza parlor were wearing *(its, their)* new uniforms.
7. On Father's Day, the children performed a one-act play for *(his or her, their)* dad.
8. Carpenter ants sometimes make *(its, their)* home in your home.
9. The puppy entertained *(itself, themselves)* with an old tennis ball.
10. The hamster slept in *(its, their)* empty food dish.

EXERCISE B On each of the lines provided, write a pronoun or a pair of pronouns that will correctly complete the sentence.

Example 1. The river overflowed ___its___ banks.

11. The siblings planned a surprise party for ______ parents' anniversary.
12. The pig raised ______ voice in a surprised squeal.
13. The captains of each team accepted ______ award.
14. Julie was proud of ______ older sister.
15. The young boy told ______ not to be afraid of the dark.

Pronoun-Antecedent Agreement B

USAGE

17q. Use a singular pronoun to refer to *anybody, anyone, anything, each, either, everybody, everyone, everything, neither, nobody, no one, nothing, one, somebody, someone,* or *something.*

17r. Use a plural pronoun to refer to *both, few, many,* or *several.*

17s. The indefinite pronouns *all, any, more, most, none,* and *some* may be singular or plural, depending on how they are used in a sentence.

EXAMPLES **Everybody** in the group wanted **his or her** own map.
Few of the photographers developed **their** own film.
Some of the bread **was** eaten, and **some** of the bananas **were** eaten, too.

EXERCISE Underline the pronoun or pronouns in parentheses that correctly complete each sentence.

Example **1.** During a fire drill, no one is allowed to remain in *(their, his or her)* classroom.

1. Many of the mice are sleeping in *(their, its)* cage.

2. Someone with muddy shoes didn't wipe *(his or her, their)* feet on the mat.

3. At my grandmother's deli, few ordered the daily special for *(his or her, their)* meal.

4. Any of the jewelry found should be returned to *(its, their)* owner.

5. Any of the jewels found should be returned to *(its, their)* owner.

6. Everything in the rooms was in *(their, its)* proper place.

7. Most of the desks have had *(their, its)* wooden surfaces revarnished.

8. Both of my sisters are successful in *(her, their)* careers.

9. Each of the teachers voted for *(his or her, their)* choice for student council.

10. Contrary to expectation, none of the treasure was worth *(their, its)* weight in gold.

11. This year most of the girls are bringing *(her, their)* lunch from home.

12. All of the boys helped clean *(his, their)* locker room.

13. In my opinion, either of the candidates would represent *(their, his or her)* district well.

14. Several of the chess players displayed *(their, his or her)* trophies in the case at school.

15. Is anybody finished with *(their, his or her)* assignment yet?

16. Anyone would enjoy riding *(their, his or her)* bike on a beautiful day like today.

17. None of the children could fit into *(their, his or her)* coats this year.

18. Both of the girls needed new shoes for *(her, their)* PE classes.

19. All of my family wants to eat dinner at *(our, its)* grandparents' house.

20. When the sun rose, several of the hikers packed *(his or her, their)* gear and started up the trail.

Pronoun-Antecedent Agreement C

17t. Use a singular pronoun to refer to two or more singular antecedents joined by *or* or *nor.*

EXAMPLE **Bill or Buddy** will lend **his** microscope to the class.

17u. Use a plural pronoun to refer to two or more antecedents joined by *and.*

EXAMPLE **Bill and Buddy** will lend **their** microscope to the class.

EXERCISE A In each sentence, underline the pronoun or pair of pronouns in parentheses that agrees in number and gender with its antecedent.

Example 1. Neither Mr. Smith nor Ms. Macelli reached *(their, his or her)* classroom on time.

1. Ants and flies found *(its, their)* way to our picnic.
2. Either Shari or April will give *(their, her)* oral report next.
3. Both Shelley and Stella promised to bring *(her, their)* cameras.
4. Did Martin or Jorge volunteer *(their, his)* time to the tutoring program?
5. Neither Paul nor Bonnie was surprised by *(their, his or her)* exam grades.
6. Mom and Dad called and said *(he, they)* are picking up pizza for us.
7. A squirrel or a bird must have found *(its, their)* way into my berry patch.
8. The band members and the fans cheered *(his or her, their)* team.
9. Will Thea or Sandra bring *(their, her)* flute?
10. Neither Jared nor Jill wants *(their, his or her)* picture on the poster.

EXERCISE B On each of the lines provided, write a pronoun or a pair of pronouns that will correctly complete the sentence.

Example 1. Either Grandma or Mom will loan ___her___ coat to me.

11. Patricia and Parker took ______________ younger brother to the park.
12. Neither Cheryl nor Gary finished ______________ sculpture.
13. Monty and Ty promised that ______________ would lead the discussion.
14. Natalie or Tabitha will tell ______________ concerns to the principal.
15. Leo and Penny said that ______________ will be here by noon.

Pronoun-Antecedent Agreement D

17v. A pronoun that refers to a collective noun has the same number as the noun.

A collective noun is singular when it refers to the group as a unit and plural when it refers to the individual members of the group.

SINGULAR The **committee** held **its** meeting in Mr. Park's classroom.

PLURAL The **committee** took **their** seats promptly.

USAGE

EXERCISE A In each of the following sentences, underline the pronoun in parentheses that agrees in number with the collective noun.

Example 1. The valuable collection resides in (*its, their*) fireproof case.

1. The brood followed closely behind (*its, their*) mother.

2. Inside the tent, the family chose positions for (*its, their*) sleeping bags.

3. The new set was placed on (*its, their*) shelf in the china cabinet.

4. The jury argued among (*itself, themselves*).

5. Before the show the chorus warmed up (*its, their*) voices.

6. This cluster, said the jeweler, has value in (*its, their*) antiquity.

7. The litter occupied (*itself, themselves*) by running, jumping, and barking.

8. The jury went (*its, their*) separate ways for lunch.

9. During the holidays, her family decorates (*its, their*) house together.

10. The emergency crew congratulated (*itself, themselves*) on the rescue.

EXERCISE B On each of the lines provided, write a pronoun that will correctly complete the sentence.

Example 1. The cleaning crew signed ___their___ time sheets.

11. Once out of the harbor, the fleet adjusted ______________ speed.

12. The audience took ______________ seats.

13. In winter the pack foraged for food near ______________ den.

14. The pack hunted on ______________ own occasionally.

15. The salary committee gave ______________ raises.

Pronoun-Antecedent Agreement E

17w. An expression of an amount may take a singular or plural pronoun, depending on how the expression is used.

SINGULAR I have **two thirds** of a pizza. Is **it** enough for your friends?

PLURAL Finding **three dollars** on the floor, I put **them** in my pocket.

17x. Even when plural in form, the title of a creative work (such as a book, song, film, or painting), the name of an organization, or the name of a country or city usually takes a singular pronoun.

EXAMPLE Where is **Hot Springs**? I don't see **it** on the map.

EXERCISE A In each of the following sentences, underline the correct pronoun in parentheses.

Example 1. If I lend you twenty dollars, will you pay *(them, it)* back next week?

1. Three fourths of the salad is left. I'm sure *(it, they)* will be eaten.
2. Have you seen *Dancers on a Bench*? Edgar Degas painted *(them, it)* in 1898.
3. Here is twenty dollars. Use *(them, it)* to get a taxi at the airport.
4. The final three miles are downhill, and *(they, it)* should pass quickly.
5. Have you read *The Exiles*? *(They, It)* tells the funny story of four adventurous sisters.
6. I'm from Grand Forks. You'll find *(them, it)* in eastern North Dakota.
7. My mother puts two tablespoons of sugar in her coffee. *(They, It)* may see like a lot to some people.
8. Much of the economy of Honduras is based on *(its, their)* export of bananas and coffee.
9. Ms. Morris gave us only two days to study. She said we'll need to use *(it, them)* wisely.
10. The shirt cost fifty dollars but is not worth *(it, them)*.

EXERCISE B On each of the lines provided, write a pronoun that will correctly complete the sentence.

Example 1. You'll need ten dollars, and you have two weeks to earn ___it___.

11. How far is two feet? Measure ______________ with the tape measure.
12. Have you seen *The Mysteries of the Horizon*? René Magritte painted ______________.
13. Here is sixteen dollars in change. Please count ______________ carefully.
14. With how many countries does the United States share ______________ borders?
15. The drama club is performing *The Merry Wives of Windsor.* William Shakespeare wrote ______________.

NAME ______________________ CLASS ______________ DATE ______________

Review A: Subject-Verb Agreement

EXERCISE A In each of the following sentences, write *C* for *correct* above the underlined verb if it agrees with its subject. If the underlined verb does not agree with its subject, write the correct form of the verb above it.

Example **1.** Neither Ms. Jamison nor Mr. Thompson *claims* claim the stray dog.

1. Where is the Mason-Dixon line?

2. The highest peak in the United States are the South Peak of Mount McKinley.

3. The Senate are in its first session of the year.

4. Several of the legends are about Hercules.

5. None of the symphony players listens to rock-and-roll.

6. Fifteen ounces are the total weight of the package.

7. Are Adrienne or Suki going to the party?

8. There is the tickets to tonight's game.

9. In the mailbox were both letters from Vicente.

10. *The Pickwick Papers* are a novel by Dickens.

EXERCISE B In each of the following sentences, underline the subject once and the verb twice. If the subject and verb agree, write *C* for *correct* above the verb. If the subject and verb do not agree, write the correct form of the verb above the incorrect verb.

Example **1.** The Association of Aquatic Enthusiasts *is* are upstairs.

11. Twenty gallons are a good size for an aquarium.

12. *Tropical Fishes* is a handy guidebook to own.

13. Neither Doyle nor Ana have an aquarium.

14. Plants in an aquarium isn't always real.

15. The local fish club is holding a meeting next Wednesday.

16. Four or five dollars are the price of a Siamese fightingfish.

17. Either neon tetras or guppies is a good choice for a home aquarium.

18. Plastic plants in the aquarium look nice.

19. A school of small fish live in this large aquarium.

20. Twelve inches is the length of tubing required for this pump.

Review B: Pronoun-Antecedent Agreement

EXERCISE A In each of the following sentences, underline the pronoun or pronoun pair that refers to the underlined antecedent. If the pronoun and antecedent agree, write *C* for *correct* above the pronoun. If the pronoun and antecedent do not agree, write the correct pronoun above the incorrect pronoun.

Example 1. Most of the members remained in his or her seats. *(their)*

1. One of my sisters thinks they will be a firefighter.
2. Each of my sisters has had plenty of time to decide on their future.
3. A person can change their career several times over a lifetime.
4. If anybody asked me, I would tell them I hope to be a doctor one day.
5. Hector or Mateo will write his report on careers of the future.
6. On Saturday I helped my grandparents in their movie rental store.
7. Someone from the career testing service left their jacket in our classroom.
8. The student body enjoyed their career fair this year.
9. White Rapids, the neighboring town, holds their harvest festival in October.
10. One of my friends sells her produce at the festival.

EXERCISE B In each of the following sentences, write *C* for *correct* above the underlined pronoun if it agrees with its antecedent. If the underlined pronoun does not agree with its antecedent, write the correct form of the pronoun above it.

Example 1. Please measure two cups of oatmeal and put them in this bowl. *(it)*

11. Either of the two sisters will bring her notebook.
12. Either a hamster or a rabbit shows affection for their owner.
13. I hope everyone remembers their lunch.
14. Each of the children will need his own permission slip.
15. Some of the girls have opened their gifts already.
16. Neither Earl nor Fred has opened their mail yet.
17. A few of the teachers want their students to make presentations.
18. One of the coaches is going to put those boys on his team.
19. Many of the students lost their flashcards.
20. Each of the contestants will do their best.

Review C: Agreement

USAGE

EXERCISE A In each of the following sentences, underline the subject and the correct verb in parentheses.

Example 1. The Society for the Care and Protection of Animals *(accept, accepts)* donations.

1. Civics *(is, are)* his favorite subject.
2. The class *(is, are)* working on their science projects.
3. You *(doesn't, don't)* have enough money for that new book.
4. The family *(is, are)* discussing their vacation plans.
5. *(Has, Have)* the jury reached a verdict?
6. Here *(is, are)* the canned goods for the food drive.
7. A machine *(doesn't, don't)* work properly unless it is oiled.
8. Ten pounds *(is, are)* a lot of weight to lose.
9. *Kelly's Heroes (is, are)* a 1970 movie starring Clint Eastwood.
10. *(Doesn't, Don't)* Thelma look great in that color?

EXERCISE B The following paragraph contains ten errors in agreement between pronouns and their antecedents. Draw a line through each error and write the correct pronoun or pronoun pair above it.

Example Both Tamara and Tomás brought ~~his~~ *their* instruments to the band's rehearsal.

Everyone has their opinion about what makes a good band. That's what I learned from its experience with a musical group. My friends and I met recently to combine their musical talents by forming a band. Tamara brought his own guitar. Tomás brought his trumpet. Rupesh and Mary brought his and her Australian didgeridoos. Unfortunately, we couldn't decide what to play. Someone suggested their favorite song, but no one else knew them. My father suggested we play her favorite song, "She'll Be Coming Round the Mountain." Each of the girls put down their instrument and laughed heartily. Everybody had their own idea of what to play. It was chaos!

Review D: Agreement

EXERCISE Underline the word or word group in parentheses that correctly completes each sentence.

Example Fans of the jazz artist Ella Fitzgerald mourned (her, their) death in 1996.

In the twentieth century, one of the best-selling vocal artists *(were, was)* Ella Fitzgerald. Newport News *(were, was)* her birthplace, and Beverly Hills *(is, are)* where she passed away at the age of 79. *(He, She)* became famous throughout the world for *(their, her)* clear, sweet voice. The city of New York *(were, was)* where she grew up. The Apollo Theatre in Harlem featured her in one of *(their, its)* amateur nights, and Fitzgerald *(were, was)* "discovered" at age sixteen. She performed in a band, and then began working with Chick Webb in *(its, his)* Chick Webb Orchestra.

The 1950s *(were, was)* good years for Fitzgerald. *(Their, Her)* manager, Norman Granz, carefully chose her singing material, and *(he, they)* provided excellent jazz instrumental support for *(it, her)*. In fact, Granz's Jazz at the Philharmonic featured Fitzgerald as *(their, its)* star attraction. Fitzgerald's singing style *(were, was)* so popular that many singers imitated Fitzgerald's style in *(his or her, their)* own performances. Fitzgerald also became famous for *(her, their)* "scat" singing. Singers of this style *(imitate, imitates)* a trumpet or saxophone with *(his or her, their)* voices. *Mack the Knife: Ella in Berlin (is, are)* one of her famed scat recordings.

Proofreading Application: Report

Good writers are generally good proofreaders. Readers tend to admire and trust writing that is error-free. Make sure that you correct all errors in grammar, usage, spelling, and punctuation in your writing. Your readers will have more confidence in your words if you have done your best to proofread carefully.

After all the work you have put into your writing, you want readers to be impressed by your work and to understand your message. Errors in agreement can make your work appear sloppy or careless and can confuse your readers. Careful proofreading will help you catch errors and ensure that you are presenting your best work to your audience.

Proofreading Activity

The following excerpt from a report on whales contains errors in subject-verb agreement. Find and correct the errors in subject-verb agreement in the following paragraphs. Use proofreading symbols such as those on page 809 of *Elements of Language* to make your corrections.

Example Whales are fascinating animals. They are mammals, but they ~~lives~~ *live* underwater.

Unlike fish, whales does not have gills. Whales need air just like other mammals. They resurface periodically and breathes through a blowhole on top of their heads. If a whale get water in its lungs, it drown.

Whales are divided into two major groups. One group are the whalebone whales. Their name come from the bony plate embedded in their upper jaw, which are called a whalebone. They eats microscopic animals called plankton, which they strains from the water through their whalebones. Whalebone whales is large and slow. Blue whales, the largest animals of all time, belongs to this group. Other members of the group is right whales, rorqual whales, and gray whales. The second major group are the toothed whales. As their name imply, they have teeth instead of a whalebone. Rather than plankton, they eat fish and squid. This group include dolphins, porpoises, beaked whales, and narwhals.

Literary Model: Dialogue

Just the sound of the name brought Slade to my eye. . . .

"I don't think it's any good to send him a bill, Mr. Baumer," I said. "He can't even read."

"He could pay yet."

"He don't pay anybody," I said.

"I think he hate me," Mr. Baumer went on. "That is the thing. He hate me for coming not from this country. I come here, sixteen years old, and learn to read and write, and I make a business, and so I think he hate me."

"He hates everybody."

Mr. Baumer shook his head. "But not to pinch the nose. Not to call Dutchie."

The side door squeaked open, but it was only Colly Coleman coming in from a trip, so I said, "Excuse me, Mr. Baumer, but you shouldn't have trusted him in the first place."

"I know," he answered, looking at me with his misty eyes. "A man make mistakes. I think some do not trust him, so he will pay me because I do. . . ."

He took his pencil from behind the ear where he had put it and studied the point of it. "That Slade. He steal. . . .He sneak things from his load. A thief, he is. And too big for me."

—from "Bargain" by A. B. Guthrie

EXERCISE A In the passage above, underline each verb that does not agree in number with its subject.

EXERCISE B

1. With regard to subject-verb agreement, how does Mr. Baumer's speech contrast with that of the other character in this passage?

____

____

____

____

2. Why do you think the author has Mr. Baumer speak in such a manner?

____

____

____

____

NAME ____________ CLASS ____________ DATE ____________

Literary Model (continued)

EXERCISE C Write a dialogue between two characters, the first a person who has a certain mastery of English grammar and the second a person who is still perfecting his or her English-language skills. Have the second character use verbs that do not agree with their subjects.

EXERCISE D

1. In what ways was writing your dialogue challenging?

2. How does the second character's use of verbs that do not agree with their subjects help to characterize him or her?

Writing Application: Report

Indefinite pronouns do not refer to a definite person, place, thing, or idea. They include words like *anybody, both, either,* and *everyone.* Some indefinite pronouns are singular, some are plural, and some can be either singular or plural depending on whether they refer to a singular or plural word. It is important to know whether an indefinite pronoun is singular or plural because the number of the pronoun determines the number of the verb it takes.

EXAMPLES Most of the play is set in the past.

Most of the characters are famous Americans in history.

The indefinite pronoun found in both the first and second sentences is singular when used with the singular noun *play* and plural when used with the plural noun *characters.*

Writing Activity

The editor of your school newspaper is planning a feature about the musical tastes of students in the different grades at your school. She has asked several students from each grade level to write a paragraph about the artists, CDs or tapes, songs, and types of music they and their friends like and dislike. Using indefinite pronouns like *everyone, nobody, many,* and *most,* tell what music you and your friends listen to and what music you can't stand. In your paragraph, include two sentences with singular indefinite pronouns as subjects, two sentences with plural indefinite pronouns as subjects, and two sentences with indefinite pronouns that can be either singular or plural as subjects.

PREWRITING Brainstorm with your friends to come up with a list of the artists, CDs or tapes, songs, and types of music you like and dislike. Depending on how long the list is, you may not be able to include every suggestion. Vote on which suggestions are most representative of your tastes.

WRITING Decide how to organize your paragraph. One possibility is to organize all your likes together and all your dislikes together. Another possibility is to organize all discussion about songs together, all discussion about CDs or tapes together, all discussion about artists together, and all discussion about types of music together.

REVISING Read your paragraph to your friends. Do they agree with your summary of the group's likes and dislikes? If not, what should you change, add, or omit?

PUBLISHING Check your summary for grammar, usage, spelling, and punctuation errors. Make sure that indefinite pronouns and verbs agree in number. Publish your report and present it to your classmates. If your class has a Web site, ask your teacher if you can post your report for students at your school to review. You might set up a page where students could post their own opinions about music.

Extending Your Writing

You may wish to develop your summary into a full-length article for your school newspaper. Instead of focusing on just what you and your friends like and dislike, conduct a survey to find out about the musical preferences at each grade level. Is there a diversity of tastes at your school, or do most of the students like the same kind of music?

NAME CLASS DATE

for **CHAPTER 18: USING VERBS CORRECTLY** pages 485–503

Choices: Investigating Verbs in Action

Here's your chance to step out of the grammar book and into the real world. You may not notice verbs, but you and the people around you use them every day. The following activities challenge you to find a connection between verbs and the world around you. Do the activity below that suits your personality best, and then share your discoveries with your class. Have fun!

GAME SHOW

Trivia Trove

You are the host of a new game show! First, use a dictionary to look up ten words from your list of irregular verbs. You are looking for words that can be used as more than one part of speech. For instance, take the word *strike*. It can be used as a noun (*a* strike *in bowling*) or as a verb (strike *up the band*). During the game, you will ask questions such as "What verb describes the act of getting a band to start playing music?" and "This same word can be used as a noun in a game of bowling." Give a point to the first person who names your verb. If that person can name the past and past participle of the verb in question, the player scores an extra two points!

BUILDING BACKGROUND KNOWLEDGE

Limit: One to a Customer

Do your classmates a favor. Create a chart of all the verb tenses. For each tense, supply a verb and, if necessary, an appropriate helping verb. In order for this chart to be helpful, you must clearly label each tense. With your teacher's permission, pass out copies of your chart for everyone in your class to keep in his or her English notebook.

CREATIVE WRITING

The Family of Tenses

Write a short play for three unnamed characters who each represent a different generation within the same family. Each character will speak in only one tense—the past, the present, or the future. You might consider having the characters discuss technological advances. With your teacher's permission, perform your play for the class. Then, have your classmates vote on the family relationship of the characters. Discuss how the content of the dialogue and the verb tenses used affected the class's understanding of the characters.

INVENTIONS

Doodads

You are an inventor who has just designed a new household appliance or tool. Write a letter to potential investors telling them about the uses of this product and encouraging them to invest in its development. In your description of what the appliance does, you'll need to use vivid and convincing verbs. In your letter, you may want to include photographs or drawings of your invention.

TECHNOLOGY

Just Trust Me

Can you trust what a computer's grammar checker says? Put that software to the test. Type in a dozen or so sentences, all with errors of verb usage. Then, run the grammar checker. Keep careful records of each message that the program gives you. Record each suggestion offered. When you've finished, study the results of your test. What kind of errors did the program miss? What kind did it catch? With your teacher's approval, report your findings to the class.

ART

Show Me the Time

A series of illustrations may help show how each of the six tenses in English are used. Draw six different illustrations that each involve a single event. In your illustrations, give creative clues to the tense of each scene. Then, after you have completed your detailed illustrations, write a sentence beneath each illustration that describes the action in that scene. In each sentence, be sure to use the appropriate tense. When you have finished your project, put your creative and artistic abilities to the test. Tape a strip of paper over each of the sentences in your illustrations. Then, give the illustrations to a classmate to see if he or she can guess the tense in each scene.

Principal Parts of Verbs

18a. The principal parts of a verb are the ***base form,*** the ***present participle,*** the ***past,*** and the ***past participle.***

BASE FORM	**walk**	**sing**
PRESENT PARTICIPLE	[is/are] **walking**	[is/are] **singing**
PAST	**walked**	**sang**
PAST PARTICIPLE	[has/have] **walked**	[has/have] **sung**

USAGE

EXERCISE A On the line next to each verb form, identify it by writing *B* for *base form, PresP* for *present participle, P* for *past,* or *PastP* for *past participle.*

Example ___PresP___ **1.** [is] fighting

_______ **1.** [is] catching

_______ **2.** drink

_______ **3.** bought

_______ **4.** [has] watched

_______ **5.** [are] cutting

_______ **6.** write

_______ **7.** [have] shone

_______ **8.** paint

_______ **9.** [is] asking

_______ **10.** jumped

_______ **11.** [have] built

_______ **12.** froze

_______ **13.** suppose

_______ **14.** taught

_______ **15.** [are] letting

_______ **16.** rang

_______ **17.** [is] growing

_______ **18.** leave

_______ **19.** drowned

_______ **20.** [has] met

EXERCISE B In each of the following sentences, identify the form of the underlined verb by writing above it *B* for *base form, PresP* for *present participle, P* for *past,* or *PastP* for *past participle.*

Example 1. The ducks have flown (PastP) south for the winter.

21. Water-resistant feathers help ducks stay dry.

22. Those ducks are swimming with their strong legs and feet.

23. These ducks have grown waterproof feathers.

24. Some ducks fed from the surface of the water.

25. Near the pond the ducks are eating seeds and insects.

NAME ______ CLASS ______ DATE ______

Regular Verbs

18b. A ***regular verb*** forms its past and past participle by adding *–d* or *–ed* to the base form.

BASE FORM	**use**	**pick**
PRESENT PARTICIPLE	[is/are] **using**	[is/are] **picking**
PAST	**used**	**picked**
PAST PARTICIPLE	[has/have] **used**	[has/have] **picked**

EXERCISE A Supply the present participle, past, and past participle for each of the following base forms.

Example 1. learn *learning* *learned* *learned*

	Present Part.	Past	Past Part.
1. watch	______	______	______
2. present	______	______	______
3. demonstrate	______	______	______
4. bandage	______	______	______
5. practice	______	______	______

EXERCISE B For each of the following sentences, write the correct present participle, past, or past participle of the verb given in parentheses.

Example 1. Cindy has *jogged* every Saturday for two months. *(jog)*

6. Today, many people are ______ for ways to improve their health. *(look)*

7. Since the middle of last semester, I have ______ to school every day. *(walk)*

8. Already, my stamina has ______. *(increase)*

9. Last year Shane ______ to do something to improve his health. *(decide)*

10. He ______ to eat junk food and spent most of his free time watching television. *(use)*

11. His mother had ______ that he had very little energy. *(notice)*

12. He also was ______ weight rapidly. *(gain)*

13. Now Shane is ______ and eating well. *(exercise)*

14. He has ______ an aerobics class that meets three times a week. *(start)*

15. Aerobic exercise has ______ to increase Shane's energy level. *(help)*

Irregular Verbs A

18c. An ***irregular verb*** forms its past and past participle in some way other than by adding *–d* or *–ed* to the base form.

BASE FORM	**eat**	**do**
PRESENT PARTICIPLE	[is/are] **eating**	[is/are] **doing**
PAST	**ate**	**did**
PAST PARTICIPLE	[has/have] **eaten**	[has/have] **done**

EXERCISE A For each of the following sentences, underline the correct verb form in parentheses.

Example **1.** This tight shoe has *(hurted, hurt)* my foot all day.

1. Calinda *(took, taked)* her sister to the rain forest exhibit at the museum.
2. Do you know what year the *Lusitania (sank, sunk)*?
3. Claudia has *(drew, drawn)* a picture of the meadow behind the cabin.
4. The camels have *(drank, drunk)* an enormous amount of water and are ready to begin their journey across the desert.
5. The three boys had *(ran, run)* as if they were being chased.
6. On Tuesday, Alfonso *(wore, worn)* the sweater that his mother gave him for his birthday.
7. Ms. Shapiro *(drove, drived)* the school bus for our field trip.
8. Small meteors have *(fell, fallen)* recently near Peekskill, New York.
9. The teacher *(rang, rung)* the bell to get the students back to their desks.
10. In the last race, gusts of wind *(blew, blowed)* a sailboat off its course.

EXERCISE B For each of the following sentences, write the past or past participle of the verb given in parentheses.

Example **1.** Salma has ____forgiven____ me for my thoughtless comment. *(forgive)*

11. The truck driver ________________ her last delivery at six o'clock. *(make)*
12. Have you ever ________________ yourself playing soccer? *(hurt)*
13. When you have ________________ the last problem on the test, you may leave. *(do)*
14. Uncle Scott ________________ the house himself and is very proud of his work. *(build)*
15. Our family has ________________ the Vierlings for more than twenty years. *(know)*

NAME ______________________ CLASS ______________ DATE ______________

Irregular Verbs B

18c. An ***irregular verb*** forms its past and past participle in some other way than by adding *–d* or *–ed* to the base form.

BASE FORM	**draw**	**break**
PRESENT PARTICIPLE	[is/are] **drawing**	[is/are] **breaking**
PAST	**drew**	**broke**
PAST PARTICIPLE	[has/have] **drawn**	[has/have] **broken**

EXERCISE A For each of the following sentences, underline the correct verb form in parentheses.

Example 1. Ouch! That mosquito *(bited, bit)* me.

1. The house mouse can be *(founded, found)* in most areas of the world.
2. The crowd cheered as the runner *(bursted, burst)* ahead of the others.
3. The plump frog quickly *(caught, catched)* a fly with its tongue.
4. Two hungry squirrels have *(came, come)* to the bird feeder.
5. Have you ever been *(bited, bitten)* by a spider?
6. A small brown sparrow *(flyed, flew)* overhead and landed on a fence post.
7. The tadpoles have *(grown, grew)* into frogs.
8. Several geese *(swum, swam)* into the reeds at the edge of the lake.
9. Near this lake, beavers have *(cut, cutted)* down trees with their teeth.
10. Yesterday evening several deer *(eated, ate)* the leaves from these bushes.

EXERCISE B For each of the following sentences, write the past or past participle of the verb given in parentheses.

Example 1. I can't believe you ____caught____ that fly ball! *(catch)*

11. Millie rudely ________________ talking before I was finished. *(begin)*
12. I have ________________ my homework with me to the library. *(bring)*
13. After I ran three miles, I ________________ tired but relaxed. *(feel)*
14. Where is my jacket? I ________________ it to you three weeks ago. *(lend)*
15. Now that the guests have ________________, we'll start cleaning the kitchen. *(leave)*

Irregular Verbs C

18c. An ***irregular verb*** forms its past and past participle in some other way than by adding *–d* or *–ed* to the base form.

BASE FORM	**hear**	**lead**
PRESENT PARTICIPLE	[is/are] **hearing**	[is/are] **leading**
PAST	**heard**	**led**
PAST PARTICIPLE	[has/have] **heard**	[has/have] **led**

EXERCISE A For each of the following sentences, underline the correct verb form in parentheses.

Example 1. The girls' soccer team has not *(losed, lost)* a game all season.

1. I *(pay, paid)* for six tickets but received only five.
2. The six of us *(met, meeted)* at our seats after I got the other ticket.
3. The new lighting system has *(litten, lit)* the entire field.
4. Gina went to the concession stand and *(got, gotten)* us some drinks.
5. Coach Simms *(sended, sent)* the team captain onto the field.
6. I have never *(saw, seen)* a more exciting game!
7. When Marta scored a goal, the fans *(stand, stood)* and cheered.
8. One of the players has *(torn, teared)* a ligament.
9. The team has *(fighted, fought)* hard for victory.
10. In the final seconds of the game, I realized our team had *(winned, won)*.

EXERCISE B For each of the following sentences, write the past or past participle of the verb given in parentheses.

Example 1. Come look at the snow fort we have ___built___! *(build)*

11. Overnight, the ponds and lakes have ________. *(freeze)*
12. Toni and her friends ________ ice-skating an hour ago. *(go)*
13. We ________ snowballs at each other until we were wet and cold. *(throw)*
14. Owen laughed as he ________ the sled down the steep hill of snow. *(ride)*
15. After building the snowman, I ________ small twigs to make its arms. *(break)*

NAME ____________ CLASS ____________ DATE ____________

Irregular Verbs D

18c. An ***irregular verb*** forms its past and past participle in some other way than by adding *–d* or *–ed* to the base form.

USAGE

BASE FORM	**lend**	**sink**
PRESENT PARTICIPLE	[is/are] **lending**	[is/are] **sinking**
PAST	**lent**	**sank**
PAST PARTICIPLE	[has/have] **lent**	[has/have] **sunk**

EXERCISE A For each of the following sentences, underline the correct verb form in parentheses.

Example 1. Father Ames has *(rang, rung)* the church bells.

1. I have *(read, readed)* every poem by Emily Dickinson.
2. At the museum, Ms. Morgan *(lead, led)* her class to the newest exhibit.
3. Who *(hitted, hit)* the emergency button for the alarm?
4. Last night the campers *(heared, heard)* eerie sounds coming from the forest.
5. Someone has *(hid, hided)* my backpack.
6. The proud teacher said to the class, "We have *(hadden, had)* a great year!"
7. As I *(holded, held)* the baby in my arms, she stopped crying.
8. Who *(letted, let)* the horses out of the corral?
9. Once again, Darryl has *(lost, lose)* his car keys.
10. Eric *(broke, breaked)* his arm when he fell on the ice.

EXERCISE B For each of the following sentences, write the past or past participle of the verb given in parentheses.

Example 1. Have you ever ___eaten___ liver and onions? *(eat)*

11. The plastic ____________ in the heat of the sun. *(shrink)*
12. In their class play last night, four enthusiastic children ____________ a funny song. *(sing)*
13. Have you ____________ to Dad about fixing the spokes on my bicycle? *(speak)*
14. I was dismayed at how much money I had ____________. *(spend)*
15. The rival football team has ____________ our mascot! No, there it is. *(steal)*

Irregular Verbs E

18c. An ***irregular verb*** forms its past and past participle in some other way than by adding *–d* or *–ed* to the base form.

BASE FORM	**shrink**	**swim**
PRESENT PARTICIPLE	[is/are] **shrinking**	[is/are] **swimming**
PAST	**shrank**	**swam**
PAST PARTICIPLE	**shrunk**	[has/have] **swum**

EXERCISE A For each of the following sentences, underline the correct verb form in parentheses.

Example 1. Kyle put on his helmet and *(ridden, rode)* away on his motorcycle.

1. Mr. Sterne *(choose, chose)* Mike to monitor the class in his absence.

2. Have I *(bought, boughten)* enough meat for the stew?

3. That fuzzy, green sweater *(cost, costed)* only fifteen dollars.

4. Whiskers *(eaten, ate)* his cat food hungrily.

5. A week passed before Marcos *(forgived, forgave)* Andy for the practical joke.

6. The seventh-grade class *(gived, gave)* coats and canned food to the homeless shelter.

7. The chef *(put, putted)* cherries and nuts on top of the cake.

8. Who *(say, said)* "Give me liberty or give me death"?

9. The pupil *(seeked, sought)* advice from his teacher.

10. The bike was *(selled, sold)* before I could save enough money for it.

EXERCISE B For each of the following sentences, write the past or past participle of the verb given in parentheses.

Example 1. The band has ___chosen___ the music for the dance. *(choose)*

11. On the playground the child climbed into the swing and ________________ as high as she could. *(swing)*

12. I have ________________ myself Spanish by watching Spanish television programs. *(teach)*

13. The auctioneer called her assistant over and ________________ him about each item. *(tell)*

14. I have always ________________ I would be good at tennis. *(think)*

15. Please open the note and read what I have ________________. *(write)*

Verb Tense

18d. The ***tense*** of a verb indicates the time of the action or of the state of being that is expressed by the verb.

USAGE

Verbs in English have six tenses: *present, past, future, present perfect, past perfect,* and *future perfect.*

PRESENT	The bird **sings.**	PRESENT PERFECT	The bird **has sung.**
PAST	The bird **sang.**	PAST PERFECT	The bird **had sung.**
FUTURE	The bird **will sing.**	FUTURE PERFECT	The bird **will have sung.**

Each tense has an additional form called the ***progressive form,*** which expresses continuing action or state of being.

EXAMPLES Nathan **is taking** a nap. [present progressive]
Carol **had been waiting** for the train. [past perfect progressive]

EXERCISE A Revise each of the following sentences by changing the verb or verbs to the tense indicated in italics.

Example 1. Our family picnic ~~took~~ *will take* place on July sixth. *(future)*

1. Alex smells the aroma of barbecued chicken. *(past)*

2. Dana will bring her famous orange marmalade cake. *(present)*

3. Trays of salads and fruit filled the picnic tables. *(present)*

4. Some corn on the cob has already disappeared from the platter. *(past perfect)*

5. Everyone at the picnic had awaited the signal for lunch. *(future)*

6. Peepers, my dog, begs for a bit of my food. *(past)*

7. Everyone will go back for second helpings. *(present perfect)*

8. The cook, my uncle Rosco, will mix more of his special sauce. *(future perfect)*

9. Carla brought her famous pasta salad. *(past perfect)*

10. I am organizing games of softball and horseshoes. *(future)*

EXERCISE B Above the underlined verb in each sentence, identify its tense by writing *present, past, future, present perfect, past perfect,* or *future perfect.* Also, indicate whether the tense is in the progressive form.

present perfect progressive
Example 1. I have been buying the supplies all week.

11. Sherri and I have registered for our own booth at the craft fair.

12. We have been making dozens of interesting and useful items this month.

13. We will sell them at reasonable prices.

14. Sherri is designing the banner for our booth.

15. We will have earned a nice profit by the end of the craft fair.

Verb Tense Consistency

18e. Do not change needlessly from one *tense* to another.

When writing about events that take place at the same time, use verbs that are in the same tense. When writing about events that occur at different times, use verbs that are in different tenses.

INCONSISTENT We sat on the porch and gaze at the stars.

CONSISTENT We **sat** on the porch and **gazed** at the stars.

EXERCISE A Each of the following sentences contains an error in consistency of verb tense. Revise each sentence to make the verb tenses consistent. Give only one answer for each sentence.

Example 1. Slowly, the sun sank below the horizon, and the sky ~~becomes~~ *became* dark.

or

Slowly, the sun ~~sank~~ *sinks* below the horizon, and the sky becomes dark.

1. Pioneers traveled west in Conestoga wagons and have endured many hardships.
2. After the president of the United States threw out the first ball, the baseball game begins.
3. The hungry child will eat some crackers and drank a cup of milk.
4. Eduardo worked in the garden while we trim the hedges.
5. By dinner I will have finished my homework, and Laurie finishes her chores.
6. After I swallowed the huge gulp of water, I will cough.
7. As the trees sway in the breeze, the birds will have sung merrily.
8. Hannah had mixed her paints before she notices a crack in her palette.
9. My parents owned a diner until last year when they sell it.
10. Tim had washed the dishes but forgets to put them away.

EXERCISE B For the following sentences, fill in each blank with an appropriate tense for the verb given in parentheses.

Example 1. Jason *has played* piano since he was five years old. *(play)*

11. She has roasted a turkey and ________________ rolls for the holiday meal. *(heat)*
12. I noticed the last bus and ________________ after it. *(run)*
13. Last weekend I ________________ Grandma and spent the afternoon with her. *(visit)*
14. Ron will do the laundry, and I ________________ the windows. *(wash)*
15. Jessie ________________ his homework before his mother came home from the store. *(finish)*

USAGE

Active and Passive Voice

A verb in the *active voice* expresses an action done *by* its subject. A verb in the *passive voice* expresses an action done *to* its subject.

ACTIVE Principal Ruiz **presented** the awards.

PASSIVE The awards **were presented** by Principal Ruiz.

EXERCISE A Above the underlined verb in each sentence, write *A* for *active voice* or *P* for *passive voice.*

Example 1. Six Nobel prizes are awarded each year. (P)

1. The Nobel Prize fund was established by Alfred Bernhard Nobel.
2. Various institutions function as prize awarders.
3. Winners are named in six categories: physics, chemistry, medicine, literature, peace, and economics.
4. The Royal Swedish Academy of Sciences awards the prizes in physics and chemistry.
5. Each award consists of a gold medal, a diploma, and money.
6. The first Nobel prizes were awarded on December 10, 1901.
7. Each year, the new winners give lectures as part of their awards ceremonies.
8. Prizes have been declined by various nominees, usually for political reasons.
9. During World Wars I and II, the prize committees couldn't gather information on nominees.
10. No Nobel prizes could be awarded during this time.

EXERCISE B Underline the verb in each sentence. Above it, write *A* for *active voice* or *P* for *passive voice.*

Example 1. Our calendar has been influenced by the early Roman calendar. (P)

11. The name *January* comes from the Roman month Januarius.
12. Janus was honored by Romans as the god of doors, gates, and new beginnings.
13. *June* is derived from the Roman month Junius.
14. Junius was named after Juno, the goddess of marriage.
15. People associate the month of May with the growth of springtime.
16. In Roman mythology, Maia reigned as the goddess of growth.
17. In Latin, *decem* means "ten."
18. The tenth month of the Roman calendar was called December.
19. *August* refers to Emperor Augustus, ruler of Rome from 27 B.C. to A.D. 14.
20. On the 15th of Februarius, a festival of purification was celebrated by Romans.

Sit and *Set*

The verb *sit* means "to be seated" or "to rest." *Sit* seldom takes an object. The verb *set* usually means "to place" or "to put (something somewhere)." *Set* usually takes an object. *Set* has the same form for the base form, past, and past participle.

EXAMPLES You cannot **sit** on that table. [no object]
I will **set** this figurine on the table. [*Figurine* is the object of *set*.]

EXERCISE A Underline the correct form of *sit* or *set* in the parentheses in each of the following sentences.

Example 1. I *(sit, set)* the treats on the counter so that the dog couldn't get to them.

1. Please *(sit, set)* your glass of water on a coaster.
2. Where will all our guests be *(sitting, setting)* for the meal?
3. *(Sit, Set)* on that chair and tell me if you think it's comfortable.
4. This longhaired cat leaves hairs wherever she *(sits, sets)*.
5. *(Sit, Set)* the groceries on the counter, please.
6. If more than two people *(sit, set)* on this old bench, it will break.
7. I am *(sitting, setting)* all the items for the garage sale on these tables.
8. Martina has always *(sat, set)* near the front of the bus.
9. With a grunt, Mel *(sat, set)* the heavy boxes on the floor.
10. On a cool evening, I *(sit, set)* in the backyard under the stars.

EXERCISE B Underline the form of *sit* or *set* in each of the following sentences. If the form is already correct, write *C* above it. If the form is not correct, write the correct form above it.

Example 1. At holiday meals, the teenagers always set together. *(sit)*

11. When our relatives arrived, they began sitting the food on the dining table.
12. I was setting quietly in a corner when I noticed my nephew Gordy.
13. His mother had sat him in a highchair near the dining table.
14. From his highchair he could reach the food that was sitting nearby.
15. He was sticking his fingers into a sweet-potato pie that set within his reach.
16. He then flung globs of pie filling into the dish of corn I had sat on the table earlier.
17. I went over to Gordy and set the pie out of reach.
18. If someone were setting beside him, maybe he would behave.
19. I sat in the nearest chair and then burst out laughing.
20. I had set on a chocolate cake that someone had carelessly left in the chair.

USAGE

Rise and *Raise*

The verb *rise* means "to move upward" or "to go up." *Rise* does not take an object. The verb *raise* means "to lift (something) up." *Raise* usually takes an object.

EXAMPLES Tina watched the hot-air balloon **rise** high into the sky. [no object]

She **raised** her hand in a gesture of farewell. [*Hand* is the object of *raised*.]

EXERCISE A Underline the correct form of *rise* or *raise* in each of the following sentences.

Example 1. The deer has *(raised, risen)* from its hiding place in the thicket.

1. April *(raised, rose)* from her seat and left the room.

2. In the back of the class, Tom *(raised, rose)* his hand to ask a question.

3. The crow flapped its wings and *(raised, rose)* above the treetops.

4. The sun *(raises, rises)* in the east.

5. Julie *(raised, rose)* to her feet when she saw the shooting star.

6. Leon *(rose, raised)* one objection to the game plan.

7. Grace and Becky slowly *(raised, rose)* the curtain.

8. On the first day of spring, I *(rise, raise)* all the windows.

9. The teenagers in the movie screamed as they watched a ghost *(rise, raise)* above them.

10. I *(rose, raised)* a white handkerchief to show that I surrendered.

EXERCISE B Underline the form of *rise* or *raise* in each of the following sentences. If the form is already correct, write *C* above it. If the form is not correct, write the correct form above it.

Example 1. My grandparents have raised (*risen*) early every morning of their lives.

11. Grain prices rose again last month.

12. Each morning when the sun raises, the farmer fills the water tank near the barn.

13. The water in the pond has raised to the top of its banks.

14. Our neighbors are rising crops of peanuts on their farm.

15. In winter the cows rise each morning to a meal of peanut hay.

16. In the barn, stacks of hay bales raise to the rafters.

17. As I gaze out into the pasture, I must raise my hand to block the sun from my eyes.

18. Rise the hood of the truck so that I can check the oil.

19. Even going slowly, the truck was rising a cloud of dust on the dirt road.

20. In the evening, sounds of the cows' moos raise in the distance.

USAGE

Lie and *Lay*

The verb *lie* generally means "to recline," "to be in a place," or "to remain lying down." *Lie* does not take an object. The verb *lay* generally means "to put (something) down" or "to place (something somewhere)." *Lay* usually takes an object.

EXAMPLES I will **lie** down for a nap now. [no object]
Will you **lay** the baby in his crib for a nap? [*Baby* is the object of *lay.*]

EXERCISE A Underline the correct form of *lie* or *lay* in each of the following sentences.

Example 1. In the summer Katy and Josh enjoy (*lying, laying*) in the sun.

1. First, they (*lie, lay*) large beach towels on chairs on the patio.
2. On a small table between the chairs are (*laying, lying*) magazines and books.
3. Katy and Josh (*lie, lay*) drowsily in the sun and talk for a while.
4. Later, they'll pick up one of the magazines that are (*lying, laying*) nearby.
5. Josh has (*lain, laid*) a bottle of sunblock on the floor within reach.
6. They are always careful to apply sunblock when they are (*lying, laying*) outside.
7. Thoughtfully, Katy (*lays, lies*) down a magazine that she had been reading.
8. As she (*lies, lays*) there, she wonders if spending so much time in the sun is an unhealthy habit.
9. The magazine says that a person who (*lies, lays*) in the sun too much can suffer from skin damage.
10. She (*lays, lies*) her hand across her eyes as she thinks about the information.

EXERCISE B Underline the form of *lie* or *lay* in each of the following sentences. If the form is already correct, write *C* above it. If the form is not correct, write the correct form above it.

laid
Example 1. I have lain the fabrics out for you.

11. You should probably lay down in the nurse's office.
12. That beautiful afghan is laying across the sofa.
13. Kendra laid the checkers on the checkerboard.
14. Sara is lying her head on her desk.
15. Brilliantly colored leaves were laying where they had fallen beneath the trees.
16. Ricky dug trenches and lay pipes for the sprinkler system.
17. Lie cold slices of cucumber on your closed eyelids for a refreshing treat.
18. Do you see that necklace that is laying in the gutter?
19. It must have lain there a long time, for it was nearly covered in mud.
20. Kelsey laid cozily in the recliner and read a new book.

USAGE

Six Troublesome Verbs

Three pairs of verbs that can be troublesome are *sit* and *set*, *rise* and *raise*, and *lie* and *lay*. The verb *sit* means "to be seated" or "to rest." *Set* means "to place" or "to put (something)." *Rise* means "to move upward" or "to go up." *Raise* means "to lift (something) up." *Lie* means "to recline," "to be in a place," or "to remain lying down." *Lay* means "to put (something) down" or "to place (something somewhere)."

EXAMPLES You **sit** and rest while I **set** the food out for lunch.
As the moon **rises,** I **raise** my eyes to gaze on it.
I will **lie** on this bench if I can **lay** a blanket there first.

EXERCISE A For each of the following sentences, underline the correct verb form in parentheses.

Example 1. The red paper was faded because it had (*lain*, *laid*) in the sun.

1. The rickety elevator was slowly (*rising, raising*) to the third floor.
2. Please (*sit, set*) up straight in your chair.
3. Rosa is (*lying, laying*) in her bed, dreaming about her future as an actor.
4. (*Lie, Lay*) the baby in his crib, Steve.
5. His expectations and goals have (*risen, raised*) with every success.
6. Chan has (*set, sat*) in that chair since noon, reading a book about dolphins.
7. Mr. Buckman's car has (*lain, laid*) in a ditch since the snowstorm last week.
8. (*Raise, Rise*) your voice so that I can hear you over all this noise.
9. Darcy (*sat, set*) the alarm clock on his desk.
10. The weary travelers (*lay, laid*) their heads on their pillows and fell asleep.

EXERCISE B The following paragraph contains five errors in verb usage. Cross out each error and write the correct verb above it.

Example 1. A jumble of equipment was ~~laying~~ *lying* at the edge of the playing field.

The audience raised to stand at attention while the flag was risen. Then everyone joined in the singing of the national anthem. When the crowd set down once again, the game began. The ball was sat at the forty-yard line for the kickoff. Soon, football players were laying in a tangled heap in the middle of the field. What an exciting game this was going to be!

Review A: Principal Parts of Verbs

EXERCISE A For each sentence below, write the present participle, past, or past participle of the regular verb given in parentheses.

Example 1. At the game yesterday I ___cheered___ until my voice was hoarse. *(cheer)*

1. Tia is ________________ for a chance to skate in the Olympic games. *(hope)*
2. The plane ________________ into the clouds and out of sight. *(soar)*
3. The town has ________________ the mayor's plan to build a homeless shelter. *(approve)*
4. Have you ________________ Lenny's snow fort? *(attack)*
5. I have ________________ my brother that I will read him a story. *(promise)*
6. The principal is ________________ the trophy in the case, where it will remain until the next competition. *(place)*
7. Babe Ruth, the famous baseball player, always ________________ to manage a baseball team. *(want)*
8. My little brother ________________ to believe in the tooth fairy. *(use)*
9. President Lyndon Johnson ________________ not to seek reelection in 1968. *(decide)*
10. Lola is ________________ me with my writing assignment. *(help)*

EXERCISE B For each sentence below, write the past or past participle of the irregular verb given in parentheses.

Example 1. These two tapestries have been ___chosen___ for display. *(choose)*

11. Alex Haley ________________ *Roots*, a book about his family history. *(write)*
12. The clever detective ________________ just where to look for the evidence. *(know)*
13. The children ________________ as they marched up and over the hill. *(sing)*
14. Mrs. Alvarez has ________________ to San Salvador to visit her granddaughter. *(go)*
15. Mom has ________________ many fruits and vegetables from the garden. *(freeze)*
16. The tennis coach ________________ Delbert his assistant. *(make)*
17. It's a terrible feeling to realize you have ________________ a family heirloom. *(break)*
18. We ________________ a murder-mystery play in which the audience helped to solve the crime. *(see)*
19. The police officer ________________ to question all the witnesses to the accident. *(begin)*
20. I can't remember to whom I ________________ my notebook. *(lend)*

Review B: **Principal Parts of Verbs**

EXERCISE A For each sentence below, write the present participle, past, or past participle of the regular verb given in parentheses.

Example 1. The hiker ___marked___ his trail as he went along. *(mark)*

1. The children _______________ their hair and brushed their teeth before they left for school. *(comb)*
2. Many of the tomato plants in our garden have _______________ because of an early frost. *(die)*
3. I am _______________ for a book about the American Revolution. *(look)*
4. Yoko _______________ she was ready for the big race. *(suppose)*
5. More than one hundred years ago, the people of the United States _______________ Ulysses S. Grant president. *(elect)*
6. Cletha has _______________ that she will make a model of the Alamo. *(decide)*
7. A petting zoo _______________ to be where that high-rise apartment building is. *(use)*
8. You have _______________ just in time to join us for dinner. *(arrive)*
9. Carl is _______________ out exactly how many days he has been alive. *(figure)*
10. Do you know who _______________ the *arroz con pollo*? *(cook)*

EXERCISE B For each of the following sentences, write the past or past participle of the irregular verb given in parentheses.

Example 1. Joanna has ___sung___ that song many times. *(sing)*

11. I have _______________ my team jacket. *(lose)*
12. My favorite pair of jeans _______________ in the wash. *(shrink)*
13. Martin _______________ that lifting that heavy carton alone would hurt his back. *(know)*
14. Tanya has _______________ so well in math this year that she has been placed in an advanced class for next year. *(do)*
15. The pitcher _______________ the ball barehanded. *(catch)*
16. My parents have _______________ us how to handle money responsibly. *(show)*
17. Kevin had _______________ five glasses of water during lunch. *(drink)*
18. The main character has not _______________ his brother for seven years. *(see)*
19. We had _______________ across the lake and back before Kelly arrived. *(swim)*
20. The rancher has _______________ out to find his lost cattle. *(ride)*

Review C: Tense

EXERCISE A Underline the verb in each of the following sentences. Then, identify its tense by writing above it *Pres* for *present*, *Past* for *past*, or *Fut* for *future*.

Example 1. Philippa joined (Past) the choir a month ago.

1. The chorus will sing a medley of Stevie Wonder's hits.
2. Many singers participated in last year's concert.
3. Ms. Das leads the chorus as well as the orchestra.
4. Mika will play a trumpet solo in tonight's concert.
5. She practiced for the performance all weekend.
6. Lionel accidentally dropped the cymbals.
7. There will be photographs of the performance available for sale.
8. The soloist sang with a strong, clear voice.
9. The principal knows the names of all the students in the choir.
10. We sold a ticket for every seat available.

EXERCISE B For each of the following sentences, write the form of the verb described in parentheses. Write the verb form in the space provided.

Example 1. I have been submitting my poetry to several contests. (present perfect progressive tense of *submit*)

11. By the time the reporters arrive, the author ____________________ her speech. (future perfect tense of *give*)
12. The editor of these books ____________________ one of them as her favorite. (past tense of *choose*)
13. Carlos ____________________ to write stories like a master storyteller. (present progressive tense of *begin*)
14. We ____________________ what happened when that book became a bestseller. (past perfect tense of *see*)
15. Tula ____________________ about this literary topic many times. (present perfect tense of *speak*)

Review D: Active and Passive Voice; Six Troublesome Verbs

EXERCISE A Above the underlined verb in each sentence, write *A* for *active voice* or *P* for *passive voice.*

Example 1. Last summer I sold vegetables at a farmer's market. (A)

1. The farmer's market holds a cooking contest each June.
2. Numerous cookies and casseroles are sampled by the judges.
3. Fruit punch, lemonade, and fruit smoothies are made by contestants.
4. Votes are cast for the tastiest items.
5. People buy ingredients to make the dishes they like the most.
6. I have frozen bags of corn and berries in my freezer at home.
7. One day I was given a slice of homemade berry tart by one of the vendors.
8. The next day I asked him for his recipe.
9. That weekend I secretly made a delicious dessert for my family.
10. "A prize should be awarded to whoever baked this!" exclaimed my father.

EXERCISE B For each of the sentences below, underline the correct verb in parentheses.

Example 1. After shopping all day, I had to (*sit, set*) with my feet up.

11. Whose bicycle is (*laying, lying*) in the driveway?
12. My parents are thrilled because all my grades have (*raised, risen*) this term.
13. The meat has been (*sitting, setting*) on the counter all day and is probably spoiled.
14. If you have any questions after the speech, please (*rise, raise*) your hand.
15. The artist had (*sat, set*) his paintings on the sidewalk for passersby to admire.
16. The colorful balloons (*raised, rose*) high up into the sky and disappeared.
17. We (*sat, set*) and waited all day for the package to arrive, but it never did.
18. (*Lie, Lay*) your clothes out the night before, and you will have a head start in the morning.
19. Mother is (*setting, sitting*) the bouquet of flowers on the table.
20. During last night's thunder storm, Lisa (*layed, lay*) on the couch and read a mystery novel by Ellis Peters.

Proofreading Application: Letter

Good writers are generally good proofreaders. Readers tend to admire and trust writing that is error-free. Make sure that you correct all errors in grammar, usage, spelling, and punctuation in your writing. Your readers will have more confidence in your words if you have done your best to proofread carefully.

People commonly make errors forming the past tense of verbs. Because most verbs are regular and form the past tense by adding *–ed* to the base form, it is easy to mistakenly apply that same rule to irregular verbs. The result is a usage error that can make a bad impression on a reader. The reader may think that the writer doesn't care enough to use the correct form or doesn't know what that form is.

In business letters and personal letters—especially letters to adults—be sure to use past-tense verbs correctly. Your reader will appreciate the effort you made to proofread your work and will think better of you for having made that effort.

PROOFREADING ACTIVITY

In the following letter, find and correct the errors in the use of past-tense verbs. Use proofreading symbols such as those on page 809 of *Elements of Language* to make your corrections.

Dear Uncle David,

I heared that you have the chickenpox. I had the chickenpox once. It was awful! I itched all over. Everyone telled me, "Don't scratch!"

I had a busy week in school. In science, Mrs. Robertson teached us about photosynthesis. We learned that plants make their own food. In language arts, we readed "The Tell-Tale Heart" by Edgar Allan Poe. It was very scary! In social studies, we seed a filmstrip about Brazil. Afterward, we drawed a map of South America.

I bought you some books at the bookstore. If you like, I would be happy to bring them by your house. I remember how you lended me some books last year when I breaked my leg and was in the hospital. With your help, I also catched up on my schoolwork. I even maked better grades that semester!

Get well soon!

Sincerely,

Ben

NAME ______________________ CLASS ______________ DATE ______________

for **CHAPTER 18: USING VERBS CORRECTLY** *pages 485–503*

Literary Model: Verb Tense

EXERCISE A By looking carefully at the verbs in Silverstein's poem, you can gather clues about when certain events occurred.

Jimmy Jet and His TV Set

by Shel Silverstein

I'll tell you the story of Jimmy Jet—
And you know what I tell you is true.
He loved to watch his TV set
Almost as much as you.

He watched all day, he watched all night
Till he grew pale and lean,
From *The Early Show* to *The Late Late Show*
And all the shows between.

He watched till his eyes were frozen wide,
And his bottom grew into his chair.
And his chin turned into a tuning dial,
And antennae grew out of his hair.

And his brains turned into TV tubes,
And his face to a TV screen.
And two knobs saying "VERT." and "HORIZ."
Grew where his ears had been.

And he grew a plug that looked like a tail
So we plugged in little Jim.
And now instead of him watching TV
We all sit around and watch him.

1. In the first stanza, identify one future tense verb and one past tense verb. Explain briefly why these two verbs have different tenses. (*Hint:* Remember that a contraction can include a verb.)

____

____

____

____

2. Re-read the second and third stanzas, paying special attention to the verbs. What is the tense of all the verbs in these two stanzas? Why do you think all the verbs in the second and third stanzas are in the same tense?

____

____

____

3. Identify the past perfect verb in the fourth stanza. Why is this verb in the past perfect tense, while all other verbs in the stanza are in the past tense?

____

____

EXERCISE B

1. In the poem's last stanza, identify one past tense verb and one present tense verb. Then, explain why these two verbs have different tenses.

____

____

Literary Model (continued)

2. In this final stanza, Shel Silverstein switches tenses in a clear and effective way. Are there any words in the last sentence that clue you in to the shift from past to present? Explain.

EXERCISE C Now it's your turn to tell a story. Write a story about an unusual or extraordinary event that either really happened to you or that you invent. You can write a poem or use regular paragraphs, but your story must include two tenses. Feel free to imitate the use of verb tense in "Jimmy Jet and His TV Set": Events that happened in the past influenced events that are happening now.

EXERCISE D Read over your story, paying special attention to the times when you switch from one tense to another. Do all of your tense shifts make sense? For example, you should not shift to the present tense while you are describing an event from the past. If any of your tense switches seem confusing or unclear, revise your sentences.

Writing Application: Narrative

One sure way to energize your writing is to avoid the passive voice and to use the active voice whenever possible. Lively active verbs can sweep readers along with your plot or argument, while ordinary passive verbs may lull them into a state of drowsiness. When you can, change the passive voice to the active voice.

PASSIVE VOICE The horses **were ridden** to the top of the cliff by the men in chaps and spurs. The train robbers **were being** relentlessly **chased** throughout the county.

ACTIVE VOICE Clad in chaps and spurs, the men **urged** the horses to the top of the cliff. Throughout the county, riders relentlessly **pursued** the train robbers.

Writing Activity

"Action!" yells the director as the cameras roll. Have you ever heard of a passive movie? That's doubtful, since *action* movies are blockbusters year after year. Many moviegoers want a plot that keeps them on the edge of their seats with thrills, chills, and spills. Readers often want the same effect, and writers can supply it by choosing colorful verbs and writing in the active voice. Try this experiment. Choose your favorite scene from an action movie. Narrate the action of this scene entirely in the passive voice, as in the first example above. Then, narrate the scene again, changing each use of the passive voice to the active voice and replacing any weak verbs with vivid, action-packed verbs.

PREWRITING You might try to rely solely on your memory as you jot down the scene you have chosen to narrate. However, memory can be spotty, even if you've seen the movie recently. View the scene in question again, several times if possible, writing down everything you see each time you watch it. You will probably catch something new on each viewing, increasing your appreciation of the movie.

WRITING Although the passive voice may creep into your writing now and then, you may find it challenging to use it in every sentence of your narrative. Use prepositional phrases with *by* and *through* to include the doers of the action, and be careful not to write run-ons, since passive voice can get a bit bulky. As you write your second narrative, in the active voice, change each of the passive constructions into active constructions.

REVISING Now that the narrative is in the active voice, read through it again, this time replacing any weak verbs with the snappiest verbs you can imagine (notice in the examples how *were ridden* becomes not *rode* but *urged*, a much more interesting and colorful verb). Consider replacing *be* verbs in particular, moving from state-of-being verbs to action verbs.

PUBLISHING Check both narratives for errors in grammar, usage, spelling, and punctuation. Watch especially for irregular past participle forms when you use the passive voice. Then, take both narratives to class, and read them aloud. After your classmates have read their narratives, discuss how the passive voice and the active voice affect readers differently. How does the use of the active voice affect the pace, directness, and liveliness of the narratives?

Extending Your Writing

This exercise could lead to a more developed writing project. As a research project, examine action movies. Why are people so drawn to action movies, even though they are not realistic? Interview people you know who are action-movie buffs, and do a little research on the Web. Then, present your ideas in an essay.

Choices: Using Pronouns Correctly

Here's your chance to step out of the grammar book and into the real world. You may not notice pronouns, but you and the people around you use them every day. The following activities challenge you to find a connection between pronoun usage and the world around you. Do the activity below that suits your personality best, and then share your discoveries with your class. Have fun!

BUILDING BACKGROUND KNOWLEDGE

Pronoun Puzzler

Use a history book to research a well-known historical figure. Then, write four sentences that each contain the figure's name and an important fact about his or her contribution to history. In at least two of the sentences, try to use the figure's name as a direct or an indirect object. Then, remove the name of the historical figure from each sentence, and replace the name with an appropriate personal pronoun. Then, give your sentences to a classmate. Challenge him or her to identify the case of the pronouns you used and to figure out the name of your historical figure.

CONTEST

On Your Mark

The pronoun has many uses. For example, you can use a pronoun as a subject or as a predicate nominative. You can also use a pronoun as an object of a preposition, an indirect object, or a direct object. Write this list of pronoun uses on the board. Then, hold a contest. Put the class in groups. The first group to write a correct sentence for each of the pronoun uses listed on the board wins. You are in charge of the prize. Make it a good one!

HISTORY

Junkyard Blues

Whatever happened to those old-fashioned pronouns *thee* and *thou*? They wound up in the junkyard of English. Sometimes, good stuff can be found at a junkyard. You could make a poster titled "Junkyard of English." On it, write (or paste in fancy fonts) words and expressions that are no longer used. (Hint: To find archaic or obsolete expressions, look through literary works from other centuries.) Don't limit yourself to pronouns. If your teacher gives you permission, hang your poster in the classroom.

STUDY AIDS

Persistence of Memory

Invent a mnemonic device, or memory aid, to help your classmates remember which pronouns are nominative case and which ones are objective case. You could write and teach a rap or song, design and produce a sticker, or compose and teach a rhyme or sentence.

REAL LIFE

The Wall of Shame?

As a group project, make a bulletin board on which you and your peers can place newspaper clippings or magazine articles that contain errors in pronoun usage. Each clipping or article should be mounted on a sheet of paper with a written explanation of the error.

ART

Reflex Action

When a reflexive pronoun is used as a direct object, it directs the action of the verb back to its subject. For example, in the sentence "He hit himself," the reflexive pronoun is used as a direct object. Write three sentences that have reflexive pronouns as direct objects. Then, create a humorous drawing for each sentence to illustrate this ability of reflexive pronouns to direct the action back to a subject.

WRITING

Who's Telling This Story?

When telling a story, a writer typically uses one of two points of view: first person or third person. Use your textbook or a dictionary to research the meaning of each of these points of view. Then, write two versions of a simple story. Each version of your story should describe the action from a different point of view, either first person or third person. Highlight the personal pronouns you use in each version.

USAGE

Case

19a. ***Case*** is the form that a noun or pronoun takes to show its relationship to other words in a sentence.

English has three cases for nouns and pronouns: ***nominative, objective,*** and ***possessive.*** The form of a noun is the same for both the nominative and the objective cases. A noun changes its form only in the possessive case, usually by adding an apostrophe and an *s*. Most personal pronouns have different forms for all three cases.

NOMINATIVE CASE	The **house** is white.	**We** are happy.
OBJECTIVE CASE	We bought the **house.**	The joke made **us** laugh.
POSSESSIVE CASE	The **house's** color is white.	**Our** laughter was loud.

EXERCISE A Identify the case of the underlined noun or pronoun in each sentence by underlining the correct option in parentheses.

Example 1. This book's accounts of inventions are interesting. (*objective* or *possessive*)

1. Yesterday I read about James C. Boyle. (*nominative* or *objective*)

2. He was a little-known inventor. (*nominative* or *objective*)

3. He invented a hat tipper in the 1890s. (*nominative* or *objective*)

4. This invention tipped a man's hat for him. (*objective* or *possessive*)

5. When Boyle greeted a woman, he would tip his hat to her. (*nominative* or *objective*)

6. A woman of that time expected this of him. (*nominative* or *objective*)

7. The hat tipper tipped Boyle's hat as he approached her. (*nominative* or *possessive*)

8. To make the tipper work, he just nodded his head slightly. (*nominative* or *objective*)

9. The patent office gave him a patent for the invention. (*nominative* or *objective*)

10. However, the invention never made him famous. (*nominative* or *objective*)

EXERCISE B Each of the following sentences needs a noun or a pronoun. The case of the needed noun or pronoun is specified in parentheses. Write your answers on the blanks provided.

Example 1. (*possessive pronoun*) Satya and Darryl have finished ___their___ homework.

11. (*possessive noun*) The ____________ large surface is covered with books and papers.

12. (*objective pronoun*) The two of ____________ have studied all afternoon.

13. (*possessive pronoun*) Satya is ____________ twin sister.

14. (*objective pronoun*) I was kind and prepared a snack for ____________ and Darryl.

15. (*possessive pronoun*) The movie was boring: ____________ plot was predictable.

The Case Forms of Personal Pronouns

19a. ***Case*** is the form that a noun or pronoun takes to show its relationship to other words in a sentence.

English has three cases for pronouns: *nominative, objective,* and *possessive.*

NOMINATIVE CASE I, you, he, she, it, we, they
OBJECTIVE CASE me, you, him, her, it, us, them
POSSESSIVE CASE my, mine, your, yours, his, her, hers, its, our, ours, their, theirs

EXERCISE A Underline the personal pronoun in each sentence. Above the pronoun, identify its case by writing *N* for *nominative, O* for *objective,* or *P* for *possessive.*

Example 1. This year we will do the holiday shopping early. (N)

1. Katie hit it out of the park.
2. We have saved money and made lists.
3. Mom has asked for a day off from her job to go shopping.
4. The family will go to the mall in our minivan.
5. It will be full of purchases by the end of the day.

EXERCISE B Each of the following sentences needs a personal pronoun. The case of the needed pronoun is specified in parentheses. Write an appropriate personal pronoun on each of the blanks provided.

Example 1. *(possessive)* Since you spilled your soup, I will give you mine.

6. *(objective)* I accidentally bumped into ____________ in the hallway.
7. *(nominative)* ____________ and I will be there soon.
8. *(possessive)* Here is yours, but where is ____________?
9. *(objective)* The wooden stair creaked when I stepped on ____________.
10. *(possessive)* That wire sculpture was ____________ project for art class.
11. *(nominative)* Nora and ____________ performed the experiment carefully.
12. *(objective)* A snake! Don't step on ____________.
13. *(possessive)* The neighbor's dog somehow got into ____________ yard.
14. *(nominative)* Are ____________ going sailing this weekend?
15. *(objective)* I blamed ____________ for ruining the evening.

USAGE

The Nominative Case A

The *nominative case* forms of personal pronouns are *I, you, he, she, it, we,* and *they.*

19b. The ***subject*** of a verb should be in the nominative case.

19c. A ***predicate nominative*** should be in the nominative case.

SUBJECTS	**We** locked the door.
	You and **they** can ride in the blue van.
PREDICATE NOMINATIVES	The last person to board the airplane was **he.**
	Our best friends in the first grade were **he** and **she.**

EXERCISE A Underline the correct form of the pronoun or pronouns in parentheses in each sentence.

Example 1. After school *(him and me, he and I)* went to the store.

1. You and *(her, she)* need to discuss the rules.
2. Amy and *(I, me)* climbed into the airplane's cockpit.
3. Yesterday *(us, we)* began reading *Nisei Daughter* for our book club.
4. Find out if the mystery man is really *(he, him).*
5. Peter and *(them, they)* are practicing skateboard tricks.
6. The membership committee will be César, Akela, and *(me, I).*
7. At what time did *(her and me, she and I)* promise to be home?
8. The students are *(them, they).*
9. *(We and they, Us and them)* will compete at the state finals.
10. The speaker from the local college is *(she, her).*

EXERCISE B Write a pronoun that can correctly replace the underlined word or words in each of the following sentences. Write your answers above the underlined words.

they

Example 1. Yesterday Terrence and Liz studied fossils at the museum.

11. Yes, the pine and the cedar are the trees to prune.
12. The man with the bulldog puppy is Max.
13. Kyron and Sherry learned to speak Spanish as children.
14. The class's most colorful dressers are Ming and David.
15. Despite her promises, Terra did not arrive on time.

USAGE

The Nominative Case B

The *nominative case* forms of personal pronouns are *I, you, he, she, it, we,* and *they.*

19b. The ***subject*** of a verb should be in the nominative case.

19c. A ***predicate nominative*** should be in the nominative case.

SUBJECTS **He** read *The Sign of the Chrysanthemum.*

We and **they** should play on the same team.

PREDICATE NOMINATIVES The man in the mask was **he.**

The best candidates for the award were **he** and **she.**

EXERCISE A Write a pronoun that can correctly replace the underlined word or words in each sentence. Write your answers above the underlined words.

Example 1. Bruce and Maria will marry in September. *she*

1. Crystal and the other sky divers checked the time.

2. The best people for the job are Kelly and Rico.

3. The dog and the cats are an important part of our family.

4. The players to watch this season are Bobbie and Cathy.

5. In the dark Joseph knocked the alarm clock off the table.

6. The Andersons and the Morgans will get to the campsite first.

7. These stray cats are not healthy, nor are these stray cats friendly.

8. Tiffany said, "Kat and Tiffany will be at her house."

9. Are you and Nilda and Rogelio taking your grandparents to dinner?

10. Cleon and Loretta and I will be the only solo singers.

EXERCISE B Read each sentence and decide whether the underlined personal pronoun is correct. If it is correct, write *C* above it. If the personal pronoun is incorrect, write the correct form above it.

Example 1. Violet and them went to the movies. *they*

11. Kelly and him started sharing a locker.

12. Dustin shouted, "Montel and I are going to win this game!"

13. I finally realized my secret pen pal was her.

14. What did you and Todd bring to the international food fair?

15. The drama instructor and me performed a one-act play for the class.

The Objective Case A

The *objective case* forms of personal pronouns are *me, you, him, her, it, us,* and *them.*

19d. ***Direct objects*** and ***indirect objects*** of verbs should be in the objective case.

USAGE

A *direct object* tells *who* or *what* receives the action of the verb. In a sentence containing an indirect object, the indirect object usually comes between an action verb and its direct object. An *indirect object* tells *to whom* or *to what* or *for whom* or *for what* the action is done.

DIRECT OBJECT The sea gull attacked **me.**

INDIRECT OBJECT The catcher gave **him** a signal.

19e. The ***object of a preposition*** should be in the objective case.

A noun or pronoun that follows a preposition is called the object of the preposition.

OBJECT OF A PREPOSITION Mario is standing between **him** and **her.**

EXERCISE A Read each of the following sentences, and identify the underlined pronoun as a direct object *(DO)*, an indirect object *(IO)*, or an object of a preposition *(OP)*.

Example 1. Don't give Darla and *IO* me any excuses!

1. The magician gave her the blindfold.

2. Toshiro photographed me in front of the state capitol.

3. With a smile, Coach handed us the first-place trophies.

4. The dog ran right by them.

5. Behind Dr. Haddad and her stood the new patient.

6. There should never be secrets between you and me.

7. "Show me your school ID," said the ticket taker at the football game.

8. I can't believe I tripped over it!

9. Give them to me, please.

10. The cafeteria serves us a different main dish each day of the week.

EXERCISE B Replace the underlined word or words in each sentence with a correct objective case pronoun. Write the pronouns above the underlined word or words.

Example 1. The circus clowns amused *them* the fans.

11. The talented gymnast performed the routine flawlessly.

12. Ice-skating is important to Deanna.

13. May I have the grapes?

14. Give Robert the shopping list.

15. At the graduation ceremony, Sue will sit between Malik and Shaun.

NAME CLASS DATE

The Objective Case B

The *objective case* forms of personal pronouns are *me, you, him, her, it, us,* and *them.*

19d. ***Direct objects*** and ***indirect objects*** of verbs should be in the objective case.

A *direct object* tells *who* or *what* receives the action of the verb. In a sentence containing an indirect object, the indirect object usually comes between an action verb and its direct object. An *indirect object* tells *to whom* or *to what* or *for whom* or *for what* the action of the verb is done.

DIRECT OBJECT Ying placed **it** in the lost and found.

INDIRECT OBJECT Archimedes gave **her** his latest invention.

USAGE

EXERCISE A Write a pronoun that can correctly replace the underlined word or words in each sentence. Write the pronoun above the underlined word or words.

Example 1. The tiger looked straight at Vince and Bertha. *her*

1. Uncle Hugo explained the fable to Doyle and me.
2. The train thundered past Justin and Clara.
3. A nurse quickly handed Emily the scissors.
4. "Just stack the books on the counter," said the librarian.
5. Photograph Aunt Shirley and me with your new camera.

EXERCISE B Use the specified verb and the object or objects in each of the following items to write an original sentence. Write your sentences on the lines provided.

Example 1. verb: throw indirect object: him direct object: towel

The basketball player threw him a sweaty towel.

6. verb: meet direct object: them

7. verb: see direct object: them

8. verb: tell indirect object: her direct object: answer

9. verb: pour direct object: it

10. verb: build direct object: fence object of a preposition: it

Nominative and Objective Case Pronouns A

19b. The ***subject*** of a verb should be in the nominative case.

19c. A ***predicate nominative*** should be in the nominative case.

19d. ***Direct objects*** and ***indirect objects*** of verbs should be in the objective case.

19e. The ***object of a preposition*** should be in the objective case.

USAGE

EXERCISE Underline the pronoun in each of the following sentences, and identify it by writing above it *S* for *subject, PN* for *predicate nominative, DO* for *direct object, IO* for *indirect object,* or *OP* for *object of a preposition.*

Example 1. Raphael tossed her (IO) the backpack.

1. The special effects impressed me.
2. The spies could possibly be they.
3. Mother and we posed for a family portrait.
4. Una borrowed the tools from the Lincolns and us.
5. Did the manager offer him a part-time job?
6. The fake ghost gave them a fright.
7. Tameka and I baby-sit the Clark children.
8. Did Carol tell you the news about the new soccer coach?
9. The class valedictorian is he.
10. She and Joey went to the library.
11. Trey doesn't believe it.
12. Give at least one clue to her.
13. The dog brought us a bone.
14. Nikota and you arrived early today.
15. Lisa and I sang the final duet.
16. The diving instructor told Sheila and him another way to work on breathing techniques.
17. They did not believe that light travels at 186,000 miles per second.
18. The bus driver turned on the radio for us.
19. Carla gave him a note after class.
20. The pouring rain drenched them to the bone.

NAME ____________________ CLASS ____________ DATE ____________

for **CHAPTER 19: USING PRONOUNS CORRECTLY** *pages 513–19*

Nominative and Objective Case Pronouns B

19b. The ***subject*** of a verb should be in the nominative case.

19c. A ***predicate nominative*** should be in the nominative case.

19d. ***Direct objects*** and ***indirect objects*** of verbs should be in the objective case.

19e. The ***object of a preposition*** should be in the objective case.

EXERCISE Decide whether the form of the underlined pronoun in each of the following sentences is correct. If it is correct, write *C* above it. If the pronoun form is incorrect, write the correct form above it.

she

Example 1. Jeremy and her tended to the horses.

1. The mayor gave us an award.
2. The most exciting match featured Tipley and he.
3. In June, you and him should go to San Juan.
4. Now the person without a partner is me.
5. The postal worker delivered a package for Harry and she.
6. My grandfather and her operated a small inn in Vermont.
7. The coach praised Manuel and he.
8. No one gave Mu Lan or I the message.
9. I felt certain that the man in the superhero costume was he.
10. The crowd cheered when the principal gave Stacy and she the trophies.
11. We've been waiting for you and him for half an hour.
12. Eddie gave the strawberries to she and Michael.
13. You must tell your dad or me if you will be out late.
14. This problem involves her and I.
15. The children and they had a great time.
16. The coach gave them an inspiring speech before the game.
17. Felicia spoke to Freddie and he.
18. The one who took the early flight was he.
19. Him and she engaged in a spirited debate.
20. Anton and they arrived late.

USAGE

Who and *Whom*

The pronoun *who* has different forms in the nominative and objective cases. *Who* is the nominative form. *Whom* is the objective form. When you are choosing between *who* or *whom* in a question, follow these steps: **(1)** Rephrase the question as a statement. **(2)** Decide how the pronoun is being used. **(3)** Determine the case of the pronoun. **(4)** Select the correct pronoun form.

EXAMPLE *(Who, Whom)* shall I invite?

Step 1 I shall invite *(who, whom).*

Step 2 The pronoun is the direct object of *invite.*

Step 3 A pronoun that is a direct object is in the objective case.

Answer **Whom** shall I invite?

EXERCISE A Underline the correct pronoun in each of the following sentences.

Example **1.** *(Who, Whom)* is calling?

1. *(Who, Whom)* did you beat in the first race?

2. To *(who, whom)* shall I send the application?

3. *(Who, Whom)* called so early this morning?

4. With *(who, whom)* did you go to the fiesta?

5. *(Who, Whom)* was the actor in the mask?

6. *(Who, Whom)* did Kathy describe the play to yesterday?

7. After dinner, *(who, whom)* will wash the dishes?

8. *(Who, Whom)* did Trevor imitate?

9. *(Who, Whom)* seemed to be the fastest runner?

10. For *(who, whom)* did you make that card?

EXERCISE B Decide whether the form of *who* or *whom* in each sentence is correct. If it is correct, write *C* above it. If it is not correct, cross it out and write the correct form above it.

Example **1.** ~~Who~~ *Whom* are you talking about, Lynn?

11. Who knows what instrument Van Cliburn plays?

12. For who was this library named?

13. Now, whom recorded the song originally?

14. With whom will you sit at the game?

15. To who shall I address this letter?

USAGE

Appositives and Reflexive Pronouns

Sometimes a pronoun is followed directly by a noun that identifies the pronoun. Such a noun is called an ***appositive*** To choose which pronoun to use before an appositive, try each form of the pronoun without the appositive.

EXAMPLE The crowd cheered *(we, us)* rodeo clowns.
(The crowd cheered we.)
(The crowd cheered us.)

CORRECT FORM The crowd cheered **us** rodeo clowns.

The ***reflexive pronouns****himself* and *themselves* can be used as objects. Do not use the nonstandard forms *hisself* and *theirselfs* or *theirselves* in place of *himself* and *themselves.*

EXAMPLE Ron saw **himself** reflected in the huge window. [not *hisself*]

EXERCISE A Underline the correct form of the pronoun in parentheses in each of the following sentences.

Example 1. They couldn't help *(theirselfs, themselves).*

1. *(We, Us)* athletes watch our diets.
2. Mr. Red Cloud told *(we, us)* Eagle Scouts how to use the Heimlich maneuver.
3. The owner always gives *(we, us)* clerks overtime pay on Saturdays.
4. The present treasurer took *(hisself, himself)* out of the election.
5. Before the next show, *(we, us)* stagehands should get better props.
6. *(We, Us)* skaters carried the flag.
7. Ian described *(himself, hisself)* as patient and dependable.
8. For the past three years, one of *(us, we)* Monteros has won first place in the county spelling bee.
9. The chaperones talked among *(theirselves, themselves)* most of the evening.
10. Maybe Kale will ask *(we, us)* photographers to judge the show.

EXERCISE B Each of the following sentences contains a pronoun error. Cross out each incorrect pronoun, and write the correct form above it.

Example 1. The winners earned ~~theirself a~~ *themselves* trophy.

11. The boys made dinner theirselves.
12. Us computer types enjoy this game.
13. Us seventh graders raised the most money.
14. Did you see Reed put hisself in front of the goal?
15. Danielle read the letter to we girls.

Special Pronoun Problems

USAGE

The pronoun *who* has different forms in the nominative and objective cases. ***Who*** is the nominative form. ***Whom*** is the objective form.

EXAMPLE In the Study Buddy program, **who** will help **whom** with math?

Sometimes a pronoun is followed by an ***appositive.*** To choose which pronoun to use before an appositive, try each form of the pronoun without the appositive.

EXAMPLE **We** [not *Us*] seventh graders have the most school spirit.

The ***reflexive pronouns*** *himself* and *themselves* can be used as objects. Do not use the nonstandard forms *hisself* and *theirselfs* or *theirselves* in place of *himself* and *themselves.*

EXAMPLE The swimmers could have hurt **themselves** [not *theirselves*] on those rocks.

EXERCISE A Underline the correct pronoun in parentheses in each of the following sentences.

Example 1. New uniforms will be given to *(we, us)* volleyball players.

1. Between games the volleyball players went to the sidelines and helped *(themselves, theirselves)* to water.
2. *(We, Us)* soccer players have parents in the stands.
3. After the game, *(who, whom)* will take you home?
4. To *(who, whom)* should I serve the ball?
5. The photographer blamed *(himself, hisself)* for the poor quality of the team photos.
6. The Blue Bees congratulated *(theirselfs, themselves)* for winning the first game.
7. Despite our loss, *(we, us)* Fighting Falcons remained positive.
8. *(Whom, Who)* would be our best player in this game?
9. Lucy, a great spiker, led the rest of *(we, us)* players to a victory in the second game.
10. The Blue Bees guaranteed *(themselves, theirselves)* a loss when they got too confident.

EXERCISE B Each of the following sentences contains an error in the use of pronouns. Cross out each incorrect pronoun, and write the correct form above it.

Example 1. She congratulated ~~we~~ *us* students on a job well done.

11. I don't know whom their coach is.
12. A coach should pride herself or hisself on the good spirit of the players.
13. During the tie-breaking game us setters worked extra hard.
14. In every play I asked myself, "Whom should spike the ball?"
15. Who were the players that set theirselves up for victory?

Review A: Nominative Case

EXERCISE A Identify the underlined pronoun in each of the following sentences by writing *S* for *subject* or *PN* for *predicate nominative* above the pronoun.

Example 1. I was shocked to learn that my secret admirer is you. PN

1. Harry and I both liked the movie.
2. After lunch, perhaps Klaus and she will help us paint the kitchen.
3. The two finalists were Fatima and I.
4. The only people to speak were they.
5. Without warning, he jumped up and pointed to the witness.
6. Then she showed me how the computer worked.
7. The only judges were Mrs. Okana and he.
8. Susana and we may be late.
9. The two finalists could be Elmore and I.
10. At the curtain call, they took another bow.

EXERCISE B In each of the following sentences, underline the correct pronoun in parentheses.

Example 1. The person who helped me research is *(her, she).*

11. This month, my classmates and *(I, me)* are supposed to write reports about Massachusetts.
12. Yesterday *(me, I)* read about the Molasses Flood of 1919.
13. The man in the clown costume was *(him, he).*
14. Charles and *(them, they)* rented canoes.
15. *(Them, They)* are the tastiest treats I have ever eaten!
16. The person on the skateboard is *(he, him).*
17. Before long, Matt and *(she, her)* had found the lost mine.
18. After the bell had sounded, Julia and *(us, we)* went home.
19. The top students were Erica and *(he, him).*
20. I thought that *(he, him)* would like to borrow my bike.

Review B: **Objective Case**

EXERCISE A Identify the underlined pronoun in each of the following sentences by writing *DO* for *direct object*, *IO* for *indirect object*, or *OP* for *object of a preposition* above the pronoun.

Example 1. Please give my best wishes to her. *(OP)*

1. The sky above him was full of clouds.
2. The gate banged against her when it closed.
3. Please pass me the atlas.
4. Melba told us something about her day at the Bluegrass Music Festival.
5. Did they give Eliot or him a surprise party?
6. A sudden storm took me by surprise.
7. The visitor saw a signal pass between the king and him.
8. The paramedic showed us a way to save someone from choking.
9. My uncle always gives my cousin and her newspaper clippings.
10. Unfortunately, the bus left without him.

EXERCISE B Read each of the following sentences, and decide whether the underlined pronoun is correct. If it is correct, write *C* above it. If the pronoun is incorrect, write the correct form above it.

Example 1. Nathan lent some paper to Ruth and I. *(me)*

11. Suzi gave thoughtful presents to Lannie and him.
12. Jenna slowly walked toward Howard and me.
13. The glowing embers of the fire warmed Rosa and she.
14. Josie's mother gave her and him a ride home from the store.
15. The speaker complimented Gary and I on our attentiveness.
16. The students read captivating stories about he and his adventures.
17. Take good care of him.
18. Clara took Todd and he to see Shakespeare's play *Othello.*
19. The one who made the generous donation was her.
20. In a flash, the skateboarder zoomed past him and she.

Review C: Special Pronoun Problems

EXERCISE A Each of the following sentences has a pronoun error. Cross out each incorrect pronoun, and write the correct pronoun above it.

Example 1. The new bike racks outside our school pleased ~~we~~ *us* bikers.

1. The gymnast first tried the new parallel bars hisself.
2. She showed we students how a diamond is cut.
3. Us left-handed people have trouble using most scissors.
4. The mayor congratulated we lifeguards for saving the child.
5. Finally, the detectives asked theirselfs the right question.
6. As he worked, Octavio talked to hisself.
7. The Mustangs lost to we Tornadoes.
8. Now us hikers have our own club.
9. The bears helped theirselves to the campers' food.
10. Us dancers practice two hours every day.

EXERCISE B Decide whether the form of *who* or *whom* in each sentence is correct. If it is correct, write *C* above it. If it is not correct, cross it out and write the correct form above it.

Example 1. ~~Who~~ *Whom* should I hug first?

11. To who should we give the money?
12. Who wants vanilla yogurt?
13. With whom can Red share a room?
14. Who has Alicia asked to help her?
15. Of all the speakers, who did you like the most?
16. Whom understands how this computer program works?
17. Who did you vote for in the last election?
18. Before Andrew Johnson, who was the President of the United States?
19. Who is this package meant for, Sabrina?
20. Whom can show us where Mexico City is on the map?

Proofreading Application: Business Letter

Good writers are generally good proofreaders. Readers tend to admire and trust writing that is error-free. Make sure that you correct all errors in grammar, usage, spelling, and punctuation in your writing. Your readers will have more confidence in your words if you have done your best to proofread carefully.

Your reader's confidence is especially important when money is at stake. When you write a letter of complaint to a business, pay particular attention to proofreading for pronouns. Such letters often describe a series of events, and your reader may not understand what has happened if you have used incorrect pronouns. What's more, your reader may not take your complaint seriously if you have made such errors in usage.

PROOFREADING ACTIVITY

In each sentence in the following letter, find and correct the error in pronoun usage. Use proofreading symbols such as those on page 809 of *Elements of Language* to make your corrections.

Example To ~~Who~~ *Whom* It May Concern:

My brother Eddie and me bought your Super Dooper Alien Robot for our younger brother and sister, who are four-year-old twins. Us children were horribly disappointed with your product.

To our shock, the big green alien yelled at my sister Lani and he and frightened them. Eddie grabbed the alien's nose; it came off right in his hand, so him dropped it on the floor. Suddenly, the nose hopped across the floor and squeaked; then little Uri jumped on it, slipped, and hurt hisself. Lani, whom had been crying, started laughing. To our relief, Uri, who the alien had frightened, soon joined her.

Even though the children did not really hurt theirselves, we want our money back. Please do not send we children another Super Dooper Alien Robot. Instead, make out a check to my brother and I in the amount of $29.89.

Literary Model: Poetry

I Am of the Earth
by Anna Lee Walters

I am of the earth
She is my mother
She bore me with pride
She reared me with love
She cradled me each evening
She pushed the wind to make it sing
She built me a house of harmonious colors
She fed me the fruits of her fields
She rewarded me with memories of her smiles
She punished me with the passing of time
And at last, when I long to leave
She will embrace me for eternity

EXERCISE A Write the six different forms of personal pronouns that appear in the poem. After each pronoun, indicate whether the pronoun is in the nominative, objective, or possessive case.

EXERCISE B The personal pronoun *she* is used repeatedly as the subject of an action verb. *Me* is used repeatedly as either the direct object or indirect object of a verb. How does this use of personal pronouns support the central message of the poem?

Literary Model (continued)

EXERCISE C Using Anna Lee Walters' poem as a model, write a poem that describes your relationship with the earth. Be sure that your poem includes many personal pronouns.

EXERCISE D

1. Circle the personal pronouns you used in your poem. How does the use of personal pronouns support or add to the meaning of your poem? Did you repeat certain pronouns as Walters did? If so, why?

2. Do you think it would be effective to use so many personal pronouns in other forms of writing—for example, in book reports, essays, or business letters? Explain.

Writing Application: Interview

In casual conversation, people often use the word *who* in place of *whom*. Though this informal usage may be appropriate in a conversation with friends, it is still important for you to know the difference between *who* and *whom*. In formal English—particularly in your writing—you should use *who* for subjects and predicate nominatives, *whom* for direct and indirect objects and objects of prepositions.

INFORMAL USAGE Who do you admire most?

FORMAL USAGE **Whom** do you admire most?

Writing Activity

Your history class has been discussing heroic figures past and present, but now the discussion has turned to "local heroes," those people whom you admire and want to be like in some way. To learn more about mentors and role models and the roles they play in people's lives, interview three people of different ages. Ask each person who his or her mentors and role models are and how they have influenced him or her. As you compile your interview questions, use *who, whom,* and *whose* formally.

PREWRITING Before interviewing someone, prepare yourself by deciding on a list of questions. Everyone is busy, so don't waste any of your gracious interviewee's time by showing up without questions. Brainstorm to create a list of five initial questions and two follow-up questions. Which questions will draw out the information you really need? Have you used interrogative pronouns correctly in each question? Set up and conduct three interviews with students in your class, teachers, parents, administrators, or others. Take notes of their responses as accurately as you can, or, with their permission, record the interviews.

WRITING Now you are ready to write up your findings in three paragraphs, one for each interviewee. Be sure to organize your paragraphs in one way or another—in order of your questions, for example. As you report the interviewees' responses, you will usually paraphrase their words, restating their ideas in your own words. Be certain that your words do not change the interviewees' ideas! Make sure you use the words *who, whom,* and *whose* at least one time each.

REVISING Although you will paraphrase most of the information you have gathered, you can make your writing interesting by including well-chosen quotations. Remember two points when you quote: First, you must give the quotations word for word—exactly as they were spoken. Second, you must use quotation marks correctly. Review their use if it has been a while since you last used them.

PUBLISHING Check each paragraph for errors in punctuation and spelling. Look especially for errors in the formal usage of *who, whom,* and *whose.* Then, write out the list of questions and the paragraphs—either on a computer or neatly by hand—in order to give your teacher a copy. Make a copy for yourself, and underline key points that you want to bring up in class discussion.

Extending Your Writing

This exercise could lead to a more extended writing project. Now that you have gathered information about role models and mentors, write a persuasive essay that suggests setting up or improving an active mentoring program at your school. When you combine your own experiences with those of your interviewees, you can write a strong argument about the importance of having role models.

NAME CLASS DATE

for CHAPTER 20: USING MODIFIERS CORRECTLY pages 531–46

Choices: Exploring Modifiers

Here's your chance to step out of the grammar book and into the real world. You may not notice modifiers, but you and the people around you use them every day. The following activities challenge you to find a connection between modifiers and the world around you. Do the activity below that suits your personality best, and then share your discoveries with your class. Have fun!

VIDEOGRAPHY

Go for Broke

Get together with a friend and test your classmates' ability to spot an incorrectly used modifier. Write a dialogue, just an ordinary everyday conversation. Fill the dialogue with double comparisons and other kinds of improperly used modifiers. Make your dialogue sound as natural as possible. Videotape your performance of the dialogue. Then, challenge your classmates to spot the incorrectly used modifiers. Have the class write down each error as the tape is played. The person who catches the most errors wins! Wins what? Well, that's up to you.

BUILDING BACKGROUND KNOWLEDGE

Wall Scrawl

Get yourself a big piece of paper and tape it to a wall or board. Then, grab a handful of colored markers and lead the class in a discussion of adverbs. Center the discussion on adverbs that might be used to describe the verb *write.* In fact, write the word *Write!* in big letters right in the middle of the paper. Invite your classmates to add whatever adverbs and graphics might be appropriate. When you're done, you'll have the beginnings of a great mural to hang on the wall.

MUSIC

Looking Good!

If you can rhyme, this is the project for you. You may want to pair up with a friend for this activity. Read over the rules for using modifiers in your textbook. Then, transform those guidelines into a song, rap, or chant with both rhythm and rhyme. Teach your song, rap, or chant to the class.

WORLD LANGUAGES

Over There

Do other languages have adjectives and adverbs? If so, how are these modifiers used? Do they appear before or after the words they modify? Do they have special endings? How do other languages express degrees of comparison? Research several word-for-word translations of appropriate sentences, and with your teacher's permission, write them on the chalkboard. Explain to your classmates the similarities and differences between the use of modifiers in English and in the other languages you researched.

TECHNOLOGY

Check It Out

Before you rely on a grammar checker, find out if it is dependable. Write ten sentences that use adjectives where adverbs should be used and ten sentences that use adverbs where adjectives should be used. Then, type the sentences into a word processor and run a grammar checker. Record each change that the checker suggests. When it's done, tally the incorrect and correct changes and report back to the class.

VISUAL

Much More Than Many

Imagine that you are a top advertising executive. Your product, Giant Gizmo, offers much to the consumer. In fact, it offers more advantages than other products. Many features distinguish it from its competitors. Your job is to create a magazine advertisement that will make Giant Gizmo the top seller in the country. To do so, you will need to correctly use all the degrees of comparison for the irregular modifiers *good, much,* and *many.*

NAME ____________________ CLASS ____________ DATE ____________

for **CHAPTER 20: USING MODIFIERS CORRECTLY** *pages 531–32*

Modifiers

A *modifier* is a word, a phrase, or a clause that makes the meaning of a word or word group more specific. The two kinds of modifiers are *adjectives* and *adverbs*.

WORDS The weather is becoming **worse.** [modifies *weather*]
The snow fell **silently.** [modifies *fell*]

PHRASES **Coating the sidewalk,** the ice sparkled in the sun. [modifies *ice*]
Shovel the snow **off the sidewalk.** [modifies *shovel*]

CLAUSES **After we went skiing,** we drank hot cocoa. [modifies *drank*]
The children **who built the snowman** live next door. [modifies *children*]

USAGE

EXERCISE A Circle each word, phrase, or clause that modifies the underlined word in each sentence. Do not include the words *a, an,* or *the.*

Example 1. Winter is the (coldest) season (of the year.)

1. The months that make up winter are December, January, and February.
2. During the winter, it sometimes snows.
3. Snow rarely falls in southern Texas.
4. Following winter, spring arrives in March.
5. Spring is the time to plant seeds.
6. The weather usually is rainy in springtime.
7. The warmest season of the year is summer.
8. Students whose school year ends in May enjoy these summer months.
9. The crisp days of autumn follow summer.
10. After the temperatures cool, leaves fall from the trees.

EXERCISE B On the line provided, write a word, a phrase, or a clause to modify the underlined word in each sentence.

Example 1. I can't decide which shirt ________ *to wear* ________.

11. Your joke was ____________________.
12. ____________________, we measured the angles of triangles.
13. I tossed my coat ____________________.
14. Will the person ____________________ please come to Lost and Found to retrieve it?
15. I admired the ____________________ colors in the painting.

NAME ______________________ CLASS ______________ DATE ______________

for **CHAPTER 20: USING MODIFIERS CORRECTLY** pages 531–32

USAGE

One-Word Modifiers

The two kinds of modifiers are adjectives and adverbs.

20a. ***Adjectives*** make the meanings of nouns and pronouns more specific.

20b. ***Adverbs*** make the meanings of verbs, adjectives, and other adverbs more specific.

EXERCISE A Circle the word that modifies the underlined word or word group in each sentence.

Example 1. Judy Blume has written much (beloved) books.

1. Judy Blume has written nearly twenty books for young people.
2. Close friendship is the subject of *Just As Long As We're Together.*
3. Stephanie and Rachel have been best friends forever, but then Alison appears.
4. If you enjoyed that book, you will eagerly read its sequel, *Here's to You, Rachel Robinson.*
5. When Rachel's older brother moves back home, her orderly life is turned upside down.
6. In *It's Not the End of the World,* Karen copes with difficult issues.
7. *Are You There God? It's Me, Margaret* is funny.
8. Young Margaret Simon talks with God about growing up.
9. The popular novel puts a funny spin on the trials of preteen girls.
10. Through her many talks with God, Margaret anxiously awaits getting older.

EXERCISE B On the line provided, write an adjective or adverb modifying the underlined word or words in each sentence.

Example 1. I can't hear you—would you speak ___louder___?

11. Talking with friends on the telephone is an ______________ part of my life.
12. We talk ______________ for hours.
13. Megan's jokes are ______________ funny!
14. After a phone call to her, I am always ______________.
15. When I'm on the phone, the time goes ______________ quickly.
16. Unfortunately, I have to share the phone with my ______________ sister.
17. She always talks in ______________ whispers.
18. She is ______________ that I'll hear what she says to her friends.
19. I am less ______________ than she is.
20. When I'm on the phone, I talk and laugh ______________.

Phrases Used as Modifiers

Like one-word modifiers, ***phrases*** can also be used as adjectives and adverbs.

EXAMPLES I have marked the chapters **to read.** [modifies *chapters*]

The puppy howled **during the thunderstorm.** [modifies *howled*]

EXERCISE A Circle the phrase that modifies the underlined word or word group in each sentence.

Example 1. Wrinkling his nose, Brad sniffed the air in the science lab.

1. This is the frog we will dissect in class today.
2. The frogs in the other trays are for the next class.
3. Please assemble your equipment on the counter.
4. These plastic gloves are the ones to wear for the best protection.
5. During the dissection, I performed most of the work.
6. Standing near our frog, my lab partner looked ill.
7. The perfect job for my lab partner was taking notes.
8. The lab windows, opened wide, allowed the odors to escape.
9. The frogs are preserved in a formaldehyde solution.
10. Working for a week, we finally finished the frog dissection.

EXERCISE B On the line provided, write an adjective phrase or an adverb phrase to modify the underlined word in each sentence.

Example 1. The vegetables, ___chopped in small pieces___, were added to the soup pot.

11. ________________, Diego put his bare feet in the water.
12. The best menu item ________________ is the corned beef hash.
13. I rearranged my room and placed the bed ________________.
14. ________________, Thania finished her test before anyone else.
15. The car, ________________, looked new again.
16. The one ________________ is Alexis.
17. The car's horn echoed loudly ________________.
18. Raymond painted his vase the color ________________.
19. ________________, Samantha flipped the pancakes.
20. The gift ________________ is the newest CD from her favorite singer.

Clauses Used as Modifiers

Like words and phrases, ***clauses*** can also be used as modifiers.

EXAMPLES Phyllis is the friend **whom I met in math class.** [modifies *friend*]

When you go out, you should take your house keys. [modifies *should take*]

EXERCISE A Circle the clause that modifies the underlined word or word group in each sentence.

Example 1. (Before Jesse went to the beach,) he grabbed his metal detector.

1. Jesse is one of those people who enjoy searching for treasure.
2. A metal detector is the search tool that he uses most.
3. A metal detector can locate metal when the metal lies beneath the ground's surface.
4. Coins and jewelry are some of the objects that a metal detector locates.
5. After they find valuable objects, many treasure seekers sell them.
6. Other hunters build special chests that hold their treasure.
7. Treasure hunters who use a metal detector must invest money in this tool.
8. High-quality metal detectors, which can cost around five hundred dollars, run on batteries.
9. The Internet is a place where you can read about other people's experiences.
10. Some treasure seekers create Web sites that show pictures of their latest finds.

EXERCISE B Underline the clause used as a modifier in each sentence. Then, draw an arrow from the clause to the word it modifies.

Example 1. Which person is the friend whom you promised a ride home?

11. Before I went to sleep, I chose my clothes for the next day.
12. Where is the coat that I loaned you?
13. Will someone who knows the answer please speak up?
14. Leticia completed her test with confidence because she had studied hard.
15. Spring is the season that I enjoy most.
16. When I removed the CD from its case, the disc cracked.
17. Did you read the e-mail that I sent you?
18. The puppy chewed on my shoes after he ate my homework.
19. Terrence is a friend whom you can trust with a secret.
20. This novel, which I read in two hours, is short and suspenseful.

Phrases and Clauses Used as Modifiers

Like one-word modifiers, phrases and clauses can also be used as adjectives and adverbs.

PHRASES Several campers gathered **around the campfire.** [modifies *gathered*]

Burned by the flames, the marshmallows were inedible. [modifies *marshmallows*]

CLAUSES The flames, **which burned the marshmallows,** glowed. [modifies *flames*]

The campers sang **while they roasted marshmallows.** [modifies *sang*]

EXERCISE A Circle the phrase or clause that modifies the underlined word or words in each sentence.

Example 1. Please pack the nylon tent (with the other camping gear.)

1. Who are the people whom you invited along?
2. They were roommates when they went to college.
3. A state park is the place to camp over the weekend.
4. I know a woman who is a park ranger.
5. Talking with her, I received some advice.
6. Campers should take plastic bags that will hold their food scraps.
7. Keep food scraps inside these bags.
8. Wild animals that wander nearby will not smell the food.
9. They will not search your campsite for the food.
10. I will pack resealable bags along with my socks and jeans.

EXERCISE B Circle the phrase or clause used as a modifier in each sentence. Then, draw an arrow from the phrase or clause to the word it modifies.

Example 1. (Skating in the competition,) Tera performed a graceful jump.

11. The grass that you planted is not growing well.
12. Please leave my bicycle in the garage.
13. The basketball court to use in the morning is the new one.
14. Before he said anything, Darnell took a deep breath.
15. Pattering against our windows, the sleet woke me.
16. The river, filled to its banks, flowed swiftly.
17. Is peach the flavor that you would like?
18. Do you know anyone who can tutor me?
19. Rae pulled her new in-line skates from their box.
20. After you leave school today, come home.

NAME ______________________ CLASS ______________ DATE ______________

USAGE

Regular Comparisons

20c. The three degrees of comparison of modifiers are the ***positive,*** the ***comparative,*** and the ***superlative.***

POSITIVE	fast	beautiful	bright
COMPARATIVE	faster	more beautiful	less bright
SUPERLATIVE	fastest	most beautiful	least bright

EXERCISE A On the lines provided, write the comparative and superlative degrees of the following modifiers. Do not include forms showing decreasing comparison.

Example 1. proudly *more proudly* *most proudly*

Positive	**Comparative**	**Superlative**
1. importantly	______	______
2. happy	______	______
3. loud	______	______
4. bravely	______	______
5. brilliantly	______	______
6. simple	______	______
7. cheaply	______	______
8. foolish	______	______
9. green	______	______
10. sad	______	______

EXERCISE B For each of the following sentences, write the form of the modifier given in parentheses.

Example 1. (comparative form of *tall*) Halley is *taller* than any other girl here.

11. (comparative form of *full*) This pail is ______ than that one.

12. (superlative form of *funny*) That is the ______ joke I know.

13. (comparative form of *rapidly*) A rabbit runs ______ than a skunk.

14. (comparative form of *small*) This piece of bread seems ______ than that one.

15. (decreasing superlative form of *difficult*) Of all school subjects, I think math is ______.

Irregular Comparisons

20c. The three degrees of comparison of modifiers are the ***positive,*** the ***comparative,*** and the ***superlative.***

The comparative and superlative degrees of some modifiers are irregular in form.

POSITIVE	bad	good	many	far
COMPARATIVE	worse	better	more	farther *or* further
SUPERLATIVE	worst	best	most	farthest *or* furthest

EXERCISE A For each of the following sentences, identify the degree of comparison of the underlined modifier by writing *P* for *positive degree,* *C* for *comparative degree,* or *S* for *superlative degree.*

Example 1. Of all the performances, I liked Brandy's most. *S*

1. Carlos likes science fiction stories better than mysteries.
2. I think Friday is the best day of the whole week.
3. More people came to the meeting than we had expected.
4. Of all the members of the team, Inez bats best.
5. My cousin was able to save more money than I.
6. Chet has delivered many newspapers.
7. After supper, I felt worse than I had felt in the afternoon.
8. We hiked farther today than we hiked yesterday.
9. Dad doesn't play much tennis.
10. This is the worst cold I have ever had.

EXERCISE B Write above the parentheses the form of the modifier given.

Example 1. Which of your two friends travels (comparative of *far*) to school? *farther*

11. In my opinion, that was a (positive of *good*) movie.
12. Lita is the (superlative of *good*) speller of the three contestants.
13. Which of the four theaters is (superlative of *far*) from your house?
14. Georgia plays all sports (positive of *well*).
15. My tennis serve is (comparative of *good*) than it was last year.
16. I'm sorry I wasn't (comparative of *much*) help to you.
17. If you practice diligently, your math skills will get (comparative of *good*).
18. Which is (comparative of *easy*) for you: memorizing dates or memorizing formulas?
19. This is the (superlative of *bad*) food I have ever eaten!
20. "How many (comparative of *many*) laps do we have to run?" I asked the coach.

NAME ______________________ CLASS ______________ DATE ______________

USAGE

Regular and Irregular Comparisons A

20c. The three degrees of comparison of modifiers are the ***positive,*** the ***comparative,*** and the ***superlative.***

Most modifiers form the comparative degree by adding *–er* and the superlative degree by adding *–est*. Some modifiers form the comparative degree by using *more* and the superlative degree by using *most*. The comparative and superlative degrees of some modifiers are irregular in form. To show decreasing comparisons, modifiers form the comparative degree by using *less* and the superlative degree by using *least*.

POSITIVE	cute	traditional	well	damp
COMPARATIVE	cuter	more traditional	better	less damp
SUPERLATIVE	cutest	most traditional	best	least damp

EXERCISE A For each of the following sentences, identify the degree of comparison of the underlined modifier by writing *P* for *positive degree*, *C* for *comparative degree*, or *S* for *superlative degree*.

Example **1.** Paulo writes fantastic reviews of fast food sold around town.

1. Paulo's articles in the school paper are read more than any other articles.

2. Paulo's reviews of local food shops usually have a fun theme.

3. Each theme is more interesting than the last one.

4. For example, last week's funny theme was "Sneeze-Inducing Meals."

5. He had eaten at a pizza parlor that used the most pepper he had ever tasted in pizza.

6. Unexpectedly, he began sneezing with loud sneezes that sounded like whistles.

7. The more eagerly Paulo ate, the more he sneezed like a train whistle.

8. The other patrons laughed quietly at first and then less quietly.

9. Between whistling sneezes, Paulo joined in the laughter more enthusiastically than anyone else.

10. Of the three pizza parlors he reviewed, this one received the fewest positive comments.

EXERCISE B Identify the degree of comparison of the underlined modifier by writing *P* for *positive degree*, *C* for *comparative degree*, or *S* for *superlative degree*.

Example **1.** Aaron behaves more independently this year than last year.

11. This recipe is simpler than the other one because there are fewer steps.

12. Although I was sorry about breaking the window, I was more sorry about breaking the vase.

13. This television show is more boring than any others I have watched this weekend.

14. "All I ask," said Coach Powell, "is that you give the best effort possible."

15. George groaned, "This is the worst haircut I have ever had!"

USAGE

Regular and Irregular Comparisons B

20c. The three degrees of comparison of modifiers are the ***positive,*** the ***comparative,*** and the ***superlative.***

Most modifiers form the comparative degree by adding *–er* and the superlative degree by adding *–est*. Some modifiers form the comparative degree by using *more* and the superlative degree by using *most*. The comparative and superlative degrees of some modifiers are irregular in form. To show decreasing comparisons, modifiers form the comparative degree by using *less* and the superlative degree by using *least*.

POSITIVE	kind	orderly	bad	dangerous
COMPARATIVE	kinder	more orderly	worse	less dangerous
SUPERLATIVE	kindest	most orderly	worst	least dangerous

EXERCISE A Above the underlined modifier in each sentence, write *D* for *decreasing comparison* or *I* for *increasing comparison*.

Example 1. As the storm intensified, the small boat rocked more wildly. *I*

1. The three children played less energetically as they grew tired.
2. That outfit looks good, but the other one looks better.
3. Of the four sales specials, this one will save us the most money.
4. I use my skateboard less often now that I ride my bike everywhere.
5. Sandra became happier after she discussed the misunderstanding with Billie.

EXERCISE B Above the parentheses in each sentence, write the form of the modifier given.

Example 1. Which is (increasing comparative of *easy*), chess or checkers? *easier*

6. "Please step back a little (increasing comparative of *far*)," said the photographer.
7. "One lamp shines (decreasing comparative of *brightly*) than all the others," said Maggie.
8. My hair is (decreasing comparative of *curly*) when it is wet.
9. Albert was relieved that today's lessons seemed (decreasing comparative of *difficult*) than yesterday's.
10. Instead of feeling better after lunch, the child felt (increasing comparative of *bad*).
11. Which is the (increasing superlative of *fast*) runner, a horse or a zebra or a gnu?
12. As computer equipment becomes more common, it often becomes (decreasing comparative of *costly*).
13. Of all the science projects, Johnny's is (increasing superlative of *fascinating*).
14. I hope the weather gets (increasing comparative of *good*) before the football game tomorrow.
15. Of all my friends' handwriting, Jenny's is the (decreasing superlative of *legible*).

Degrees of Comparison A

20c. The three degrees of comparison of modifiers are the ***positive,*** the ***comparative,*** and the ***superlative.***

(1) The ***positive degree*** is used when at least one thing is being described.
(2) The ***comparative degree*** is used when two things are being compared.
(3) The ***superlative degree*** is used when three or more things are being compared.

POSITIVE A boxer is a **big** dog. [one thing]
COMPARATIVE A mastiff is **bigger** than a boxer. [two things]
SUPERLATIVE A Great Dane is the **biggest** dog of the three. [three or more things]

EXERCISE A Underline the correct form of the modifier in parentheses in each sentence.

Example 1. I think that having the flu is (*worse, worst*) than having a cold.

1. Of all the players, Pete kicks the ball (*more forcefully, most forcefully*).
2. Please pet the cat (*more gently, most gently*) than that.
3. The Yukon River is (*longer, longest*) than the Rio Grande.
4. It rained (*hard, harder*) yesterday than it did today.
5. Of the six department stores in the mall, this one is the (*larger, largest*).

EXERCISE B Above the underlined modifier in each sentence, write *1, 2,* or *3 or more* to tell how many things are being described or compared. Then, identify the underlined modifier by writing *P* for *positive degree, C* for *comparative degree,* or *S* for *superlative degree.*

3 or more—S
Example 1. Who is the tallest basketball player on the team?

6. Which is heavier—a pound of feathers or a pound of nails?
7. Of the lion, tiger, and cheetah, the cheetah can run fastest.
8. Maura is the least qualified candidate who ever ran for president.
9. Michael dances more gracefully than I do.
10. This chemistry problem seems extremely difficult.
11. Of all my friends, Albert works most carefully.
12. Does Leigh live farther from the library than LaShawna?
13. Julia sings in the choir very often.
14. Which story in the collection do you like best?
15. Miriam is less familiar with using a globe than I.

Degrees of Comparison B

20c. The three degrees of comparison of modifiers are the ***positive,*** the ***comparative,*** and the ***superlative.***

(1) The ***positive degree*** is used when at least one thing is being described.
(2) The ***comparative degree*** is used when two things are being compared.
(3) The ***superlative degree*** is used when three or more things are being compared.

POSITIVE Brian read his lines **convincingly** for the audition. [one thing]
COMPARATIVE Oscar read his lines **more convincingly** than Brian. [two things]
SUPERLATIVE Of all the actors, Ramiro read his lines **most convincingly.** [three or more things]

EXERCISE A Underline the correct form of the modifier in parentheses in each sentence. Then, identify the underlined modifier by writing *P* for *positive degree, C* for *comparative degree,* or *S* for *superlative degree.*

Example 1. Are oranges *(higher, highest)* in vitamin C than broccoli is? C

1. Which tastes *(good, better)* with frozen yogurt—fresh fruit or oatmeal crumble?
2. The jicama is a large *(white, whiter)* root that can be eaten raw or cooked.
3. Of these fruits—mango, papaya, and pineapple—I think pineapple is *(sweeter, sweetest).*
4. The guava is a *(smallest, smaller)* fruit than the melon.
5. Of the four kinds of berries in the market, the blueberries are *(riper, ripest).*

EXERCISE B Above the underlined modifier in each sentence, write *1, 2,* or *3 or more* to tell how many things are being described or compared. Then, identify the underlined modifier by writing *P* for *positive degree, C* for *comparative degree,* or *S* for *superlative degree.*

Example 1. I think the blue betta fighting fish is prettier than the goldfish. 2—C

6. The bite of the tarantula can be deadly to mice.
7. The blue whale is the largest animal ever to have lived on earth.
8. To me, a snake is scarier than a spider.
9. The bison population in North America was once more numerous than the population today.
10. The garter snake is harmless.
11. Warm regions are better habitats for scorpions than colder regions.
12. Over short distances, the cheetah is the fastest land animal of all.
13. Is a dog more loyal than a cat?
14. Of my three parrots, Mr. Chatty is the most talkative.
15. Which is more likely to be a good pet for children, a golden retriever or a Great Dane?

NAME CLASS DATE

Degrees of Comparison C

20c. The three degrees of comparison of modifiers are the ***positive,*** the ***comparative,*** and the ***superlative.***

(1) The ***positive degree*** is used when at least one thing is being described.
(2) The ***comparative degree*** is used when two things are being compared.
(3) The ***superlative degree*** is used when three or more things are being compared.

POSITIVE This curry sauce tastes **spicy.** [one thing]
COMPARATIVE The salsa tastes **less spicy** than the jalapeño sauce. [two things]
SUPERLATIVE Of the three sauces, the salsa tastes the **least spicy.** [three or more things]

USAGE

EXERCISE Underline the correct form of the modifier in parentheses in each sentence. Then, identify the underlined modifier by writing *P* for *positive degree,* *C* for *comparative degree,* or *S* for *superlative degree.*

Example **1.** Of the two students, Lori worked the math problem *(most quickly, more quickly).* C

1. Which of your three friends has the *(earlier, earliest)* curfew?

2. Of all the members in my writing group, I am *(less interested, least interested)* in poetry.

3. The toddler walked *(aimlessly, more aimlessly)* around the playground.

4. This new computer game is *(less fun, least fun)* than the game I already had.

5. What is the *(more interesting, most interesting)* book of all those on the list?

6. Grandpa's computer store is open *(later, latest)* than his competitor's.

7. Would the subway be *(fastest, faster)* than the bus?

8. When I cook chicken, I use *(less, least)* oil than Dad uses.

9. The kite flew merrily in a *(brisk, brisker)* summer breeze.

10. Selena is *(more comfortable, most comfortable)* speaking in public than her brother.

11. Don't buy that potted plant—it looks the *(least healthy, less healthy)* of them all.

12. Listen to this joke—it's the *(funnier, funniest)* one I've heard all week!

13. This abandoned house is *(spooky, spookier).*

14. We'll watch this movie tonight since it is *(shortest, shorter)* than the other one.

15. Vic is the *(most loyal, more loyal)* friend I have known.

16. Every grocery store promises that its fish counter has the *(freshest, fresher)* fish in town.

17. My front yard has the *(taller, tallest)* trees on the block.

18. Which is *(farther, farthest)* away, the library or the park?

19. Jeanette is *(more punctual, most punctual)* than her sister Julia.

20. Wearing a hat is the *(better, best)* way to stay warm.

USAGE

Good and *Well*

20d. Use ***good*** to modify a noun or a pronoun in most cases. Use ***well*** to modify a verb.

Although ***well*** is usually an adverb, *well* may also be used as an adjective meaning "in good health" or "satisfactory."

EXAMPLES Barbara is a **good** artist. [*Good* is used as an adjective to modify the noun *artist*.]
Barbara paints **well.** [*Well* is used as an adverb to modify the verb *paints*.]
I was sick, but now I am **well.** [*Well* is used as an adjective to modify the pronoun *I*.]

EXERCISE A Underline the correct modifier in parentheses to complete each sentence.

Example **1.** Do you know Sophie *(good, well)*?

1. The orchestra sounds *(good, well)* tonight.
2. Ruthie handles herself *(good, well)* in a crisis.
3. The Chang twins play the piano very *(good, well)*.
4. You look *(good, well)* now that your cold is gone.
5. How *(good, well)* did you do on the spelling test?
6. Because she has the flu, she doesn't feel *(good, well)* today.
7. The directions say to stir the ingredients until they are *(good, well)* blended.
8. Despite what Mike says, I think this is a *(good, well)* plan.
9. I have earned *(good, well)* grades for six weeks.
10. She speaks so quietly that I cannot hear her very *(good, well)*.

EXERCISE B Each sentence below uses either *good* or *well*. If *good* or *well* is used correctly, write *C* above it. If *good* or *well* is not used correctly, cross it out and write the correct word above it.

Example **1.** I haven't been feeling ~~good~~ *well* all day.

11. You did a good job on this essay for history class.
12. If this plan doesn't work good, we will try the backup plan.
13. Alfred writes really good short stories.
14. I didn't know you could dance so good!
15. Doesn't the poem sound well?

NAME CLASS DATE

Choosing Adjectives or Adverbs

20e. Use adjectives, not adverbs, after linking verbs.

EXAMPLES I feel **bad** [not *badly*] about my mistake.
The homemade bread tastes **good** [not *well*].

USAGE

EXERCISE A Underline the correct modifier in parentheses to complete each sentence.

Example 1. Rodolfo felt (*sad, sadly*) about the tragedy.

1. Eduardo was (*quick, quickly*) in solving problems.
2. The team's performance seemed (*weak, weakly*) in the final quarter.
3. This whole situation is (*confusingly, confusing*).
4. The milk smelled (*bad, badly*).
5. The actor felt (*happy, happily*) about getting the part in the play.

EXERCISE B In each sentence below, if the underlined modifier is used correctly, write *C* above it. If the modifier is not used correctly, cross it out and write the correct word above it.

Example 1. In class, Jonah's behavior seemed ~~strangely~~ *strange*.

6. Lanelle feels badly about the misunderstanding.
7. That song sounds greatly.
8. Yesterday you seemed cheerful when I saw you.
9. Karen appeared nervously for some reason.
10. All afternoon, Mario looked distracted.
11. Coffee smells wonderfully.
12. Mailou grimaced because the soup tasted so salty.
13. The baby grew quickly.
14. During the movie, the kids looked curious at the old theater.
15. Please feel freely to look around the store.
16. The lecture at the auditorium was lengthily.
17. Is it me, or do you feel coldly also?
18. Rufina's new hairstyle is curly.
19. The note Katy received from a secret admirer was unexpectedly.
20. "Are you ready for your surprise?" asked Javier excitedly.

USAGE

Double Comparisons

20f. Avoid using double comparisons.

A ***double comparison*** is the use of both *–er* and *more* (or *less*) or *–est* and *most* (or *least*) to form a comparison. When you make a comparison, use only one form, not both.

NONSTANDARD I have just read Stephen Hawking's most latest book.

STANDARD I have just read Stephen Hawking's **latest** book.

EXERCISE A Underline the correct modifier in parentheses in each of the following sentences.

Example 1. The skies are (*sunnier, more sunnier*) today than yesterday.

1. I am (*busier, more busier*) this week than I was last week.
2. It's the (*most scariest, scariest*) book I have ever read.
3. This salsa tastes (*less spicy, less spicier*) than the salsa I make.
4. He is (*more smarter, smarter*) than he thinks.
5. It is (*easier, more easier*) to jump than it is to dive.
6. This is the (*most shortest, shortest*) song on the album.
7. This dress is (*bluer, more bluer*) than the color I requested from the dressmaker.
8. This is the (*most latest, latest*) Chuck has ever been for practice.
9. At the dog show, Marcella's dog performed (*funnier, more funnier*) tricks than my dog.
10. This is the (*cutest, most cutest*) mouse in the pet store.

EXERCISE B Cross out any errors in the use of modifiers in the following sentences. Then, write the correct form of the modifier above each error.

Example 1. We fenced in the yard so it would be ~~more safer~~ *safer* for my younger brothers.

11. I have two brothers who are more younger than I.
12. Mick is the most friendliest little boy you will ever meet.
13. Mark, on the other hand, is more shyer than Mick.
14. Of all of us, Mark is the most quietest.
15. When Mick and Mark are together, however, they are both more louder than you would expect.
16. We recently moved into a house with a more larger yard than our previous house had.
17. Of all the houses we saw, this one was most best because of the large yard.
18. During the more warmer days this autumn, we will play ball in the backyard.
19. I am teaching Mick and Mark the most best way to catch a softball.
20. They are more curiouser, however, about the treehouse I am building than about softball tips.

USAGE

Double Negatives

20g. Avoid using double negatives.

A ***double negative*** is the use of two or more negative words to express one negative idea. Common negative words include *barely, hardly, neither, never, no, nobody, not, nothing,* and *scarcely.* To express a negative idea, use only one of these words, not two.

NONSTANDARD I haven't never read a book by Madeleine L'Engle.

STANDARD I **have never** read a book by Madeleine L'Engle.

I **haven't ever** read a book by Madeleine L'Engle.

EXERCISE A Underline the correct choice to complete each of the following sentences.

Example 1. I don't know *(nothing, anything)* about engines.

1. No fish *(were, weren't)* biting in the stream this morning.
2. Nobody *(was, wasn't)* disappointed with the results of the fund-raiser.
3. The fable didn't mean *(nothing, anything)* to him.
4. You *(can, can't)* hardly find this type of pen in stores.
5. Don't go *(nowhere, anywhere)* until I get back.
6. It *(was, wasn't)* scarcely dark before the bats flew out of their cave.
7. On Mondays, Sheila *(can, can't)* barely make it to school on time.
8. I can't hear *(anything, nothing)* because of that hammering from the construction.
9. I promise I didn't tell *(no one, anyone)* your secret.
10. Nate didn't call, and he didn't write *(neither, either)*.

EXERCISE B The following paragraph contains ten double negatives. Cross out each error and, if necessary, write a correction above it. Although sentences can be corrected in more than one way, you need to give only one correction.

Example I ~~can't~~ *can* hardly wait to play the piano professionally.

Nobody never taught me how to play the piano, so I wasn't hardly prepared for the surprise. At first, I played a few notes very softly. I didn't want no one to hear me playing. When I didn't feel shy no more, I played less softly. I still wasn't taking no lessons. I didn't go nowhere without thinking about the next time I could practice. I didn't scarcely go out on the weekends when I could stay inside and practice. Then my grandmother asked me, "Wouldn't you like to take no lessons?" I didn't barely wait a second to shout "Yes!" I could scarcely believe it. I hadn't never been so excited before.

Misplaced Prepositional Phrases

20h. Place modifying words, phrases, and clauses as close as possible to the words they modify.

Place a prepositional phrase used as an adjective or as an adverb near the word it modifies. Avoid placing a prepositional phrase so that it seems to modify either of two words.

MISPLACED The dog belongs to that man with the black spots.

CLEAR The dog **with the black spots** belongs to that man.

MISPLACED We talked about the football game in the locker room.

CLEAR **In the locker room,** we talked about the football game.

MISPLACED We decided on Tuesday we would visit you.

CLEAR **On Tuesday,** we decided we would visit you.

CLEAR We decided we would visit you **on Tuesday.**

EXERCISE A Underline the prepositional phrase in each sentence. Then, draw an arrow from the phrase to the word that the phrase modifies.

Example 1. I studied the fish in the aquarium.

1. The woman in the red car is Ms. Prasad, my principal.
2. I found your bracelet under the sofa.
3. With a map, we found our way home.
4. We used glue to repair the chair with the broken leg.
5. On Monday afternoon she told us that she had scored the game's winning goal.

EXERCISE B Each of the following sentences contains a misplaced prepositional phrase. Underline the prepositional phrase. Then, draw a caret (^) to show where the phrase should be placed.

Example 1. In the stew pot I salted the vegetables^.

6. The parrot spoke three words to my mother in the brass cage.
7. We sat at the table and talked about our fishing trip in the kitchen.
8. In the game I scored two points at the high point.
9. I read about the lost puppy that was found in today's newspaper.
10. The runner twisted her ankle with the blue T-shirt.
11. The rancher lassoed the steer in a cowboy hat.
12. I promised before the test on Friday I would help you with math.
13. The student with polka dots is painting his pottery.
14. In a ballerina costume Todd photographed the dancer.
15. I said during the break she should visit the nurse.

USAGE

Misplaced and Dangling Participial Phrases

20h. Place modifying words, phrases, and clauses as close as possible to the words they modify.

A *participial phrase* consists of a present participle or a past participle and its modifiers and complements. A participial phrase that is not placed near the noun or pronoun it modifies is called a *misplaced modifier.* A participial phrase that does not sensibly modify any word in the sentence is called a *dangling modifier.*

MISPLACED MODIFIER I saw a robin walking home.
CORRECT **Walking home,** I saw a robin.
DANGLING MODIFIER Walking to school, the morning was pleasant.
CORRECT Walking to school, I found the morning pleasant.

EXERCISE A Underline the misplaced modifier or dangling modifier in each sentence. Above the modifier, write *M* for *misplaced* or *D* for *dangling.*

Example 1. Hitting a home run, the crowd cheered. D

1. I spoke softly to the horse sitting in the saddle.
2. Munching on popcorn, the movie was enjoyable.
3. Frosted with a fruit glaze, I couldn't wait to eat the muffin.
4. Painted red, I noticed the new fire lanes.
5. Miguel saw a rabbit jogging in his new sneakers.

EXERCISE B Each of these sentences contains a misplaced or dangling modifier. On the lines provided, revise the sentences so that they are clear. You may need to add words so that the sentences make sense.

Example 1. Munching on carrot sticks, the lunch period went quickly. *Munching on carrot sticks, I thought the lunch period went quickly.*

6. Modene did not hear the ringing telephone taking a shower. ________

7. The missing baseball card was found cleaning my closet. ________

8. Making the bed, my cat burrowed under the pillows. ________

9. Sitting in its nest, I saw a bluebird. ________

10. Running to catch the bus, a dog barked at me. ________

USAGE

Misplaced Adjective Clauses

20h. Place modifying words, phrases, and clauses as close as possible to the words they modify.

An *adjective clause* modifies a noun or a pronoun. Most adjective clauses begin with a relative pronoun—*that, which, who, whom,* or *whose.* An adjective clause should generally be placed directly after the word it modifies.

MISPLACED The book was about insects that we read.

CORRECT The book **that we read** was about insects.

EXERCISE A Underline the adjective clause in each of the following sentences. Then, draw an arrow from the clause to the noun or pronoun that the clause modifies.

Example 1. The person who called at midnight was my aunt.

1. The president whom I respect the most is Abraham Lincoln.
2. I would like to hike up a mountain that has a snow-covered peak.
3. The player who scores the most goals will be elected Most Valuable Player.
4. We drove to Springfield, which is about an hour away.
5. My best friend is Elbert, whose father was in the army with my father.

EXERCISE B Each sentence below contains a misplaced adjective clause. Underline the adjective clause in each sentence. Then, draw a caret (^) where the clause should be placed in the sentence.

Example 1. The dog ^ lives in the house that has the red collar.

6. I served the food to the athletes that had been made for lunch.
7. Mom chose the puppy as a gift for my little brother that has brown fur.
8. The actor gave me his autograph who starred in the film.
9. I put the camera in the closet that my uncle gave me.
10. My cousin gave me a parakeet who goes to college in Alabama.
11. The candles came from the corner store that I bought.
12. The people have arrived at the skating rink whom I invited to my skating party.
13. The strange thumping remained a mystery that I heard in the night.
14. The software crashed my computer system that I installed.
15. This poem is for your personal scrapbook, which I wrote myself.

NAME ______________________ CLASS ______________ DATE ______________

Misplaced and Dangling Phrases and Clauses A

20h. Place modifying words, phrases, and clauses as close as possible to the words they modify.

MISPLACED Barking loudly, Sasha looked out the window at the dog.

CORRECT Sasha looked out the window at the dog **barking loudly.**

MISPLACED The package is crushing the pansies that I set near the door.

CORRECT The package **that I set near the door** is crushing the pansies.

EXERCISE Each of these sentences contains a misplaced modifier or a dangling modifier. On the lines provided, revise the sentences so that they are clear. You may need to add, delete, or rearrange words.

Example 1. Squinting into the sun, the dusty road seemed endless. *Squinting into the sun, I thought the dusty road seemed endless.*

1. Flipping through the yearbook, Jordan's picture leaped out at me. ______________________

2. Understanding the problem, a solution suddenly became clear. ______________________

3. The room belongs to my brother with the blue walls. ______________________

4. Caught in the net, I examined the sandy starfish. ______________________

5. Ben carelessly left it lying on the bus, who borrowed my CD. ______________________

6. Painted with dyes made from berries, the archaeologist was fascinated with the pots. ______________________

7. Jan hid her dirty dishes when Alfredo unexpectedly visited behind the bookcase. ______________________

8. Here are the instructions for the baby sitter that I jotted down. ______________________

9. I promised the girl I would help her find her bird who wore a red dress. ______________________

10. The cat surprised Uncle Fred trotting by with feathers in his mouth. ______________________

Misplaced and Dangling Phrases and Clauses B

20h. Place modifying words, phrases, and clauses as close as possible to the words they modify.

MISPLACED The photographer studied the lush oasis setting up his camera.

CORRECT **Setting up his camera,** the photographer studied the lush oasis.

MISPLACED The atlas shows several pictures of the Sahara that I bought.

CORRECT The atlas **that I bought** shows several pictures of the Sahara.

EXERCISE If a sentence contains a misplaced modifier or a dangling modifier, write a revision on the line provided. You may need to add, delete, or rearrange words. If the sentence needs no change, write *C*.

Example 1. The pizza should be delivered to this address with anchovies. *The pizza with anchovies should be delivered to this address.*

1. The skater thanked the judges who won the competition. ______

2. Cliff suggested after lunch we shoot some hoops. ______

3. Boiling in hot water, Alberto stirred the rice. ______

4. The dust won't be visible to our guests under the rug. ______

5. Covering more than three million square miles, the Sahara is in North Africa. ______

6. I handed the basket to the lucky recipient filled with fruit, nuts, and a cheese log. ______

7. The stale bread was eaten by birds that I tossed into the yard. ______

8. I can't reach the spices that I need for the recipe on the top shelf. ______

9. Divided by an island, Niagara Falls breaks into two different waterfalls. ______

10. I gave the stuffed animal to the cute toddler that I won at the carnival. ______

NAME ____________________ CLASS ____________ DATE ____________

for **CHAPTER 20: USING MODIFIERS CORRECTLY** *pages 532–35*

Review A: **Comparative and Superlative Forms**

USAGE

EXERCISE A Underline the correct form of the modifier in parentheses in each sentence.

Example 1. After eating the entire falafel sandwich, I didn't feel (*good, well*).

1. Trains can travel (*faster, more faster*) than horses.
2. I think swimming is (*excitinger, more exciting*) than baseball.
3. Hamid is the (*smarter, smartest*) boy that I know.
4. That was the (*better, best*) movie that we have ever seen.
5. I feel (*badder, worse*) than I did this morning.
6. Rats are (*larger, more large*) than mice.
7. Of all the trees in the forest, the pines are the (*more beautiful, most beautiful*).
8. This book is the (*most interesting, more interesting*) of the two.
9. Hector felt (*bad, badly*), so he went to see a doctor.
10. This is the (*best, goodest*) pasta salad that I've ever eaten.

EXERCISE B On the lines provided, complete the following chart. For each modifier given, write the corresponding modifiers in the other degrees of comparison. Do not include forms showing decreasing comparison.

Example 1. thoughtfully — *more thoughtfully* — *most thoughtfully*

	Positive	**Comparative**	**Superlative**
11.	near	____________	____________
12.	many	____________	____________
13.	____________	more terrific	____________
14.	safe	____________	____________
15.	____________	more silently	____________
16.	bad	____________	____________
17.	much	____________	____________
18.	suddenly	____________	____________
19.	____________	____________	most intelligent
20.	far	____________	____________

Review B: Special Problems in Using Modifiers

EXERCISE A Each of these sentences contains an error in the use of modifiers. Cross out each error, and write a correction above it.

Example 1. I ~~couldn't~~ *could* hardly fit the tiny ring on my finger.

1. Nobody doesn't like to be late for school.

2. That's the most silliest story I've ever heard.

3. Joanna works good with others.

4. I couldn't hardly recognize Jorge in his costume.

5. The people who live in that house aren't never home.

6. Of all the roads leading into the canyon, this one is the most steepest.

7. Toshi seems more bravely than Sid.

8. We didn't have nothing to do.

9. I've never felt more sadly.

10. I couldn't hardly move the heavy carton.

EXERCISE B Correctly complete each of the following sentences with the correct modifier given in parentheses. Write the correct modifier on the line provided.

Example 1. *(interesting, interestingly)* Frogs are more *interesting* than most people realize.

11. *(beautifully, beautiful)* The pond where we saw the frogs looks ________________.

12. *(good, well)* Barry, who does ________________ in science class, told me that frogs lay eggs in water.

13. *(younger, more younger)* A tadpole is ________________ than a frog.

14. *(good, well)* The tadpole's tail can propel it ________________.

15. *(not hardly, not)* The tiny tadpole does ________________ look like the frog it will become.

Review C: Misplaced and Dangling Modifiers

USAGE

EXERCISE A Underline the misplaced prepositional phrase in each sentence. Then, draw a caret (^) to show where the phrase should appear in the sentence.

Example 1. ^I saw a lion drinking water through the telescope.

1. Elena called while you were taking a shower from Texas.
2. My uncle made a table for my aunt with carved legs.
3. In the soup, Miriam ate all the noodles.
4. In a hurry, the drive seemed longer than usual to the reporter.
5. Over the buildings, Marcel and I saw a blimp flying by.
6. Vernon gave a fish to his friend with purple fins.
7. He wrote her name on the envelope with the fountain pen.
8. Stormy wants the bike for her birthday in the store window.
9. In the frying pan Elia scrambled some eggs.
10. In my report, I wrote about hurricanes for my science class.

EXERCISE B Each sentence below contains a misplaced or dangling modifier. Rewrite the sentences to make them clear and correct. Delete, add, and rearrange words as necessary.

Example 1. Lapping at the shore, the sound was peaceful. *Lapping at the shore, the waves made a peaceful sound.*

11. The house is about a mile from Dunbar High School that my parents want to buy. ____________
12. My pen pal wants a dog who lives in Kansas. ____________
13. That dog needs a bath covered with dirt. ____________
14. Tired and sleepy, the bed seemed very comfortable. ____________
15. The woman owns a horse who is Angelo's teacher. ____________

Review D: Modifiers

EXERCISE A Underline the misplaced phrase or clause in each sentence. Then, draw a caret (^) to show where the phrase or clause should appear in the sentence.

Example 1. ^Mr. Gallego announced on Monday class was canceled.

1. Overgrown and full of weeds, I found the garden.
2. I was interrupted by a visitor eating my lunch.
3. Henry was reading a book about the grizzly bear relaxing in his armchair.
4. Interrupting the movie, the audience began to glare at the noisy children.
5. Recorded on the surveillance tape, the inspector searched for a suspect.
6. Stuck in a scrapbook, my uncle has several old photographs.
7. We saw the Grand Canyon flying home.
8. Chopped into small pieces, Ahmad put onions in the stew.
9. Give the sandwich to your friend that I toasted.
10. The artist painted a picture of lions in his studio.

EXERCISE B Each sentence contains an error in the use of modifiers. Rewrite each sentence so that it is clear and correct.

Example 1. Wow! That was the most easiest exam I have ever taken! *Wow! That was the easiest exam I have ever taken!*

11. I didn't never see that wall in the rearview mirror. ______

12. Tommy scored the harder goal of the entire game. ______

13. The telephone seemed more loudly than a siren. ______

14. I turned around quickly, but didn't see no fire engine. ______

15. Shaped like a camel's head, Mi Kyung saw a huge boulder. ______

Proofreading Application: Scientific Journal Entry

Good writers are generally good proofreaders. Readers tend to admire and trust writing that is error-free. Make sure that you correct all errors in grammar, usage, spelling, and punctuation in your writing. Your readers will have more confidence in your words if you have done your best to proofread carefully.

Every year that you are in school, you will write more and more. Very likely, you are already required to have and write in at least one journal. You may even have two or three journals—one for science, English, history, and even mathematics. Some of these journals may be private; others will be read by your teacher and sometimes by your classmates. Writing these journals prepares you for a career. Scientists, for instance, must make regular and careful notes in their journals. Scientists, like many adults, work in teams. Journals enable teammates to understand the methods, criticisms, and results of experiments. Proofread this type of journal carefully to avoid errors that could confuse teammates and botch future experiments.

Proofreading Activity

Find and correct the errors in the use of modifiers. Use proofreading symbols such as those on page 809 of *Elements of Language* to make your corrections.

Example To make a waterwheel, ^we need paper cups and plastic foam plates and tape ~~are needed~~.

The new design worked pretty good. In fact, it was the better of the three designs. However, the duct tape on the axle that was wrapped several times around was troublesome. The axle wobbled real bad and slowed down the whole process. Less duct tape and more better and careful application should be used on the next model.

I also suggest that we tilt the cups so that the water drains out more quicklier. To tilt the cups, a small bit of tape could be placed under the lip of each cup. Also, water comes out too slowly to turn the wheel from the hose. We just can't get no water pressure. Before performing the experiment again, the water pressure must be increased.

Literary Model: Using Modifiers in a Poem

A wondrous portal opened wide,
As if a cavern was suddenly hollowed;
And the Piper advanced and the children followed,
And when all were in to the very last,
The door in the mountainside shut fast.
Did I say all? No! One was lame.
And could not dance the whole of the way;
And in after years; if you would blame
His sadness, he was used to say,—
"It's dull in our town since my playmates left!
I can't forget that I'm bereft
Of all the pleasant sights they see,
Which the Piper also promised me.
For he led us, he said, to a joyous land,
Joining the town and just at hand,
Where waters gushed and fruit trees grew.
And flowers put forth a fairer hue,
And everything was strange and new;
The sparrows were brighter than peacocks here,
And their dogs outran our fallow deer,
And honeybees had lost their stings,
And horses were born with eagles' wings;
And just as I became assured
My lame foot would be speedily cured,
The music stopped and I stood still,
And found myself outside the hill,
Left alone against my will,
To go now limping as before,
And never hear of that country more!

—from "The Pied Piper of Hamelin" by Robert Browning

EXERCISE A

1. List eight adjectives in the positive degree in the excerpt above. ____________

2. List two adjectives in the comparative degree in the excerpt above. ____________

3. List five adverbs in the excerpt above. ____________

EXERCISE B Read the passage aloud, omitting the adjectives and adverbs. Then, compare the original passage to the one without modifiers. How are they different?

USAGE | Language in Context: Literary Model

Literary Model (continued)

EXERCISE C Write a poem about a strange occurrence or a strange place. Use positive and comparative forms of adjectives and adverbs to describe the occurrence or place and to compare it to an ordinary one.

EXERCISE D How would your poem be different if you had used only positive forms—no comparative forms? Explain.

Writing Application: How-To Poster

"Lift the barbell with flexed muscles. Lowering the barbell, it is necessary to inhale slowly through the nose." These sentences sound a little funny because both have modifier problems. How can a barbell have muscles, flexed or otherwise? In the first sentence, the modifier *with flexed muscles* is clearly out of place. In the second sentence, who is lowering the barbell? The dangling modifier *lowering the barbell* has nothing to modify. Be sure that your modifiers are firmly tied to the words they modify.

REVISED With your muscles flexed, lift the barbell. Lowering the barbell, you should inhale slowly through the nose.

WRITING ACTIVITY

Your school has just purchased new weight-lifting equipment, and students in gym class are compiling information on proper training techniques. Students will make posters with text and illustrations to guide their peers in weight-lifting exercises. Choose one exercise to describe for a poster, and write instructions for the exercise. Use at least four correctly placed modifiers to help students perform the exercise safely and effectively.

PREWRITING Here's an unusual prewriting technique: Since you are describing physical activity, perform that activity yourself and note what you do. Get your P.E. teacher to demonstrate the correct lifting technique so that you, too, will perform it safely. Notice what part of the exercise is hardest, what part tempts the lifter to cheat a little, and where your body feels the stress of the activity. Then, while the activity is fresh in your mind, describe it in writing.

WRITING You are writing a miniature how-to explanation, so a chronological organization is probably best. What do lifters do first, next, last? As with any how-to writing, point out potential mistakes so that readers can avoid them without ever having to make them. Use brief, clear sentences in your instructions; and since you are describing activity, use active voice.

REVISING The best test of a set of instructions is a trial run. Ask several friends to perform the exercise based on your instructions. Refine your instructions if your friends have trouble following them. Use correctly placed modifiers to clarify the instructions.

PUBLISHING Check your instructions for errors in punctuation and spelling. How embarrassing it would be if these were displayed on a poster board for all to see! Then, create the poster board drawings and instructions for posting in the weight room.

EXTENDING YOUR WRITING

This exercise could lead to a more developed writing project. Everyone knows that exercise helps the body. Beyond physical fitness, however, exercise brings other benefits. For the weight-room bulletin board, prepare an encouraging list of reasons to exercise beyond a healthy physique. Research these other reasons by interviewing health professionals and reading good books and Web sites.

Choices: Exploring Usage

Here's your chance to step out of the grammar book and into the real world. Examples of standard English usage appear in your life every day. The following activities challenge you to find a connection between usage and the world around you. Do the activity below that suits your personality best, and then share your discoveries with your class. Have fun!

LITERATURE

Outlaws of the English Language

As the old saying goes, "You've got to break eggs if you want to make an omelet." Very likely, there are no great writers who have not, at one time or another, broken an established usage rule. However, they usually do so for good reason. Find some examples of this outlaw streak that runs through literature. Then, for each of your examples, write a few sentences that explain whether or not you think the author broke usage rules for an acceptable reason. Also, write a brief biographical note that provides a few interesting facts about one author. Be sure to include any important dates.

BRAINSTORMING

'Round Here

What usage errors are common among the students in your school and the people in your community? With your teacher's permission, get together with a group of friends and brainstorm a list of ten usage errors that are common in your community. Keep in mind that expressions that seem quite natural may be grammatically incorrect. If an expression is questionable, look it up in a usage dictionary. Then, make your own glossary of usage. Pass out copies to your classmates.

DISCUSSION

Beg to Differ

You've probably been speaking English for quite a while now, and you've spent a number of years in school. Surely you have an opinion about the usage errors listed in the glossary of your grammar text. Do any of these errors particularly annoy you when you come across them? Do any of the usage rules seem out-of-date to you? If so, which ones? After you've thought about these questions, list five of your least favorite usage rules. Then, ask permission to lead a discussion of them with the class.

ART

Picture This

Some errors are easy to see but hard to hear. Help everyone see these errors by illustrating two or three pairs of words from the glossary of usage. For instance, you could draw two cartoons illustrating the words *accept* and *except* or *bring* and *take*. With your teacher's permission, post your illustrations in the classroom.

WORD PROCESSING

If You Want Something Done Right

Some computer word processors will automatically correct certain mistakes for you. However, you may not wish to rely too heavily on this feature. Investigate a computer's automatic-correction feature. Identify the kinds of errors the feature can detect. Also, identify the times when this feature is appropriate and the times when it is best turned off. With your teacher's permission, present your findings to the class.

MEMORY DEVICE

Easy to Remember

Help your friends (or yourself) remember the solution to one or two troublesome usage problems. Write a rap, a riddle, or some other rhythmic lines. Then, teach your memory device to the class.

WRITING

Seen But Not Heard

Several usage errors are easier to see than they are to hear. After all, who can hear the difference between *alot* and *a lot*? Help your classmates see the difference. Begin by making a list of several errors that may not be easily heard. Write a sentence for each one. Your sentence should use each entry correctly. With your teacher's approval, make posters to hang in the classroom.

Glossary of Usage A

Review the glossary entries on pages 553–557 of your textbook for information on the correct usage of the following words or phrases:

a, an	*anyways, anywheres, everywheres, nowheres, somewheres*	*bust, busted*
accept, except		*can't hardly, can't scarcely*
ain't	*at*	*could of*
all right	*bad, badly*	*fewer, less*
a lot	*between, among*	*good, well*
already, all ready	*bring, take*	*had ought, hadn't ought*

EXERCISE Underline the word or word group that is correct according to formal, standard usage.

Example 1. When the water balloon hit the ground, it *(busted, burst)*.

1. The wallpaper looked *(alright, all right)* to him.
2. We need to get Crissy *(all ready, already)* by the time Dad gets home with the camping gear.
3. Mom said we *(can't scarcely, can scarcely)* afford the private music lessons.
4. Will you *(bring, take)* me a soda when you come back from the kitchen?
5. Adeola didn't skate *(bad, badly)* the first time she was on ice skates.
6. I made a two-dimensional map for *(a, an)* history project.
7. We have *(fewer, less)* sopranos in the chorus than we did last year.
8. Donald told Professor Trapp that we *(ain't, aren't)* finished with the assignment yet.
9. Those crickets are *(everywheres, everywhere)*!
10. Larry does not eat *(a lot, alot)* of red meat.
11. Tommy explained the difference *(among, between)* adjectives, adverbs, and verbs.
12. Jay has *(less, fewer)* money than Amy does today, so she will buy the popcorn for the movie.
13. The three friends all agreed that Stan's plan for the outing was *(well, good)*.
14. Carmen gladly *(accepted, excepted)* the warm sweater from her father.
15. Dad was a few minutes late because he could not figure out where his car keys *(were at, were)*.
16. When you visit Grandmother, please *(bring, take)* this package to her.
17. The consensus *(between, among)* the faculty was that the school should dismiss early.
18. After the water pipe *(busted, burst)*, water flooded the room.
19. Rosa bragged that she *(could of, could have)* made the basketball team if she had tried out.
20. Jean *(hadn't ought to, shouldn't)* wear those hard-soled shoes on the basketball court.

USAGE

Glossary of Usage B

Review the glossary entries on page 559 of your textbook for information on the correct usage of the following words or phrases:

he, she, they
hisself, theirself, theirselves
how come
its, it's
kind, sort, type

EXERCISE A Underline the word or word group that is correct according to formal, standard usage.

Example 1. I have always liked (*these kinds, these kind*) of outdoor sports.

1. The kitten has been chasing (*it's, its*) tail, and now the poor thing is dizzy.
2. The members of the drama club produced the play (*theirselves, themselves*).
3. (*Why do, How come*) the experiments need to be conducted in a vacuum?
4. (*This types, This type*) of fruit has seeds in the center.
5. This morning Dad cut (*hisself, himself*) when he was shaving.

EXERCISE B Each of the following sentences has an error in formal, standard usage. Cross out the error and write the correct usage above it.

Example 1. ~~Its~~ *It's* been over five hundred years since Columbus first came to America.

6. Those type of hats and coats were popular during the late 1900s.
7. Abraham Lincoln dedicated hisself to a career in law and politics.
8. The members of the Iroquois Confederacy they were North American Indians who lived in an area of New York state.
9. How come those bears hibernate?
10. In 1959, Alaska took it's place as the forty-ninth state of the United States.
11. The English Puritans who immigrated to North America in 1620 sought to gain more religious freedom for theirselves.
12. The Smithsonian Institution engages in these sort of activities: research, publication, and preservation.
13. Samuel Morse he is given credit for creating the electric telegraph and its code.
14. I enjoy reading this magazine because its both informative and fascinating.
15. Betsy Ross she is credited with making the first American stars and stripes flag.

USAGE

Glossary of Usage C

Review the glossary entries on page 560 of your textbook for information on the correct usage of the following words or phrases:

kind of, sort of	***leave, let***	***like, as if, as though***
learn, teach	***like, as***	

EXERCISE A Underline the word or word group that is correct according to formal, standard usage.

Example 1. I tried to straighten the garage, but it is still *(kind of, somewhat)* messy.

1. The baby is *(kind of, rather)* cranky today because she hasn't had a nap.
2. My skating instructor can *(teach, learn)* me how to skate backward on one foot.
3. I'd like to learn how to use a calculator *(like, as)* my math teacher does.
4. In cold weather, we all become *(sort of, rather)* irritable if we stay inside for several days.
5. *(Leave, Let)* me do the dishes, and you go out with your friends.
6. If you practice *(like, as)* we do, you'll learn to dance in no time.
7. When we looked out the window, we saw that the sky was *(kind of, somewhat)* overcast.
8. At the camp I'm attending, the recreation teacher will *(teach, learn)* us to water-ski.
9. You look *(as though, like)* you've seen a ghost.
10. *(Let, Leave)* the parcel on the stoop.

EXERCISE B Some of the following sentences have an error in formal, standard usage. Cross out each error and write the correct usage above it. If a sentence has no error, write *C* at the end of the sentence.

Example 1. At their birthday party, the twins felt ~~like~~ *as though* they were princesses.

11. Jaime is kind of scared of dogs, so we keep Buster in his kennel when Jaime visits.
12. My sister will learn me how to do a back flip at the pool this afternoon.
13. Barbara asked if I would let her borrow my portable CD player.
14. Written by Betsy Byars, *The Burning Questions of Bingo Brown* looks like it will be fun to read.
15. Carol is sort of shy around people she doesn't know.
16. My instructor said we would all learn how to dance the two-step.
17. Those trumpet players look like they have been practicing all day.
18. Leave her stay home if she doesn't want to go shopping.
19. This shoe looks like a size eight.
20. Frank told me that he would learn me how to eat with chopsticks.

USAGE

Glossary of Usage D

Review the glossary entries on pages 562–564 of your textbook for information on the correct usage of the following words or phrases:

of	*some, somewhat*	*their, there, they're*	*this here, that there*
real	*than, then*	*them*	*try and*

EXERCISE A Underline the word or word group that is correct according to formal, standard usage.

Example **1.** Bettina watched the cardinals and blue jays that were *(outside of, outside)* the window.

1. Bettina said she would *(try and, try to)* build a bird feeder for our patio.

2. When birds are nearby, *(their, there, they're)* always visiting a neighbor's bird feeder.

3. By leaning over the patio railing, I can see the birds *(somewhat, some).*

4. It would be *(real, really)* nice, however, if they were right outside our own window.

5. She said that if we set out our own bird feeder, *(than, then)* birds would come to our patio.

6. Bettina decided to place a feeder over *(their, there, they're)* by the potted ivy.

7. Do you think *(those, them)* birds will be drawn to the seeds and nuts?

8. *(This, This here)* chair will have to be moved to allow space for the feeder.

9. We eventually placed the chair *(inside, inside of)* the apartment next to the window.

10. We are delighted now because more birds visit our patio *(than, then)* we ever expected.

EXERCISE B Some of the following sentences have an error in formal, standard usage. Cross out each error and write the correct usage above it. If a sentence has no error, write *C* at the end of the sentence.

Example **1.** I noticed an interesting picture, and ~~than~~ *then* I read the article beside it.

11. The article said that the secretary bird is real unusual.

12. Protruding behind the secretary bird's head are feathers that look some like quill pens.

13. Them ink pens are made of feather quills.

14. Secretary birds run in a zigzag fashion after there prey.

15. Their predators of snakes.

16. The bird in that there picture used its foot to attack the snake.

17. Secretary birds can beat a snake with their wings.

18. Them birds are found in Africa.

19. They're habitat is in the part of the continent that is south of the Sahara.

20. This here bird is really tall; it grows to four feet in height!

Glossary of Usage E

Review the glossary entries on pages 566–567 of your textbook for information on the correct usage of the following words or phrases:

use to, used to	*when, where*	*who, which, that*	*without, unless*
way, ways	*where*	*whose, who's*	*your, you're*

EXERCISE A Underline the word or word group that is correct according to formal, standard usage.

Example 1. Kano *(use to, used to)* take ballet classes, but now she prefers gymnastics.

1. Saint Bernards, *(which, who)* are very large dogs, can be trained to rescue people.
2. Never cross the street *(unless, without)* you look both ways first.
3. When I was nine or ten, I *(use to, used to)* play outside in the rain.
4. Carlos traveled a long *(way, ways)* to get to this country.
5. A square dance is *(when you dance, a dance)* with four couples grouped in a square.
6. Lorena will be part of *(your, you're)* writing group in English class.
7. *(Whose, Who's)* car is parked in your driveway?
8. A simile is *(a comparison that, when a comparison)* uses *like* or *as.*
9. JoAnne is the one *(which, who)* showed me how to make candles.
10. It's a long *(way, ways)* from the school to my house.

EXERCISE B Some of the following sentences have an error in formal, standard usage. Cross out the error and write the correct usage above it. If a sentence has no error, write *C* at the end of the sentence.

Example 1. Tooling leather is ~~when you create~~ *creating* designs on leather with special tools.

11. The produce market is only a short ways from my house.
12. A pair of stone lions use to stand outside this library.
13. I can't stay overnight at your house without I get my mother's permission.
14. Watercolor painting is when you use water-based paint on paper or fabric.
15. Clarissa can run a long ways without getting tired.
16. These are the hyenas who need to be relocated.
17. There's nothing better than an unexpected smile when your spirits are low.
18. I saw on the bulletin board where we will get a half-day holiday on Friday.
19. Karen asked, "Whose in charge of decorating the gym?"
20. Ms. Roth is the person which schedules the yearbook photos.

Review A: Common Usage Problems

USAGE

EXERCISE A Underline the word or word group that is correct according to formal, standard usage.

Example 1. Harry Houdini was an entertainer *(which, who)* performed magic tricks.

1. For a few days, the student could not *(accept, except)* being cut from the soccer team.

2. Last winter, I built *(them, those)* birdhouses.

3. There are *(less, fewer)* people in the cafe now than there were an hour ago.

4. We were *(already, all ready)* sitting on the train when Corinne raced up to the ticket counter.

5. Ira explained that you cannot travel outside the country *(unless, without)* you have a passport.

6. Francine and Kurt play *(alot, a lot)* of miniature golf.

7. When Maryam tries to dress *(like, as)* her older sister does, she looks a little silly.

8. José is trying to teach *(you're, your)* sister Gloria to swim.

9. The squid that I bought yesterday is *(kind of, somewhat)* tough, so I will pound it with a meat tenderizer before I cook it.

10. Can you tell whether that dog has a collar around *(its, it's)* neck?

EXERCISE B Some of the following sentences have an error in formal, standard usage. Cross out each error and write the correct usage above it. If a sentence has no error, write *C* at the end of the sentence.

Example 1. The award was ~~a~~ *an* unexpected honor for Sergeant Colmes.

11. When you go home today, please bring that book with you.

12. Although the gumbo is cold, it tastes alright.

13. The violin is one instrument that sounds really badly until you know how to play it.

14. There are less patches of snow on the mountain this year than there were last year.

15. If you have already painted a watercolor, why don't you try oil painting for your next project?

16. Gazing through the binoculars, Ted asked where the island was at.

17. Helen taught me how to write a anagram.

18. Hana's project didn't turn out exactly like she thought it would.

19. Although we were nervous, we should of knocked on the door of the senator's office.

20. You hadn't ought to try to walk until your sprained ankle is better.

Review B: Common Usage Problems

EXERCISE A Underline the word or word group that is correct according to formal, standard usage.

Example 1. Please come to my desk and (bring, *take*) your report with you.

1. The queen decided that she would never *(accept, except)* any man's offer of marriage.
2. The milk smelled *(bad, badly)*, so we had to throw it away.
3. If you take *(less, fewer)* money to the store, maybe you'll keep more in the bank.
4. I don't know *(how come, why)* the lawn sprinklers won't work.
5. I'd like to go to Niyatee's house now—Stacey and Maddie are already *(their, there, they're)*.
6. Skimming is *(when you read, reading)* quickly to get the general idea of a piece of writing.
7. Kendra and Alex walked a long *(way, ways)* to get to school from their parents' farm.
8. Most of the speeches were interesting, but a few were *(kind of, rather)* boring.
9. Before the car was invented, people *(use to, used to)* travel by horse and carriage.
10. Dina read in the article *(that, where)* the mayor has decided to run for a seat in the senate.

EXERCISE B Some of the following sentences have an error in formal, standard usage. Cross out each error and write the correct usage above it. If a sentence has no error, write *C* at the end of the sentence.

Example 1. All the foliage ~~accept~~ *except* the pine needles was gone from our trees by December.

11. The sheep pressed theirselves together against the cold.
12. The talented actress cried like her heart would break—on cue.
13. I looked everywheres for the key but couldn't find it.
14. Can you believe that there cat is two years old?
15. Susan didn't feel good this morning.
16. A snake ain't the kind of pet that I want.
17. If you teach me how to knit, I will show you how to crochet.
18. In the ballet that our teacher planned, some of the dancers move like fish move in water.
19. I can't hardly find a ripe peach among all these green ones.
20. Janet wants to try and play the song in a minor key.

NAME CLASS DATE

Review C: Common Usage Problems

USAGE

EXERCISE Underline the word or word group that is correct according to formal, standard usage.

Example 1. I decided to (*let, leave*) her borrow my paints.

1. The cat is licking (*its, it's*) paw because it has a splinter.

2. The figure skater was (*real, very*) disappointed with her performance in the final round.

3. Hold your head high (*as, like*) a swan does, and your back will be straight.

4. I enjoy playing volleyball (*some, somewhat*).

5. Helen's glass fell (*off, off of*) the counter.

6. Jana's watch (*busted, broke*) when she accidentally stepped on it.

7. I don't (*except, accept*) criticism very well, but I do listen when someone is praising me!

8. To me, blue cheese tastes (*bad, badly*), but Bobby really likes it.

9. Please put (*their, there*) art projects on the table.

10. Kara's kindergarten teacher reported that the child plays (*well, good*) with others.

11. Whatever is making that noise has to be (*somewhere, somewheres*) around here.

12. I can tell the cake is done because (*its, it's*) top springs back when I press it.

13. I decided to (*let, leave*) my sister borrow my green sweater.

14. Marge is the person (*who's, whose*) horse was found wandering downtown.

15. I (*use to, used to*) be clumsy at all sports, but now I'm fairly good at baseball.

16. Everybody except him was shorter (*then, than*) six feet.

17. A marathon covers a little over twenty-six miles; that is a long (*way, ways*) to run.

18. Never play in a pile of leaves (*without, unless*) the leaves are off the street.

19. Mrs. Evans, (*which, who*) is running for mayor, visited our class yesterday.

20. A patent is (*when you have a right to, a right to*) an invention.

Proofreading Application: Video Presentation

Good writers are generally good proofreaders. Readers tend to admire and trust writing that is error-free. Make sure that you correct all errors in grammar, usage, spelling, and punctuation in your writing. Your readers will have more confidence in your words if you have done your best to proofread carefully.

A video camera is ideal for certain projects: It allows you to communicate ideas that may be difficult to communicate through the written word alone. However, the fact that on a video your words will be heard—not read—does not mean that you should throw formal, standard usage out the window. Usage errors, even when heard on a video, can make a poor impression. Therefore, before you videotape a project, you should write down what you or others will say so that you can proofread for mistakes in usage.

Proofreading Activity

Find and correct the errors in formal, standard usage in the following introduction to a video presentation. Use proofreading symbols such as those on page 809 of *Elements of Language* to make your corrections.

Example *You'll have to go a long ~~ways~~ way to find a better school.*

The Beel Middle School Ostriches welcome you to this here school! In this video, we're going to try and show you our school: the grounds, the building, the library, and the cafeteria. We have some real good teachers here. They can learn you a whole lot in no time at all. Our school it has some swell students, too; here are some right now. There ain't a school in the county with a better library than ours. We even have a awesome comic-book section; doesn't it look good? Here's the cafeteria; most students just make theirselves at home here. You won't find better food anywheres! We can't hardly wait to meet you!

NAME ______ CLASS ______ DATE ______

for **CHAPTER 21: A GLOSSARY OF USAGE** ***pages 553–67***

Literary Model: Nonfiction

In this excerpt, Jane Goodall describes her studies of chimpanzees.

As the weeks went by the chimpanzees became less and less afraid. . . .

On the eighth day of my watch David Graybeard [one of the chimpanzees] arrived again, together with Goliath, and the pair worked there for two hours. I could see much better: I observed how they scratched open the sealed-over passage entrances [of a termite mound] with a thumb or forefinger. I watched how they bit the ends off their tools when they became bent, or used the other end, or discarded them in favor of new ones. Goliath once moved at least fifteen yards from the heap to select a firm-looking piece of vine, and both males often picked three or four stems while they were collecting tools, and put the spares beside them on the ground until they wanted them.

Most exciting of all, on several occasions they picked small leafy twigs and prepared them for use by stripping off the leaves. This was the first recorded example of a wild animal not merely using an object as a tool, but actually modifying an object and thus showing the crude beginnings of toolmaking.

—from *In the Shadow of Man* by Jane Goodall

EXERCISE A

1. Does Jane Goodall apply the usage rule regarding the words *there, their,* and *they're*? List any examples of these words that appear in this excerpt. Then, explain whether or not Goodall used each of these words correctly.

______

______

______

______

2. Review the usage rule regarding the word *of.* Then, search Goodall's excerpt carefully to find the sentence in which she correctly demonstrates this rule. Write the sentence on the lines below.

______

______

3. Goodall understands the rule about avoiding the phrases *this here* and *that there*. Find the example of Goodall's correct use of this rule. Write the sentence on the lines below.

______

______

Literary Model (continued)

EXERCISE B

1. What one word best describes the tone, or overall sound, of this excerpt? Would the tone be different if the excerpt contained many instances of usage errors? Explain.

2. Why do you think it is important for Goodall and other researchers to avoid usage errors in their writing? Be specific.

EXERCISE C Pretend that you are a writer for a scientific journal, and describe in detail an interesting event you have observed—a family at the airport or a group of dogs playing at the park, for example. Your article should be at least two paragraphs long. Be sure your article includes at least five examples of correct usage, as outlined in the glossary of usage in your textbook.

EXERCISE D What one word best describes the tone of your article? How do you think your usage might affect your readers' reactions to what you wrote? Explain.

Writing Application: Certificate

Read a typical diploma, professional license, or certification, and you will hear the most formal English imaginable:

TYPICAL DIPLOMA BethAnn Mistrot, having successfully completed the Course of Study as prescribed by the Faculty of the College, has been granted the Degree of Doctor of Veterinary Medicine and is entitled to all the rights and privileges appertaining to that Degree, in testimony whereof, the undersigned have subscribed their names and affixed the Seal of the University.

The great degree of formality speaks to Dr. Mistrot's accomplishments and the serious responsibilities that come with her degree. Writers seldom use such formal English, but when they do, it performs a useful service by calling our attention to and celebrating important occasions.

Writing Activity

How appropriate that National Teachers Day falls in May, as the school year comes to an end. Pretend that students at your school are preparing a special luncheon to thank teachers for their year of hard work. Your task is to write the text for certificates of appreciation to be given to each teacher. In formal English, write five lines of text to appear on the certificates.

PREWRITING Two prewriting exercises will prepare you for this task. First, find and read some awards and certificates that use formal English, such as that used in the above example. You could even check an etiquette source—book or Web site—to get a feel for this special style of writing. Second, brainstorm a list of the ways teachers help students. You may wish to cooperate with other students to generate ideas for the text of the certificate.

WRITING If you are worried about the formal language, don't let it block your writing. Instead, create the text first in less formal English. Write about fifteen sentences thanking and praising teachers. Then, choose the five sentences that best communicate students' appreciation. Make sure that your prewriting ideas show up in the sentences you choose. Finally, decide on the best order for the sentences. Often, certificates begin with the recipient's name, followed by a listing of the recipient's helpful activities and the name of the people or group presenting the award. Don't forget to include on the certificate the presentation date.

REVISING Now that you have the text in place, you can concentrate on formalizing the language. Refer to the glossary of usage in your textbook to make sure that the language of your certificate is formal and correct. You should also compare your text to the formal texts that you read during the prewriting stage. As you turn up the formal tone of your certificate, get feedback from other students and a few adults.

PUBLISHING Check your text—and let others check it, too—for errors in punctuation and spelling. Such errors would be embarrassing if printed up for all to see. After you have corrected errors in the text of the certificate, work with your classmates to produce a copy of the certificate to present to your teacher.

Extending Your Writing

This exercise could lead to a more developed writing project. In honor of National Teachers Day, you could write a profile of a teacher who has inspired you, for publication in the school or local paper.

Choices: Exploring Capital Letters

Here's your chance to step out of the grammar book and into the real world. You may not notice capital letters, but you and the people around you use them every day. The following activities challenge you to find a connection between capitalization and the world around you. Do the activity below that suits your personality best, and then share your discoveries with your class. Have fun!

ETYMOLOGY

Check Up

Look up the word *capital* in a dictionary. From what language did this word originate? What are its roots and their meanings? How many meanings does *capital* have? Find the answers to these questions. Then, write a memo telling your classmates about your research. With your teacher's permission, share your findings with your class.

LISTING

My Hometown

For each capitalization rule in this chapter, find a real-life example from your town. Then, write each rule along with the corresponding hometown example. Ask for approval to post your work on a bulletin board.

RESEARCH

Winnie-the-Pooh

A. A. Milne, the author of the Winnie-the-Pooh series, often used old-style capitalization rules in which anything important might be capitalized. Investigate how he used capitals. Then, look for other works that use capitals in the old style. The writings of the U.S. Founders will be fruitful for this project. Make a poster that illustrates the old style, and ask to hang it in the classroom.

GRAPHIC DESIGN

Construction Supervisor

Prepare a capitalization exhibit. Include examples of modern poetry using few or no capitals. Modern art sometimes uses words with capital letters, so works such as Andy Warhol's famous soup cans would be good candidates, too. Computer programs, some of which are created in all capitals, would also be a great addition. What else can you add? When your exhibit is complete, ask for permission to display it in the classroom.

REAL LIFE

In the Diplomatic Corps

Find a good secretarial dictionary, and check out the variety of titles that people have all over the world. How are these titles capitalized? Make a list of them, paying particular attention to interesting ones as well as ones that you might actually have the need or opportunity to use in your life. With your teacher's approval, pass out copies of the list to your classmates.

HISTORY

Da Vinci to Picasso

Have you ever seen the fabulous, ancient paintings that decorate the walls of caves? We do not know the names of the artists who drew these masterpieces. We do, however, know the names of many other great artists. Who are they? Make a list of the world's great artists. Include at least one from every century since 1500. Include one from each continent of the world. For each artist, include his or her country, a brief biography, and the title of one famous painting. Post your notes (and illustrations, if possible) on a time line. Ask your history or art teacher to let you display your time line in his or her classroom.

GEOGRAPHY

Great Plains

How well do you know this country? Get a map of the good old *U S* of *A*. Choose a black-and-white map or make a black-and-white copy. Make a list of all the regional names that you have ever heard—Deep South, Midwest, and Great Plains, for instance. Then, get a U.S. geography book and learn about other regions. Use colored markers, paint, or pencils to outline or shade in each region. Use proper capitalization when you label each region. Hang your map in the classroom, or make copies for everyone in the class.

First Words and *I*

22a. Capitalize the first word in every sentence.

22b. Capitalize the first word in both the salutation and the closing of a letter.

22c. Capitalize the pronoun *I*.

EXAMPLES **T**he picture that **I** am painting is almost finished.
She said, "**P**lease help me plan the costumes for the school play."
Yours truly

MECHANICS

EXERCISE A In the following sentences, circle each incorrectly used lowercase letter.

Example 1. Will it sound too formal if (i) begin with the salutation "(d)ear Sir"?

1. the letter began, "dear friends of our fair city."

2. Helen asked, "may i borrow that book when you're finished?"

3. picking up a murder mystery, i wondered if Ms. Jay would approve it for my book report.

4. Luis wrote, "dear Jim Arnosky, i was fascinated by your recently published book."

5. my teacher asked me to write a poem beginning with the line "roses are red; violets are blue."

6. Wondering who the guests would be, i asked, "whom did you invite to our dinner party?"

7. When i saw the latest bestseller, i eagerly grabbed it.

8. Tom began reciting his poem: "falling, spinning, whirling—the dream had just begun."

9. During lunch, Robin jotted a letter to Amy and signed it, "your friend, Robin."

10. Christine raised her hand and asked, "may i read my short story to the class?"

EXERCISE B In the following letter, underline each word that incorrectly begins with a lowercase letter.

Example Mr. Jiménez said to the class, "<u>write</u> a letter to the author of this book."

dear Louis Sachar,

we read your novel *Holes* in class, and i am writing to say I loved this book! when Mr. Jiménez said, "in this story, Stanley Yelnats is mistakenly sent to a juvenile detention camp," i thought, "maybe I'll skip this one." When we started reading, however, I couldn't wait to finish. the mysterious holes the boys had to dig kept me in suspense. keep up the fantastic work!

sincerely,

Leo Bellman

NAME ______ CLASS ______ DATE ______

Proper Nouns A

22d(1). Capitalize the names of persons and animals.

PROPER NOUNS Denzel Washington, Lassie, Alexander the Great
COMMON NOUNS actor, dog, ruler

EXERCISE A In the following sentences, circle each incorrectly used lowercase letter.

Example 1. Let's meet at touch of spice, the restaurant near my house.

1. I just got the new CD by lauryn hill.
2. My favorite rabbit is peter cottontail.
3. Justine took her cat smokey to the vet.
4. Did you hear michael feldman on the radio this weekend?
5. My dentist, Dr. larry lane, always gives me free dental floss.
6. Tracy enjoys taking her dog bandit to the park.
7. Our neighbors, the garzas, are hosting the block party this year.
8. Did you read this biography of catherine the great?
9. One of my favorite authors is J.r.r. Tolkien.
10. Why did you name your parrot khan?

EXERCISE B Write proper nouns that correspond to each of the following common nouns.

Example 1. dog *Fido*

11. actor ______
12. president ______
13. teacher ______
14. parent ______
15. cat ______
16. scientist ______
17. athlete ______
18. brother ______
19. horse ______
20. student ______

Proper Nouns B

22d(2). Capitalize geographical names.

EXAMPLES **N**ew **M**exico, **O**hio **R**iver, the **W**est, the **U**nited **S**tates of **A**merica, **M**ount **R**ainier
state, river, west of town, nation, mountain

MECHANICS

EXERCISE A On the lines provided, write a geographical name for each of the following common nouns.

Example 1. region *the Southwest*

1. continent ______
2. country ______
3. city ______
4. state ______
5. island ______
6. body of water ______
7. street ______
8. park ______
9. mountain ______
10. region ______

EXERCISE B In the following sentences, circle each incorrectly used lowercase letter.

Example 1. My family is going to big bend national park in texas.

11. There is a rocky island in the atlantic called st. helena.
12. On June 30, 1998, a volcano named korovin erupted on atka island in alaska.
13. Thomas is drawing a map of africa and has marked the location of the equator.
14. Ships use the panama canal to pass between the Caribbean sea and the pacific ocean.
15. Although you may think lake charles is just a lake, it is also a city in louisiana.
16. I spoke with a woman from laos, which is a country between vietnam and thailand.
17. Sanya's class toured the museum located at 249 dixon parkway.
18. The island of puerto rico, which is in the west indies, covers nearly 3,500 square miles.
19. Located in two states, death valley contains the lowest point in the western hemisphere.
20. Kay enjoys spending time in her home on fifty-third st. in minneapolis.

Proper Nouns C

22d(3). Capitalize names of organizations, teams, institutions, and government bodies.

EXAMPLES **W**estwood **B**allet **C**enter, **H**ouston **C**omets, **U**niversity of **C**alifornia at **L**os **A**ngeles, the **H**ouse of **R**epresentatives

EXERCISE A In the following sentences, circle each incorrectly used lowercase letter.

Example **1.** Doesn't your sister go to california institute of technology?

1. Brandon is helping to coach the broncos, which is a little league team.

2. In 1947, the Central intelligence agency was founded to coordinate the intelligence activities of government groups.

3. Margaret Thatcher was elected to the British parliament in 1959.

4. Has Julian done his research for the oral report on united way?

5. The buffalo bills were runners-up in the Super Bowl four years in a row, from 1991 to 1994.

6. The United States congress was established in 1789.

7. When Paula turns fourteen, she plans to volunteer at Marshall memorial hospital.

8. Normally we use the school library, but today we're going to the sherman public Library.

9. The United States senate is composed of two senators from each state.

10. Did you hear the results of the vote in Durant city council today?

EXERCISE B The following sentences contain errors in capitalization. Circle each incorrectly used lowercase letter.

Example **[1]** Neil Armstrong taught aerospace engineering at the university of cincinnati from 1971 to 1979.

[11] The national aeronautics and space administration was formed in 1958. **[12]** Eleven years later, nasa had landed the first people on the moon. **[13]** Neil Armstrong, who studied aeronautical engineering at purdue university, was the astronaut who first stepped onto the moon. **[14]** In Cape Canaveral, Florida, space flights for nasa are launched from the john f. kennedy space center. **[15]** Space flights with crews are controlled from the lyndon b. Johnson space center in Houston, Texas.

Proper Nouns D

22d(4). Capitalize the names of historical events and periods, special events, calendar items, and holidays.

EXAMPLES the **R**enaissance, the **A**utumn **F**estival, **F**riday, **A**pril **F**ools' **D**ay

22d(5). Capitalize the names of nationalities, races, and peoples.

EXAMPLES a **B**razilian, **P**akistanis, **H**ebrews, the **H**opi

EXERCISE In the following sentences, circle each incorrectly used lowercase letter.

Example 1. My goal is to speak the language like a native (i)talian.

1. The bedouins are nomadic arabs in Arabia, Syria, and North Africa.
2. The class's thanksgiving party is this friday at noon.
3. It has been over half a century since world war II ended.
4. Last saturday I met a jamaican who was here to tour a nearby college.
5. Marcos and his horse will lead the tyler fourth of july parade.
6. Why don't we get together to watch the super bowl?
7. My friend Mark Nguyen is a third-generation asian american.
8. Horace and Tamara both have birthdays in february, but mine is in august.
9. In the 1500s, a religious movement called the reformation led to Protestantism.
10. Mr. Paik is teaching us some interesting facts about the industrial revolution.
11. What does the groundhog's shadow mean on groundhog day?
12. Many descendants of the maya live in Mexico and Guatemala.
13. The lead role in the movie called for an african american of around twenty years of age.
14. The U.S. civil war is also called the war between the states.
15. The war of 1812, which lasted from 1812 to 1815, was between the americans and the british.
16. Everyone is looking forward to the next outdoor jazz concert, called blues on the green.
17. The spring flight of fancy is a dance held every spring at my school.
18. Courtney enjoyed meeting the australian who spoke at her school.
19. "Are you going to watch the olympics?" asked Lucas.
20. Were the dark ages in Europe a time of poverty, lack of knowledge, and cultural decline?

Proper Nouns E

22d(6). Capitalize the names of businesses and the brand names of business products.

EXAMPLES **A**ardvark **A**nt **C**ontrol, **B**est **B**uy, **H**ewlett-**P**ackard **D**eskJet 500

22d(7). Capitalize the names of ships, trains, aircraft, and spacecraft.

EXAMPLES USS ***M****innow,* ***O****rient* ***E****xpress,* ***B****lue* ***T****rickster,* ***E****ndeavour*

EXERCISE A In the following sentences, circle each incorrectly used lowercase letter.

Example 1. For their fiftieth anniversary, my grandparents took a cruise on the *silver mermaid.*

1. I have shopped for clothes from the gap on the store's Web site.
2. My homeroom teacher has a coffee cup from dunkin' donuts on her desk.
3. Aaron and his friends met at taco hut before the basketball game.
4. The steamship *great britain,* which sailed in the 1840s, was driven by propellers.
5. Have you seen that television series about the spacecraft *voyager*?
6. My sister has several gund stuffed bears.
7. Should we get the xerox copier or the ricoh aficio 200, which also works as a printer?
8. For Tina's birthday party, her grandmother threw a surprise party at baskin-robbins.
9. Charles Lindbergh made the first solo nonstop flight from New York to Paris in the *spirit of st. louis.*
10. Casey was pleased about his job as a teller at bank of north america.

EXERCISE B In the following paragraph, circle each incorrectly used lowercase letter.

Example [1] The advertisement featured the new nike air garnett III shoes.

[11] Each week my mailbox overflows with circulars advertising barbies and magnavox boom-boxes at target, hewlett-packard fax machines at office depot, and cruises on ships such as the *royal princess.* **[12]** Once, I received a brochure for a railway tour on the *midwestern express.* **[13]** Another time I received a voucher to fly on the President's private airplane, *air force one,* but that was a joke concocted by my friend Charlie. **[14]** The Sunday paper is stuffed with ads for macintosh computers and minute maid orange juice. **[15]** If I bought all the stuff advertised by j. c. penney and the other stores, I would have to fly to outer space on *columbia* to find the space to store it all!

Proper Nouns F

22d(8). Capitalize the names of buildings and other structures.

EXAMPLES **W**hite **H**ouse, **T**ower of **L**ondon, **G**reat **W**all of **C**hina

Do not capitalize such words as *hotel, theater,* or *high school* unless they are part of the name of a particular building or institution.

22d(9). Capitalize the names of monuments, memorials, and awards.

EXAMPLES **W**ashington **M**onument, **A**lex **H**aley **M**emorial **S**tatue, **P**urple **H**eart

EXERCISE In the following sentences, circle each incorrectly used lowercase letter.

Example 1. Daniel was surprised to receive the (m)ost (v)aluable (p)layer award.

1. The mayor's office is located downtown in city hall.

2. The gateway arch in St. Louis, Missouri, rises 630 feet high.

3. We do our holiday shopping at the galleria mall.

4. A distinctive structure in San Francisco is the golden gate bridge.

5. The leaning tower of pisa, a bell tower in Italy, leans ten degrees off center.

6. The frederick douglass national historic site honors the famous African American leader.

7. The colossus of rhodes was one of the Seven Wonders of the World.

8. Jennifer and Matt's wedding reception will be held at the plaza hotel.

9. On our way home, we passed shepton middle school.

10. Christiane Nüsslein-Volhard won the nobel prize in medicine in 1995.

11. We have tickets to a performance at the metropolitan opera house.

12. During our visit to London, we went to see big ben, a famous clock.

13. Clara studied the photograph of mount rushmore national memorial closely.

14. The volleyball game will take place in the harriet johnson gymnasium.

15. My uncle, who is a Vietnam veteran, visited the vietnam veterans memorial yesterday.

16. English monarchs are crowned in westminster abbey.

17. My father's office is on the tenth floor of georgetown towers.

18. Someone with a sense of humor named the bridge near my house rickety bridge.

19. David will play in a piano recital to be held at the denver civic center.

20. In the seventh-grade talent show, Vivica won an award called the sensational sevens.

Proper Nouns G

22d(10). Capitalize the names of religions and their followers, holy days and celebrations, sacred writings, and specific deities.

EXAMPLES **I**slam, **M**uslims, **H**anukkah, **T**almud, **B**uddha

22d(11). Capitalize the names of planets, stars, constellations, and other heavenly bodies.

EXAMPLES **O**rion, **N**eptune, **N**orth **S**tar, **B**ig **D**ipper

MECHANICS

EXERCISE A In the following passage, circle each incorrectly used lowercase letter.

Example 1. A follower of (i)slam is called a (m)uslim.

1. Many religions, including christianity, judaism, buddhism, and others, stress the importance of moral integrity in one's conduct.
2. For example, christians follow the teachings of jesus christ, which are recorded in the holy bible.
3. Guided by the hebrew bible and the torah, jews strive to act with mercy and justice.
4. Students of the buddha (buddhists) as well as hindus are taught dharma, which is right conduct, or duty.
5. Followers of a particular religion join together to celebrate events such as easter, lent, advent, passover, or other holy days that remind them of their religious heritage.

EXERCISE B In the following sentences, circle each incorrectly used lowercase letter.

Example 1. I can always find the constellation (a)ndromeda in the night sky.

6. The planet nearest the sun is mercury.
7. On a cloudless night, I studied pisces, a constellation in the north sky.
8. The brightest star in the constellation Centaurus is Alpha centauri.
9. That planet with a thin, icy ring system around its equator is saturn.
10. "First, locate the constellation gemini," said Professor Hermann.
11. "Then, look for the brightest star in Gemini, which is pollux," he said.
12. The Milky way is a galaxy formed of stars and interstellar gas.
13. Looking up at the northern Cross, Kendra began planning an oil painting of the five stars.
14. The largest planet of the solar system carries the same name as the Roman god of thunder: jupiter.
15. "Is that a bright star, or is that venus?" asked Michelle as she gazed upward.

Proper Adjectives and Course Names

22e. Capitalize proper adjectives.

A *proper adjective* is formed from a proper noun.

PROPER NOUNS China, William Shakespeare, the Confederacy
PROPER ADJECTIVES a Chinese scientist, a Shakespearean play, a Confederate soldier

22f. Do not capitalize the names of school subjects, except course names followed by numerals and names of language classes.

COURSE NAMES art, French, History II

EXERCISE A In the following sentences, circle each incorrectly used lowercase letter.

Example 1. When you're at the bookstore, pick up an italian newspaper and a french magazine.

1. My mother bought an african lamp made of teakwood for my aunt.
2. My japanese friend took latin american history and enjoyed it.
3. Yesterday, a famous guest came to visit our music 102 class.
4. My british pen pal, Sarah, sent me an irish friendship ring.
5. I told my mother that the best way for me to practice speaking spanish is to talk with my argentinian friend every night.
6. The spanish explorers sailed up the florida coast.
7. According to the korean exchange student, english class is very different in this country.
8. Isak Dinesen was a danish author who wrote a story about a european girl named Babette.
9. When I go to college, I plan to take biology 101 and swimming I, II, and III.
10. Everyone who is in my english class is also in my math 202 class.

EXERCISE B In the following sentences, circle each incorrectly used capital or lowercase letter.

Example 1. I have Study Hall between social studies and french.

11. As an interior decorator, Molly enjoys adding peruvian Rugs to a room's decor.
12. When Roberto left Science class, he went to his locker to pick up a book for English class.
13. In History class, we saw pictures of victorian children.
14. We brought back some beautiful Mexican Pottery from our vacation in Mexico.
15. Next year I hope to enroll in advanced computer programming IV.

First Words, *I*, and Proper Nouns and Adjectives A

Review Rules 22a–22f for information on the correct capitalization of first words, the pronoun *I*, proper nouns, and proper adjectives.

EXERCISE A Identify each underlined word or word group by writing above it *CN* for *common noun*, *PN* for *proper noun*, or *PA* for *proper adjective*. Then, rewrite any underlined word that should be capitalized but is not.

Example 1. American <u>history</u> (CN) is covered in <u>history I</u> (PN—History I).

1. The Marquis de Lafayette was a <u>french</u> soldier and diplomat.
2. He came to <u>america</u> in 1777 to join the <u>staff</u> of George Washington.
3. He helped the <u>american</u> <u>colonists</u> in their struggle for independence.
4. He persuaded <u>king louis XVI</u> to send <u>soldiers</u> and <u>ships</u> to help, too.
5. <u>Lafayette</u> fought in many <u>battles</u> of the American Revolution.

EXERCISE B In the following sentences, circle each incorrectly used lowercase letter.

Example 1. (m)illie, a girl who sits next to me in (e)nglish class, wrote a funny poem that begins, "(t)he banana peel came out of nowhere."

6. Last january, i moved away from arizona.
7. it takes several days to drive from utah to pennsylvania.
8. After dinner, my friend arlis and i swam in the gulf of mexico.
9. During my vacation last summer, i took a picture of a statue of Dr. martin luther king, jr., in montgomery, alabama.
10. Pola said, "this is such a pretty city. let's stop for the night here."
11. our book club always meets on the second wednesday of the month.
12. As I walked through the front door, Dad asked, "would you rather have vegetable spaghetti or baked fish for dinner?"
13. Hilda said, "let's try that new restaurant that serves mediterranean food."
14. ms. Williams said, "your assignment is to write a poem using the line 'some people don't understand.'"
15. When i attend savannah college of art and design after high school graduation, i'm going to study roman architecture.

MECHANICS

First Words, *I*, and Proper Nouns and Adjectives B

Review Rules 22a–22f for information on the correct capitalization of first words, the pronoun *I*, proper nouns, and proper adjectives.

MECHANICS

EXERCISE A Identify each underlined word by writing above it *CN* for *common noun, PN* for *proper noun,* or *PA* for *proper adjective.* Then, rewrite any underlined word that should be capitalized but is not.

Example 1. "This is a composition by mozart," Ms. Davis told us. (CN above composition; PN–Mozart above mozart)

1. Wolfgang Amadeus Mozart was born in salzburg, austria.
2. By the age of four, Mozart had already shown great musical genius.
3. He toured the european courts, performing on the violin and organ.
4. This austrian became one of the world's greatest composers.
5. Mozart wrote many operas, including *The Marriage of Figaro* and *The Magic Flute.*

EXERCISE B The following paragraph contains errors in capitalization. Circle each word that is incorrectly capitalized or lowercased.

Example [1] most People are unaware of how many american tourist attractions exist.

[6] sherry and i took a trip one weekend. **[7]** On friday, we arrived in atlanta, georgia, where we stopped for lunch at a place called priscilla's pantry. **[8]** then, we went to burlington, North carolina. **[9]** Sherry wanted to see the monument to Charles drew, the famous doctor. **[10]** I decided that i would learn more about dr. drew once we got back home. **[11]** That night, we stayed in a Hotel on the Roanoke river. **[12]** Then, on saturday, we went to Gettysburg, pennsylvania. **[13]** I learned that Gettysburg was founded by james gettys. **[14]** The Battle of Gettysburg, an important battle in american History, was fought here. **[15]** After the Battle, abraham lincoln delivered the Gettysburg Address. **[16]** a version of this speech appears on a plaque in the Lincoln Memorial, which is located in Washington, d.c. **[17]** Because I had memorized this speech in History class, I was able to recite it. **[18]** As we traveled home on sunday, we admired the pennsylvania countryside. **[19]** When we reached the Ohio river, we knew our trip was almost finished. **[20]** After we got home, Sherry said, "we should take trips together more often."

Personal Titles and Titles Showing Family Relationships

22g. Capitalize titles.

(1) Capitalize the title of a person when the title comes before a name.

(2) Capitalize a word showing a family relationship when the word is used before or in place of a person's name.

Do not capitalize a word showing a family relationship if it follows a possessive word.

EXAMPLES My **d**ad is a close friend of **C**hief Bradley.

My **u**ncle Frank planned a birthday party for **A**unt Flora.

MECHANICS

EXERCISE A In the following sentences, circle each incorrectly used lowercase letter. If a sentence is already correct, write *C* after it.

Example 1. Arthur enjoys talking with (p)rofessor Bleau about archaeology.

1. For her birthday, my uncle Derwood gave aunt Bonnie a pair of earrings.

2. My grandpa owns stables where he boards and trains horses.

3. On Thursday, mayor Wilkins will be visiting our school.

4. Each morning, principal McVicar reads announcements.

5. Vickie listened with interest to a speech made by commissioner Jackson.

6. "Please ask Carlton whether he'd like to spend the night here," said dad.

7. My mom wrote a note to excuse me from class for my appointment with dr. Lanier.

8. When you see mrs. Davenport, please ask her if she has seen my mom.

9. Is that a drawing of president Washington on the one-dollar bill?

10. As Douglas approached the table, he said, "Good afternoon, uncle."

EXERCISE B The following sentences contain errors in capitalization. Circle each letter that is incorrectly capitalized or lowercased.

Example 1. Kenneth asked his (D)ad for permission to go see a movie with Mike.

11. Our committee should speak with the Principal about the dates for the party.

12. Before his birthday, I asked my Brother to give me a list of items he wanted.

13. I asked my neighbor, mr. Elton, if he would hire me to mow his lawn.

14. Jenny has always enjoyed spending time with aunt Pattie.

15. The fire marshal and mayor Kniffin worked together on the parade committee.

NAME CLASS DATE

Titles and Subtitles

22g(3). Capitalize the first and last words and all important words in titles and subtitles.

Unimportant words in titles include articles, coordinating conjunctions, and prepositions of fewer than five letters.

EXAMPLES *The **N**ew York **T**imes, **T**he **O**ld **M**an and the **S**ea, **M**asterpiece **T**heater*

MECHANICS

EXERCISE A In the following sentences, circle each incorrectly used lowercase letter. If a sentence is already correct, write *C* after it.

Example 1. Please open your books to the poem "(o)de to a (n)ightingale."

1. Because I enjoy reading short articles, I subscribe to *reader's digest*.

2. Justin used the lyrics of the song "vincent" for his poetry analysis.

3. In the *tampa tribune*, I read about a statement made by President Clinton.

4. Morton decided to subscribe to *sports illustrated*.

5. Do you know the words to "the battle hymn of the republic"?

6. My mother really liked Raul Julia in the movie *the addams family*.

7. Dale bought himself a tape of the musical play *cats*.

8. A popular movie during the holidays is *It's a Wonderful Life*.

9. Once I started reading *the giver* by Lois Lowry, I couldn't put it down.

10. Jeremy prepared an oral report on the textbook's tenth chapter, "the structure of cells."

EXERCISE B Circle each incorrectly lowercased or capitalized letter.

Example 1. For my birthday, Joey got me a copy of *Stories (a)bout (g)hosts*.

11. One of my favorite movies is *king kong*.

12. At the bookstore, Mitzi browsed the racks of Magazines looking for *national geographic*.

13. Paulie often stays up late watching old movies on the television Program *film classics*.

14. The game *Sonic the hedgehog* is on sale at the computer software store.

15. The ballad "the cremation of Sam McGee" is funny and unforgettable.

16. Does our homework include answering the questions at the end of "The American poets"?

17. Sandra lay on the couch and laughed as she watched *the simpsons*.

18. Would you help me find a copy of the declaration of independence on the Internet?

19. May I borrow your copy of *everlasting love* by CeCe Winans?

20. Carrie bought a black-and-white print by Ansel Adams called *Birds On A beach*.

NAME ______________ CLASS ______________ DATE ______________

for **CHAPTER 22: CAPITAL LETTERS** *pages 586–88*

Titles A

22g(1). Capitalize the title of a person when the title comes before a name.

22g(2). Capitalize a word showing a family relationship when the word is used before or in place of a person's name.

22g(3). Capitalize the first and last words and all important words in titles and subtitles.

EXAMPLES The camping trip was organized by **D**ad, **U**ncle James, and **M**r. Johnson.
We are reading ***O**de: **I**ntimations of **I**mmortality,* a long poem by Wordsworth.

MECHANICS

EXERCISE In the following sentences, circle each incorrectly used lowercase letter. If a sentence is already correct, write *C* after the sentence.

Example 1. Last night I rented the movie *(t)he Sound of (m)usic.*

1. Marge admired the painting *Four Seasons—autumn.*
2. Rao enjoys watching broadcasts of the meetings of our United States senators.
3. Betsy said, "Andy, will you tell dad that I'm still at aunt Marge's house?"
4. Tom Hanks and Tim Allen provided voices for the animated film *toy story.*
5. I enjoyed reading Washington Irving's story "the legend of sleepy hollow."
6. My favorite song on Charlotte Church's CD *Charlotte church* is "Porgy and Bess: summertime."
7. After detective sergeant Desai spoke to our class, I decided to become a detective.
8. Kelly and Alex turned on the television to watch a new episode of *7th Heaven.*
9. *The cherry Orchard* is a play by Anton Chekhov.
10. This biography about President Carter reveals what the daily life of a president is like.
11. In "a Scandal in bohemia," Sherlock Holmes solves a mystery involving Irene Adler.
12. Jared worked for weeks to complete a poem he titled "Lone Wolf in the Wilderness."
13. Drew says he learns a lot from reading the magazine *popular mechanics.*
14. My favorite part of the *Houston chronicle* is the comics.
15. Which doctor examined your eyes for contacts, doctor Mae or doctor Phillips?
16. When I was learning to play the piano, I practiced "ode to joy" every day.
17. This sculpture, *couple dancing,* was created by a student in my art class.
18. Would you hand me the sports section from the *Los Angeles Times,* please?
19. I'll go next door and ask señora Ruiz if she can spare some eggs.
20. On the wall of my room, I hung a copy of the painting *the starry Night.*

NAME ______________________ CLASS ______________ DATE ______________

for **CHAPTER 22: CAPITAL LETTERS** *pages 586–88*

Titles B

22g(1). Capitalize the title of a person when the title comes before a name.

22g(2). Capitalize a word showing a family relationship when the word is used before or in place of a person's name.

22g(3). Capitalize the first and last words and all important words in titles and subtitles.

EXAMPLES The chaperones for the dance are **M**om, **A**unt Trina, and **M**rs. Warshawski.
Pete read aloud Adrienne Rich's poem "**A**unt **J**ennifer's **T**igers."

MECHANICS

EXERCISE Circle words that are incorrectly capitalized or lowercased.

Example 1. My (Mom) called (grandmother) from the supermarket.

1. My brother has read Jack London's *white fang* several times.

2. "Tell general Foster that his plane is ready," said the major.

3. Alfred spent his weekend reading *the Horse and his Boy,* which is a book by C. S. Lewis.

4. Becky said, "When are you taking your lunch break, doctor?"

5. Since I want to design rides for amusement parks, I was pleased to find *Roller coaster Tycoon* at the software store.

6. Does anybody know the words to our school song, "oh, westwood"?

7. My Cousin is working on mayor O'Shey's reelection campaign.

8. Many famous actors provided voices for the animated movie *a bug's life.*

9. I always read the comics page to follow the adventures of the Gumbo family in *rose is rose.*

10. When Janet entered the store, a clerk asked, "May I help you, ms. Monsanto?"

11. Are we eating Easter dinner at grandpa Olson's house or at grandpa Hulen's house?

12. The next chapter in the book is titled "the track of a storm."

13. Lying in the sun, Lisa read the latest issue of *vogue.*

14. Uncle Enrique gave me a CD by Branford Marsalis, *renaissance.*

15. Does *ERA* stand for *equal rights amendment*?

16. *The Fellowship Of The Ring* is the first book in Tolkien's trilogy.

17. Looking through his collection of video games, Raul selected *chess master.*

18. The author of this book, professor Simkins, is a friend of my Stepfather.

19. The church that Rosa attends is named after saint Mark.

20. The most exciting chapter of the book is "trouble at sea."

NAME ______________________ CLASS ______________ DATE ______________

for **CHAPTER 22: CAPITAL LETTERS** pages 574–88

Review A: **Using Capital Letters**

EXERCISE A In the following sentences, cross out each word that contains an error in capitalization. Above the error, write the word correctly.

Example 1. We spent the day swimming and picnicking at the ~~Lake~~. *lake*

1. Sophomores at lincoln high school take world history II.
2. Mount whitney is one of the highest mountains in north america.
3. the author of the book *A tale of Two cities* is charles dickens.
4. I saw an exhibit of paintings by the mexican artist josé orozco.
5. Then, aunt clara began to sing the song "silver threads among the gold."
6. The Cineplex Theater is two blocks North of our high school.
7. My Grandmother lives on the banks of The Ohio river.
8. there will be a full Moon on my birthday, september 14.
9. Harrison Ford stars in the Movie *Raiders Of The Lost Ark*.
10. Your aunt modene will take you to your appointment with dr. Block.

EXERCISE B Rewrite each of these word groups, using capital letters as needed. If the word group is capitalized correctly, write *C*.

Example 1. Declaration Of Independence *Declaration of Independence*

11. the united states senate ______________________
12. a puerto rican engineer for design, inc. ______________________
13. 145 spring avenue, munster, indiana ______________________
14. tuesday, the fourteenth of november ______________________
15. the book *a day no pigs would die* ______________________
16. a beautiful river in north dakota ______________________
17. a south american jungle ______________________
18. a pizza from the restaurant known as mama leone's ______________________
19. a summer trip to the beach ______________________
20. my cousin hannah ______________________

MECHANICS

Review B: **Using Capital Letters**

EXERCISE A Rewrite each of these word groups, using capital letters as needed. If the word group is already capitalized correctly, write *C*.

Example 1. an asian american comedian ___an Asian American comedian___

1. water from the salton sea ________

2. general ulysses s. grant ________

3. a hispanic doctor, alex rodriguez ________

4. a quarterback for the chicago bears football team ________

5. 897 cricket avenue, fort worth, texas ________

6. a picnic at the beach on long island ________

7. the book *the collected poems of w. b. yeats* ________

8. a winter vacation in a warm climate ________

9. a legend about a monster in lake superior ________

10. my grandmother, minnie robinson ________

EXERCISE B Each sentence contains one error in capitalization. Circle the word that is incorrectly capitalized or lowercased.

Example 1. Eva helped distribute programs in the (Theater's) lobby.

11. My cousin Sheila asked, "what time does the play begin?"

12. I glanced at my timex watch and told her the time.

13. She and i were planning to go to the Lillian Beaumont Theater.

14. I had seen the play *King Lear* there last november.

15. This time, Sheila had Tickets to see the musical play *Evita*.

16. It's the story of Eva Peron, a legendary figure in the history of argentina.

17. I had become interested in Eva Peron after studying her in History class.

18. Sheila and I had both read a biography of Peron, *Evita: An Intimate Portrait Of Eva Peron*.

19. After seeing *Evita,* I realized that she had led a fascinating Life.

20. I decided to ask mr. Mitchell if we could practice singing songs from the show in music class.

Review C: Using Capital Letters

EXERCISE Circle each letter that is incorrectly capitalized.

Example 1. Many barges and ships pass through the panama canal.

1. Juniors at elkton high school must take world history.
2. The larkspur hotel is just north of an exit on the turnpike.
3. The poet t. s. Eliot wrote the poem "The love Song of j. Alfred Prufrock."
4. The planets Saturn and jupiter are much larger than Earth.
5. My uncle Patrick works as a dentist in missouri.
6. On tuesday, brazilians will vote for a new president.
7. Drive west on Third avenue until you come to the Burger Barn.
8. We saw a program about the planet mercury last Sunday night.
9. Celine Dion sang "o Canada."
10. Robin Williams played a modern peter pan in the movie *hook.*
11. The birthday of queen Elizabeth II is celebrated with a Parade in the united kingdom.
12. The window of blum's bakery was full of italian bread and french pastries.
13. Tennessee williams, a playwright from the south, wrote *The Night Of the Iguana.*
14. I read an article about the persian gulf war in *The Philadelphia Inquirer.*
15. Babe ruth was a great baseball Player for the new york Yankees.
16. Native American indians joined the Pilgrims at the first thanksgiving feast.
17. At certain points in its orbit, Pluto is the farthest planet from the Sun.
18. The british composer Andrew lloyd-Webber wrote the musical play *The Phantom Of the Opera.*
19. Did you read Ellen Goodman's column in the sunday *boston globe*?
20. The butler insurance company has its Headquarters in akron.

MECHANICS

NAME CLASS DATE

Proofreading Application: Letter

Good writers are generally good proofreaders. Readers tend to admire and trust writing that is error-free. Make sure that you correct all errors in grammar, usage, spelling, capitalization, and punctuation in your writing. Your readers will have more confidence in your words if you have done your best to proofread carefully.

Capitalization has many functions in writing: It announces the beginning of a sentence; it indicates a proper noun; and it is used in the salutation and closing of a letter.

Proofreading Activity

Find and correct the errors in capitalization. Use the proofreading symbols in the chart on page 809 of *Elements of Language* to make your corrections.

Example My ~~M~~other has always wanted to take a european vacation.

dear beth,

Today, we arrived in london. We flew out of John F. Kennedy airport in new york and landed at heathrow airport in london. We took the Underground, which is the name of the subway system, to our Hotel. After checking in, we were ready for some sightseeing.

First, we went to see buckingham palace, where queen elizabeth II lives. My sister, lisa, took my picture in front of its gates. Then, we visited westminster abbey. The english kings and queens have been crowned there since 1066! Afterward, we went to the tower of london, where the Crown Jewels are housed. We saw not only fabulous crowns, scepters, and swords, but golden saltcellars and spoons as well. By the time we were finished there, we were tired and went back to the Hotel.

We are resting up tonight for another busy day tomorrow. In the morning we are going to great russell street to visit the british museum. Then, in the afternoon we are going to the london zoo. I hear it has a wide variety of animals.

your friend,

Anne

Literary Model: Capital Letters in a Fable

Long ago, the mice had a general council to consider what measures they could take to outwit their common enemy, the Cat. Some said this, and some said that; but at last a Young Mouse got up and said he had a proposal to make which he thought would meet the case. "You will all agree," said he, "that our chief danger consists in the sly and treacherous manner in which the enemy approaches us. Now, if we could receive some signal of her approach, we could easily escape from her. I venture, therefore, to propose that a small bell be procured and attached by a ribbon round the neck of the Cat. By this means we should always know when she was about and could easily retire while she was in the neighborhood."

This proposal met with general applause, until an Old Mouse got up and said, "That is all very well, but who is to bell the Cat?" The mice looked at one another and nobody spoke. Then the Old Mouse said:

"It is easy to propose impossible remedies."

—"Belling the Cat," retold by Joseph Jacobs

EXERCISE A

1. Write the words in the fable that do not follow standard conventions of capitalization.

2. Which standard conventions of capitalization were not followed?

EXERCISE B Why do you think the writer who retold this fable chose not to follow the standard convention of capitalization?

Literary Model (continued)

EXERCISE C A fable teaches a useful lesson, called a moral, about human behavior. The characters in a fable are usually animals. Create a short, original fable that includes animal characters. In it, use capitalization for effect, as Joseph Jacobs does in "Belling the Cat." The following list of morals may help you get started, or you can think of your own moral.

- It is best to prepare for the days of necessity.
- Do not trust flatterers.
- Be sure you can better your condition before you seek to change it.
- There are many who pretend to despise and belittle things beyond their reach.

EXERCISE D

1. What effect did you try to achieve with your use of capitalization? How would your fable read differently if you had not used capitalization the way you did?

2. In which other forms of writing might capitalization that does not follow standard conventions be effective? Explain your answer.

Writing Application: Genealogy

Following the rules of capitalization will help you communicate clearly with the widest possible audience. When you write names and titles, you should be careful to write them correctly.

Writing Activity

Your social studies class is learning about genealogy, which is the study of family histories. Last week the class created charts with students' family trees. This week your teacher has asked you to write a short essay telling about three people in your family. You are to include at least the following information about each person: his or her full name, his or her birth date and birthplace, his or her occupation, and something special about him or her. Make sure to capitalize each person's full name properly. In your discussion, use a word showing a family relationship, such as *aunt* or *father,* in place of or as part of each person's name at least once. Also, at least once in your essay, use a possessive in front of a word showing a family relationship for each person.

PREWRITING Decide which three relatives you will discuss. Write down everything you know about each person. Look at your information, and make a list of what else you need to find out. If you can, visit or call the people you are writing about and interview them. If one of your subjects is no longer alive or lives far away, ask a parent or another relative about the person.

WRITING Try to do more than just list facts about your relatives. You are sketching a brief story of each person's life. Create a narrative with smooth transitions between topics. Feel free to include additional details to round out your portraits.

REVISING Have one of your parents or another relative review your essay. Are your facts accurate? Have you left out any important information about your family members?

PUBLISHING Check your essay for correct spelling and punctuation. Have you capitalized people's names and words showing family relationships accurately? With your teacher's approval, gather your essay and your classmates' essays into a booklet. Make a copy for each member of the class.

Extending Your Writing

You may wish to learn more about your family history. Perhaps you and a parent or grandparent could compile photographs of family members in an album and write short biographical sketches of each family member.

NAME ________________ CLASS ________ DATE ________

for CHAPTER 23: PUNCTUATION pages 598–620

Choices: Exploring Punctuation

Here's your chance to step out of the grammar book and into the real world. You may not notice punctuation marks, but you and the people around you use them every day. The following activities challenge you to find a connection between punctuation marks and the world around you. Do the activity below that suits your personality best, and then share your discoveries with your class. Have fun!

ETYMOLOGY

Detective Work

What does the word *comma* mean? What is its root word? Find out. Go to your school library, and ask the librarian for a dictionary and any reference books that explain the history of words. Then, prepare a handout for your class that gives the information that you have found.

ART

All in One

Get a piece of poster board and draw a giant comma on it. Inside the borders of the comma, write each comma rule and an example for each. You could use different colors for different rules. With your teacher's permission, display your poster in the classroom.

WRITING

Truth, Pure and Simple

Too many adjectives can be boring, especially when they always seem to come in the same place—before a noun. Show your classmates how to juggle adjectives. Write a poem in which you show the versatility of adjectives. Include adjectives before and after the nouns they modify. Use predicate adjectives as well. Be sure to have a series of adjectives that does not require commas and a series that does. With your teacher's approval, read the poem aloud to the class and post it on the bulletin board as a reference.

HISTORY

Once upon a Time

Pick an end mark. Then, find out how it began. When and where was it first used? Did it change over the years? Answer these questions. Then, prepare notes and illustrations to post on a time line. Be ready to explain your notes to the class.

STUDY AID

Rhyme Time

Devise a rhyme, rap, or some other kind of musical mnemonic (*mnemonic* means "memorizing") device to help your classmates remember the rules regarding colons. Write your own lyrics and melody. Enlist some of your classmates to help choreograph a routine for the presentation.

VISUAL ANALYSIS

Alike and Different

Why do we bother to have both commas and semicolons? What's the difference? Think about it. Make a chart with two columns: one labeled "Similarities" and the other labeled "Differences." Then, brainstorm ways in which commas and semicolons are alike and the ways in which they are different. Consider using sentences as examples. When you have finished your chart, copy your chart on poster board and ask for permission to place it where the class can read it.

ART

Around and Around They Go

Make a mobile or a wind chime of punctuation marks. You could use metal, ceramic, wood, or a mixture of media. Go ahead and add a word or two if you want. After you get approval from your teacher, hang your finished project in the classroom. Then, take a bow!

CREATIVE WRITING

A Checkered Past

Make up your own story about how semicolons came to be. Consider the following questions as you write your semicolon creation story. Why is their relationship to the comma not mentioned in their name? What is their relationship to the colon? Which do you think came first, the colon or the semicolon? Why?

End Marks

An *end mark* is a mark of punctuation placed at the end of a sentence.

23a. Use a period at the end of a statement.

23b. Use a question mark at the end of a question.

23c. Use an exclamation point at the end of an exclamation.

23d. Use either a period or an exclamation point at the end of a request or a command.

EXAMPLES Charles Dickens is my favorite author**.**
Who can ever forget Oliver Twist**?**
What a likable character he is**!**
Please return this book for me**.**

EXERCISE A Write the necessary end mark for each of the following sentences.

Example 1. What an exciting way to end a book that is!

1. The library opens at 10:00 A.M. tomorrow
2. Did Randall finish the Stephen King mystery
3. Many movies are based on King's books
4. What scary movies they are
5. I missed seeing the latest one when it was in theaters
6. Garth and Towanna saw it three times
7. How I wish I could have seen it
8. Have you read any mysteries by Sara Paretsky
9. Chicago is the setting for many of her stories
10. You should read one of these exciting mysteries

EXERCISE B Write end marks as needed in the following passage.

Example What is the title of the latest selection in Oprah's Book Club?

You have probably seen or heard about Oprah Winfrey's television show and book club Do you know how she earned this recognition and success As a child, Oprah struggled with problems of poverty, obesity, and abuse What a tragic childhood this was At age thirteen, however, she began living with her father, a devoted parent Have you heard of Tennessee State University This is the college that Oprah attended while working as a news anchor What an interesting after-school job that must have been She began hosting a talk show in 1984 The rest, as they say, is history

Abbreviations

23e. Many abbreviations are followed by a period.

Some abbreviations, such as those for government agencies, are written without periods and are capitalized.

EXAMPLES Dr. Zhivago Video Corp. UN
10 Downing St. 1 qt TV

EXERCISE A Add the necessary periods to abbreviations in the following sentences. If a sentence is already correct, write *C* to the left of the item number.

Example 1. I'm working on an oral report on C.S. Lewis.

1. Al Unser, Jr, won the Indianapolis 500 in 1994.

2. Ms Dexter is here to see you.

3. *Winnie-the-Pooh* was written by A A Milne.

4. Alvin said, "Come watch this television special on the CIA!"

5. The letterhead says "Alma Rd." not "Elma Dr"

6. "Shoes, Inc" is the name of the new store.

7. Please address the letter to 338 Norton Ln in Boston.

8. I think the schedule says "Tues," not "Thurs," Alan.

9. The shopping list says "one lb of apples."

10. I want to work at Johnson Computer Corp, which offers weekend jobs to teenagers.

EXERCISE B Some of the following sentences contain abbreviations that have not been correctly punctuated or capitalized. Cross out each incorrectly written abbreviation, and write the correct form above it.

Example Some materials for the school play were shipped by ~~ups.~~ UPS

ANNOUNCEMENT: The pta of Green Valley Jr High will meet in the Dr Fitzhugh Auditorium at 7:00 on Thursday night. The address of the auditorium is 379 Fourth Ave, Lexington, K.Y. Refreshments will be provided by Ms Kingston, Mr Purdell, and Mrs Garza. Helen McKinnet will be collecting donations for the seventh-grade play. Below is a list of items the seventh-graders still need.

8 yds. of light blue taffeta

ten in of silver metallic cord

red velvet around 3 ft by 2 ft in size

black paint

End Marks and Abbreviations

23a. Use a period at the end of a statement.

23b. Use a question mark at the end of a question.

23c. Use an exclamation point at the end of an exclamation.

23d. Use either a period or an exclamation point at the end of a request or a command.

23e. Many abbreviations are followed by a period.

EXAMPLES Capt**.** Erickson will pilot our flight today**.**
I can't wait to go to Portland to see my cousins**!**
Who invented the term UFO**?**
Look out for that falling rock**!**

MECHANICS

EXERCISE A Insert periods, question marks, and exclamation points where they are needed in the following sentences. If a sentence is already correct, write *C* to the left of the item number.

Example 1. Don't leave yet!

1. Please set the clock on the VCR for me
2. The listing says "6:30 on ch 5," but I'll be at the gym then.
3. We will record the film and watch it later
4. It is about Dr Martin Luther King, Jr
5. Send your request to the following address: 1010 Butler St, Orlando, FL 32887.
6. What fascinating classes hers must be
7. Sara read one of her poems at Mr Bannerjee's retirement party
8. Have you read *I Know Why the Caged Bird Sings*
9. Oh no—watch out
10. Pick up those clothes, Rita

EXERCISE B Insert periods, question marks, and exclamation points where they are needed in the following paragraph.

Example I was up late working on my presentation for Dr**.** Johnson's class.

What a crazy day this has been The Cedar Ave bus left early Wasn't I lucky that Dr and Mr Moreno came by and drove me to school We got to school by 8:00, but it was closed because of a heating problem The principal, Martin Crowe, Sr, stood out front and sent everyone home I hope this means that I can give my UNICEF presentation next Friday

Commas A

23f. Use commas to separate items in a series.

23g. Use a comma to separate two or more adjectives that come before a noun.

WORDS IN A SERIES	Dad's garden produced **carrots, beans,** and **cucumbers.**
PHRASES IN A SERIES	Irene walked **around the corner, across the street,** and **to the store.**
CLAUSES IN A SERIES	I want to know **who will be there, how long the event will last,** and **how much the food will cost.**
ADJECTIVES	Ten **hungry, chirping** birds landed near our blanket.

EXERCISE A Insert commas as needed in the following sentences.

Example 1. I need tortillas, grated cheese, and ground beef.

1. Cars trucks and buses were stranded by the storm.
2. Mrs. Ortega won more votes than Mr. Harris Miss Steinberg or Dr. Gladstone.
3. Scallops oysters herring and shrimp are displayed in the fish-market window.
4. One tall weary man wearing a hat dropped a silver coin into the kettle hanging by the door.
5. The chairperson's responsibilities included calling the meeting to order asking for the minutes and announcing new officers.
6. Howie's dogs are friendly obedient and loyal to him and his family.
7. The zoo director had to feed the animals guide visitors and keep the grounds safe and clean.
8. A sleek powerful submarine slipped into the sea.
9. Many white purple and yellow crocuses grew on the hill.
10. Todd's uncle asked who Rory was when she had arrived and why she was asleep on the porch.

EXERCISE B Insert commas as needed in the following paragraph.

Example I plan to spend a long, happy afternoon at the mall.

Have you heard about the new shopping mall? It is a big exciting place! It has department stores with clothing furniture and sporting goods. It even has specialty shops, such as those that sell only music boxes rare comic books organic health food shoes, or baseball caps. It has a noisy crowded food court that is filled with the smell of warm French bread. This weekend my father sister and I are going to find running shoes a music box with a ballerina, and crunchy trail mix. Why don't you come with us?

Commas B

23h. Use a comma before *and, but, for, nor, or, so,* or *yet* when it joins independent clauses in a compound sentence.

EXAMPLES Joshua's uncle drove us to the skating rink, and he decided to skate with us.
Ariel took her umbrella, for it looked like rain.

EXERCISE A Underline the conjunction in the sentences that follow. Then, add commas where necessary. If a sentence needs no comma, write *C* to the left of the item number.

Example 1. Some people enjoy long car trips, but others get restless in the car.

1. Our family planned a driving trip so we needed maps.
2. Mom looked carefully but couldn't find Elgin.
3. She put on glasses for the print was tiny.
4. The scenery was great yet my sister was restless.
5. Is that normal or is something wrong with the car's engine?
6. Carla noticed I forgot my pencil so she lent me one of hers.
7. My cousin Cary writes music and plays in a band.
8. He invited us to listen but we had no time.
9. Who woke us up and why must we leave early?
10. Yoko is not a good traveler nor am I.

EXERCISE B Combine two sentences to make a compound sentence. Include commas as needed.

Example 1. Rain was pouring down. The football game continued. *Rain was pouring down, yet the football game continued.*

11. I brought a new camera. It broke. ____________________

12. It rained on Sunday. We were disappointed. ____________________

13. The mountains were snowy. The weather didn't seem very cold. ____________________

14. I can borrow skis. Maybe I can rent some. ____________________

15. Mariana spotted a fire tower. Dad saw a deer. ____________________

MECHANICS

Commas C

23i. Use commas to set off an expression that interrupts a sentence.

Use commas to set off nonessential participial phrases, nonessential subordinate clauses, nonessential appositives, and nonessential appositive phrases.

NONESSENTIAL PARTICIPIAL PHRASE	The spring picnic**, planned for months,** is on Thursday.
NONESSENTIAL SUBORDINATE CLAUSE	My favorite aunt**, who is a teacher,** will drive the bus.
NONESSENTIAL APPOSITIVE	Jason's younger brother**, Steve,** is eight years old.
NONESSENTIAL APPOSITIVE PHRASE	Mr. Tarkov**, Dad's new boss,** will be an umpire.

MECHANICS

EXERCISE A Each of the following sentences contains a nonessential phrase or clause. Insert commas as needed.

Example 1. Swimming, my favorite sport, is great exercise.

1. The Johnston City pool built ten years ago is a great place to swim.

2. City residents who are allowed to swim free use the pool all summer.

3. Our annual swim meet which was postponed will be next month.

4. Did you see Sheri my neighbor do a triple flip?

5. Mr. Epstein who is a retired firefighter teaches the beginning swimmers.

EXERCISE B Identify each underlined phrase or clause in the following sentences by writing above it *N* for *nonessential* or *E* for *essential.* Then, add commas to the nonessential phrases and clauses.

Examples 1. Parents who know how to swim can join the group. (E)

2. Lana, the one who's laughing, wants her mother to swim with her. (N)

6. The park equipped with a pool is the one we choose.

7. The pool water sparkling in the sunshine invites me to jump in.

8. Only students who have paid their fees can attend.

9. How would you an experienced instructor educate swimmers about safety?

10. Should we ask Mrs. Sims who walks every day to join us?

11. The lifeguard wearing blue shorts is the strictest one.

12. He stresses good behavior which is important for everyone's safety.

13. A child who is frightened can usually be calmed.

14. The third diving board which is the highest is reserved for experienced divers.

15. Nina Parks the Sentryville Middle School swimming champion is swimming laps.

Commas D

23i. Use commas to set off an expression that interrupts a sentence.

Use commas to set off words that are used in direct address and to set off parenthetical expressions.

EXAMPLES Yes**,** **Tina,** I have extra notebook paper.
The best player**, in my opinion,** is Roberto.

EXERCISE A The following sentences contain words used in direct address or as parenthetical expressions. Insert commas before, after, or both before and after the words as needed.

Example 1. The omelet**,** to tell the truth**,** tasted scorched.

1. The time of our club meeting by the way has been changed.
2. Juan the glove on the other hand of the mannequin does not match this one.
3. The landscape architect said, "These pansies for example would look wonderful there."
4. I didn't know Lorena that you could sing so beautifully!
5. I suppose that you Rudolfo will fill in for Perrin while she is on vacation.
6. On the other hand that old barn looks quite picturesque.
7. Marina may I borrow a pencil?
8. You must of course be home by curfew.
9. In fact these are the cathedral's original stained-glass windows.
10. I'm not sure Kelly whether I want to go to the game.

EXERCISE B Insert commas as needed in the following paragraph.

Example Tell me**,** Edna**,** about your involvement in Habitat for Humanity.

Habitat for Humanity first caught my attention I suppose with its Web site. Victor do you know how to search for information on the Internet? To tell the truth searching on the Internet is quite simple. I will however e-mail you the URL you need. On this Web site Victor you will find lots of information. Habitat for Humanity for example welcomes volunteers to help build houses. You see the main purpose of the organization is to supply affordable housing to people who need it. The future homeowners of course help to build their houses. I thought that you Victor would be especially interested in this organization. Your goal of becoming an architect I think would be compatible with working for Habitat for Humanity.

Commas E

23j. Use a comma after certain introductory elements.

INTRODUCTORY WORD **Yes,** I'm the one who called.

INTRODUCTORY PHRASES **Feeling confident and prepared,** Sara decided to enter the contest.
In the backyard by the alley, I found this old horseshoe.

INTRODUCTORY CLAUSE **After Tyrone wrote the essay,** he checked it for errors.

MECHANICS

EXERCISE A Insert commas as needed in the following sentences.

Example 1. Why, I see you cut your hair!

1. Under the picnic table beside the tent Frisky slept peacefully.

2. Hiding behind the bush during a game of hide-and-seek she scared me.

3. Well look who's here!

4. Beyond that mountain with a snowy peak there's a small cabin.

5. No it burned down last summer.

6. Although the air was muggy we turned off the air conditioner.

7. Oh look at all those birds!

8. Since their leaves stay green all year those trees are called evergreens.

9. After we ate we explored the woods surrounding the campground.

10. Why I wish all views were as beautiful as this!

EXERCISE B Insert commas as needed in the following paragraph.

Example Browsing Web sites on the Internet, I found some interesting information.

In the final month of the twentieth century *Time* magazine named Albert Einstein the Person of the Century. After I read the article by Frederic Golden I agreed with the choice. Yes Einstein won the distinction, but Franklin Roosevelt and Mohandas Gandhi were close runners-up. Although Einstein was a brilliant scientist everyday people recognize his name and photo. As a matter of fact you may even own a poster of Einstein. With his amazing intellect and his flyaway hair Einstein is a beloved figure in American culture. Indeed his ideas influenced more than just science. As Frederic Golden pointed out Einstein's ideas have influenced the arts as well. In fact artists and poets have studied Einstein, and filmmakers have portrayed his life and ideas. Although he died in 1955 Einstein seems very much alive today.

NAME CLASS DATE

Commas F

23f. Use commas to separate items in a series.

23g. Use a comma to separate two or more adjectives that come before a noun.

23h. Use a comma before *and, but, for, nor, or, so,* or *yet* when it joins independent clauses in a compound sentence.

23i. Use commas to set off an expression that interrupts a sentence.

23j. Use a comma after certain introductory elements.

EXAMPLES I sketched **castles, dragons,** and **horses.**
Heavy, gray clouds filled the sky**, and** rain began to fall.
Splashing in the pool, the children were**, of course,** enjoying themselves.

EXERCISE A Insert commas as needed in the following sentences.

Example 1. Since my boots are muddy, may I borrow yours?

1. This mild creamy cheese will taste good on toast.
2. No one claimed the lost dog that I found so I decided to keep her.
3. My school has a tennis court a baseball diamond and a jogging track.
4. Where are we eating lunch Maxine?
5. "He can shake hands he can roll over and he can play dead," Scruffy's trainer told us.
6. Before I can watch television I have to finish my homework.
7. A landscape painting in my opinion would look better in this room than a portrait.
8. I bought the latest issue and I eagerly read every article.
9. Your clothing designs Cheryl are very promising.
10. Running across the lawn a squirrel attracted Alex's attention.

EXERCISE B Insert commas as needed in the following paragraph.

Example I missed the game on television, but Stephanie told me about it.

Smiling from ear to ear Stephanie had spectacular wonderful news. Yes the Bears won their fifth game! In the second half of the game they were awesome. When she told us we yelled jumped for joy and hugged each other. I pasted team pictures in my bedroom inside my locker on the refrigerator and on my notebook cover.

Commas G

23f. Use commas to separate items in a series.

23g. Use a comma to separate two or more adjectives that come before a noun.

23h. Use a comma before *and, but, for, nor, or, so,* or *yet* when it joins independent clauses in a compound sentence.

23i. Use commas to set off an expression that interrupts a sentence.

23j. Use a comma after certain introductory elements.

EXAMPLES **We hiked, we rafted,** and **we swam** at the state park.
The **soggy, overcooked** vegetables didn't appeal to me**, nor** did the meatloaf.
After she got the camera, Katy**, who is twelve,** developed her own film.

EXERCISE A Insert commas in the following sentences as needed.

Example 1. Taught golf as a toddler**,** Tiger Woods was destined for greatness.

1. Tiger Woods's parents Earl and Kultida had Tiger playing golf at age two.
2. When Tiger was fifteen he won the U.S. Junior Amateur championship.
3. The dedicated gifted Tiger went on to win the 1992 and 1993 championships as well.
4. In each of the following three years he won the U.S. Amateur championship.
5. Tiger enrolled in Stanford University in 1994 but he did not give up golf.
6. Turning pro in August of 1996 Tiger left college.
7. He golfed in numerous events that year if I'm not mistaken.
8. He won two titles earned almost $800,000 in prize money and was named outstanding rookie.
9. Tiger is well known for his golf swing which is graceful and accurate.
10. Tiger, in 1997, won the Masters Tournament a highly prestigious event.

EXERCISE B Insert commas as needed in the following paragraph.

Example Haunted houses**,** in Leon's opinion**,** really do not exist.

The grand old mansion fascinated neighborhood teenagers. Situated at the top of a hill it looked very stately. An iron fence which was covered with vines encircled the property. The teenagers discovered that they could part the vines peek through the fence and see a garden maze in the yard. One of the children Leon wanted to climb the fence. When he put his foot on the fence the other children shook their heads. Looking disappointed Leon said that he guessed the maze should remain a mystery.

Commas H

23k. Use commas in certain conventional situations.

Use commas to separate items in dates and addresses. Use a comma after the salutation of a personal letter and after the closing of any letter.

EXAMPLES My grandfather was born on May 4, 1948, in Philadelphia.
His first apartment was at 32 Walton Street, Dayton, Ohio.
Dear Grandpa,
Sincerely yours,

EXERCISE A Insert commas as needed in the following sentences.

Example 1. The new wing of the school was dedicated on April 4, 2000.

1. The public library in New Falls South Dakota received an anonymous donation.
2. You'll find the bakery at 719 Pixel Avenue Louisville.
3. Mary signed the letter, "Yours truly Mary Roberts."
4. Spring Break will begin March 1 2002.
5. Cory wrote, "Dear Mrs. Reszke I am writing to volunteer for math tutoring."
6. I have a pen pal who lives in North Platte Nebraska.
7. What were you doing on December 31 1999 when the clock struck midnight?
8. My mom's address is P.O. Box 338 Bangor Maine.
9. The movie theater at 462 Locust in Avery Montana is closing down.
10. Charlene's uncle will graduate from law school on May 17 2003.

EXERCISE B Insert commas as needed in the following letter.

Example Margo's address is 432 State Street, Tampa, Florida.

December 30 2001

Dear Margo

I'm catching up on my letters. No, I didn't forget your camp form. The camp's office moved from 1234 Howard Street Springfield Missouri. Now they're at 16 Rogers Road Deerfield Missouri. Camp starts on June 15 2001, but our forms need to be mailed by March 15 2001. Good news—they need counselors! I hope we both get jobs. Oh—use my new address when you write me back: P.O. Box 977 Fayetteville Arkansas.

Your pal

Nichola

Commas I

Review the rules on pages 602–15 of your textbook for information on using commas with items in a series, independent clauses, introductory elements, nonessential clauses and phrases, words used in direct address, parenthetical expressions, dates, addresses, and letters.

EXERCISE Insert commas as needed in the following sentences. If a sentence needs no commas, write *C* after it.

Example 1. VCR**,** CD**,** and DVD are abbreviations we hear often.

1. I often rent a movie pop some popcorn and invite a friend over.
2. When I rent a movie I rent a copy on videotape.
3. If I had a DVD player I could rent the movie on DVD.
4. The abbreviation *DVD* stands for either "digital video disc" or "digital versatile disc."
5. The DVD which is a newer technology than the videotape was introduced in 1996.
6. Consumers were curious about DVDs but they did not have access to them until 1997.
7. DVD players were widely available by December 1 1999.
8. You may remember Anthony how many holiday season advertisements featured DVD players that year.
9. I wonder how many kids wrote letters saying, "Dear Grandma Please give me a DVD player."
10. The DVD a flat shiny disc looks much like a music CD or a computer CD-ROM.
11. A CD-ROM stores 650 million bytes of data but the DVD can store over 4 billion bytes.
12. Well imagine the difference in quality between a movie on videotape and one on DVD.
13. The DVD as you know has a much higher capacity for data storage.
14. It has higher quality video it has better sound and it can contain multiple movies.
15. Yes that's right.
16. With the technology of the DVD a filmmaker can provide several versions of a movie on one DVD.
17. Different endings different languages and other variations can be offered.
18. The DVD player which is still rather costly for my budget is now a familiar sight in stores.
19. For now on movie night I will continue using my trusty VCR.
20. Maybe I'll ask Grandma for a DVD player next year and sign the letter, "Your DVD-deficient grandson Chad."

Commas J

Review the rules on pages 602–15 of your textbook for information on using commas with items in a series, independent clauses, introductory elements, nonessential clauses and phrases, words used in direct address, parenthetical expressions, dates, addresses, and letters.

EXERCISE Insert commas as needed in the following sentences. If a sentence is already correct, write *C* on the line provided.

Example ______ **1.** These roofing shingles**,** which are made of wood**,** should be replaced.

______ **1.** They washed vegetables they baked chicken and they packed a picnic basket.

______ **2.** When did you write this poem Muriel?

______ **3.** The farmer's market will open for this summer on May 31 2002.

______ **4.** Students who have finished their assignments may leave early.

______ **5.** Under the bushes by the back fence a small cottontail rabbit sat perfectly still.

______ **6.** Whenever you host one of your karaoke parties I laugh for days afterward.

______ **7.** Laura sings and Ricardo dances.

______ **8.** Santiago wrote, "Dear Grandmother I'm writing to wish you a happy birthday."

______ **9.** The vice president of our class Jane Ellen has an announcement to make.

______ **10.** Ba Thi is not interested in soccer nor is he interested in hockey.

______ **11.** This brown fuzzy fruit is a kiwi.

______ **12.** There are campaign posters in the hallways in the cafeteria and on the locker doors.

______ **13.** This is the correct answer right?

______ **14.** Planted in early spring the seeds soon sprouted.

______ **15.** Shel Silverstein's book *The Giving Tree* is my favorite of his works.

______ **16.** Across a field and down a hill the horse galloped at full speed.

______ **17.** The letter was signed mysteriously, "Yours forever Your Secret Admirer."

______ **18.** For information write to the manufacturer at 2407 Smyth Ave. Bismarck, ND.

______ **19.** These floors by the way are made of Italian marble.

______ **20.** Sure go ahead and have the last muffin.

Semicolons A

23l. Use a semicolon between independent clauses if they are not joined by *and, but, for, nor, or, so,* or *yet.*

23m. Use a semicolon rather than a comma before a coordinating conjunction to join independent clauses that contain commas.

EXAMPLES Anna Mary Robertson Moses had a goal**;** she wanted to be an artist.
I called Chung Sook, Van, and Ray**;** and Sam called Marva.

MECHANICS

EXERCISE A Insert semicolons as needed in each of the following sentences.

Example 1. Many people love Grandma Moses's paintings; others, though, find them too simple.

1. Hector's mother is a painter she told him about Grandma Moses.
2. Anna Mary Robertson Moses began painting in the 1930s she was in her late seventies.
3. You won't see her full name on her paintings instead, you'll see the name Grandma Moses.
4. Some people like folk art others like abstract art.
5. Simone, Rita, and Hector are taking Art I Anita is taking Art II.

EXERCISE B Some of the following sentences need semicolons. Above the sentence, write the semicolon and the words before and after it. In some sentences, semicolons will replace commas. If a sentence already has correct punctuation, write *C* on the line provided.

Examples ______ 1. Jeremy and Thad returned early, LaVerne was late. (*early; LaVerne*)
C 2. You help Dad, and I'll help Uncle Seymour.

______ 6. First, I delivered papers, then I practiced soccer.
______ 7. Dan, I know you are tired, but the laundry is waiting.
______ 8. Phillip, Homer, and Carla wrote poetry, Luis wrote a play.
______ 9. The steady rain continued, yet nobody cared.
______ 10. Helen, please sing the soprano part Jean will sing the alto part.
______ 11. Some of us marched others, like John, rode on a float.
______ 12. Ethel saw the danger she shouted a loud, clear warning.
______ 13. I like checkers, charades, and dominoes, and he likes chess.
______ 14. Nicknames are fun some, however, can embarrass you.
______ 15. Lila forgot her umbrella Janet, of course, had hers.

Semicolons B

23l. Use a semicolon between independent clauses if they are not joined by *and, but, for, nor, or, so,* or *yet.*

23m. Use a semicolon rather than a comma before a coordinating conjunction to join independent clauses that contain commas.

Semicolons are also used between items in a series when the items contain commas.

EXAMPLES Don't use those oil paints**;** use these watercolors instead.

My relatives live in Nashville, Tennessee**;** Atlanta, Georgia**;** and Austin, Texas.

MECHANICS

EXERCISE A Insert semicolons as needed in the following sentences. Above the sentence, write the words before and after the semicolon. In some sentences, semicolons will replace commas.

California; Lima Peru; and

Example 1. I would like to visit San Diego, California, Lima, Peru, and Athens, Greece.

1. I declined Larry's offer of a ride home I wanted to walk.

2. Please wash the car's windshield, I will fill the tank with gasoline.

3. My brothers were born on March 10, 1984, July 28, 1986, and September 4, 1991.

4. Save those newspapers, we will need them when we pack the dishes.

5. I saw Ms. Norris and Ms. Carson, the chaperones, but, as I said, I did not see the principal.

EXERCISE B Insert semicolons in the following sentences as needed. In some sentences, semicolons will replace commas. Above the sentence, write the words before and after the semicolon.

carefully; it

Example 1. I handled the clock carefully, it was an antique.

6. There are international airports in Miami, Florida, Chicago, Illinois, and New York City.

7. Tina always does homework at the kitchen table, however, her mom is setting the table for dinner.

8. I cheered when I crossed the finish line, it was my first victory.

9. At the market Flora selected strawberries, which were on sale, a pineapple, which is her favorite fruit, and blackberries, which Todd had requested.

10. Please walk the dog, he hasn't been out in several hours.

11. The team leaders are Janet, Terrence, and Phil, Roy will fill in if one of them is absent.

12. Fallen leaves cover the front yard, I should rake them soon.

13. Georgia enjoys reading, her sister is more interested in writing.

14. We need lots of ice for the party, let's go to the corner market to get some.

15. I sent valentine cards to three people: Monica, my stepmom, Bertie, my pen pal, and Kat, a close friend.

Colons

23n. Use a colon before a list of items, especially after expressions such as *the following* or *as follows.*

23o. Use a colon between the hour and the minute.

23p. Use a colon after the salutation of a business letter.

23q. Use a colon between chapter and verse in Biblical references and between all titles and subtitles.

EXAMPLES For the picnic we need the following**:** fruit, sodas, cheese, and crackers.
8**:**00 P.M. 2**:**15 A.M.
Dear Mrs. Cramer**:** To Whom It May Concern**:**
Matthew 3**:**1–4 *Robert Frost**:** The Official Biography*

EXERCISE A Insert colons as needed in the following sentences.

Example 1. The finalists are the following students: Aidan, Rowan, and Rebecca.

1. Our bus leaves at 6 23 A.M.
2. The languages the exchange student speaks are as follows English, German, French, and Spanish.
3. Dear Mayor Winston
4. Please read Luke 3 7–8.
5. At 7 04 P.M. the spacecraft was launched.
6. Uncle Jerry likes the following authors Alex Haley, Mark Twain, and Willa Cather.
7. Our reading assignment is the following a short story by O. Henry, pages 4–18 in our text, and two newspaper editorials.
8. These students won awards Tasha Zimmer, Blake Sanders, and Sam Reyes.
9. Carol titled her essay "Time How to Make the Most of It."
10. Remember these tips when you drive courtesy, caution, and judgment.

EXERCISE B Add colons as needed in the following memo.

Example The speech is titled "Workplace Friendships: Strength in Numbers."

To All Employees

You are invited to a luncheon at 1 30 P.M. on Friday. The speakers are as follows Dr. Perez, Mr. Feldman, and Mrs. Puccini. Bring these items a notebook, a pen or pencil, and your list of questions for the speakers. The event will be over by 3 00 P.M.

Review A: End Marks and Abbreviations

EXERCISE A Add a period, a question mark, or an exclamation point to each sentence.

Example 1. Look at this hilarious cartoon!

1. Are you familiar with Gary Larson's work

2. What a talented cartoonist he is

3. Have you seen *The Far Side*

4. The characters are sometimes animals who act like people

5. How did he become a cartoonist

6. When he was a child, Larson liked to draw dinosaurs and gorillas

7. In college, he wanted to save the world from boring advertising

8. How funny that is

9. Be sure to read his cartoon collections

10. You'll like the dogs who wear glasses

EXERCISE B Add periods, question marks, and exclamation points as needed in the following sentences.

Example 1. Col. Mustard committed the crime with a candlestick in the library!

11. Please tell Mrs Neziri that we accept her party invitation

12. Oh no, stop that

13. Isn't this movie based on a book by E M Forster

14. The school's PTA will host a concert in June

15. Dr Nelson said that the Petrified Forest in Arizona covers over 93,000 acres

16. We need help over here, Dr Taylor

17. Does Facts by Fax, Inc close at 5:00 on weekdays

18. Ella's older sister goes to a college in Morgantown

19. What year did E Annie Proulx win a Pulitzer Prize for *The Shipping News*

20. Spot, let go of Ms Sherling's glove *now*

Review B: Commas

EXERCISE A Add commas as needed in the following sentences.

Example 1. Putting on her sneakers, Megan prepared for the basketball game.

1. Albert what makes a sneaker comfortable?
2. I think support comfort and cushioning are three important things.
3. Our track team buys only one brand but it's not easy to get all sizes.
4. My brother always wants the latest greatest style of shoe.
5. He plays basketball he plays tennis and he runs track.
6. In fact he has several pairs of sneakers for these sports.
7. Since I jog almost every day I am most concerned with the shoe's comfort.
8. I do however shop for a style and color that I like.
9. Dark blue my favorite color is always my first choice.
10. This sale on athletic shoes ends August 31 2002.

EXERCISE B Add commas as needed in the following sentences. If a sentence is already correct, write *C* on the line provided.

Examples ______ **1.** Thumper, my pet rabbit, eats all of our vegetable scraps.

__C__ **2.** The person who made this holly wreath is Andrea Morton.

______ **11.** Covered with a layer of fluffy snow the sidewalk was completely hidden.

______ **12.** I don't really like asparagus but I ate it to be polite.

______ **13.** Dad relaxed beside the fireplace was reading a Thomas Hardy novel.

______ **14.** Over the weekend we shopped we talked and we ate dinner.

______ **15.** Those dusty grimy windows should be washed thoroughly.

______ **16.** The equation that I found most challenging was the fifth one.

______ **17.** Ms. Hoffmann the art teacher always dresses colorfully and with style.

______ **18.** The salad on the other hand would be more healthy than the fried shrimp.

______ **19.** Under the weeping willow beside the lake we spread our blanket for the picnic.

______ **20.** Because he loves adventure Ronny rode the tallest roller coaster at the park first.

Review C: Semicolons and Colons

EXERCISE A Add semicolons and colons as needed in the following sentences.

Example **1.** We will arrive at the museum at 1:30 P.M.

1. Here is London's famous wax museum, Madame Tussaud's it dates back to 1835.

2. This is a weird but interesting place I'm sure we'll enjoy our tour.

3. The Grand Hall features the following popes, politicians, and villains from history.

4. I want a picture of Ari, Ben, and myself but I didn't bring a camera.

5. This letter from the Friends of the Museum begins, "Dear Wax Enthusiasts Welcome."

6. I asked one of the guards a question then I realized he was made of wax!

7. Some of us know that's true others can hardly believe it.

8. A queen donated a gown a king gave his cape.

9. Wax models are made using these materials fiberglass, real hair, acrylic, and other materials.

10. Sandy says that she's been to wax museums in New York, New York Las Vegas, Nevada and Salem, Massachusetts.

EXERCISE B Add semicolons and colons as needed in the following letter.

Example My plans for the afternoon include the following: writing letters, doing homework, and working on my Web site.

March 1, 2001

Dear Professor Rumbaugh

I will be in Finland on the following dates March 10 through March 17. I know that Spring Break does not begin until March 12 that's why I'm writing you this letter. I will miss your lecture, "Farming Communities Life on the Land," on March 11 but I am really interested in the topic. Could I stop by your office around 10 30 A.M. on Thursday to discuss the topic?

You see, I'm going to work on a farm in Finland I plan to write my term paper, "Small-Scale Farming America's Future," about the things I learn there. Before I go, I'd like to ask you some questions I think you'll have some good advice. For instance, I think I'll need to take the following items work clothes, a wide-brimmed hat, and boots. I'm not sure about the other supplies.

Thank you very much.

Sincerely,

Karen Kent

Review D: End Marks, Commas, Semicolons, and Colons

EXERCISE A Add periods, question marks, exclamation points, and commas as needed in the following sentences.

Example 1. Gazing at the stars, I wondered if scientists had ever counted them all.

1. Do you enjoy looking at the stars
2. What a wonderful sight that will be
3. Kurt have you seen the Big Dipper
4. The Big Dipper a group of seven stars is in Great Bear.
5. Isn't that a constellation
6. Did your parents see Halley's comet in 1986
7. It was named for Edmond Halley an astronomer who died in 1742
8. Does *Halley* rhyme with *daily valley* or *crawly*
9. Halley's comet won't be back until 2062 I believe
10. After I finish my research I plan to write an essay about Halley's comet

EXERCISE B Add end marks, commas, semicolons, and colons as needed in the following sentences.

Example 1. I'll invite Trish, Veronica, and Max; and you, please, invite the other people on this list.

11. Are you ready for some summer fun
12. What has the following things in common water music friends and food?
13. You guessed it
14. You're invited to a Splash Party on Thursday May 26 2001
15. Come to my house at 2 00 call if you need a ride.
16. Look for a sign for Apt 215
17. Bring the following items bathing suit sandals towel and sunscreen lotion.
18. If possible bring some CDs then we can dance
19. My older brother and sister who are both college students will chaperone the party
20. Oh you don't have to bring anything drinks and food will be provided

MECHANICS

NAME _______________ CLASS _______________ DATE _______________

Proofreading Application: Written Announcement

Good writers are generally good proofreaders. Readers tend to admire and trust writing that is error-free. Make sure that you correct all errors in grammar, usage, spelling, and punctuation in your writing. Your readers will have more confidence in your words if you have done your best to proofread carefully.

No matter how carefully you choose your words, incorrect punctuation can confuse your readers. Punctuation conveys a lot of information beyond the basic meaning of the words in a sentence. For example, punctuation tells whether a sentence is a statement or a question, it shows how to separate words and phrases, and it indicates abbreviations.

PROOFREADING ACTIVITY

The following announcement contains errors in punctuation. Find the errors and correct them, using the proofreading symbols in the chart on page 809 of the Quick Reference Handbook to add or replace punctuation marks.

Example In order to raise the money needed for new equipment, we need to hold a fund-raiser.

To: Soccer Team

From: Fund-raising Committee

We need your help The soccer team is holding a bake sale at the River City Mall on Saturday October 13, 2001 to raise money to buy new equipment. We need volunteers to bake bread brownies cookies muffins and other goodies. Of course we also need people to work at our sales table. There are three shifts available 1130 A.M. to 130 P.M. 130 P.M. to 330 P.M., and 330 P.M. to 530 P.M. If you are creative we could use your help on the advertising committee. Can you write draw or paint. Help us design posters! If you can help please see Mrs Adams. She is scheduling volunteers and she will also answer any questions you may have.

NAME _______________ CLASS _______________ DATE _______________

Literary Model: Punctuation in Poetry

in Just-
by E. E. Cummings

in Just-
spring when the world is mud-
luscious the little
lame balloonman

whistles far and wee

and eddieandbill come
running from marbles and
piracies and it's
spring

when the world is puddle-wonderful

the queer
old balloonman whistles
far and wee
and bettyandisbel come dancing

from hop-scotch and jump-rope and

it's
spring
and
the

goat-footed

balloonMan whistles
far
and
wee

EXERCISE A How do you think Cummings wants you to feel about spring? Use information from the poem to support your answers.

EXERCISE B

1. Rewrite this poem, adding end marks and commas and formatting it in a more traditional manner. You may want to delete one or two of the conjunctions that appear in the original poem.

2. Why do you think Cummings chose to write this poem the way he did instead of the way you rewrote it? Does Cummings' style—his untraditional approach to punctuation and formatting—help create the feeling you described in Exercise A? Explain.

Literary Model (continued)

EXERCISE C Using E. E. Cummings' poem as a model, write a poem about your favorite season of the year. To create a particular feeling about the season you choose, use little or no punctuation. Also, experiment with the formatting of the words on the page.

EXERCISE D How might the lack of punctuation and the nontraditional formatting of your poem affect how the reader feels about the season you chose?

Writing Application: Letter

Sometimes a writer interrupts a sentence with a nonessential expression that is used to modify an element in the sentence. This kind of expression is not part of the main idea of the sentence; it just provides the reader with a little more information. To show that an expression is an aside rather than part of the main sentence, a writer sets off nonessential expressions by using commas. A single comma is used with an expression at the end of a sentence. Two commas are used with an expression in the middle of a sentence.

INCORRECT I went to the movies with Becky who is my best friend.

CORRECT I went to the movies with Becky**,** who is my best friend.

INCORRECT *The Secret Garden* which was written by Frances Hodgson Burnett is my favorite book.

CORRECT *The Secret Garden***,** which was written by Frances Hodgson Burnett**,** is my favorite book.

Notice how the meaning of the main part of each sentence would be the same if the clause were omitted. Each clause just provides some extra detail.

Writing Activity

Pretend that you are attending a summer camp on the moon. Write a letter telling your parents or a friend about the people you have met, the games you have played, the interesting sights you have seen, and anything else that would interest them. You may need to interrupt your narrative to add short explanations of who people are, how a particular game is played, or what a particular place looks like. Remember to set off these interruptions with commas. In your letter, use commas to set off at least six expressions that interrupt sentences.

PREWRITING Make a list of people you have met, places you have gone, and activities in which you have participated. Which items on your list will you need to clarify for your parents? Write down your explanations.

WRITING As you write your letter, decide where you will insert each of your explanations: at the beginning, the middle, or the end of each sentence. Where does it make the most sense to add the information? Where does it sound the most natural?

REVISING Let your parents or a classmate read the letter. Do they have any questions about who people are, what a certain game is, and so on? How could you add those details?

PUBLISHING Check your letter for errors in grammar, usage, spelling, and punctuation. Pay close attention to the use of commas with expressions that interrupt a sentence. After you have revised your letter, have some fun. Mail it and wait for a response.

Extending Your Writing

Consider using your letter as the basis of a science fiction story. Throughout the course of your story, develop interesting characters who face challenging conflicts. Be sure that your story has a beginning, middle, and end. As in your letter, you may need to insert short explanations about the people, places, or activities about which you are writing.

Choices: Examining Punctuation Marks

Here's your chance to step out of the grammar book and into the real world. You may not always notice punctuation, but examples of it appear in your life every day. The following activities challenge you to find a connection between pronouns and the world around you. Do the activity below that suits your personality best, and then share your discoveries with your class. Have fun!

FOREIGN LANGUAGES

The Case for Other Cases

Interview several people who can speak a foreign language, and ask them about the use of possessives in the language. How do these languages handle possessives? Do they have possessive cases? If so, do they have apostrophes? If a language does not have apostrophes, how does it indicate possession? Tell your classmates the answers.

CREATIVE WRITING

Time's a Wastin'

Writers can create characterization and tone in a story by using shortened words. By simply dropping the last *g* in a word like *going* and inserting an apostrophe, a writer can create a casual atmosphere and a more realistic dialogue. Try your hand at this skill. Write a dialogue that uses words shortened by apostrophes. Then, ask for volunteers to perform your dialogue.

INTERNET

:) or :(

Do you like to surf the World Wide Web or write e-mail? You can find some interesting punctuation in e-mail. Find out as much as you can about e-mail and the customs associated with it. Then, tell (and show) your classmates how punctuation marks are used in e-mail. For example, why is it considered bad *netiquette* (etiquette, or manners, associated with Internet use) to use all capital letters?

RESEARCH

Hy•phen•at|ed

Examine your dictionary to determine how it marks the best places to hyphenate a word. Does your dictionary mark where not to hyphenate a word? If so, how? Find out. Then, find five hyphenated words that appear in a printed source. Look up these words in your dictionary. Did your source print the words correctly? Tell your classmates what you learned.

OBSERVATION

She Said *That*!

You may have noticed that writers sometimes use italics for emphasis. Find a few examples, and read them (with emphasis, of course) to the class. Then, write several sentences of your own. Use your sentences to demonstrate to your classmates how italics may be used for emphasis. You should be able to move the italics around in your sentences as in the following examples: She *said* that! *She* said that! She said *that*! How does the meaning change when you move the italics? Report your observations to the class.

SURVEY

"The Secret of Life"

Ask each of your classmates to make up a title for a magazine article. The title should be special. It should be a title for an article that would be fun to write and would capture the readers' attention. When you have a title from each classmate, prepare a table of contents for a special magazine that you, yourself, will title. If you want, you can design a cover for the proposed magazine. Later, students can use your list to get ideas for essays.

STUDY AID

Memorization Made Easier

It takes some time to memorize which titles to italicize and which to place in quotation marks. Speed up the process. Do a bit of research on mnemonics. Then, write a few mnemonics to help your classmates remember what to do with which titles. Unveil your mnemonics in a presentation in which you also explain how mnemonics can be a great study aid.

Underlining (Italics) A

24a. Use underlining (italics) for titles and subtitles of books, plays, periodicals, films, television series, works of art, and long musical works.

EXAMPLES *A Raisin in the Sun, The New York Times, Aladdin, Mona Lisa, The Nutcracker*

EXERCISE A In the following sentences, underline each title that should be italicized.

Example 1. Winnie and Carlo enjoy watching This Old House on television.

1. Mom reads The Wall Street Journal every morning.
2. Norman Rockwell created covers for The Saturday Evening Post.
3. Does your library have a copy of Raiders of the Lost Ark?
4. My brother subscribes to Ebony.
5. One of Puccini's operas is Madama Butterfly.
6. National Geographic had an interesting article about butterflies.
7. The famous statue by Auguste Rodin is called The Thinker.
8. During dinner, we listened to a long work by George Gershwin called Rhapsody in Blue.
9. Did you think the film Little Women accurately represented the book?
10. Roberta admired the photograph of the famous statue Venus de Milo.

EXERCISE B Add underlining as needed in the following conversation.

Example [1] Marianne opened TV Guide to find today's listings.

[11] Marianne asked Paula, "Do you want to watch a rerun of Home Improvement? **[12]** The Miami Herald wrote about the show."

[13] Paula replied, "So did The Morning Advocate. **[14]** But I have to finish my book report on To Kill a Mockingbird."

[15] "That was a movie, too," Marianne said. "We watched it along with The Black Stallion last weekend."

Underlining (Italics) B

24b. Use underlining (italics) for the names of ships, trains, aircraft, and spacecraft.

24c. Use underlining (italics) for words, letters, and numerals referred to as such.

EXAMPLES *Queen Elizabeth 2, Midwest Express, Skyglider II, Endeavour*
Did you know that *aloha* means both "hello" and "goodbye"?
Kareem often forgets to cross his *t*'s and dot his *i*'s.

MECHANICS

EXERCISE A In the following sentences, underline each word or item that should be italicized.

Example 1. My brother built a model of the USS <u>Enterprise</u>.

1. Shalom can mean "welcome" as well as "farewell."
2. Have you seen photographs of Sputnik 1?
3. The speech therapist is helping Sheila learn to pronounce s's without lisping.
4. Your passage has been booked on the Ocean Princess.
5. Stacey's first word was Mama.
6. I've always found it difficult to write the capital letter Q in cursive.
7. Marty is writing a mystery that takes place on a train called American Majesty.
8. Boris draws a line through the stem of his 7's.
9. At age 77, John Glenn served as part of the crew of the space shuttle Discovery.
10. On weekends, I am helping to rebuild an old boat, the Fly by Night.

EXERCISE B Add underlining as needed in the following paragraph.

Example [1] There are two <u>4</u>'s, two <u>8</u>'s, and one <u>9</u> in Aunt Rita's ZIP code.

[11] "How many s's are in the word Mississippi?" Jean asked her sister. **[12]** Jean was writing a letter to her aunt to ask her about a ship named Aurelia. **[13]** In July, Jean and Aunt Rita will take a riverboat cruise on the Spirit of Mississippi. **[14]** They are also considering an ocean cruise on the Atlantis. **[15]** They decided to save a train tour on the Sleek Mystique for future vacations.

Underlining (Italics) C

24a. Use underlining (italics) for titles and subtitles of books, plays, periodicals, films, television series, works of art, and long musical works.

24b. Use underlining (italics) for the names of ships, trains, aircraft, and spacecraft.

24c. Use underlining (italics) for words, letters, and numerals referred to as such.

EXAMPLES *The Adventures of Tom Sawyer, National Geographic, Apollo 8*
Roll your *r*'s when you say *burrito* in Spanish.

EXERCISE In the following sentences, underline each word or item that should be italicized.

Example 1. The Dawn Treader is a ship in one of C. S. Lewis's books.

1. I'm going to spend the afternoon reading The Last of the Really Great Whangdoodles.

2. Gilligan and the Skipper are the crew of the SS Minnow.

3. At the art supply store, Megan bought stencils for the letters a, e, g, m, and n.

4. I bought four tickets to the musical Grease.

5. Tanya glanced at the headlines of USA Today.

6. Drew Barrymore starred in E.T.: The Extra-Terrestrial.

7. Does your apartment number end in one 6 or two 6's?

8. Sonya and her mother always watch Providence together.

9. Liberation, an artwork by M. C. Escher, shows triangles transforming into flying birds.

10. Terrence read about a space mission of the Endeavour.

11. The seventh-grade class will tour the Blue Rose, a yacht in the nearby harbor.

12. Squinting at the faded sign, Karla could make out only an H and a P.

13. We'll get there faster if we buy railway tickets on the Midwest Express.

14. Martha named her small plane Amelia in honor of Amelia Earhart.

15. Have you ever seen The Phantom of the Opera?

16. Is this the letter l or the number 1 in your e-mail address?

17. May I read your copy of The Importance of Being Earnest?

18. Gustavo enjoys reading about current films and books in Entertainment Weekly.

19. I usually comes before e except in words such as neighbor and weigh.

20. Taylor studied Georgia O'Keeffe's painting called Ram's Skull With Brown Leaves.

Punctuating Direct and Broken Quotations

24d. Use quotation marks to enclose a ***direct quotation***—a person's exact words.

24e. A direct quotation generally begins with a capital letter.

EXAMPLE Mr. Colby said, **"T**he *Titanic* will never sink.**"**

24f. When an expression identifying the speaker interrupts a quoted sentence, the second part of the quotation begins with a lowercase letter.

EXAMPLE **"**The *Titanic,***"** said Mr. Colby, **"w**ill never sink.**"**

24g. A direct quotation can be set off from the rest of the sentence by one or more commas or by a question mark or an exclamation point, but not by a period.

24h. A comma or a period should be placed inside the closing quotation marks.

24i. A question mark or an exclamation point should be placed inside the closing quotation marks when the quotation itself is a question or an exclamation. Otherwise, it should be placed outside.

EXAMPLES **"**What a fabulous ship**!"** Mrs. Colby exclaimed.
"Let's go**,"** suggested her husband**, "**and join the others for dinner**."**
Roberto asked**, "**Where are we going**?"**

EXERCISE Use quotation marks, commas, and capital letters where they are needed in each of the following sentences. If a sentence is already correct, write *C* above it.

Examples **1.** "~~did~~ *Did* you enjoy your dinner?" asked Mrs. Colby.
C
2. Mr. Colby said that the *Titanic* would never sink.

1. The captain announced that dancing begins at midnight.

2. how can we dance if the sea gets rough? Mrs. Colby asked.

3. My dear her husband replied, we'll just move with the waves.

4. What is that ahead? asked Clive.

5. A steward said that it looked like an iceberg.

6. The captain asked what's causing the commotion?

7. A short while later, a telegraph operator said I heard a distress signal.

8. Someone asked where the signal originated.

9. I'm trying to figure that out he answered, but I'm not sure.

10. It might be coming from the *Titanic* another operator said.

Quotation Marks and Paragraph Breaks

24j. When you write dialogue (a conversation), begin a new paragraph every time the speaker changes.

EXAMPLES "After lunch," said Mrs. Ochoa, "we will read the end of the story." The tale, growing more mysterious every day, had captivated the class.

"Will it have a happy ending?" asked Grace. The room was silent, and all eyes gazed intently at the teacher. No one moved, but somebody's pencil rolled onto the floor.

"You will have to wait to find out," Mrs. Ochoa replied.

EXERCISE In the following dialogue, insert paragraph symbols (¶) wherever a new paragraph should begin.

Example Stanislav exclaimed, "I'll take Swiss cheese anytime."¶ "Is that your favorite cheese?" asked Jeanne.

As he wrote on the chalkboard, Mr. Kaplan asked, "Does anyone know what causes the holes in Swiss cheese?" "I know the answer!" exclaimed Stanislav. "It's the gas bubbles." "How did you know that?" asked Mr. Kaplan. "My grandfather makes cheese," answered Stanislav. "I've watched him many times. He adds bacteria for flavor, and adding bacteria makes gas bubbles." "What happens next?" Alicia wanted to know. "When the cheese gets hard, the bubbles remain as the holes we see in Swiss cheese," added Stanislav. "I never knew that," said Jeanne. "I wish I hadn't learned it," whispered Alicia, "because that process doesn't sound very appetizing to me." "What do you mean? I think it's interesting," Jeanne told her, "and it doesn't change the fact that Swiss cheese tastes good." "I agree," Stanislav said. Nodding his head, Mr. Kaplan looked at Stanislav and told him, "Thanks for sharing your story with the class."

Quotation Marks in Dialogue

24j. When you write dialogue (a conversation), begin a new paragraph every time the speaker changes.

EXAMPLES "I wish I could attend the ball," said Cinderella.

"Sorry, my dear. You must stay home and finish your chores," replied her stepmother.

"It seems that I'm the only one working around here," Cinderella complained.

24k. When a quotation consists of several sentences, put quotation marks only at the beginning and the end of the whole quotation.

EXAMPLE "Everybody knows this is totally unfair! But if I finish quickly, maybe I'll have a chance to go. Who knows? I might even dance with the prince."

24l. Use single quotation marks to enclose a quotation within a quotation.

EXAMPLE "Did she say 'dance with the prince'?" one of the sisters asked.

MECHANICS

EXERCISE Insert any quotation marks that are needed in each of the following sentences. When the speaker changes, draw a paragraph symbol (¶) to show where any new paragraphs should begin.

Examples Ramona asked, "Why do you have that odd look on your face, Whitney?"

¶ "Yeah, I was wondering that, too," said Christopher.

Looking slowly around the room, Whitney stopped and said, Listen! Did you hear a noise? No, I didn't hear anything. Do you think you might be imagining things? Ramona answered quietly. I'm worried, Christopher whispered. I heard a strange noise, too. Maybe someone is standing on the back porch! exclaimed Whitney. Let me check the back door, said Christopher in an unsure tone. I'll go with you, volunteered Whitney. Shaking her head, Ramona said, Oh, you two. Nobody's standing outside on the porch. Let's just stay where we are. Christopher teased, Are you afraid to stay in here by yourself? No, silly! she answered. You're the one who said I'm worried. You know, Whitney replied, our cat does walk around on the porch in the evenings. Now that I think about it, he sometimes makes sounds exactly like the one we just heard.

Quotation Marks with Titles

24m. Use quotation marks to enclose the titles of short works such as short stories, poems, songs, episodes of television series, essays, articles, and chapters and other parts of books.

EXAMPLES "The Gift of the Magi"
"The Raven"
"I've Been Working on the Railroad"
"How to Improve Your Bowling"
"Using End Marks"

MECHANICS

EXERCISE Add quotation marks where they are needed in the following sentences.

Example 1. Turn to the fourth chapter, "The Solar System."

1. The band plays Hail to the Chief for the president.

2. Jack London's To Build a Fire is the first story in this book.

3. Man on the Moon is *Nova's* program tonight.

4. What's New in Videos is a daily column in our newspaper.

5. Nikki Giovanni's poem Train Rides is about the power of love.

6. The Magic Barrel by Bernard Malamud is a short story about Leo Finkle and a matchmaker.

7. Uncle Rick likes to watch *Scientific American Frontiers;* his favorite episode is Journey to Mars.

8. In 1999, Santana's song Smooth was the longest running number-one single.

9. Did you read Top Ten Music Camps: A Comprehensive Report in the newspaper?

10. I enjoyed Mark Twain's short story called The Notorious Jumping Frog of Calaveras County.

11. The test had a section on The Aftermath of the Civil War, the chapter we studied last week.

12. My mom always reads Dear Abby aloud at the breakfast table.

13. The school newspaper is printing Crystal Stream, my haiku.

14. Did you see the episode of *Frontline* called High Stakes in Cyberspace?

15. This article, Speed-Reading Made Easy, is interesting.

16. Of Mr. Booker T. Washington and Others is an essay by W.E.B. DuBois.

17. Love-Charm Song is one of the songs in *Chippewa Music.*

18. I'm writing about Denise Chávez's story The Last of the Menu Girls.

19. Rodney worked all afternoon writing a song he titled Sunday Serenade.

20. This article, No Lockers: No Tardies, recommends that schools remove student lockers.

Quotation Marks Review

Review the rules on pages 630–36 of your textbook for information on using quotation marks with direct quotations, broken quotations, punctuation and end marks, dialogue, a quotation within a quotation, and titles of short works.

EXERCISE A Add quotation marks, capital letters, punctuation, and end marks where they are needed in the following sentences.

Example 1. Who said, "Money can't buy happiness"?

1. Carlton asked his aunt what's your secret recipe for oatmeal bread?
2. Try reading your essay aloud, Dennis said the teacher.
3. I enjoy reading Places To Go, Things To Do in the Sunday newspaper.
4. Ouch Thea exclaimed as she pulled a splinter from her finger.
5. Melanie said, Last night my dad told me, Laughter is the best medicine.
6. Today's episode of *Nature* is called Yellowstone Otters.
7. I've decided to re-landscape the front yard said Mom, but I'll need help.
8. Did you hear Trina, who is on the trampoline, shouting Look at me
9. Ron said, what's that? Did someone say we need to bring a side dish to the picnic? I'll make fruit salad.
10. In 1986, said Ms. Mendell, Li-Young Lee wrote his poem Persimmons

EXERCISE B Add quotation marks where they are needed in the following sentences. When the speaker changes, draw a paragraph symbol (¶) to show where a new paragraph should begin.

Example [1] "Amber, look at this!" Ramon said. ¶"Look at what?" she replied.

[11] Do you know that tigers are an endangered species? asked Ramon, sitting at the library computer. **[12]** Here's an amazing Web site about photographing tigers. **[13]** Tigers are beautiful animals, Amber replied. **[14]** Show me the site! **[15]** Michael Nichols photographed tigers up close so people will pay more attention to the problem, Ramon told her. **[16]** His photos are on the *National Geographic* site. **[17]** Did you say *Geographic World*? **[18]** No. Here's the URL. Check it out! **[19]** You are right, said Amber. **[20]** This is a wonderful way to learn more about tigers!

Apostrophes A

24n. To form the possessive case of a singular noun, add an apostrophe and an *s*.

EXAMPLES the sun**'s** rays James**'s** scooter the city**'s** mayor

24o. To form the possessive case of a plural noun that does not end in *s*, add an apostrophe and an *s*.

EXAMPLES people**'s** votes men**'s** shirts the children**'s** toys

24p. To form the possessive case of a plural noun ending in s, add only the apostrophe.

EXAMPLES the classes**'** election the Petersons**'** snowmobile

EXERCISE A Above each underlined noun, write the correct possessive form.

weeks'
Example 1. four <u>weeks</u> supply

1. three <u>doctors</u> opinions
2. <u>Mrs. King</u> business
3. <u>Chris</u> bicycle
4. the <u>mice</u> favorite hiding place
5. in ten <u>years</u> time
6. the <u>women</u> locker room
7. the <u>team</u> beloved mascot
8. <u>New Orleans</u> jazz scene
9. two <u>sisters</u> secret
10. the <u>Wilsons</u> house

EXERCISE B In each sentence, underline the word that should be in the possessive case. Above the word, write its correct possessive form.

winners'
Example 1. The five <u>winners</u> photographs are on page one of the newsletter.

11. The Mount Vernon Chorus sang Jason favorite songs.
12. One student brother had a minor accident in that big blue car.
13. The Garcias new neighbor is Sandra Johnson.
14. The banjo with broken strings is Jennifer.
15. Carlotta voice was hoarse from cheering for the volleyball team.
16. The raindrops patter could be heard on the tin roof.
17. We brought a day supply of granola bars, water, and sandwiches.
18. The photographer won an award for that picture of the wolves den.
19. Do you know Carlos e-mail address?
20. This weekend homework is written on the chalkboard.

Apostrophes B

24q. Do not use an apostrophe with possessive personal pronouns.

EXAMPLES The red car is **theirs.** **Whose** car is that?

24r. To form the possessive case of some indefinite pronouns, add an apostrophe and an *s.*

EXAMPLES somebody**'s** notes everyone**'s** idea

EXERCISE A Above each pronoun, write the correct possessive form. If a pronoun is already correct, write *C.*

Examples **1.** somebody lost puppy (*somebody's*)

2. its new paint (*C*)

1. anyone guess

2. everybody friend

3. her money

4. your skates

5. neither basketball

6. someone science book

7. anybody opportunity

8. The car is theirs.

9. no one first choice

10. Those books are yours.

EXERCISE B In the following paragraph, underline each possessive personal pronoun and each indefinite pronoun. Then, above each indefinite pronoun, write the correct possessive form.

Example **[1]** Someone trash is another person's treasure, in my opinion. (*Someone's*)

[11] Everybody unwanted items can bring in a few coins at a garage sale. **[12]** When my family organized our garage sale, everybody attention was devoted to the project. **[13]** One night, someone dreams even focused on our garage sale! **[14]** We spent several days writing down anyone ideas. **[15]** We finally decided to make a list of everyone items for sale. **[16]** Soon, a friendly disagreement occurred when two different people thought the iron was theirs. **[17]** Dad claimed it was his, but Tanya was sure it was hers. **[18]** In the end, of course, no one possessions made him or her rich. **[19]** We set out everybody items together during the garage sale and then equally divided the profit. **[20]** We were all quite happy with our success.

Apostrophes C

24n. To form the possessive case of a singular noun, add an apostrophe and an *s.*

24o. To form the possessive case of a plural noun that does not end in *s,* add an apostrophe and an *s.*

24p. To form the possessive case of a plural noun ending in *s,* add only the apostrophe.

EXAMPLES dog's bark the oxen's food four brothers' band

EXERCISE In each of the following sentences, underline the noun that needs an apostrophe or an apostrophe and an *s.* Then, above the underlined word, write the correct possessive form.

Grimm's

Example 1. Which of Grimm fairy tales should I read tonight?

1. Jacob Grimm was Wilhelm older brother.

2. Only thirteen months time separated their births in 1785 and 1786.

3. The brothers enjoyed storytellers tales.

4. At that time, storytellers held audiences attention by telling stories aloud.

5. The brothers goal was to write down these stories.

6. They carefully recorded the folk tales content.

7. The Grimms notes for their work have been studied by other storytellers.

8. Each written story words were very close to the original, spoken version.

9. Have you read the story of Rapunzel long hair?

10. Do you know about Snow White friends, the seven dwarfs?

11. One of my sister favorites is the story of Hansel and Gretel.

12. She particularly enjoys hearing about the old woman cottage.

13. The cottages walls were made of gingerbread.

14. Many people favorite story is the tale of Cinderella.

15. Other stories appeal lies in their funny and fantastic scenes.

16. For example, consider Rumpelstiltskin promise to turn straw into gold.

17. Tom Thumb tiny size makes him another interesting character.

18. Some readers favorite stories are those that resemble their own lives.

19. A reader favorite story may present life as he or she wishes it were.

20. These fairy tales are certainly a beloved part of children literature.

Apostrophes D

24s. Use an apostrophe to show where letters, words, or numerals have been omitted (left out) in a contraction.

The word *not* can be shortened to *n't* and added to a verb, usually without any change in the spelling of the verb.

EXAMPLES I am—I'm of the clock—o'clock
1998—'98 do not—don't she would—she'd

MECHANICS

EXERCISE A On the lines provided, write the contraction for each set of words.

Example 1. should not _shouldn't_

1. where is ______
2. we are ______
3. they will ______
4. has not ______
5. she is ______
6. could not ______
7. you will ______
8. does not ______
9. might have ______
10. they are ______

EXERCISE B The following sentences have errors in the use of apostrophes in contractions. An apostrophe may be missing or in the wrong place. Underline each error. Then, above the error, write the contraction correctly.

Example 1. _They've_ Theyv'e been reading quietly in their room.

11. Theres a hobby you may find interesting.
12. Its' called in-line skating.
13. Why have'nt I heard about it?
14. Here is a magazine article from October 99'.
15. Youll have to finish reading it this afternoon.
16. I promised to meet Jessie tomorrow morning at eight oclock and lend it to her.
17. Lets all go in-line skating this weekend!
18. I know we do'nt have skates yet.
19. Ben and Phoebe said theyre not using theirs and will lend them to us.
20. I think well find in-line skating difficult but fun.

Apostrophes E

24t. Use an apostrophe and an *s* to form the plurals of letters, numerals, and symbols, and of words referred to as words.

EXAMPLES Paula forgot to dot the *i*'**s** and cross the *t*'**s.**
Mr. Johanson writes *1*'**s** that look like *7*'**s.**
Use fewer *so*'**s** in your writing.

EXERCISE A Above each underlined item in the following sentences, write the item in its plural form.

Example 1. Did you get any A's (written above underlined A) on your progress report?

1. Count the *yes* and the *no*.
2. How many *n* and *e* are in the word *Tennessee*?
3. My telephone number has two *2* and two *8*.
4. Sakura's *4* look like *9*.
5. There are too many *or* and *but* in that paragraph.
6. Be sure to write clearly, so people can tell your *m* and *n* apart.
7. The *l* in the word *parallel* are parallel to each other.
8. Don't forget to use double *s* and *p* in the word *Mississippi*.
9. All the *4*, *5*, and *6* are blurred.
10. The *why* and *wherefore* will be covered later.

EXERCISE B The following letter contains errors in apostrophes in plurals. Insert apostrophes where they are needed, and draw a line through the apostrophes that are not needed.

Example [1] Your capital *Y*'s look like lowercase *r*'s in these note/s to Juan.

Dear Juan,

[11] I'm writing to tell you why 7s are lucky! **[12]** One of the nearby theaters' had a contest. **[13]** How many bean's were in the jar? **[14]** It's hard to tell by looking, but I decided to try—no *if*s, *and*s, or *but*s about it. **[15]** My guess was 7,777, which is a lot of 7s. **[16]** Of all the guesses' submitted, mine won! **[17]** The prize was, as you might guess, seven movie ticket's. **[18]** Are you free to go to the movies' with me? **[19]** Get ready for more 7s': The first movie is on July 7 at 7:00 P.M. **[20]** Maybe next time 9s will be lucky, and I'll win nine ticket's!

Your friend,

Emily

Apostrophes F

Review the rules on pages 638–45 of your textbook for information on using apostrophes with singular nouns, plural nouns that do not end in *s*, plural nouns that do end in *s*, some indefinite pronouns, contractions, and the plurals of letters, numerals, symbols, and words referred to as words.

EXAMPLES book**'s** cover children**'s** toys students**'** holiday
someone**'s** bicycle can**'**t several *H***'s**
six *8***'s** three *$***'s** too many *very***'s**

EXERCISE A For each of the following sentences, add apostrophes where needed. Cross out apostrophes that are not needed.

Example 1. Who chooses hurricanes' name's?

1. One person doesnt choose a hurricanes name.
2. Theyre chosen by scientists' from all over the world.
3. Who'se idea was it to give hurricanes peoples names?
4. Probably its an international groups idea.
5. Theres a list of names' for each coast.
6. *A*s and *B*s begin the names of the first hurricane's of each season.
7. Hurricane Andrew was scientists choice of name for a hurricane in 1992.
8. I do'nt think Id want that hurricane to have the same name as I have.
9. Andrews costly destruction caused many people to see *$*s in their heads!
10. The damage caused by Andrew cost around fifteen billion dollar's—there are a lot of *0*s in that number!

EXERCISE B For each of the following sentences, add apostrophes where needed. Cross out apostrophes that are not needed. If a sentence is already correct, write *C* after the sentence.

Example 1. How many *e*'s are in that girl's name?

11. The shells' of these pecan's are hard to crack.
12. They'll be pleased that you accepted their invitation.
13. I dont usually care for soup, but Theresas chicken soup is irresistible!
14. If you don't use an apostrophe when referring to several *a*s, the word looks like *as*.
15. In her class notes, Norma writes *&*s instead of *and*s.

Hyphens

24u. Use a hyphen to divide a word at the end of a line.

INCORRECT When the school year ends each summer, I am always ready for a v–acation. By the end of summer, I'm ready for school again.

CORRECT When the school year ends each summer, I am always ready for a vaca–tion. By the end of summer, I'm ready for school again.

24v. Use a hyphen with compound numbers from *twenty-one* to *ninety-nine* and with fractions used as modifiers.

EXAMPLES twenty-seven votes two-thirds majority

24w. Use a hyphen with the prefixes *ex–*, *self–*, *all–*, and *great–* and with the suffixes *–elect* and *–free.*

EXAMPLES ex-player self-cleaning wheat-free

EXERCISE A On the line following each word, write the word with a hyphen added to show how you would divide the word at the end of a line. If the word cannot be divided, write *DND* for *do not divide.*

Examples **1.** luggage *lug-gage*

2. tiny *DND*

1. rocky ______

2. railroad ______

3. track ______

4. station ______

5. through ______

6. discount ______

7. jumping ______

8. seat ______

9. overnight ______

10. ticket ______

EXERCISE B In the items below, cross out each number and write above it the spelled-out version. Cross out each word that needs a hyphen, and write above it the correctly hyphenated word.

Examples **1.** ~~25~~ *twenty-five* penguins

2. ~~selfemployed~~ *self-employed* writer

3. a ~~seven eighths~~ *seven-eighths* response rate

11. sugarfree gelatin

12. a three fourths success rate

13. 39 years

14. ex favorite dessert

15. greatgrandfather clock

16. 52 points

17. governorelect of Montana

18. selfmotivated student

19. all female soccer team

20. one third minority

Parentheses, Brackets, and Dashes

24x. Use parentheses to enclose material that is added to a sentence but is not considered of major importance.

EXAMPLE Two thirds of our class **(**most are athletes**)** voted for afternoon games.

24y. Use brackets to enclose an explanation added to quoted or parenthetical material.

EXAMPLE Lucy told us, "I wasn't expecting it **[**the surprise birthday party**]** today!"

24z. Use a dash to indicate an abrupt break in thought or speech.

EXAMPLE It's your turn**—**even though it *is* your birthday**—**to do the dishes.

EXERCISE A Add parentheses and brackets where they are needed in the following sentences.

Examples **1.** Shoshanna (Shanna) and I attended the outing together.

2. Shanna said, "Isn't this [the picnic] as much fun as I said it would be?"

1. Read the article the one on page 5 about keeping dogs as pets.

2. Our school's mascot that's Anne's Newfoundland dog won an award for bravery.

3. The dog otherwise known as Newfie once saved a boy from drowning.

4. Anne said, "Newfie Anne's dog has always loved people."

5. We were paddling a canoe it feels as if it happened yesterday the day of our big outing.

6. Nigel fell overboard everyone was scared and shouted for help.

7. Of everyone children, adults, and pets who was there, only our mascot leapt in to save Nigel.

8. Afterward Nigel said, "He Newfie seemed to come out of nowhere!"

9. Newfie happily chewed on his award a rawhide chew toy while Nigel rested.

10. Both of them Nigel and Newfie are doing well.

EXERCISE B In the following sentences, draw a caret (∧) to show where a dash is needed. Then, write the dash above the caret.

Example **1.** Would you like my opinion—I know you didn't ask for it—about a gift?

11. We found the perfect gift Mother will love it to give her on her birthday.

12. I can't believe even though I've seen it that we actually found it.

13. Aren't you surprised I know I am I thought of it first?

14. Let's not tell Dad he won't believe it anyway until she opens the box.

15. Can you keep a secret it's hard to do, I know until next Monday?

Review A: Underlining (Italics) and Quotation Marks

EXERCISE Add underlining and quotation marks as needed in the following sentences.

Example 1. The poem "My Last Duchess" is one of my favorites by Browning.

1. Many Walt Disney films, such as Bambi and The Jungle Book, are back again.
2. Sometimes I listen to Ravel's famous Boléro when I study.
3. Aunt Fran sent our family a subscription to the magazine Birds and Blooms.
4. Dad suggested, Read the article called Best Buys in Bicycle Helmets.
5. Byron's long poem titled Don Juan fills an entire book!
6. Here's my copy of Anne of Green Gables, said Mother.
7. USA Today covers the news of all fifty states.
8. Did Columbus sail on the Santa María or on another ship? asked Larry.
9. Everybody Loves Raymond is Uncle Emil's favorite television series.
10. Kelly exclaimed, Look, that hockey game we saw is on the cover of Sports Illustrated!
11. Listen to this recording of The Rite of Spring.
12. When I was a child, said Aunt Minnie, the U.S. flag had forty-eight stars.
13. The episode showing tonight is Crisis in Central City.
14. His article, How to Excel in Soccer, will be published soon.
15. Who said, It's one thing to build castles in the air; it's another thing to live in them?
16. One third of my cousin's shelf is filled with Seventeen magazines.
17. I need two more weeks, she said, to finish reading them all.
18. Poems such as Edward Lear's The Owl and the Pussycat are nonsense poems.
19. When I return The Yearling, I'll owe the library about twenty-five cents.
20. Did you finish reading it? Mrs. Casper asked.

Review B: Apostrophes

EXERCISE A On the lines provided, rewrite the phrases in the possessive case, inserting apostrophes as needed.

Example 1. the meeting of the teachers *the teachers' meeting*

1. the strategy of the opponent ______
2. the fears of the men ______
3. the tracks of the deer ______
4. the trips of the family ______
5. the victories of the candidates ______
6. the giggles of the children ______
7. the lines of the poem ______
8. the shouts of the girls ______
9. the worries of the parents ______
10. the population of Alaska ______

EXERCISE B Insert apostrophes where they are needed in the following paragraphs. Delete any apostrophes that are incorrectly placed.

Example [1] I'm glad we're working together on our report's, Chen.

[11] "Im sure well make *A*s on our report's!" said Chen. **[12]** "Were sure to hear *oh*s and *ah*s from the class, too."

[13] "Youre right," agreed Latitia. **[14]** "Ill bet our scores will be in the 90s. **[15]** Im going to tell about an article I read. **[16]** Its about a twelve-year-old boy who climbed Mount McKinley."

[17] Chen asked, "Isnt Mount McKinley North Americas highest mountain?"

[18] "Thats right. Its over 20,000 feet high! There are a lot of *0*s in that number."

[19] "My papers about weight lifting," Chen responded. **[20]** "Of our two papers topics, your's is much more interesting, Latitia—no *maybe*s about it!"

Review C: Hyphens, Parentheses, Brackets, and Dashes

EXERCISE A On the line following each word, write the word with a hyphen added to show how you would divide the word at the end of a line. If the word cannot be divided, write *DND* for *do not divide.*

Examples **1.** telephone *tele-phone*

2. sticky *DND*

1. pencil _______________

2. notebook _______________

3. shiny _______________

4. principal _______________

5. marks _______________

6. things _______________

7. flagpole _______________

8. weary _______________

9. conduct _______________

10. enough _______________

EXERCISE B Add parentheses, brackets, or dashes to each sentence, as needed. Draw a caret (∧) to show where a dash belongs, and then write the dash above the caret.

Examples **1.** The Olympics (the winter games) are happening this week.

2. Dad said, "They [the athletes] are inspiring!"

3. Where has the television schedule—the guide you bought yesterday—been placed?

11. Our entire family likes to watch who doesn't? the Olympics.

12. Do we have a blank videotape I hope so to record our favorite events?

13. Maddie commented, "Even Rex and Zippy our dog and kitten seem to like the competition."

14. Do you think they understand I'm not sure if I always do what's going on?

15. Rex stares with great concentration it's so cute at the ice-skating events.

16. My dad's favorite event and mine, too is speed skating.

17. Mom said, "My favorite event alpine skiing is scheduled for tomorrow."

18. Addie Sue wants to join us that is, if you agree to watch tomorrow night's games.

19. Help me move this table I know it's heavy so we can put the television on it.

20. I have always dreamed of winning believe it or not an Olympic medal.

Review D: Punctuation Marks

EXERCISE A Add underlining, quotation marks, apostrophes, and parentheses where needed in the following dialogue. Draw a paragraph symbol (¶) to show where a new paragraph should begin.

Example **[1]** My dad, Jamal (our neighbor), and I were talking about cartoons.

[1] "Guess whos celebrating his sixtieth birthday? **[2]** Goofy! said Dad. **[3]** He went on to say that hed read about it in The Pleasanton Times our local newspaper. **[4]** "Isnt Goofy pals with Mickey Mouse? asked Jamal. **[5]** Thats right, I answered. Grandpa said that Goofy first appeared in a movie called Mickey's Revue. **[6]** He was known as Dippy Dawg in those days. **[7]** Jamal nodded and said, That was in 1932." **[8]** I remember him in the 1950's, said Dad. **[9]** "He was in films that taught safety. **[10]** "Lets watch his daily TV show, I said. Its called Goof Troop."

EXERCISE B Add hyphens, brackets, and dashes where needed in the following sentences.

Example **1.** The critic wrote, "It [*Songbirds: A Photographic Journey*] is stunning!"

11. Troy's outstanding skills at soccer are selftaught.

12. The gift I hope you like it is outside on the lawn.

13. I agree with Abrams when he writes, "They the waters of the Caribbean are a scuba diver's dream."

14. The all amateur cast performed with unusual talent.

15. The juice there is orange or cranberry is in the refrigerator.

16. Jen said, "Take this a lantern and hang it from that high branch."

17. Booker was elected class treasurer by a four fifths majority.

18. I've collected twenty five pounds of aluminum cans for the recycling bin at school.

19. I saw my favorite actress yes, this is a true story in Manhattan yesterday!

20. If you divide *mistletoe* at the end of a line, divide it like this: mistletoe.

NAME ______________ CLASS ______________ DATE ______________

for **CHAPTER 24: PUNCTUATION II** *pages 628–50*

Proofreading Application: Book Report

Good writers are generally good proofreaders. Readers tend to admire and trust writing that is error-free. Make sure that you correct all errors in grammar, usage, spelling, and punctuation in your writing. Your readers will have more confidence in your words if you have done your best to proofread carefully.

More than any other type of writing, book reports require the correct use of italics, quotation marks, and apostrophes. In book reports, you may also find yourself using other less common marks of punctuation such as hyphens, parentheses, and dashes.

When you are assigned a book report, you are invited to give and support your opinion of a book. Regardless of your opinion, be very sure that you proofread carefully.

Proofreading Activity

In each sentence below, find and correct the error in the use of italics, quotation marks, apostrophes, hyphens, parentheses, or dashes. Use proofreading symbols such as those on page 809 of *Elements of Language* to make your corrections.

Example "No," I said, "I did not care for the book."

Lord Evan Poughkeepsie Smithfields *Autobiography of a Gentleman* is too detailed and too pointless to be worthwhile. This, his last work 1813, covers the period between Smithfields birth in 1752 and his retirement in 1807. In his famous essay Winter and Decay he views every tiny event in his life as monumental. For example, the author's descriptions of his breakfast foods toast, kippers, and finnan haddie are not necessary.

For a detailed list of the author's offenses, see Matthew Wellington's book of criticism Literature in My Day. Like Wellington, I grew weary of hearing over and over the words my dear reader. As Wellington so aptly puts it, "If Smithfield's readers were, in fact, dear, he would not address them so."

In conclusion, I heartily agree with Wellington, who recommends this book only to someone I would not wish this fate on anyone shipwrecked on a desert island. I make this recommendation, as Wellington says, "merely because the book is thick enough to serve as furniture.

Literary Model: Dialogue

"You can't come in," he [the sick son] said. "You mustn't get what I have."

I [the father] went up to him and found him in exactly the position I had left him, white-faced, but with the tops of his cheeks flushed by the fever, staring still, as he had stared, at the foot of the bed. . . .

"Your temperature is all right," I said. "It's nothing to worry about."

"I don't worry," he said, "but I can't keep from thinking."

"Don't think," I said. "Just take it easy."

"I'm taking it easy," he said and looked straight ahead. . . .

I sat down and opened the Pirate book and commenced to read, but I could see he was not following, so I stopped.

"About what time do you think I'm going to die?" he asked.

—from "A Day's Wait" by Ernest Hemingway

EXERCISE A

1. Look back at the dialogue, and find the contractions. On the lines below, write each contraction that appears in the excerpt.

2. Read over the narration, and write the three clauses in which contractions could have been used but were not. (Do not include clauses from the characters' speech.)

EXERCISE B

1. What can you generalize about the use of contractions in this passage?

2. Why do you think the author chose to use contractions in this manner?

Literary Model (continued)

EXERCISE C Using this excerpt as a model, write a passage in which the narrator is also a character. Have the narrator talk to a child who is afraid. The passage should contain both narration and dialogue. Include many contractions in the characters' speech. Do not include any contractions in the narration.

EXERCISE D

1. Choose two of the sentences you wrote that contain contractions. Rewrite them, eliminating the contractions.

2. If you were to rewrite your passage so that it contained no contractions, how would the style of your passage change?

Writing Application: Analysis of Song Lyrics

Music can be silly or serious, but it is almost always meaningful. Songs can inspire us and show us a new way of looking at the world. Like poetry, the words to songs—called lyrics—have a special meaning to the author, as well as to those who listen to the song.

Like song titles, song lyrics show up in quotation marks when we use them in writing. When quoting a song's lyrics in your writing, be sure to put end marks in the right position when quotation marks end a sentence.

EXAMPLES Do you know the song that begins "Oh, how lovely is the evening"?

Yes, it's called "Campfire Song."

I'd like to learn the lyrics to "Strike Up the Band."

Writing Activity

While studying poetry in your English class, your teacher has asked you to write about the lyrics of a song that you like. (After all, lyrics are poems set to music.) Write a few paragraphs about these lyrics and the reasons that they stand out to you. In your writing, you will need to include some of the song's lyrics. Be sure to quote them accurately and punctuate them correctly. Then, play an excerpt of the song for your class, and share some of your observations.

PREWRITING Start by choosing a song: Look for one of your favorites (your song can be serious or funny) that you would feel comfortable sharing with the whole class. Read a copy of the lyrics section by section, and jot down notes about why you're drawn to the words.

WRITING First, make a list of reasons why the song you chose is important to you. You could tell about the first time you heard the song, explain whether your understanding of the song has changed over time, or describe how the music reinforces the lyrics' meaning. Outline your comments about the lyrics before you begin drafting. Be thinking about the best way to organize your paragraphs.

REVISING In a personal response to a favorite song, you will naturally want to use first person, and that's fine. There's no need, however, to say again and again "I think" or "I feel." Your classmates take for granted that your words are your thoughts and feelings. Also, when you quote lines from the poem in your writing, remember to keep the excerpts brief—a line here, a phrase there. A few carefully chosen words can carry the feeling of the poem into your paragraphs.

PUBLISHING Check your paragraphs for errors in punctuation and spelling, paying special attention to quotation marks. Then, decide how you will present your paragraphs to the class. For example, you could give your presentation using note cards that you've prepared or a poster that you've created. Practice your presentation a few times before taking it to class.

Extending Your Writing

This exercise could lead to a more developed writing project. Think of a play or animated movie that uses music in a powerful way. Choose one scene that effectively connects a certain song to the story's action, and write an essay about the scene. Include song lyrics in your writing, and explain how the song influenced the drama of the scene.

NAME _______________ CLASS _______________ DATE _______________

for **CHAPTER 25: SPELLING** *pages 655–77*

Choices: Exploring Spelling

Here's your chance to step out of the grammar book and into the real world. You may not notice spelling rules, but you and the people around you use them every day. The following activities challenge you to find a connection between spelling and the world around you. Do the activity below that suits your personality best, and then share your discoveries with your class. Have fun!

REAL LIFE

Bakers and Weavers

How did we get last names, anyway? We didn't always have them, so how did they come to be? What circumstances or events made them seem necessary? Research the history of surnames, and fill your classmates in on the story. While you're at it, find out what your own last name means. Investigate a few other surnames, too. With your teacher's permission, present your findings to the class.

LINGUISTICS

Pore, Poor, and *Pour*

The homonyms that you see in your textbook are not the only ones in English. What are some of the other homonyms that are often confused? Make an alphabetized list of at least fifteen of these word sets and their definitions. Be sure to make copies to hand out to your classmates.

REAL LIFE

Across the Pond

Have you ever noticed that some books spell *labor* and *color* with a *u* before the *r*? What's with these writers and editors? Don't they have dictionaries? Well, they do, but they are British dictionaries. British spelling and American spelling differ in several ways. Find out how and why. Then, give your classmates the lowdown.

HISTORY

Mass Production

Scholars say that the invention of the printing press greatly influenced spelling. Why on earth should they say so? Look in encyclopedias and history books, and find out. Mark any relevant dates on a time line. Then, use the time line as you explain to your class how and why the printing press influenced spelling.

INVENTION

Phydeau

What? You can't pronounce this word? It's a made-up spelling for the name *Fido.* Because English has borrowed so many words from other languages, spelling can be confusing. Take advantage of the situation! Invent new ways to spell at least ten words. Your inventions must follow an acknowledged pattern of spelling. Make a list of your new spellings, and see how many of your classmates can understand them.

GRAPHICS

Color Highlights

Some letter combinations tend to cause spelling problems. Survey your classmates or your teacher for the twenty most common spelling errors in your class. Then, make a poster of these words, spelled correctly, of course. Use a highlighter to emphasize the letter combinations that cause the most trouble. With your teacher's permission, hang your poster where everyone can see it. If you have a computer and a color printer, you could simply print the troublesome letters in a contrasting color and hand out copies of your list to your classmates.

STUDY AID

Day by Day

Take all of the entries in the words-often-confused list and use them to create a month-long vocabulary calendar. You'll need a piece of poster board on which to print or paste your typed entries. Some days will have more than one entry, especially if you want to take weekends off. Whenever possible, paste appropriate illustrations on the poster. With your teacher's permission, hang your poster in the classroom.

NAME _______________ CLASS _______________ DATE _______________

Good Spelling Habits

Practicing the following techniques can help you spell words correctly.

- To learn the spelling of a word, pronounce it, study it, and write it.
- Use a dictionary. When you find that you have mispelled a word, look it up in a dictionary.
- Spell by syllables. A ***syllable*** is a word part that is pronounced as one uninterrupted sound.
- Proofread for careless spelling errors.
- Keep a spelling notebook.

EXAMPLES Jan-u-ar-y, plas-tic, pep-per, di-ver-si-ty, dic-tion-ar-y

EXERCISE A In each of the following sentences, determine whether the underlined word is misspelled. If it is misspelled, write the correctly spelled word above it. If the word is already correct, write *C* above it.

Example 1. One of my hobbies is <u>studing</u> bats. *(studying)*

1. Did you watch the <u>documentry</u> about bats?
2. There are many <u>difrent</u> kinds of bats.
3. One <u>exspert</u> said that photos make bats look vicious.
4. If the bat was caged, it <u>probably</u> was scared.
5. A scientist's <u>labotory</u> isn't a bat's favorite roosting place!
6. Bats <u>preffer</u> dark, peaceful shelters such as caves.
7. They come out after sunset to search <u>fer</u> insects.
8. People <u>livin</u> in cities rarely, if ever, see bats.
9. You can, <u>however</u>, see bats at some state parks.
10. Another option is to watch programs on <u>telivision</u>.

EXERCISE B Divide each of the following words into syllables by drawing lines between the syllables. Use a dictionary if necessary.

Example 1. ex|per|i|ment

11. atrocious
12. frightened
13. habitat
14. research
15. scientist
16. insects
17. nighttime
18. wingspan
19. flying
20. beautiful

Words with *ie* and *ei*

25a. Write *ie* when the sound is long *e*, except after *c*.

EXAMPLES yi**e**ld, chi**ef**, pi**e**rce rec**ei**ve, c**ei**ling
EXCEPTIONS s**ei**ze, l**ei**sure, n**ei**ther, prot**ei**n

Write *ei* when the sound is not long *e*, especially when the sound is long *a*.

EXAMPLES **ei**ght, sl**ei**gh, w**ei**gh
EXCEPTIONS fr**ie**nd, misch**ie**f, anc**ie**nt, p**ie**

MECHANICS

EXERCISE A Above the underlined word in each of the following sentences, rewrite the word correctly if it is misspelled. If the word is already spelled correctly, write *C* above it. Use a dictionary if necessary.

Example 1. Can your eyes decieve you? *(deceive)*

1. Jason is one of my nieghbors.
2. Jason's chief interest is magic tricks.
3. It all began when he recieved a book for his birthday.
4. Would you beleive that it was about famous magicians?
5. There's a breif story about Harry Blackstone, Jr.
6. In one mischievous trick, he seemed to turn his wife into a tiger!
7. The audience was releived when she came out for a bow.
8. Some tricks are called "slieghts of hand."
9. Jason tried to hide eight scarves in his sleeve.
10. He iether lost one or miscounted.

EXERCISE B For each incomplete word in the following paragraph, add the letters *ie* or *ei* so that the word is spelled correctly.

Example [1] Here is the rec *ei* pt for your groceries, Mr. Liu.

Here's something to do in your **[11]** l_____sure time. Maybe you and a **[12]** fr_____nd can start a service. It is many people's **[13]** bel_____f that assisting others is a rewarding **[14]** exper_____nce. Offer to take an elderly **[15]** n_____ghbor shopping. In the store, you may be able to reach items at a greater **[16]** h_____ght than an elderly person can. You can also help this person by carrying all items of heavy **[17]** w_____ght. **[18]** S_____ze this opportunity to help an older person relax. Although your shopping trips may be **[19]** br_____f, let's hope this idea will **[20]** y_____ld success!

Words with –*cede,* –*ceed,* and –*sede*

25b. The only English word ending in –*sede* is *supersede.* The only English words ending in –*ceed* are *exceed, proceed,* and *succeed.* Most other words with this sound end in –cede.

EXAMPLES pre**cede** con**cede** inter**cede** se**cede**

EXERCISE A Underline the correctly spelled word in parentheses in each of the following sentences.

Example 1. Yes, I *(conceed, concede)* that your intentions were good.

1. Shantel's goal is to *(exsede, exceed)* her teachers' expectations.
2. Training typically *(anteceeds, antecedes)* a promotion.
3. In a good relationship, your needs do not always *(supersede, superseed)* the other person's.
4. After a five-minute review, we will *(proceed, procede)* to take the test.
5. Lawyers *(intercede, interceed)* with the judge for their clients.
6. I always knew you would *(succeed, succede)* in your goal of forming a band.
7. If you no longer want to be a member, you may *(secede, sesede)* from the club.
8. Later, the tide will *(resede, recede).*
9. The *(prosedes, proceeds)* from each sale will go to the church's soup kitchen.
10. We always meet or *(exceed, exsede)* our sales quota.

EXERCISE B Above the underlined word in each of the following sentences, rewrite the word correctly if it is misspelled. If the word is already spelled correctly, write *C* above it.

Example 1. Didn't disagreements over slavery, tariffs, and states' rights preceed [*precede*] the American Civil War?

11. From 1860 to 1861, eleven states announced that they would seceed from the Union.
12. President Lincoln would not acceed to the secession.
13. Jefferson Davis decided to intersede on behalf of the South.
14. The eleven Southern states would prosede to elect Davis their president.
15. Over the next four years, the lines of battle would advance and receed numerous times.
16. The great destruction caused by the war would surely exceed the expectations of many.
17. As you know, these Southern states did not succede in their withdrawal from the Union.
18. By the end of the war, the goals of the North would supersede the desires of the South.
19. In 1865, the South was finally forced to consede victory to the North.
20. The North's victory was decreed on April 26, 1865; the Southern states would not secede.

Prefixes

25c. When adding a prefix to a word, do not change the spelling of the word itself.

EXAMPLES dis + similar = dis**similar** re + elect = re**elect** mis + spell = mis**spell**

EXERCISE A For each of the following items, add the prefix given to form a new word. Write the new word on the line provided.

Example 1. over + run = *overrun*

1. in + direct = ____________
2. dis + locate = ____________
3. re + open = ____________
4. il + legal = ____________
5. un + safe = ____________
6. over + take = ____________
7. un + natural = ____________
8. mis + state = ____________
9. im + possible = ____________
10. dis + service = ____________

EXERCISE B On the line in each of the following sentences, rewrite the prefix and word in parentheses as a single word.

Example 1. *(un + pack)* Behruz had to *unpack* his suitcase.

11. *(re + wind)* Please ____________ the videotape.
12. *(over + cooking)* Aunt Manuela was upset about ____________ the stew.
13. *(Dis + respect)* ____________ is an attitude I cannot tolerate.
14. *(mis + spell)* Did I ____________ your name on the invitation?
15. *(in + visible)* Helga wrote a story about an ____________ woman.
16. *(dis + contented)* Francine wondered why the baby seemed so ____________ today.
17. *(un + nerved)* The loud, cheering crowd ____________ the timid gymnast.
18. *(over + estimated)* Philip ____________ the cost of the old coin he found.
19. *(re + cycle)* Please stack the newspapers over there; I ____________ them.
20. *(un + wind)* Bettina could not ____________ the tangled fishing line.

Suffixes A

25d. When adding the suffix *–ness* or *–ly* to a word, do not change the spelling of the word itself.

EXAMPLES kind + ness = **kind**ness total + ly = **total**ly

Exception: For most words that end in *y*, change the *y* to *i* before *–ly* or *–ness.*

EXAMPLES day + ly = **daily** lonely + ness = lone**liness**

EXERCISE A For each of the following items, add the suffix given to form a new word. Write the word on the line provided.

Example 1. silly + ness = *silliness*

1. beautiful + ly = ______

2. routine + ly = ______

3. busy + ness = ______

4. main + ly = ______

5. neat + ness = ______

6. tardy + ness = ______

7. urgent + ly = ______

8. forgetful + ly = ______

9. scary + ness = ______

10. shy + ness = ______

EXERCISE B In the following paragraph, add the suffix to the word given in parentheses to make a single word. Write the new word on the line provided.

Example [1] I have *avidly* (*avid + ly*) read all of Edgar Allan Poe's stories.

Some people would say there is an element of **[11]** ______ (*creepy + ness*) in the stories of Edgar Allan Poe. I **[12]** ______ (*certain + ly*) think so, and to speak **[13]** ______ (*truthful + ly*), I like it! I **[14]** ______ (*particular + ly*) enjoy the **[15]** ______ (*spooky + ness*) of the characters and events in "The Fall of the House of Usher." The **[16]** ______ (*ghostly + ness*) of Madeline Usher's character is riveting. In the story, it **[17]** ______ (*gradual + ly*) becomes clear that Madeline's twin brother has sealed her in the family vault before she is **[18]** ______ (*actual + ly*) dead. The **[19]** ______ (*wild + ness*) of the weather reflects the **[20]** ______ (*stormy + ness*) of the emotions inside the house. Is it something supernatural or is it the weather that causes the Ushers' house to collapse?

Suffixes B

25e. Drop the final silent *e* before adding a suffix beginning with a vowel.

EXAMPLES like + able = **lik**able skate + ing = **skat**ing

Exception: Keep the silent *e* in words ending in *ce* and *ge* before a suffix beginning with *a* or *o*.

EXAMPLES notice + able = notic**eable** courage + ous = courag**eous**

25f. Keep the final silent *e* before adding a suffix that begins with a consonant.

EXAMPLES care + ful = care**ful** state + ly = state**ly**

EXCEPTIONS argue + ment = argu**ment** true + ly = tru**ly**

MECHANICS

EXERCISE A For each of the following words, add the suffix given to form a new word. Write the new word on the line provided.

Example 1. share + ing = *sharing*

1. shake + er = ______ **6.** sore + ly = ______

2. exterminate + or = ______ **7.** broke + en = ______

3. sedate + ly = ______ **8.** freeze + ing = ______

4. admire + able = ______ **9.** retire + ment = ______

5. argue + ing = ______ **10.** advantage + ous = ______

EXERCISE B Cross out each misspelled word in the following paragraph. Above the word, rewrite it correctly. Hint: Some sentences contain more than one misspelled word.

Example [1] ~~Gazeing~~ *Gazing* at the photos, I thought about our camping trip.

[11] The remotness of our camping site did not stop us. **[12]** We would not give in to a little discouragment. **[13]** The uniquness of this opportunity appealed to us, and we welcomd it. **[14]** We had packed all the camping gear that had been stord in our basments, including tents, shovels, an inflateable mattress, and a few crates of supplies such as ropes, matches, and canned food. **[15]** The trip was so amazeing, we're already planning the next camping trip.

Suffixes C

25g. For words ending in *y* preceded by a consonant, change the *y* to *i* before any suffix that does not begin with *i*.

EXAMPLES happy + ness = happ**iness** carry + er = carr**ier**

Words ending in *y* preceded by a vowel generally do not change their spellings before a suffix.

EXAMPLES play + ed = play**ed** array + ing = arra**ying**

EXCEPTIONS lay + ed = la**id** pay + ed = pa**id**

EXERCISE A For each of the following words, add the suffix given to form a new word. Write the new word on the line provided.

Example 1. hairy + ness = *hairiness*

1. scary + ness = ______
2. marry + ing = ______
3. coy + ness = ______
4. inlay + ed = ______
5. dirty + ness = ______
6. contrary + ness = ______
7. scurry + ing = ______
8. employ + able = ______
9. spray + ing = ______
10. deploy + able = ______

EXERCISE B Cross out each misspelled word in the following sentences. Then, above the word, write it correctly. Hint: Proper nouns are spelled correctly.

Example 1. Because of the sofa's ~~heavyness,~~ *heaviness* we'll need three people to lift it.

11. Who is that mysteryous stranger?
12. The children's enjoiment of his story pleased Miguel.
13. Janesha sayed that she'd be here by noon.
14. Luther is repaing me by teaching me how to pitch a knuckle ball.
15. Have you ever read funnyer poems than Shel Silverstein's?
16. Alfred plaied the antique violin beautifully.
17. Kendra is triing to memorize her lines for the play.
18. "The winds are varyable," stated the weather announcer.
19. Is Tara envyous of Tina's awards?
20. We will be compliing with the fire code by placing fire extinguishers in the building.

Suffixes D

25h. Double the final consonant before adding *–ing, –ed, –er,* or *–est* to a one-syllable word that ends in a single consonant preceded by a single vowel.

Do not double the final consonant in words ending in *w* or *x.*

EXAMPLES swim + ing = swi**mm**ing chop + ed = cho**pp**ed fax + ed = fa**x**ed

For one-syllable words ending in a single consonant that is not preceded by a single vowel and for most words of more than one syllable, do not double the consonant before adding *–ing, –ed, –er,* or *–est.*

EXAMPLES roam + ing = roa**m**ing retain + er = retai**n**er

MECHANICS

EXERCISE A For each of the following words, add the suffix given to form a new word. Write the new word on the line provided.

Example 1. tan + ing = *tanning*

1. win + er = ______

2. fast + est = ______

3. drum + er = ______

4. mat + ed = ______

5. mold + ing = ______

6. repair + ed = ______

7. mop + ing = ______

8. run + er = ______

9. tow + ed = ______

10. fit + est = ______

EXERCISE B In each of the following sentences, underline the correct spelling of the word in parentheses.

Example 1. We are *(traping, trapping)* spiders to study in science class.

11. A mirror with a carved wooden frame was *(centered, centerred)* over the fireplace.

12. I have *(maped, mapped)* out the route to the city lake.

13. What is a *(gildded, gilded)* cage, anyway?

14. Which is more *(relaxing, relaxxing)*, reading or watching TV?

15. "Thank you for *(treatting, treating)* us to grape juice," Felix said.

16. When I gently *(petted, peted)* the kitten, she began to purr.

17. I think the lawn *(mower, mowwer)* is in the toolshed.

18. "Is this a *(snaping, snapping)* turtle?" asked Wanda.

19. At the market, I selected the *(redest, reddest)* apples from the display.

20. Mindy, *(knitting, kniting)* a sweater, sat before the fireplace.

Suffixes Review

25d. When adding the suffix *–ness* or *–ly* to a word, do not change the spelling of the word itself.

25e. Drop the final silent *e* before adding a suffix beginning with a vowel.

25f. Keep the final silent *e* before adding a suffix that begins with a consonant.

25g. For words ending in *y* preceded by a consonant, change the *y* to *i* before any suffix that does not begin with *i*.

25h. Double the final consonant before adding *–ing, –ed, –er,* or *–est* to a one-syllable word that ends in a single consonant preceded by a single vowel.

MECHANICS

EXERCISE A In each of the following sentences, underline the correct spelling of the word in parentheses.

Example [1] *Jai alai,* which is *(pronounced, pronounceed)* "hi u li," means "merry festival."

This **[1]** *(fascinating, fascinateing)* handball game is played in a three-walled court. The court is **[2]** *(approximately, approximatly)* fifty-three meters long by fifteen meters wide, and the three walls are at least twelve meters high. **[3]** *(Spectateors, Spectators)* may watch the **[4]** *(excitment, excitement)* of the game from bleachers at the fourth side of the court, which is open. On the court, players catch and throw a hard rubber ball with long, **[5]** *(curved, curveed)* wicker scoops that are **[6]** *(straped, strapped)* to one arm. One player begins by **[7]** *(serving, serveing)* the ball against the front wall so that the ball lands in a designated serving zone. **[8]** *(Quickkly, Quickly),* before the ball touches the floor more than once, the opponent catches and throws the ball back at the wall in one continuous motion. A **[9]** *(truly, truely)* **[10]** *(envyable, enviable)* return would be to bounce the ball off the front wall with such speed and spin that the opposition cannot return it and loses the point.

EXERCISE B Cross out each misspelled word in the following sentences. Then, above the word, write it correctly.

Example 1. Last weekend, we ~~campped~~ *camped* out in the backyard.

11. The inventivness of Jerry's idea appealed to me.

12. Before dark, we worked on the placment of the tent.

13. Next, useing a ring of rocks and some logs, Jerry's father built a fire for us.

14. We finished eatting and cleaned up the site.

15. Then we sat beneath the beautyful moon and played our guitars.

NAME _______________ CLASS _______________ DATE _______________

Plurals of Nouns A

25i. Observe the following rules for spelling the plurals of nouns.

(1) To form the plural of most nouns, add *–s.*
(2) Form the plurals of nouns ending in *s, x, z, ch,* or *sh* by adding *–es.*
(3) Form the plurals of nouns ending in *y* preceded by a consonant by changing the *y* to *i* and adding *–es.*
(4) Form the plurals of nouns ending in *y* preceded by a vowel by adding *–s.*

EXAMPLES tree—tree**s** wish—wish**es** baby—bab**ies** tray—tray**s**

EXERCISE A Write the plurals of the following nouns on the lines provided.

Example 1. boss *bosses*

1. branch ______________ **6.** buzz ______________
2. crayon ______________ **7.** desk ______________
3. monkey ______________ **8.** lady ______________
4. mix ______________ **9.** turkey ______________
5. country ______________ **10.** crush ______________

EXERCISE B Cross out each misspelled word in the following sentences. Then, above the word, write it correctly. If a sentence is already correct, write *C* on the line provided.

Example ______ **1.** Samantha's ~~hobbys~~ *hobbies* have always included drawing and painting.

______**11.** Samantha likes to paint old churchs.

______**12.** She uses delicate brush strokes to create realistic details.

______**13.** Some of her paintinges have a dark, gothic tone.

______**14.** For instance, she painted angels on the roof of one church.

______**15.** She has also developed wayies of creating a soft, peaceful tone.

______**16.** Creating beautiful works, she said, helps relieve her worrys and stress.

______**17.** She uses different brushs to achieve different effects.

______**18.** She also arranges the draperyes in her studio so that the perfect amount of light enters.

______**19.** Samantha's future involves no uncertaintys or guesses.

______**20.** She plans to take art courses in college and later open a gallery.

NAME _______________ CLASS _______________ DATE _______________

Plurals of Nouns B

25i. Observe the following rules for spelling the plurals of nouns.

(5) Form the plurals of most nouns ending in *f* by adding *–s.* The plural form of some nouns ending in *f* or *fe* is formed by changing the *f* to *v* and adding *–es.*
(6) Form the plurals of nouns ending in *o* preceded by a vowel by adding *–s.*
(7) The plural form of many nouns ending in *o* preceded by a consonant is formed by adding *–es.*

EXAMPLES belief—belief**s** wolf—wol**ves** video—video**s** fiasco—fiasco**s**

EXERCISE A Write the plurals of the following nouns on the lines provided.

Example 1. gulf *gulfs*

1. elf _______________
2. rodeo _______________
3. studio _______________
4. leaf _______________
5. roof _______________
6. potato _______________
7. calf _______________
8. igloo _______________
9. wife _______________
10. piano _______________

EXERCISE B In each of the following sentences, underline the correct spelling of the word in parentheses.

Example 1. Several (*chefs, cheves*) worked to prepare a meal for the sailors.

11. One chef chopped several (*tomatoes, tomatos*) for a stew.
12. She then carefully cleaned and stored away the sharp (*knifes, knives*).
13. The crew of the submarine prided (*themselves, themselfs*) on running a tight ship.
14. Each sailor stores his or her clothes on the assigned (*shelfs, shelves*).
15. (*Torpedos, Torpedoes*) can be detonated by impact and by sound.
16. A lighthouse sat atop the (*bluffs, bluves*) overlooking the sea.
17. Some of the men and women studied training (*videoes, videos*).
18. Others discussed some beautiful coral (*reefs, reeves*) they had seen recently.
19. Some of our national (*heros, heroes*) have served aboard submarines.
20. Several battery-operated (*radioes, radios*) were given to the sailors.

NAME ______________ CLASS ______________ DATE ______________

Plurals of Nouns C

25i. Observe the following rules for spelling the plurals of nouns.

(8) The plurals of some nouns are formed in irregular ways.
(9) For most compound nouns written as one word, form the plural by adding *–s* or *–es.*
(10) For compound nouns in which one word is modified by the other word or words, form the plural of the word modified.

EXAMPLES foot—**feet** footrest**s** brother**s**-in-law

EXERCISE A Write the plurals of the following nouns on the lines provided.

Example 1. sergeant-at-arms *sergeants-at-arms*

1. child ______________
2. mother-in-law ______________
3. bookcase ______________
4. man ______________
5. backpack ______________
6. ox ______________
7. seashell ______________
8. rack of lamb ______________
9. love seat ______________
10. woman ______________

EXERCISE B Cross out each incorrect plural in the following sentences. Then, above the error, write the correct plural. If a sentence is already correct, write *C* on the line provided.

Example ______ **1.** The restaurant had several ~~coats rack~~ *coat racks* behind the reservations desk.

______ **11.** The childs will eat earlier in the evening than the adults.

______ **12.** I really enjoy spending time with my two brother-in-laws.

______ **13.** The three mouses headed in three different directions when the cat showed up.

______ **14.** The dentist said that I have no cavities in my tooths.

______ **15.** Use one of the step stools to reach the top shelf.

______ **16.** Several videos game are on sale at the computer store.

______ **17.** Put the baseballs in this bag, and I'll grab some bats.

______ **18.** All editor in chiefs will attend a meeting in June.

______ **19.** I do not have a sister, but I have three wonderful sisters-in-law.

______ **20.** How many gooses are in a gaggle?

Plurals of Nouns D

25i. Observe the following rules for spelling the plurals of nouns.

(11) Some nouns are the same in the singular and the plural.
(12) Form the plurals of numerals, letters, symbols, and words referred to as words by adding an apostrophe and *s*.

EXAMPLES deer—deer 1900—1900**'s**
A—*A*'**s** &—&'**s** *very*—*very*'**s**

EXERCISE A Write the plurals of the following items on the lines provided.

Example 1. *hurrah* hurrah's

1. 1950 ______
2. *Z* ______
3. * ______
4. *goodbye* ______
5. Vietnamese ______
6. # ______
7. sheep ______
8. *thank you* ______
9. Sioux ______
10. moose ______

EXERCISE B Above the underlined item in each sentence, write the item's plural form. If the plural form is the same as the singular, write *C.*

Examples 1. I heard several *ah* [ah's] as the magician pulled a dove out of a hat.

2. From the tracks, I knew several deer [C] had passed by.

11. I gasped when I saw how many *0* were on the price tag.
12. You have accidentally typed two *the* in a row in this sentence.
13. When do the salmon swim upstream?
14. The play takes place sometime in the late 1600.
15. Are @ used in e-mail addresses?
16. Several sheep are grazing in the farmyard.
17. Some people draw a line through their *Z*.
18. They do this to distinguish them from *2*.
19. When giving a speech, try to eliminate all *um*.
20. The Sioux make their home in the northern United States and southern Canada.

Plurals of Nouns Review

Review the rules on pages 663–66 of your textbook for information on forming the plurals of nouns.

EXAMPLES

pen + s = pen**s**	leaf + s = lea**ves**	mouse—**mice**
lunch + es = lunch**es**	ratio + s = ratio**s**	salmon—**salmon**
fairy + es = fair**ies**	potato + es = potato**es**	1980**'s**
tray + s = tray**s**	piano + s = piano**s**	*A***'s**
grief + s = grief**s**	sister-in-law + s = sister**s**-in-law	&**'s**
		*so***'s**

EXERCISE A Write the plurals of the following items on the lines provided.

Example 1. *hero* heroes

1. table ________

2. watch ________

3. cranberry ________

4. journey ________

5. belief ________

6. sheaf ________

7. patio ________

8. veto ________

9. soprano ________

10. woman ________

11. editor in chief ________

12. spacecraft ________

13. salmon ________

14. *X* ________

15. @ ________

16. *and* ________

17. four-wheeler ________

18. knife ________

19. wax ________

20. moss ________

EXERCISE B Cross out each incorrect plural in the following sentences. Then, above the word, write it correctly.

Example [1] Did you see Alvin's sketch of the ~~wolfs~~ wolves with their two cubs?

[21] I don't know any other fourteen-years-old who can draw as well as Alvin. **[22]** He has several sketchesbook full of watercolors and pen-and-ink drawings. **[23]** His mooses and oxen are especially realistic, but I prefer his landscapes and seascapes. **[24]** Alvin also makes drawings using nothing but #s and &'s. **[25]** If I could draw as well as Alvin does, I'd spend my weekends sitting on park benchs with a sketch pad in my hand.

Words Often Confused A

Review the Words Often Confused covered on pages 666–68 of your textbook for information on the correct spelling and usage of the following words:

accept, except	*already, all ready*	*altogether, all together*
advice, advise	*all right*	*brake, break*
affect, effect	*altar, alter*	

EXERCISE For each sentence below, underline the word or words in parentheses that correctly complete the sentence.

Examples **1.** Would you *(advice, advise)* me to buy this jacket?

2. Yes, take my *(advice, advise)* and buy it.

1. How did your test score *(affect, effect)* your final grade?

2. I *(already, all ready)* have an A for the semester!

3. Will you follow Dwayne's *(advice, advise)* about your project?

4. I was *(already, all ready)* to buy it, but then I saw another one.

5. My mood *(affects, effects)* what I buy.

6. If we *(alter, altar)* the collar, the shirt will look much better.

7. Did Ms. Rubio *(advice, advise)* you to take cheerleading?

8. She needs us *(altogether, all together)* for daily practice.

9. What were the *(affects, effects)* of the war with Iraq?

10. Dad, is it *(allright, all right)* that I told Mr. Valdez you'd bring snacks to the open house?

11. Patrick squeezed the hand *(brake, break)* on his bicycle to slow down.

12. I hope that our older cat will *(accept, except)* the two new kittens.

13. It's *(altogether, all together)* too silly for me!

14. Do you need more time, or are you *(already, all ready)?*

15. Marguerite has finished all of her homework *(accept, except)* the history questions.

16. My mom said it's *(alright, all right)* if you come over after school.

17. Would you place these candles on the *(alter, altar)* please?

18. I packed the crystal vase in layers of bubble wrap so it would not *(brake, break).*

19. I like all of these hats *(accept, except)* the one with orange flowers on it.

20. Edwina's kind note had a positive *(affect, effect)* on my mood today.

Words Often Confused B

Review the Words Often Confused covered on pages 668–70 of your textbook for information on the correct spelling and usage of the following words:

capital, capitol	***coarse, course***	***councilor, counselor***
choose, chose	***complement, compliment***	***desert, desert, dessert***
cloths, clothes	***council, counsel***	

EXERCISE A Underline the word in parentheses that correctly completes each sentence.

Example 1. Three new *(councilors, counselors)* were elected to the city council.

1. Our computer *(coarse, course)* sometimes baffles me.

2. You know what a spreadsheet is, of *(coarse, course)*.

3. Joyce is a respected member of the student *(council, counsel)*.

4. I'm writing about Washington, the *(capital, capitol)* of the United States.

5. After college, I plan to work as a student *(councilor, counselor)* at a middle school.

6. Mom invited me to help her *(choose, chose)* new curtains for the family room.

7. When I think of the *(desert, dessert)*, I think of sand, camels, and hot sun.

8. The Colorado *(capital, capitol)* has a gold dome.

9. I decided to *(complement, compliment)* Antonia on the success of her party.

10. I used soft *(cloths, clothes)* to clean the TV screen and porcelain figurines.

EXERCISE B Choose words from the list at the top of the page to complete each sentence correctly.

Example 1. Would you like strawberry yogurt for ___*dessert*___?

11. I organize the ______ in my closet by color and season.

12. She thinks this fabric is too ______ for a prom dress.

13. I knew you would ______ me in my time of crisis.

14. Harvey's deep green sweater ______ his green eyes.

15. The town's planning committee, ten ______ in all, met last night.

16. At the plant nursery yesterday, I ______ several potted plants for my room.

17. What city is the ______ of your state?

18. An oasis is a welcome sight to any ______ traveler.

19. Instead of criticizing failures, Mr. and Ms. Kent ______ us on our successes.

20. Kaveh's favorite ______ this year is Spanish.

Words Often Confused C

Review the Words Often Confused covered on pages 671–73 of your textbook for information on the correct spelling and usage of the following words:

formally, formerly *lead, led, lead* *passed, past* *hear, here*
loose, lose *peace, piece* *its, it's*

EXERCISE A Underline the word in parentheses that correctly completes each sentence.

Example 1. *(Lead, Led)*-based paint can be unsafe.

1. Look at that *(peace, piece)* of material on the shelf.

2. Miranda, did you *(hear, here)* about the test?

3. I think *(its, it's)* warm enough outside to go swimming!

4. Luis bought a special key rack so that he wouldn't *(loose, lose)* his keys.

5. The trainer expertly *(lead, led)* the horse along the path.

6. We will dress *(formally, formerly)* for the dance.

7. In the mall, a woman *(passed, past)* out perfume samples.

8. The seven-year-old wiggled his *(loose, lose)* tooth.

9. This plant is admired for *(its, it's)* large red blossoms.

10. Can you *(lead, led)* me to the picnic spot you found?

EXERCISE B In each of the following sentences, underline the word in parentheses that correctly completes the sentence. Then, write a new sentence using the other word correctly.

Example 1. Instead of dwelling on the *(passed, past)*, I dream about the future.

I am so happy I passed the spelling test!

11. Have you found the missing *(peace, piece)* of that model train? ____________________

____

12. This new restaurant was *(formally, formerly)* a dry cleaner's store. ____________________

____

13. *(Lead, Led)* is a chemical often used in batteries. ____________________

____

14. This tree shed *(its, it's)* leaves later than the others did. ____________________

____

15. If you move your bed over *(hear, here)*, you'll have more floor space. ____________________

____

Words Often Confused D

Review the Words Often Confused covered on pages 673–75 of your textbook for information on the correct spelling and usage of the following words:

plain, plane	*shone, shown*	*than, then*
principal, principle	*stationary, stationery*	*their, there, they're*
quiet, quite		

MECHANICS

EXERCISE A Underline the word in parentheses that correctly completes each sentence.

Example 1. Do you want *(plain, plane)* yogurt or flavored yogurt for breakfast?

1. Your project is not *(quiet, quite)* completed.
2. You've already *(shone, shown)* me how to work the math problem.
3. For her birthday, I gave Leigh a box of *(stationary, stationery)*.
4. Who is the new student sitting alone over *(their, there, they're)*?
5. Grandma always says, "It's as *(plain, plane)* as the nose on your face!"
6. First, practice dribbling, and *(than, then)* do some layups.
7. Try to be as *(quiet, quite)* as a mouse.
8. The *(principal, principle)* of my school likes to say he is our pal.
9. Uncle Henry uses a hammer and a *(plain, plane)* in his carpentry jobs.
10. The lights in the harbor *(shone, shown)* brightly.

EXERCISE B Choose words from the list at the top of the page to complete each sentence.

Example 1. The Campbells had ___*their*___ house repainted.

11. We were ______________ how to sort the glass for recycling.
12. This box of books is ______________ heavy.
13. Ruben saw the Statue of Liberty from the window of the ______________.
14. Our teacher asked us to be ______________.
15. Shirley says that the golden rule is a good ______________ by which to live.
16. Ask Aunt Fern and Uncle Dale if ______________ going to the game with us.
17. Is our team ranked higher ______________ our rival's?
18. Bison once roamed this ______________.
19. A spotlight ______________ on center stage.
20. You must remain ______________ until the swelling in your ankle goes down.

Words Often Confused E

Review the Words Often Confused covered on pages 675–77 of your textbook for information on the correct spelling and usage of the following words:

threw, through *waist, waste* *weather, whether* *your, you're*
to, too, two *weak, week* *who's, whose*

EXERCISE A For each sentence below, underline the correct word in parentheses.

Example 1. (*Who's, Whose*) going to coach girls' basketball next year?

1. My walkie-talkie is too (*weak, week*) to pick up their voices.
2. Susan casually tied the sweater around her (*waist, waste*).
3. The criminal (*threw, through*) away the evidence.
4. I don't know (*weather, whether*) I'll try out for cheerleading or not.
5. (*Who's, Whose*) jacket was left on my desk?
6. I was so thirsty that I drank (*to, too, two*) glasses of water.
7. It will take a (*weak, week*) to get my watch repaired.
8. I was able to reach him (*threw, through*) a friend.
9. Will this project take more than one (*weak, week*)?
10. These potatoes are (*to, too, two*) salty for my taste.

EXERCISE B In each of the following sentences, underline the word in parentheses that correctly completes the sentence. Then, write a new sentence using the other word correctly.

Example 1. Your dentist appointment is next (*weak, week*). ______

Because I have the flu, I am too weak to go to school.

11. My mom always says, "(*Waist, Waste*) not, want not." ______

______

12. Will the recycling drive last all (*weak, week*)? ______

______

13. Do you know the way (*to, too*) Jared's house? ______

______

14. Which is (*your, you're*) favorite subject in school? ______

______

15. Loretta (*threw, through*) out some bread crumbs for the birds. ______

______

NAME ______ CLASS ______ DATE ______

for **CHAPTER 25: SPELLING** *pages 656–66*

Review A: **Spelling Rules**

EXERCISE A For items 1–5, spell the word correctly, adding the given prefix. For items 6–10, write the plural form of the word given.

Examples **1.** un + necessary = *unnecessary*

2. *B (plural)* = *B's*

1. re + write = ______

2. un + healthy = ______

3. over + turn = ______

4. im + mature = ______

5. mis + inform = ______

6. veto *(plural)* = ______

7. wolf *(plural)* = ______

8. box *(plural)* = ______

9. 10 *(plural)* = ______

10. man *(plural)* = ______

MECHANICS

EXERCISE B Cross out any misspelled word in each of the following sentences. Above the word, write it correctly. If a sentence is already correct, write *C* on the line provided.

Example ______ **1.** It was ~~hopless~~ *hopeless* for Marta to win, since she didn't practice.

______ **11.** In all fairrness, the judge will hear the case.

______ **12.** Much to our astonishement, Manfred won a trophy!

______ **13.** Finaly, the team has a chance for first place.

______ **14.** A sudden storm caused a postponment of the picnic.

______ **15.** When did Henry VIII riegn over England?

______ **16.** Who owns that adoreable little kitten?

______ **17.** My cousin's directions were worthless, so we got lost.

______ **18.** The clock in the hall chimes hourely.

______ **19.** What busyness do you have at the bank?

______ **20.** Aunt Thelma won the acheivement award.

Review B: **Words Often Confused**

EXERCISE A For each of the following sentences, underline the word or words in parentheses that correctly complete the sentence.

Example 1. I believe *(its, it's)* your turn to rake the leaves.

1. The legislature meets on the second floor of the *(capital, capitol).*

2. Willard took his sister's *(advice, advise)* and went to the party.

3. The coach said we're not *(quiet, quite)* ready to compete.

4. Are you *(already, all ready)* for your trip?

5. I hope you counted every *(peace, piece)* of luggage.

6. When I had the flu, I felt very *(weak, week).*

7. The small *(plane, plain)* flew over the Grand Canyon.

8. Can you *(hear, here)* me?

9. I hope to take a cooking *(coarse, course)* this summer.

10. That decision might *(affect, effect)* your job.

EXERCISE B In the following paragraphs, underline the word or words in parentheses that correctly complete each sentence.

Example [1] Would you like to *(hear, here)* about the play *Macbeth* by William Shakespeare?

The **[11]** *(principal, principle)* character, Macbeth, is **[12]** *(altogether, all together)* too ambitious for his own good. When he hears a prediction that he will be the new king, he **[13]** *(accepts, excepts)* it as the truth. His wife, Lady Macbeth, greatly **[14]** *(affects, effects)* Macbeth's **[15]** *(coarse, course)* of action.

When the king visits Macbeth's castle, Macbeth and his wife are ready to proceed with **[16]** *(their, there, they're)* plan. While the king sleeps, Macbeth slips **[17]** *(past, passed)* the guards and does a terrible deed.

Macbeth mistakenly believes that nothing now can **[18]** *(altar, alter)* his plan to be king. He gains the throne but **[19]** *(looses, loses)* his **[20]** *(peace, piece)* of mind. Lady Macbeth loses her sanity.

MECHANICS

Review C: Spelling Rules

EXERCISE A For items 1–5, spell the word correctly, adding the given prefix. For items 6–10, write the plural form of the word given.

Examples **1.** il + legible = illegible

2. 1900 *(plural)* = 1900's

1. un + real = ____________________ **6.** hoof *(plural)* = ____________________

2. re + tell = ____________________ **7.** deer *(plural)* = ____________________

3. in + secure = ____________________ **8.** woman *(plural)* = ____________________

4. mis + spell = ____________________ **9.** fox *(plural)* = ____________________

5. over + run = ____________________ **10.** C *(plural)* = ____________________

EXERCISE B In each of the following sentences, underline the correct spelling of the word in parentheses.

Example **1.** I'm *(writeing, writing)* to tell you some good news.

11. My older sister Holly has known her boyfriend since they were *(childs, children).*

12. Holly and Dirk talked about their *(engagement, engagment)* last night.

13. They'll announce it *(formaly, formally)* in the newspaper.

14. We hope the wedding turns out to be a *(joyous, joious)* event.

15. The whole family is sharing their *(happiness, happyness).*

16. Tomorrow, Mom will help Holly shop for a dress and *(veil, viel).*

17. You will *(recieve, receive)* your wedding invitation in a few weeks.

18. I'm sure that Holly and Dirk will *(succede, succeed)* in planning a special ceremony.

19. My little cousin Mary will *(preseed, precede)* Holly down the aisle as flower girl.

20. Close *(friends, freinds)* will be bridesmaids and groomsmen.

MECHANICS

NAME ____________________ CLASS ____________ DATE ____________

for **CHAPTER 25: SPELLING** *pages 656–77*

Review D: **Words Often Confused and Spelling Rules**

EXERCISE A In each of the following sentences, underline the word in parentheses that correctly completes the sentence.

Example 1. Have you (*already, all ready*) adopted a kitten from the animal shelter?

1. It is only July, but that store has a large display of winter (*cloths, clothes*) such as coats and scarves.
2. "Both candidates for senator have very clear (*principals, principles*)," my father said.
3. The forecasters don't know (*weather, whether*) the blizzard will hit our area tonight.
4. Dan said he is (*quiet, quite*) sure that the movie is too violent for his taste.
5. According to the sign, we have just (*passed, past*) the entrance to Lion Country Safari.
6. If you pull that cord too hard, it will (*brake, break*).
7. If you want my (*advice, advise*), you should buy a mountain bike, not a ten-speed.
8. "(*Its, It's*) a shame that you can't go to the play," said Ahmed.
9. Yes, if enough people truly work at it, (*piece, peace*) on earth is possible, don't you think?
10. The fabric on the couch in the waiting room is (*coarse, course*) and scratchy.

EXERCISE B Cross out the misspelled word in each of the following sentences. Then, write the word correctly above the error. Hint: All proper nouns are already spelled correctly.

Example 1. I am ~~planing~~ *planning* to write a short report about the history of food.

11. Most of us probably beleive that food is one of the greatest subjects!
12. There's no deniing that wheat and barley were the leading grains in ancient Egypt.
13. The rich land in the Nile Valley allowed the Egyptians to succede in farming.
14. Olives, raw beans, and figs were often included in Roman dishs long ago.
15. The dayly diet of many Romans also included a cereal mixture called polenta.
16. Spices were extremly popular during the Middle Ages and the Renaissance.
17. Ships from the New World haulled potatoes to Europe.
18. To me, the strangeest thing is that potatoes were not known in Europe before then.
19. The beginning of canned food is not unoted in history books.
20. Truthfuly, canned food was developed in the 1800's; the can opener came later.

NAME ______________________ CLASS ______________ DATE ______________

for **CHAPTER 25: SPELLING** *pages 655–77*

Proofreading Application: Public Notice

Good writers are generally good proofreaders. Readers tend to admire and trust writing that is error-free. Make sure that you correct all errors in grammar, usage, spelling, and punctuation in your writing. Your readers will have more confidence in your words if you have done your best to proofread carefully.

Errors in spelling are particularly embarrassing in public notices. In English, there are a number of words that are often confused with one another. These words sound alike but are spelled differently. When you write a public notice and misspell these words, they jump out at your readers. These misspelled words can make readers doubt the worth of your service, product, or event.

PROOFREADING ACTIVITY

Find and correct the errors in spelling in the following public notice. Use proofreading symbols such as those on page 809 of *Elements of Language* to make your corrections.

Example Friends and ~~nieghbors~~ [neighbors], do yourselves a favor.

Its that time again!

Spring-cleaning time is hear!

The days of cold whether are over.

Snow and sleet have all past us by.

Get you're car ready for those nice, warm spring days!

Better yet, let the student's of Niceville Middle School do it for you!

We're having a car wash from 9:00 A.M. too 3:00 P.M. on Saturday, March 1.

The cost is two dollares per car, three for trucks and vans.

Come to Big Ralph's Vegetable Stand at the corner of Central Avenue and Mississippi Street if you truely want to have the cleanest car in town!

Child care is available, and we have plenty of childrens' toys to amuse your young ones.

Literary Model: Spelling in a Poem

from "When the Frost Is on the Punkin"
by James Whitcomb Riley

The husky, rusty russel of the tossels of the corn,
And the raspin' of the tangled leaves, as golden as the morn;

. . . .

The strawstack in the medder, and the reaper in the shed;
The hosses in theyr stalls below—the clover overhead!—
O, it sets my hart a-clickin' like the tickin' of a clock,
When the frost is on the punkin and the fodder's in the shock!

Then your apples all is gethered, and the ones a feller keeps
Is poured around the celler floor in red and yeller heaps;

. . . .

I don't know how to tell it—but ef sich a thing could be
As the Angels wantin' boardin', and they'd call around on *me*—
I'd want to 'commodate 'em—all the whole indurin' flock—
When the frost is on the punkin and the fodder's in the shock!

EXERCISE A After reading the poem aloud, write at least ten words that the poet has spelled using nonstandard spelling conventions. (Hint: Do not include words in which an apostrophe indicates that a letter has been left out.)

EXERCISE B

1. Rewrite lines 25 and 26 using standard spelling conventions.

Literary Model (continued)

2. Why do you think the author used nonstandard spelling conventions in the poem? Would the poem sound different if he hadn't? Explain your answers.

EXERCISE C ***Dialect*** is a form of speech belonging to a particular region or to a particular group of people. Think of a dialect you have heard in a movie, on television, or in real life. Write a paragraph spoken by someone who uses this dialect. Use nonstandard spelling conventions to help represent the dialect.

EXERCISE D

1. Will the nonstandard spelling conventions you used help your reader "hear" your speaker? Explain your answer.

2. In what types of writing would the use of nonstandard spelling conventions help you express what you want to express? In what types would it not help you? Explain your answers.

Writing Application: Definitions

Many sets of words in English are pronounced and spelled almost the same way, so it's easy to mix them up. When you're in doubt, look up the word in question in a dictionary or on a spelling list like the one in this chapter. Watch out especially for words that are new to your vocabulary. Otherwise, you may come up with embarrassing bloopers like these.

EXAMPLES I found the solution in *around about* way. (in a roundabout way)

The baseball player behaved like a *pre-madonna*. (like a prima donna)

The statues had survived for two centuries *in tacked*. (intact)

I am *a custom* to getting up early. (accustomed to)

Writing Activity

Your class is planning a spelling bee for fifth- and sixth-graders. These students may be younger than you, but they are a smart bunch, and you want to challenge them with words worthy of their knowledge. Each student in your class must choose seven words that writers frequently misspell. For each word, you must write your own definition. Then, write a sentence using the word correctly. (This sentence will be read to the student who must spell the word.) Finally, if you know any tips for remembering the correct spelling, write them down, too. Put each word on a 3×5 index card so that it can be shuffled with the other students' choices and drawn at random during the bee. You may use the spelling lists in this chapter or choose words that you have had trouble with in the past.

PREWRITING Prewriting for this assignment is straightforward: list the seven words you've chosen, and check the dictionary for exact definitions of each. Then, rewrite each definition in your own words. Be sure to note the part of speech for each word, too. *Effect,* for example, can be a noun or a verb, and its meaning depends on how you use it.

WRITING Now write your sentences to go with each word. The sentences should make the meaning of each word clear, and they should not challenge the spellers' comprehension—no trick questions. You may need to write several example sentences for each word so that you can then pick the clearest and most helpful example. Finally, attach to each word any tips you have identified to help remember how the word is spelled.

REVISING Enlist a couple of fifth and sixth graders who are not contestants to listen to your sentences (not to read them, since the contestants won't have that luxury, either). Which sentences most consistently prompt your listeners to spell the word correctly? Refine your sentences based on their feedback. Then, ask them not to leak any sensitive spelling bee secrets!

PUBLISHING Check your words and sentences for errors in grammar, usage, punctuation, and (of course) spelling. Then neatly prepare the 3×5 cards, and give them to the spelling bee reader.

Extending Your Writing

This exercise could lead to a more developed writing project. The spelling of words in English hasn't always been so fixed. In fact, not too long ago, writers had more liberty to spell words as they heard them. For a history class, do some research into how and when English spelling began to be regularized. You may be surprised at what you find. You may decide that you prefer the older methods of spelling words to our modern dictionary spellings!

for **CHAPTER 26: CORRECTING COMMON ERRORS** *pages 684–717*

Choices: Exploring Common Errors

Here's your chance to step out of the grammar book and into the real world. You may not notice them, but you and the people around you use grammar, usage, and mechanics every day. The following activities challenge you to find a connection between common errors and the world around you. Do the activity below that suits your personality best, and then share your discoveries with your class. Have fun!

PUBLISHING

Roll the Presses

Your classmates have created some great stuff for English class! Now it's time to form a committee to choose the best of the best and publish them in your class newsletter or on the class Web site. Assign someone to interview your teacher and get his or her opinion of the projects. Include a few photographs as well. When you have finished, you will have something really special to help you remember this exciting year.

DRAMA

What a Character!

You have probably noticed that errors in English usage are sometimes funny. Have you also noticed that certain errors can be used for characterization? For instance, you can use sentence fragments to characterize a scatterbrained person—someone who never finishes a thought. Write a brief comedy sketch. Include at least one character who makes as many language errors as possible. For contrast, have at least one character who never makes an error. Plot your sketch so that all of the characters are friends in the end. Select actors, and perform the sketch for the class.

MEMORY

Flashcards

Irregular verb forms can be tricky to remember. Help your classmates out by making a class set of flashcards. Choose several irregular verbs that have past and past participle forms that are hard to remember. Make a flashcard for each verb. On the front of each card, write the base form of your verb. On the back, write the past-tense form near the top edge of the card and the past participle form near the bottom edge. Then, test your classmates.

DISCUSSION

Pet Peeves

Just about everybody has an opinion about what the most horrible language error is. For some it's spelling, for others it's sentence fragments, and for still others it's incorrect pronoun references. Do you have a pet peeve? Do your classmates? Do your teachers? Find out by taking a survey of your classmates and teachers. Ask your parents, neighbors, and relatives, too. Then, use the results of your survey to lead a discussion on the errors that bug people the most.

WRITING

Who Says Friends Are All Alike?

Find out how different two friends (or three, four, or five friends) can be. Divide your class into groups of five or fewer, making sure that everyone has a pencil and a few sheets of paper. Have each group member write down the following sentence fragment: "before they went to dinner." Each person's job is to write a complete sentence by adding words to the beginning or end of the fragment. No consulting allowed! When everyone is finished, have each person read his or her sentence to the group. Repeat the exercise using a few fragments of your own.

ART

Fast, Faster, Fastest

If you like to draw or paint, you may be the best person to show your class how important modifiers can be. For example, when you draw a picture of three basketball players, you can make it easy for others to tell which player is tall, which one is taller, and which one is tallest. Now, pick your own set of modifiers and illustrate them. Make sure that your artwork has a caption that contains the modifiers you have brought to life.

Sentence Fragments and Run-on Sentences A

EXERCISE On the line provided, identify the following word groups by writing *SF* for *sentence fragment*, *RO* for *run-on sentence*, or *S* for *sentence*.

Examples SF 1. Buying school supplies at the office supply store.

RO 2. I chose self-stick flags and notes in different colors, I use these when I study.

S 3. Have you ever marked pages in your books with reusable sticker flags?

______ 1. Available in different colors, such as red, yellow, green, blue, and purple.

______ 2. At my school, we cannot write or highlight in our textbooks.

______ 3. I use small sticker flags to mark important passages I write notes on larger self-stick slips of paper.

______ 4. A color-coded system for marking different types of information.

______ 5. Occasionally a teacher will say, "This will be on the test."

______ 6. Marking the page with a red sticker immediately.

______ 7. Red stickers are for high-priority passages, and yellow stickers are for low-priority passages.

______ 8. Green is the color of growth I use green flags for difficult topics requiring extra study.

______ 9. As a reminder of my own possible intellectual growth in this topic.

______ 10. Blue, the color of smooth sailing.

______ 11. Important information is not always difficult to understand I mark this type of passage with a blue flag.

______ 12. Education, above all, should be challenging and inspiring.

______ 13. Always looking for interesting or fascinating topics and ideas.

______ 14. The purple flags for these creative topics.

______ 15. For example, after reading a brief reference to ostrich farms.

______ 16. I marked the reference with a purple flag that weekend I investigated ostrich farms.

______ 17. Free access to the Internet at the public library near my apartment.

______ 18. The Internet has become a useful tool for my research, I find information for tests and papers as well as information for my personal interest and enjoyment.

______ 19. The three-inch-square, yellow self-stick notes.

______ 20. On these, I write short notes about my teacher's comments.

Sentence Fragments and Run-on Sentences B

EXERCISE A On the lines provided, revise each sentence fragment by (1) adding a subject, (2) adding a verb, or (3) attaching the fragment to a complete sentence.

Example 1. A new sport available this year at school. *A new sport available this year at school is golf.*

1. Because I enjoy sports of any kind.

2. Never played golf before.

3. Coach Mabry, the other players in seventh grade, and I.

4. That walking long distances is a part of golf.

5. On the golf course on a beautiful, sunny day.

EXERCISE B On the lines provided, revise each of the following run-on sentences by (1) making two sentences or (2) using a comma and a coordinating conjunction to make a compound sentence.

Example 1. I have always been interested in interior decorating my friends and family trust my advice. *I have always been interested in interior decorating, and my friends and family trust my advice.*

6. I carefully study interior design magazines I then make sketches of my own ideas.

7. One of my specialties is window treatments this category includes drapes and blinds.

8. You can't forget about the details for example, candlesticks or pillows brighten a room.

9. If I had to give one piece of advice, it would be about color choose neutral furniture colors.

10. Then, accent the room with colorful pillows or rugs these items are less costly to update.

Sentence Fragments and Run-on Sentences C

EXERCISE On the line provided, identify each of the following word groups by writing *SF* for *sentence fragment, RO* for *run-on sentence,* or *S* for *sentence.* Then, revise any sentence fragments or run-on sentences to create complete sentences.

Example 1. The planet Earth has been around for a long time scientists estimate it is 4.6 billion years old. *RO. The planet Earth has been around for a long time; scientists estimate it is 4.6 billion years old.*

1. Formed at the same time as the sun, from materials left over from the sun's formation. ______

2. At first, Earth was extremely hot it then cooled. ______

3. Earth maintained a central core of iron and nickel it developed a middle layer of liquid metal and an outer crust. ______

4. Above the crust, an atmosphere, which constantly revolves. ______

5. Earth's oceans appeared quickly once the planet cooled they have existed ever since. ______

6. Single-celled algae, the first form of life, after about 3.5 billion years. ______

7. Some fossils 570 million years old. ______

8. Dinosaurs lived in the Mesozoic Era, 225 million to 65 million years ago, *mesozoic* means "middle life." ______

9. How long have human beings existed? ______

10. The present era is the Cenozoic, *cenozoic* means "recent life." ______

Subject-Verb Agreement A

EXERCISE A In each of the sentences below, underline the form of the verb in parentheses that agrees with its subject.

Examples 1. Carmina and Gerald *(read, reads)* a book called *Some of the Kinder Planets.*

2. The stories in this book *(was, were)* written by Tim Wynne-Jones.

1. A boy in one of the stories *(fear, fears)* he has been abducted by aliens.
2. The "aliens" *(is, are)* actually a family living in a high-tech geodesic dome.
3. What *(does, do)* the planet Mars and the pomegranate fruit have in common?
4. If you *(read, reads)* "The Night of the Pomegranate," you will find out.
5. Everyone *(has, have)* been ill at one time or another.
6. In "Tashkent," a boy nearly *(die, dies)* from a mysterious illness.
7. Then, in a very unusual way, he *(begin, begins)* to plan a trip to an exotic city.
8. Either you or your friends *(has, have)* probably written an essay about a vacation.
9. An imaginative boy and his friend *(creates, create)* an alternative to this assignment.
10. The story that tells about their activities *(is, are)* "Tweedledum and Tweedledead."

EXERCISE B In each of the following sentences, write *C* above the underlined verb if it agrees with its subject. If the underlined verb does not agree with its subject, write the correct form of the verb above it.

Example 1. Does you or a friend want to live forever at the same age you are now? *(Do)*

11. Winnie Foster, in *Tuck Everlasting,* face this exact choice.
12. Winnie, while playing in the woods, find a beautiful, clear stream of water.
13. Before she can take a drink, however, she is kidnapped by a very nice family.
14. When the Tuck family kidnap Winnie, she doesn't expect magic.
15. The spring of water, these people tell her, are magical.
16. A tiny sip from this spring hidden among the trees give everlasting life.
17. Every one of the Tucks are immortal because they drank from the spring.
18. Over the years they have formed a definite opinion about their situation.
19. Winnie, faced with the opportunity of drinking from the spring, make a surprising decision.
20. Meanwhile, a mysterious stranger suspect Winnie's secret.

Subject-Verb Agreement B

EXERCISE A Underline the verb in each of the following sentences. If the subject and verb do not agree, write the correct form of the verb above it. If the subject and verb agree, write *C* above the verb.

Example 1. Has you considered the role of heroes in the lives of young people? *(Have considered)*

1. Not everyone nowadays have a personal hero.
2. Some people just hasn't thought about the subject.
3. Others have not found an ideal hero.
4. Either people from history or someone alive today make a good choice for a personal hero.
5. For example, Helen Keller or Anne Frank may inspire people in difficult circumstances.
6. On the other hand, one of your own classmates are also a good candidate for a hero.
7. Have someone in your school been an "unsung hero"?
8. Each day peoples' decisions affect the lives of people around them.
9. Has someone affected your life in a positive way?
10. That are the sign of a hero!

EXERCISE B In each of the following sentences, underline the subject once and the verb twice. If the subject and verb do not agree, write the correct form of the verb above the verb. If the subject and verb already agree, write *C* above the verb.

Example 1. The first of six successful lunar landings by the U.S. Apollo program were achieved on July 20, 1969. *(was achieved)*

11. One of the Apollo astronauts, Neil Armstrong, were the first human on the moon.
12. None of the early Soviet Sputnik satellites was designed for a moon landing.
13. Both Orville and Wilbur Wright was responsible for the first airplane flight, in North Carolina in 1903.
14. Computer-created images and touch sensations is often called virtual reality.
15. Pakistan, along with Bangladesh, were freed from British rule in 1947.
16. Neither Dan nor Jill know the capital of Canada.
17. The Philippines is an island system in the southwestern Pacific.
18. Qatar, one of many Middle Eastern countries, have made use of its oil resources.
19. Gu and Thy is planning a party for their uncle's visit.
20. San Salvador, the largest of El Salvador's cities, have suffered from recurring earthquakes.

Pronoun-Antecedent Agreement A

EXERCISE A In each of the following sentences, underline the word or word group in parentheses that creates pronoun-antecedent agreement.

Example 1. The doll, forgotten in an attic for years, is in *(their, its)* original box.

1. Have you tried in-line skating? *(It is, They are)* a fun outdoor activity.
2. Either Darren or Marco will present *(their, his)* report in Spanish.
3. One of my cats uses *(its, their)* paws to eat.
4. Angela and Trisha enjoyed *(her, their)* soccer team practice.
5. Neither of the bicycles still has *(its, their)* original tires.
6. One of our neighbors played *(their, her)* sitar for us.
7. The smaller of the two tables needs *(its, their)* top polished.
8. Everyone contributed *(their, his or her)* ideas during the brainstorming session.
9. Roy's bedroom needs *(his, its)* walls repainted with a fresh, new color.
10. After a while, this chewing gum loses *(its, their)* flavor.

EXERCISE B In the following sentences, cross out each pronoun that does not agree with its antecedent. Above it, write the correct pronoun. If a sentence is already correct, write *C* after the sentence.

Example 1. Here is the microscope, but where are ~~their~~ *its* lenses?

11. Each science student is choosing their own project.
12. Both Jorge and Diana chose insect study as his or her projects.
13. Diana plans to study medicine when she is in college.
14. Jorge, unlike Diana, plans on making art their major in college.
15. Jorge will make sure that the photographs in their report provide good visual support.
16. Few of the other students are as sure about his or her career goals.
17. For many seventh-graders, choices about college are still far in their future.
18. Many students view the project as a way to explore his or her interests.
19. Perhaps someone in our class will realize their dream to become a scientist.
20. The idea of studying the world around me appeals to me. They would be an interesting career.

Pronoun-Antecedent Agreement B

EXERCISE A In each of the following sentences, underline the pronoun or pair of pronouns in parentheses that agrees with the antecedent.

Example 1. One of the sled's blades is loose, and *(it, they)* should be tightened.

1. Did someone that you know leave *(their, his or her)* umbrella at our house?

2. The roads are safe for travel because *(its, their)* surfaces have been cleared of ice.

3. Either Leona or Barbara can use these skis on *(his or her, her)* ski trip.

4. One of the girls, wearing *(their, her)* raincoat, splashed happily in the puddles of rain.

5. Because *(its, their)* surface is frozen, the small lake looks eerily motionless.

6. Josh and his brother Jake worked all morning to clear *(his, their)* driveway of snow.

7. No one enjoys having *(their, his or her)* car doors frozen shut.

8. Both Charlene and Kristin are spending *(their, her)* afternoon at the ice rink.

9. Icicles are beautiful, but *(its, their)* sharp points can be dangerous.

10. Winter is my favorite of all four seasons, and I always look forward to *(them, it)*.

EXERCISE B On the line in each sentence below, write a pronoun or pair of pronouns that agrees with the antecedent.

Example 1. Is anyone able to share ___his or her___ encyclopedia with me?

11. Either Lucy or Maxine will lend you ______ encyclopedia.

12. Birds fascinate me because ______ have the freedom of flight.

13. I'm sure the Wright brothers, who invented the first successful airplane, spent some of ______ time watching and envying birds.

14. Everyone has ______ own hobby; mine is ornithology, which is the study of birds.

15. Encyclopedias are great sources of information because ______ have interesting articles and accurate drawings.

16. For example, I learned that penguins are birds, but ______ cannot fly.

17. In ______ oral presentation, Janice described a bird called the shoebill stork.

18. The shoebill stork has a distinctive bill; ______ resembles a scoop or shovel.

19. Janice said that the bird looks clumsy on land, but ______ is graceful in flight.

20. A few of my classmates asked Janice questions; ______ share my interest in birds.

COMMON ERRORS

Verb Forms A

EXERCISE A In each of the following sentences, write the correct past or past participle form of the verb in parentheses.

Example 1. Have you ___*seen*___ any films made in Hong Kong? *(see)*

1. LaShonda ______ the honor roll again this semester. *(make)*

2. Bright green leaves ______ after last week's rain. *(grow)*

3. Yesterday I ______ sushi for the first time. *(eat)*

4. My uncle ______ me a harmonica for my last birthday. *(give)*

5. Maria ______ me a card for Hanukkah last week. *(send)*

6. Has Mr. Kung already ______ you the story about that Chinese vase? *(tell)*

7. The principal has ______ highly of the seventh-graders' charity work. *(speak)*

8. Last weekend, my family ______ to the opera. *(go)*

9. Pedro has ______ in this race each year since he was nine. *(run)*

10. I have ______ to my senator about the issue. *(write)*

EXERCISE B In the following sentences, cross out any incorrect past or past participle verb forms. Write the correct form above the error. If a sentence is already correct, write *C* after it.

Example 1. Pamela ~~speaked~~ *spoke* to me about her plans for earning money.

11. She is only thirteen years old, but she has begin to develop a good reputation for hair care.

12. For the past year, Pamela has run an informal hair salon in her kitchen on Saturdays.

13. She has ringed up enough sales to buy quality scissors and other equipment.

14. She says she has knowed for a long time that she will open her own salon after high school.

15. Pamela has builded up a strong base of knowledge about hair care.

16. She has always weared her hair in the latest fashion.

17. Last year, I taked her advice about cutting my bangs.

18. Pamela herself did the work.

19. I feeled great about the new look!

20. I gladly payed Pamela's reasonable charge for the haircut.

COMMON ERRORS

Verb Forms B

EXERCISE A In each of the following sentences, underline the correct verb form in parentheses.

Example **1.** I was *(give, given)* swimming lessons before I was six years old.

1. I recently *(heard, hear)* about the first woman to swim across the English Channel.

2. Gertrude Ederle, an American, *(swam, swum)* the Channel on August 6, 1926.

3. She *(break, broke)* the current record by nearly two hours.

4. She *(hold, held)* the new record of fourteen hours, thirty-one minutes.

5. During the 1920s, Ederle *(become, became)* a well-known figure in sports.

6. In the early 1920s, she had *(setted, set)* women's freestyle records for distances from 100 to 880 yards.

7. In 1924, she *(win, won)* an Olympic gold medal as a member of the U.S. women's 400-meter relay team.

8. After the record-setting swim across the English Channel, however, she *(lost, lose)* some of her hearing.

9. After that, she *(teach, taught)* swimming and designed clothing.

10. With her many achievements, Gertrude Ederle *(leave, left)* her mark on the world of sports.

EXERCISE B In each of the following sentences, cross out any incorrect past or past participle verb forms. Write the correct form above the error. If a sentence is already correct, write *C* after it.

Example **1.** Tony's parents ~~gived~~ *gave* him a Dalmatian for his birthday.

11. The dog growed into a friendly, helpful companion.

12. Tony teached the dog to catch tennis balls.

13. He has had the dog nearly a year now.

14. During that time, Tony has seeked out information about Dalmatians.

15. People have finded that Dalmatians make good guard dogs.

16. Shepherds have chose Dalmatians to help herd flocks of sheep.

17. You may have read about fire departments that have a Dalmatian as a mascot.

18. At one time in history, Dalmatians were send to war as war dogs.

19. I have always thinked that Dalmatians' spotted coats are beautiful.

20. Tony told me that Dalmatians can grow to almost two feet in height.

COMMON ERRORS

Pronoun Forms A

EXERCISE In each of the following sentences, underline the correct pronoun in parentheses.

Example **1.** *(We, Us)* kids always enjoy a good party.

1. My neighbor asked all the families nearby to celebrate the Fourth of July with *(he, him)*.

2. Mr. Cardenas has several grandchildren, and he invited *(them, they)* as well.

3. Before the party started, he asked my sister and *(I, me)* to help him with a project.

4. He gave *(us, we)* dozens of red, white, and blue balloons.

5. We filled *(them, they)* with water and tied them tightly at the top.

6. When kids arrived for the party, *(them, they)* were ready for fun.

7. Mr. Cardenas, my sister, and *(me, I)* asked half the kids to hold the edges of a large quilt so that it stretched out like a tablecloth, about three feet above the ground.

8. We gathered the other kids and had *(them, they)* hold another quilt in the same way.

9. Since the ones who would begin the game were *(them, they)*, I joined that group.

10. Mr. Cardenas named us the Reds and named *(they, them)* the Blues.

11. Then he tossed a water balloon toward *(we, us)* Reds.

12. Those of *(we, us)* holding this quilt moved in unison to position our quilt to catch the balloon.

13. Then our team held the quilt stretched nearly flat and raised it quickly to toss the water balloon toward *(them, they)*.

14. We laughed as we watched *(them, they)* scramble to catch the water balloon in their quilt.

15. One girl stumbled when someone bumped into *(she, her)*, but the team didn't lose the balloon.

16. Mr. Cardenas stood watching on the sidelines, and some of the parents joined *(him, he)*.

17. Those who now had to scramble to catch the balloon were *(we, us)*.

18. Unfortunately, the others and *(I, me)* missed catching the balloon by a few inches, and it burst.

19. The Blues cheered because the ones to score the first point were *(them, they)*.

20. *(We, Us)* Reds weren't worried; we knew we would win the next point!

Pronoun Forms B

EXERCISE A Underline the correct pronoun in parentheses in each of the following sentences.

Example 1. One of the best tennis players in the history of the game was *(her, she).*

1. The committee is going to give the award to *(she, her)* now.

2. The principal and *(I, me)* cheered loudly at the soccer game.

3. *(He, Him)* and the other boys are planning to go to the Holocaust museum.

4. The recorder for the group assignment is *(she, her).*

5. Mr. Wu gave the sheet music to the flute players and *(us, we).*

6. Francine and *(she, her)* practice their snare drums in the band hall.

7. Felipe lent his comic books to Eddie and *(I, me).*

8. The president of the student council is *(she, her).*

9. Mr. Chee will award the trophy to you and *(he, him).*

10. The finalists read their poems to the teachers and *(we, us).*

EXERCISE B In each of the following sentences, cross out each error in pronoun usage. Above the error, write the correct pronoun form. If a sentence is already correct, write *C* after it.

Example 1. I wasn't sure ~~who~~ *whom* I would ask to the dance.

11. The football players congratulated theirselves on their victory over our rivals.

12. This secret must remain between you and I.

13. We seventh-graders have more school spirit than anyone!

14. Karen thanked me for helping she and Kevin with the science homework.

15. Whom is the singer who performed at the awards ceremony?

16. The principal hisself will cut the ribbon at the building dedication.

17. Vicky and them are going to the frozen-yogurt shop after school.

18. Give your ballots to us ballot counters.

19. Danny, David, and me are going to the ball field.

20. From who did you get these beautiful flowers?

COMMON ERRORS

Comparative and Superlative Forms A

EXERCISE A For each of the following modifiers, write the two missing forms of comparison on the lines provided.

Example 1. *stormy* *stormier* stormiest

	Positive	Comparative	Superlative
1.	______	fluffier	______
2.	______	______	least impressive
3.	good	______	______
4.	______	______	worst
5.	______	less tempting	______
6.	salty	______	______
7.	______	more entertaining	______
8.	childlike	______	______
9.	______	______	smoothest
10.	______	kinder	______

EXERCISE B Underline the correct form of the modifier in parentheses in each of the following sentences.

Example 1. This is the *(less expensive, least expensive)* camera I could find at the store.

11. The food at this restaurant tastes *(better, best)* than the food at the diner.

12. That is the *(tragicest, most tragic)* story I have ever read!

13. Next time I will cook the eggs *(more thoroughly, thoroughlier)*.

14. Which of the fifty states has the *(mildest, milder)* climate?

15. Which is *(farthest, farther)* from here, Kassy's house or Harrison's apartment?

16. Which dog is *(most interesting, more interesting)*, Lassie, Wishbone, or Scooby-Doo?

17. When choosing among red meat, poultry, and fish, I choose red meat *(less often, least often)*.

18. Janine, this essay is your *(better, best)* work all year!

19. I have to catch the school bus thirty minutes *(early, earlier)* than Shane does.

20. The farmers' market boasts the *(fresher, freshest)* produce in town.

Comparative and Superlative Forms B

EXERCISE A For each of the following sentences, write the correct comparative or superlative form of the underlined word. Write your answer on the line provided.

Example ___*best*___ **1.** Of all the stores, Freeman's Sports offers the good price on tennis rackets.

______ **1.** São Paulo is the big city in Brazil.

______ **2.** Mount McKinley is the high mountain in North America.

______ **3.** Which do you like well, Ugli fruit or mangoes?

______ **4.** Belgium, the Netherlands, and Luxembourg have often fared the bad in wars between their bigger neighbors in Europe.

______ **5.** The capital of Nepal, Katmandu, is also the country's large city.

______ **6.** Who do you think is famous worldwide: Michael Jordan or the Brazilian soccer star Ronaldo?

______ **7.** Neanderthal remains are old than the Cro-Magnon remains.

______ **8.** Of everyone's scores on the quiz, Clara's is close to one hundred.

______ **9.** Many people believe that solar power is the clean of all energy sources.

______ **10.** Is it important to feel good or to look good?

EXERCISE B On the lines provided, write the comparative and superlative degrees of the following modifiers.

Example 1. ambitious ___*more ambitious*___ ___*most ambitious*___

Positive	Comparative	Superlative
11. gently	______	______
12. possible	______	______
13. quiet	______	______
14. curly	______	______
15. interesting	______	______
16. simple	______	______
17. funny	______	______
18. foolish	______	______
19. purple	______	______
20. sunny	______	______

COMMON ERRORS

Double Comparisons and Double Negatives

EXERCISE Each of the following sentences contains a double comparison or a double negative. Cross out the word or words in error, and write a correction above the error.

Example 1. Jeff can't believe in ~~no such thing~~ *something such* as ESP.

1. You'll never guess who ran more farther than anyone else today!
2. I'm not going to no movies until I save up more of my allowance.
3. This dog's coat is the most dirtiest I've ever seen it.
4. Miguel has hardly allowed any goals in neither of his two seasons as goalkeeper.
5. Dwayne can't hardly wait for the tennis state semifinals.
6. Don't buy your CDs at that store—their prices are the most highest in town.
7. Mr. Ali doesn't never let a day go by without exercising.
8. Wei-Lin is much more better at painting than she is at sculpting.
9. Both my parents drink coffee, but I don't think I'll never like this beverage.
10. On the final day of the school year, the students were more livelier than they had been all year.
11. Cynthia hasn't never invited me to one of her parties.
12. Nobody wasn't surprised when Mark's cow won first place at the livestock show.
13. My new alarm clock has the most loudest alarm you can imagine.
14. We should mix more yellow with the green to make the paint more yellower.
15. I wasn't scarcely ready for school when my dad shouted, "Time to leave!"
16. You will never find a more cuter puppy than Freckles.
17. The officers didn't tell no one outside the police department about the new evidence.
18. I don't feel like eating a fish sandwich, but a salad isn't appetizing neither.
19. I'm trying to keep my room more cleaner now that my friends come over more often.
20. Don't put the keys nowhere where I can't find them, please.

Misplaced Modifiers A

EXERCISE A Underline the misplaced modifier in each of the following sentences. Then, draw a caret (^) to show where the modifier should be.

Example 1. ^I read a play written by Thornton Wilder relaxing on a Sunday.

1. I learned in 1938 that Wilder wrote the play *Our Town*.
2. Set in the early 1900s, I enjoyed the play's story line.
3. The play named Grover's Corners is about everyday events that take place in a small town.
4. Doing homework in her room each evening, George can see Emily from his window.
5. Talking to him through her window, George gets some homework help from Emily.
6. Their mothers spend their days doing housework, cooking, and caring for their families who are Mrs. Gibbs and Mrs. Webb.
7. The teenagers' fathers go off to work each day who are a doctor and a newspaper editor.
8. The events are intended to show what life was like in the early 1900s in the play.
9. I think that everyday life is—and will be—different from the play in the early 2000s.
10. Homework, housework, and office work will, however, remain familiar to people which occupy nearly everyone's time at some point in life.

EXERCISE B Each of the following sentences contains a misplaced modifier. Revise each sentence so that its meaning is clear and correct.

Example 1. The ranch owner trains the horses who shook your hand. *The ranch owner who shook your hand trains the horses.*

11. We saw geese flying south from our porch. ______________________

____

12. Wearing their robes, Bryan saw the Buddhist monks enter the room. ______________________

____

13. Sitting at the bottom of her lunch sack, Brenda found her sandwich. ______________________

____

14. Recently given a fresh coat of paint, Ms. Chan admired the fence. ______________________

____

15. The Nguyens saw majestic buffaloes and huge moose on vacation. ______________________

____

Misplaced Modifiers B

EXERCISE Each of the following sentences contains a misplaced modifier. Revise each sentence so that its meaning is clear and correct.

Example 1. Covered in a soft fuzz, Marcus selected a fresh peach from the bin. *Marcus selected a fresh peach, covered in a soft fuzz, from the bin.*

1. This story that helps his master solve mysteries is about a dog. ______________________

2. Running around the track, the crowd cheered for the athletes. ______________________

3. I said on Tuesday I would be there. ______________________

4. Students may sign up for next semester's classes whose last names begin with the letters *A–F.* ______________________

5. The yellow-and-black butterfly would make a good specimen on that flower. ______________________

6. Clicking his heels together playfully, the photo captured a young man. ______________________

7. The joke across her face caused a wide grin to spread. ______________________

8. Meet me by the school under the oak tree. ______________________

9. Painted a warm yellow now, I thought the kitchen was much brighter than before. ______________________

10. I placed a kitchen chair to watch the falling rain on the wide front porch. ______________________

Standard Usage A

EXERCISE A In each of the following sentences, underline the word or words in parentheses that are correct according to the rules of formal, standard English.

Example 1. I looked (*everywhere, everywheres*) for the earring but couldn't find it.

1. Justin was sure he (*could of, could have*) won the chess game if he had concentrated harder.
2. Professor Shipley said we (*shouldn't, hadn't ought to*) worry about the test.
3. (*These types, This type*) of math problem always confuses me but not Karmisha.
4. Everyone chose photos of (*theirselves, themselves*) to include in the yearbook.
5. Watching the art teacher carefully, Phillippa sculpted her clay (*as, like*) he did.
6. These instructions look (*like, as though*) they will be simple to follow.
7. I promised that I would (*try and, try to*) keep my room cleaner.
8. Would you hand me (*them, those*) books from the top shelf?
9. Students should bring (*their, there, they're*) signed permission slips in by Friday.
10. Waking up to bright rays of sunlight, I thought, "(*Its, It's*) going to be a great day!"

EXERCISE B If the underlined word or phrase in each sentence below is used incorrectly according to standard English usage, write the correct usage above the error. If the word or phrase is already correct, write *C* above it.

Examples 1. Our neighbor is learning (*teaching*) us how to make shish kebabs.

2. I always enjoy learning (*C*) new ways of making tasty food.

11. We read where there's going to be a Thanksgiving Day parade.
12. Them candles must have been difficult to make.
13. I can understand how come people view the United States as a land of opportunity.
14. My uncle is someone who's interested in pioneer times.
15. "Let's try and preserve our heritage," he always says.
16. It looks like I'll be going to the art exhibit on Saturday.
17. After recuperating from a long illness, Mr. Dahl finally felt good again.
18. Its complex rhythms are what makes Jamaican music so fun.
19. After running in the marathon, Julia felt kind of tired.
20. Tim would rather go swimming then spend the day indoors.

COMMON ERRORS

Standard Usage B

EXERCISE A In each of the following sentences, underline the word or words in parentheses that are correct according to the rules of formal, standard English.

Example 1. *(This, This here)* calf is the one we feed with a bottle.

1. Let the dog *(inside, inside of)* the back porch before the rain starts.
2. This painting is *(real, really)* expensive!
3. Keidron was happier *(than, then)* Kelly was about their move to a new town.
4. Don't go to the movies *(unless, without)* you invite me!
5. Ms. Corbett is the one *(which, who)* will organize the book sale.
6. Five miles is a long *(way, ways)* to walk, so I'll ride my bike.
7. I *(use to, used to)* play on the basketball team, but I prefer tennis now.
8. Melissa is a friend *(whose, who's)* always kind and supportive.
9. When *(your, you're)* friends are here, I'll prepare some snacks.
10. *(That, That there)* bush blocks the sunlight from my window.

EXERCISE B In each of the following sentences, cross out the error in the use of formal, standard English. Above the error, write the correct usage.

Example 1. I read in a magazine ~~where~~ *that* the juice of the aloe vera plant is good for cuts.

11. Yes, I'll leave you stay out a half hour later tonight.
12. I need someone to learn me how to fix a leaky faucet.
13. I thought the lecture today was kind of interesting.
14. Pick the leaves of the herb when it's blossoms have just opened.
15. How come the game is canceled?
16. Yodeling is when you sing meaningless syllables.
17. I think we should get these kind of pepper plants to grow at home.
18. Did we have less quizzes this month than last month?
19. I hear about that actress everywheres I go.
20. Is dinner already?

COMMON ERRORS

Capitalization A

EXERCISE A Above each of the following items, rewrite the item using correct capitalization. If an item is already correct, write *C* above it.

the Western Hemisphere
Example 1. the western hemisphere

1. west tenth street
2. a chinese proverb
3. Winter in Alaska
4. Wednesday, June 8
5. american indian
6. a government agency
7. senator Gonzales
8. the far East
9. a pair of nikes
10. West hills hiking club

EXERCISE B In each of the following sentences, cross out each word that contains a capitalization error. Then, above the word, write it with correct capitalization. If a sentence is already correct, write *C* after it.

saying Great
Examples 1. Have you ever heard the ~~Saying~~ "~~great~~ minds think alike"?

2. "If Mr. Roy approves," said Terry, "my report will be on these two men." *C*

11. One great proponent of nonviolent protest was mohandas k. gandhi in india.
12. He was also known as *mahatma,* which means "great soul."
13. In History class, we learned that gandhi's peaceful methods led to indian independence from great britain.
14. India finally gained independence after world war II.
15. another great leader who advocated nonviolent methods was dr. martin luther king, jr.
16. In the united states during the 1950s and 1960s, dr. king led nonviolent protests as a part of the movement for civil rights.
17. His famous publication "letter from birmingham jail" outlined his peaceful strategies.
18. in 1964, the civil rights act was passed by congress, and in the same year king won a nobel peace prize.
19. These two great men were not the first to think of fighting injustice with nonviolence, however.
20. The Nineteenth-century american author henry david thoreau described many of the same principles in his essay "civil disobedience."

COMMON ERRORS

Capitalization B

EXERCISE A Above each of the following items, rewrite the item using correct capitalization. If an item is already correct, write *C* above it.

a lake in Michigan
Example 1. a Lake in Michigan

1. going east on the freeway
2. *The hunchback of Notre Dame*
3. the Civil war
4. four Chapters
5. Tuesday morning
6. thai food
7. my Uncle Frank
8. Venezuelan coast
9. the big dipper
10. a story, "Stan's stupendous Saturday"

EXERCISE B In each of the following sentences, circle each letter that should be capitalized.

Example 1. (h)ave you read (n)icholasa (m)ohr's *(e)l (b)ronx (r)emembered: (a) Novella and Stories?*

11. When i read books, i enjoy reading about people who show me a view of life i haven't seen before.
12. Judith Ortiz Cofer published *an Island like you: stories of the Barrio* in 1995.
13. one character comments, "dating is not a concept adults in our barrio really get."
14. the stories are about kids in puerto rican families.
15. Many of the kids speak both english and spanish.
16. They live in an american city, which is paterson, new jersey.
17. Some of the kids miss puerto rico, which seems as far away as mars.
18. if you like poetry, you should read *Cool Salsa: bilingual poems on growing up latino in the united states.*
19. Poems such as "school days" and "hard times" are written partly in english and partly in spanish or are printed twice—once in each language.
20. If you like these poems, look for the bilingual magazine named *azul,* which means "blue" in spanish.

COMMON ERRORS

Commas A

EXERCISE In each of the following sentences, insert commas where they are needed and underline the word before the comma. If a sentence is already correct, write *C* after it.

Example 1. The Incan empire, once centered in what is now Peru, had a highly developed civilization.

1. Often called the father of history Herodotus wrote an account of the Persian invasion of ancient Greece.

2. Julius Caesar supposedly described one of his victories by simply saying, "I came I saw I conquered."

3. Montezuma II a sixteenth-century Aztec emperor was overthrown by the Spanish conquistadors.

4. The Japanese surrender that ended World War II occurred on September 6 1945.

5. During World War II more than 22 million people died and more than 34 million were wounded.

6. Aren't red white and blue also the colors of the French flag?

7. In 1992 Sarajevo came under a bloody siege by Bosnian Serbs.

8. The region of Indochina includes Cambodia Laos Malaysia Myanmar Thailand and Vietnam.

9. How excited you must be about taking vacation in Santiago Chile!

10. Well I'm not sure who is the prime minister of England.

11. Dear Friends Mr. Thompson's seventh-grade class is hosting an international food fair.

12. I'd like to ask you Ms. Robertson about the field trip to Gettysburg Pennsylvania.

13. On the shelf beneath the window you'll find the new globe.

14. Because I enjoy water sports and bright sunshine I want to visit Hawaii this summer.

15. Imported tea was costly in 1773 yet colonists dumped shipments of tea into the Boston harbor in protest of British taxes on tea.

16. The Seven Hills of Rome which are on the eastern bank of the Tiber river mark the site of ancient Rome.

17. The continents of the earth are Africa Asia Australia Europe North America and South America.

18. Oh, I forgot to name Antarctica as one of the earth's continents.

19. You can address your letter to the President of the United States 1600 Pennsylvania Ave. Washington D.C. 20500.

20. On May 29 1848 Wisconsin was granted statehood.

COMMON ERRORS

Commas B

EXERCISE In each of the following sentences, insert commas where they are needed, and underline the word before the comma. If a sentence is already correct, write *C* after it.

Example 1. A lunar eclipse**,** which occurs when the earth casts its shadow on the moon**,** will occur tonight.

1. The letter she found was dated November 16 1950.
2. If Leilani plans to go she will need to sign up.
3. June July, or August will be the best month for the swim party.
4. Since Hank is not very hungry he will eat only half a bagel.
5. In my opinion students should decide for themselves.
6. Most salmon which live in salt water swim upstream and lay eggs in fresh water.
7. Most of the food that you see on the table was prepared by Mr. Khan.
8. Noticing a misspelled word Raymond looked up the correct spelling in his dictionary.
9. Monica was vacationing in Toronto Canada but she has returned.
10. Captain Martinez who owns the ship, has been sailing for thirty years.
11. Katrina my sister's college roommate is spending the holidays with my family.
12. In the back corner of a dusty toy store I found an antique marionette.
13. The soccer players intent on their exciting game did not notice the storm clouds approaching.
14. Chili powder in my opinion should be used sparingly.
15. I'll sweep the floor straighten the living room and make sandwiches if you'll pick up Cecilia from the airport.
16. Yes these are the baseball cards I want to trade.
17. When you hear your cue move to center stage Aaron.
18. Jorge who is an animal rights supporter volunteers at the humane society organizes pet adoptions and always takes in stray dogs and cats.
19. Christie you can go bowling with your brothers or you can go to the opera with Sandy and me.
20. The drab boring walls of my room were transformed when I hung posters photos awards and a calendar.

Semicolons and Colons

EXERCISE A Insert semicolons and colons where they are needed in the following sentences. If a sentence is already correct, write *C* after it.

Example 1. The Spanish colonized many parts of Latin America and South America; they brought the Spanish language to these regions.

1. I'll tell Ricky, Sue, and Rao about the field trip and you tell the others.

2. The Spanish Club will meet in front of the school at 7 15.

3. Mr. Fuentes will be there earlier he wants to oversee the loading of the bus.

4. The field trip should be a success last year, it went very smoothly.

5. Bring the following items lunch money, notepad, and a hat.

6. I would love to go however, I have conflicting plans.

7. The chaperones are these parents Mr. Kobek, Ms. Lee, and Mrs. Dayle.

8. I have pen pals in Monterrey, Mexico San Juan, Puerto Rico and Buenos Aires, Argentina.

9. This article, "In Demand Bilingual Workers," raises some interesting points.

10. Dear Members of the Spanish Club Prepare for a day of fun, food, and friends.

EXERCISE B Insert semicolons and colons where they are needed in the following formal letter.

Example The students' interests are these: pioneer Americans, war heroes, and athletes.

Dear Ms. Simiyu

Thank you for inviting me to speak to your class I will be there on Tuesday promptly at 10 00 A.M. I plan to speak about the following people Marshall Taylor, an African American cyclist Solomon Butcher, a photographer in pioneer times and Deborah Sampson, a woman who fought (disguised as a man) in the American Revolution. Your students are welcome to ask questions about other people from history almost everyone has a favorite historical figure. They have probably heard at least a little about Molly Bloom, Anne Frank, and Captain Cook and I can include some information on these people. Also, I will talk about a couple of my favorite books *Astrid Lindgren Storyteller to the World* by Johanna Hurwitz; and *Stonewall* by Jean Fritz, which is about General "Stonewall" Jackson.

Sincerely,

C. J. LeBeaux, Head Librarian

Centerville Public Library

Quotation Marks and Other Punctuation A

EXERCISE A Add underlining, quotation marks, and parentheses where they are needed in the following sentences. Circle any letters that should be capitalized or made lowercase.

Example 1. Tranh said to his friend Kate, "How's it going?"

1. "Do you have permission to go tomorrow? Kate smiling broadly asked him.
2. "Go where? Tranh replied. is there a field trip?"
3. "You're kidding!" Kate exclaimed. you don't remember!
4. Sure I do, Tranh hedged, "But remind me anyway."
5. "Tomorrow is the free concert, Kate said. I hear there will be a didgeridoo!
6. "Oh, yes," Tranh said. "I read about that in the Weekly Entertainer.
7. The didgeridoo a hollow wind instrument originated in Australia.
8. I read the book Didgeridoo: Ritual Origins And Playing Techniques by Dirk Schellberg.
9. If you've never heard a didgeridoo being played, you could listen to Didgeridoo Dreamtime, a CD of music performed by Mark Atkins.
10. The two friends Tranh and Kate enjoyed the didgeridoo concert.

COMMON ERRORS

EXERCISE B Add hyphens, brackets, dashes, and quotation marks where they are needed in the following sentences.

Example 1. My homework—I finished it already—is in my notebook.

11. These talented poets Langston Hughes, Shel Silverstein, and Jean Little wrote about friendship.
12. I see my exEnglish teacher, Ms. Sellers, going into that bookstore.
13. This poem I don't know who wrote it is about unrequited love.
14. The mayor announced, "They the winners of the Young Poetry Contest will be announced at noon tomorrow."
15. I read twenty five poems before I found the one I want to write about for class.
16. A two thirds majority of my classmates prefer humorous poems to serious ones.
17. The president elect of our writer's guild is Emilio Bennett.
18. These poems they're known as limericks are really funny!
19. Mr. Canon said, You'll find Stopping by Woods on a Snowy Evening on page fifty.
20. He continued, "All of these the poems by Robert Frost are well loved by many readers."

Quotation Marks and Other Punctuation B

EXERCISE A Add underlining, quotation marks, and parentheses, and brackets where they are needed in the following sentences. Circle any letters that should be capitalized or made lowercase.

Example **1.** Isaac put down his copy of Motor Cross when Tina walked up.

1. "Did I ever tell you about my uncle Bernie? Tina asked.

2. Yes, you told me about his stamp collection, said Isaac.

3. Tina said, no, that was my Grandfather.

4. Oh, said her friend, I thought your grandfather collected baseball cards.

5. He collects both, Tina said, But Uncle Bernie works for Amnesty International.

6. Isaac nodded; he had read about Amnesty International in the Los Angeles Times.

7. He said, I read about it the organization and thought it was interesting."

8. He continued, you have an active family. Didn't one of your other relatives sail on the Queen Elizabeth 2?

9. "Yes, and he wrote a book about it called Sailing with the Queen.

10. Do you see the pun play on words in the book title?

EXERCISE B Add hyphens, brackets, and dashes where they are needed in the following sentences.

Example **1.** Michael is a self-motivated student, and I admire him.

11. Have you ever eaten a cheese free pizza?

12. Here is how you should divide *competition* at the end of a line: competition.

13. Serve each guest a one eighth portion of the quiche.

14. "I didn't know anything about it the donation to the school until we received the check," said a happy Principal Thomas.

15. You can get two notepads for ninety nine cents at the Corner Cupboard.

16. Chad, would you prepare the turnips I know they're not your favorite vegetable for dinner?

17. Sally proclaimed, "I don't wear anything made of that substance leather."

18. The automatic sprinkler system we installed it last summer makes yard care much easier.

19. When I was a child, I was certain my mother was all seeing and all knowing!

20. Casey was proud of the score of eighty eight that he earned on the math test.

COMMON ERRORS

Apostrophes

EXERCISE A Add apostrophes where they are needed in the following items. If an item is already correct, write *C* above the item.

Example 1. the Californians' flag

1. didnt study
2. Brandons skates
3. how you write *r*s
4. womens league
5. both of the books titles
6. borrowing yours
7. the Chavezs house
8. youre my best friend
9. children's voices
10. after theyre through

EXERCISE B Add apostrophes where they are needed in the following sentences. Circle apostrophes that do not belong.

Example 1. Juan can't find his neighbor's lost dog.

11. Its been missing since the neighborhood party held at the Merrills house.
12. Their party wasnt that long ago—only yesterday—but Juan couldnt help worrying.
13. He played with the neighbor's dog as much as if it were his'.
14. It's name is Boo-Boo, which Juan at first thought was spelled with two *u*'s.
15. The neighbors got Boo-Boo in 95.
16. Finally, Juan found the dog in the backyard of the Changs', whose hedge had been trimmed and shaped to form a maze.
17. The hedge, formed in a pattern of repeating *s*s, had confused the dog.
18. Juan had called out several *Boo-Boo*s when the dog finally responded.
19. Juans face relaxed into a smile he couldnt repress.
20. At exactly four oclock, Boo-Boo had been found!

All Marks of Punctuation A

EXERCISE A Add underlining, end marks, commas, semicolons, and colons where they are needed in the following sentences.

Example 1. Mr. Sizemore, my photography teacher, showed us some works by Dorothea Lange.

1. Lange a famous photographer decided while still a teenager to pursue photography
2. As a teenager in Manhattan Lange explored the city with the eyes of a photographer she promised herself she would one day take pictures for a living
3. What an ambitious admirable teenager she was
4. Lange did in fact become a professional photographer she took portraits of wealthy residents of San Francisco
5. When the Great Depression struck the country she began photographing migrant workers for the California State Emergency Relief Administration
6. Her goal was this to show the inhuman housing conditions in which these people lived
7. In a similar job for the Farm Security Administration she photographed farmers sharecroppers and other poverty-stricken groups
8. Referring to photography Lange once said "You go in over your head, not just up to your neck"
9. Do you feel this passionately about anything
10. Go to the library bookstore or Internet look at some of Lange's work in Dorothea Lange Photographs of a Lifetime

EXERCISE B Add apostrophes, quotation marks, hyphens, parentheses, brackets, and dashes where they are needed in the following sentences.

Example 1. I'm going to the party—I think I mentioned it—with a friend.

11. Duncan had been looking forward to the party the one at the ice rink for days.
12. When Chris he's Duncan's best friend had invited Duncan, hed said, "Id love to come.
13. Ill meet you there the party location."
14. Chriss great uncle and two of his aunts they are all quite friendly had helped plan the party.
15. Everyone all of the seventh grade class would enjoy three hours worth of skating, eating, and having fun.

All Marks of Punctuation B

EXERCISE A Add underlining, quotation marks, commas, and parentheses where they are needed in the following sentences. Circle any letters that should be capitalized or made lowercase.

Example 1. Here is a photograph of the space shuttle Columbia, Erin.

1. There are too many very's in your paper, A Day in the Life of the President.
2. Casablanca check listings for show times is highly acclaimed by critics.
3. We have new students from Topeka Kansas and Portland Oregon.
4. When you pick up Ruthie from school Jane said would you also get some sandwiches?
5. Have you ever tasted cantaloupe? asked Horace. It tastes delicious. I like it.
6. The stories in this book I'm almost finished reading it have been quite entertaining.
7. Malcolm said, when you're at the museum, look at Broken Bridge & Dreams by Salvador Dali.
8. I sat in one of the swings in the park and I watched my younger brother play.
9. John Hancock 1737–1793 was the first signer of the Declaration Of Independence.
10. Hanging from the strongest limb of the tree a swing made from an old tractor tire swayed in the breeze.

EXERCISE B Add apostrophes, hyphens, brackets, and dashes where they are needed in the following sentences. Then, add the necessary end mark for each sentence.

Example 1. A job—you know, work—is one of the best ways to become self-sufficient.

11. The childrens dance class is performing for their parents entertainment
12. Last week this is so funny twenty five clowns skated down Main Street
13. My cousin said, "Ill call and tell you about it summer camp after I get there"
14. I didnt know you're full of surprises that you knew how to dance the salsa
15. Everyones vote counts equally in the Students Choice Award
16. The award in case you dont know shows appreciation for a teachers outstanding work
17. Are these zs or 2s? I cant tell
18. His mother-in-laws decision is final she will not sell her house this year
19. The final exam will be all encompassing that means comprehensive and will have seventy five questions on it
20. Someones car alarm is going off, and it couldnt be louder

Spelling A

EXERCISE A On the line provided, spell each of the following words correctly or write *C* if it is already correct.

Example 1. resede *recede*

1. sheild ________

2. father-in-laws ________

3. cheif ________

4. wolfs ________

5. puting ________

6. disallow ________

7. heros ________

8. childs ________

9. lovelier ________

10. succede ________

EXERCISE B For each of the following items, add the prefix or suffix given to form a new word. Write the new word on the line provided. Some letters may need to be changed, added, or dropped.

Example 1. over + run = *overrun*

11. in + operable = ________

12. dis + satisfaction = ________

13. open + ness = ________

14. il + legible = ________

15. safe + ly = ________

16. tan + ed = ________

17. beauty + ful = ________

18. mis + understand = ________

19. im + possible = ________

20. argue + ment = ________

Spelling B

EXERCISE A In each of the following items, one word is misspelled. Underline that word, and write the correct spelling above the error.

Example 1. potatos (potatoes) moose receipt

1. statehood	misspent	unatural
2. wiegh	emptiness	radios
3. taxes	waxxes	fazes
4. business	arguement	rarely
5. purly	oxen	daily
6. knifes	independent	happier
7. succeed	piece	mother-in-laws
8. mischeif	probably	government
9. foxes	carried	procede
10. Joneses	hobbys	highways

EXERCISE B Above the underlined items in each of the following sentences, write the plural form.

Example 1. How many s (s's) and i (i's) are in *Mississippi*?

11. My grandmother grows tomato and pea in her backyard garden.

12. All the *Wednesday* on this calendar except the one on the final two pages are misspelled.

13. Did you see any moose or wolf on your trek in the wilderness?

14. Should I make the bouquet from rose or pansy?

15. The story was illustrated with paintings of fairy and elf.

16. Both of my sister-in-law have piano in their houses.

17. The woman in this photograph are wearing clothing from the 1800.

18. Both of the lawyers placed their legal brief in their briefcase.

19. Two mouse scurried under the bush along the fence.

20. Replace all the *really* in this paper with more interesting word choice.

Words Often Confused

EXERCISE In each of the following sentences, underline the correct word or words in parentheses.

Example 1. The bright blue painting *(complements, compliments)* the decor of the room.

1. It has always been my *(principal, principle)* to treat people as I want to be treated.

2. Elena told them that *(their, there, they're)* accents differ from those of South American Spanish speakers.

3. Jason doesn't know *(weather, whether)* to go swimming or ride his bicycle.

4. *(Its, It's)* not my fault a stray dog ate our lunches!

5. Whenever I try to wear my older brother's clothes, they are too *(loose, lose)*.

6. Gifts to the judges will not *(affect, effect)* their decisions.

7. I followed your *(advice, advise)* about getting plenty of sleep before the day of the test.

8. Camels are well-known for their endurance in the heat of the *(desert, dessert)*.

9. The students had their photograph taken as they stood on the steps of the *(capital, capitol)*.

10. Which person from your *(passed, past)* would you most want to see again?

11. It is the *(principal, principle)* who calls the assembly each week.

12. The letter was written on formal business *(stationary, stationery)*.

13. There are *(to, too, two)* many details for one lesson; we'll cover the rest tomorrow.

14. I found *(your, you're)* bracelet where you had left it in the locker room.

15. I'll *(accept, except)* your help with the yard work if you will join me for frozen yogurt later.

16. "Your visit is *(altogether, all together)* unexpected," said Grandma, "but you are welcome nevertheless."

17. Be sure to engage the parking *(brake, break)* if you park the car on a hill.

18. The texture of this sandpaper is too *(coarse, course)* to use for our project.

19. Martin has contributed a number of wonderful ideas to the school's *(council, counsel)* on fitness.

20. Someone always *(looses, loses)* the remote control to the TV.

COMMON ERRORS

NAME ______________________ CLASS ______________ DATE ______________

Spelling and Words Often Confused

EXERCISE A For each of the following items, add the prefix or suffix, or write the plural form of the word on the line provided. Some letters may need to be changed, added, or dropped.

Examples **1.** rare + ly = *rarely*

2. & + *(plural)* = *&'s*

1. un + real = ______________________

2. journey + *(plural)* = ______________________

3. curly + ness = ______________________

4. leaf + *(plural)* = ______________________

5. train + able = ______________________

6. drive-in + *(plural)* = ______________________

7. rate + ings = ______________________

8. approximate + ly = ______________________

9. 1950 + *(plural)* = ______________________

10. busy + ness = ______________________

EXERCISE B In each of the following sets of words, underline the misspelled word. Then, write the correct spelling above it.

Example **1.** serving *daily* <u>dayly</u> readily

11. unatural	intercede	dancing
12. believe	envyable	tapping
13. taxxes	conceit	argument
14. supersede	proceed	succede
15. openness	reddest	wieght
16. employable	crazyness	freezing
17. admireable	yield	impossible
18. cheif	dislocate	changing
19. formally	discount	conceed
20. loneliness	routinly	fiercest

Review A: Standard Usage

EXERCISE A Each of the items below contains one of the following errors: a sentence fragment, a run-on sentence, a lack of agreement between subject and verb, a lack of agreement between pronoun and antecedent, or a misplaced modifier. Revise each sentence to correct any errors.

Examples 1. Everyone in the bleachers waved ~~their~~ *his or her* school banners.

2. Around the curve in the road *the house was* hidden from view.

1. The bird had a red crest on their head.
2. After wiping the tables, I swept the floor the diner would be ready to open.
3. Our football team are going to the conference playoffs.
4. Hot and fluffy from the oven, the delicious muffin filled with raisins.
5. The candle sits on the nightstand that smells of berries.
6. Either Sarah or Lisa will share their book with you, but please bring your own book tomorrow.
7. The pages are the ones I wanted you to read with the corners folded over.
8. We planned a theme for the Valentine's Day dance it was "famous couples from literature."
9. Shopping for school clothes each August before school starts.
10. All members of the debate team is expected to attend the practice session.

EXERCISE B Each item below contains an error in verb form, in pronoun form, in comparative or superlative form, or a double comparison or double negative. Underline the error and write a correction above it.

Example 1. I'm not sure of the answers to none (*any*) of these equations.

11. These jeans must have shrinked in the dryer.
12. Which of these four movies was interestinger?
13. In this fog I can't hardly see the road before us.
14. Mr. McKay said that us volunteers are needed in the red tent.
15. Hockey practice today was the most longest it's ever been.
16. Which are warmer: wool coats, leather coats, or down-filled coats?
17. It is more rapider to write your paper on a computer than by hand.
18. Several eggs bursted when the carton fell to the ground.
19. The author of the lead story in the school newspaper is her.
20. I don't remember nothing about the rules for playing solitaire.

COMMON ERRORS

Review B: Mechanics

EXERCISE A The items below contain errors in capitalization and punctuation. Circle each letter that should be capitalized or made lowercase, and add punctuation where it is needed.

Example **1.** I saw my Teacher at the grocery store and said, "Hello, Ms. Williams."

1. Have you ever read O. Henry's story The Gift Of The Magi

2. The ingredients are as follows peanut butter, jelly, bread, and bananas.

3. look out for the angry wasp

4. Which street do you live on JoEllen

5. "I can offer you iced tea, said our hostess, Or I can offer you lemonade."

6. My Mom works at Arlington Memorial hospital.

7. Answer the first twenty five questions in the third chapter of your History book

8. I called Travis Sela and Gordon but none of them were home.

9. One of my favorite books is Something Wicked This Way Comes by Ray Bradbury.

10. The calligraphy teachers instructions are to practice writing *A*s *B*s and *C*s.

EXERCISE B In each of the following sentences, underline the correct word or words in parentheses.

Example **1.** You can get a refund if you still have your *(reciept, receipt)*.

11. I enjoy the *(piece, peace)* and quiet of a lazy summer day.

12. Do you *(truely, truly)* believe I'll win the audition?

13. The Robinsons have planted colorful marigolds in *(their, there, they're)* flower beds.

14. The *(facilities, facilitys)* include a weight room, an aerobics studio, and an indoor track.

15. Are the dogs *(already, all ready)* for the show?

16. The movers *(padded, paded)* the furniture with protective quilts.

17. James has *(shone, shown)* the new student around the school.

18. Let's take our *(sleds, sledds)* to the top of the hill.

19. The Jacksons *(formally, formerly)* lived in North Carolina.

20. Please be *(carful, careful)* when dusting the glass figurines.

Review C: Standard Usage and Mechanics

EXERCISE A Each item below contains an error in sentence structure, subject-verb agreement, pronoun-antecedent agreement, placement of a modifier, verb forms, pronoun forms, or formal, standard English. Revise each sentence to correct any errors.

Examples 1. The ones who are interested in your band are ~~them~~. *they*

2. *I saw Tasha f*illing the vase with carnations, irises, and ferns before the party.

1. I watered the lawn before leaving for school the sun would be hot today.

2. Neither Frederick nor Heidi know when the package arrived.

3. Making a chain out of the paper clips in his desk.

4. Each of the gymnasts performed their routine for the coach.

5. Hidden in the bottom of a large red toolbox, Jamie finally found the pliers.

6. Someone ringed the doorbell, and Felicity hurried to the door.

7. Shelby, Carrie, and me are playing miniature golf on Saturday.

8. Natasha asked Jamud how come he decided against running for class treasurer.

9. Since the mail carrier had already delivered mail to the large yellow house.

10. Valued for their friendly personality, the golden retriever makes a good pet.

EXERCISE B In the sentences below, underline the errors in capitalization, spelling, and word usage. Then, write a correction above each underlined error. Also, add any missing punctuation.

Example 1. the *(The)* clerk in the dress store announced, "all cloths *(All clothes)* on this rack are on sale today."

11. the teachers meeting included some announcements from the principle.

12. The school councilor helped me with my college applications said Josephine

13. for everyones comfort, this is a smoke free establishment

14. How did you earn fifty nine dollars asked Margaret.

15. The donations from my family are these Bens skates moms winter coat and dads extra basketball.

16. the marching band put on quiet a show the crowd loved the new routines.

17. Someday i plan to visit Paris France Rome Italy and London England.

18. These boxxes wiegh to much please help me lift each of them Rodney.

19. Meet me at 7 30 in front of the school and Ill help you memorize Genesis 1 1–10.

20. For my report on coral reeves I'm using a book called Underwater Life and an article titled Coral in tropical seas.

COMMON ERRORS

Proofreading Application: Report

Good writers are generally good proofreaders. Readers tend to admire and trust writing that is error-free. Make sure that you correct all errors in grammar, usage, spelling, and punctuation in your writing. Your readers will have more confidence in your words if you have done your best to proofread carefully.

Many times in your school and work careers, you will be required to evaluate the writings of your peers. Whether your evaluation is graded or not, take care to proofread it carefully. If your evaluation is full of errors, your classmate will certainly not take your comments, criticisms, and suggestions seriously.

PROOFREADING ACTIVITY

Find and correct the errors in usage and mechanics. Use proofreading symbols such as those on page 809 of *Elements of Language* to make your corrections.

Example This report fascinated me, but was difficult to read.

I knew that African Americans had influenced American music but I had not realized the importance of music in African life. The list of stringed instruments was helpful, but the lack of commas between items on the list confuse me. The instruments on this list was not familiar to me, so I wasn't sure if its names were one word or two. Take, for instance, the lute in the first paragraph that was mentioned. Was this a lute or a bow lute.

Moving on to the rest of the report. The section on african wind instruments was fascinating. The writer handled this material well, not an easy task for he or she. When all is said and done the biggest problem in this report was the spelling. I hope the author takes the time too proofread more carefully the next time.

Literary Model: Sentence Fragments in Haiku

The lightning flashes!
And slashing through the darkness,
A night-heron's screech.
—Bashō

A dragonfly!
The distant hills
Reflected in his eyes
—Issa

Broken and broken
again on the sea, the moon
so easily mends
—Chosu

EXERCISE A

1. Which of the three haiku contains only sentence fragments?

2. Which one contains only a complete sentence?

3. Which one contains a complete sentence and a sentence fragment?

EXERCISE B Haiku often try to evoke a particular moment or a particular sensation. Why might someone writing haiku choose to use sentence fragments?

Literary Model (continued)

EXERCISE C Write three haiku on the lines below. Make each one three lines long. Some people write haiku with five syllables in the first line, seven syllables in the second line, and five syllables in the third line. Try writing at least one of your haiku that way.

EXERCISE D

1. Underline any fragments you used. What kinds of things, if any, did you use fragments to express? For instance, did you use them to express ideas, images, sensations, actions, or other things?

2. Underline twice any complete sentences you used. What kinds of things, if any, did you use sentences to express?

Writing Application: Dialogue

From now on, you will probably hear teachers warn you to avoid sentence fragments. These teachers are correct. Fragments should not appear in most writing contexts, so writers must know the difference between a fragment and a complete sentence. One writing context, however, demands that writers use fragments: dialogue. Speakers often use fragments—pausing, losing track of the sentence, backtracking, changing their minds—and always expecting listeners to keep up and fill in the gaps. Listen to your own speech and that of your friends, and you will hear many fragments, especially when a conversation gets heated.

EXAMPLES "Am not." "Are too!" "No way" "Bad dog!"

Writing Activity

In your drama class, you are exploring the special type of writing called script writing, the kind that is used in movies and television shows. For an exercise in how fragments can make dialogue more real, you will write two versions of a heated scene. First, write entirely in complete sentences; then, write in a mix of complete sentences and fragments. Other students will act out the roles in both versions of the scene. Then, the class will discuss which version works better in a script and why. The assigned scene involves a small group of friends watching a close game between two sports teams. Some of the friends are die-hard fans of one team, and the other friends have sworn loyalty to the opposing team.

PREWRITING First, decide on your particulars. How many friends are gathered around the television? What are their names? What sport are they watching? What teams are playing (real or fictional)? Who's cheering for which team? What's the score? Set the scene in which the dialogue will be played out, and give one of the characters a line that challenges the fans of the opposing team.

WRITING You're not creating an entire plot for this exercise, just a scene. Don't worry about coming up with the traditional beginning, middle, and end sequence of events. Instead, focus on who says what about the teams. Write the first version of your dialogue, the one that contains complete sentences.

REVISING Now put the dialogue you've just written in front of you and prepare to abridge it. When should you use fragments instead of complete sentences? The goal is to keep the dialogue's content *the same* while altering the way the content is expressed. Have a little fun with this version—"hear" these friends debating as you write. Then, identify each fragment you used by underlining it.

PUBLISHING Check your two dialogues for errors in punctuation and spelling—even a fragment should have good grammar otherwise. Then type your dialogues out or write them very neatly, so that your classmates can read them easily. In class, listen to the performances, and then discuss which version of each pair sounds more convincing, more true to life.

Extending Your Writing

This exercise could lead to a more extended writing project. Team loyalty is an interesting concept. For a sports class, explore the idea of life-long, or at least long-term, allegiance to a sports team. Interview some true fans, asking them why their teams mean so much to them. Talk also to a few avid sports fans who don't play favorites. What are the loyalists getting out of their teams? Are you yourself a fan (short for *fanatic*, of course) of a particular team or player? Present your research to the class, and see who's on your team and who's not.

Writing Application: Dialogue

Writing Activity

Extending Your Writing